ENCYCLOPAEDIA OF GENETICS-II

PHYSICAL BASIS OF INHERITANCE

By

Dr. Arvind N. Shukla

School of Studies of Zoology & Biotechnology

Vikram University

Ujjain

DISCOVERY PUBLISHING HOUSE PVT. LTD.

NEW DELHI-110 002

First Published-2009

ISBN 978-81-8356-393-2

Published by:

DISCOVERY PUBLISHING HOUSE PVT. LTD.
4831/24, Ansari Road, Prahlad Street,
Darya Ganj, New Delhi-110002 (India)
Phone: 23279245 • Fax: 91-11-23253475
E-mail: dphbooks@rediffmail.com
dphtemp@indiatimes.com

Printed at:
Sachin Printers, Delhi

Preface

The present title *"Physical Basis of Inheritance"* is an exciting, and dynamic branch of science and offers the finest approach to teaching genetics through the integration of the molecular and chemical subdisciplines. It prepares the students to learn to formulate genetic hypothesis and apply critical thinking skill necessary for problem solving, while also gaining a sense of the social and historical context in which genetics has developed. This text also has a completely novel way to illustrate the one or two experiments in each chapter that are rigorously examined according to the scientific method. It starts with the premise that the syllabus for a university course in genetics should reflect the major research issues of the new millennium rather than those topics that were in vogue during the last decades of nineteenth century.

The text covers both the basic and practical aspects of Genetics. Fundamental knowledge is developed within the context of applied relevance. Principles are supplemented with examples. This is done to maintain student interest, which is essential for learning any subject.

In the preparation of this book large number of books and research papers have been consulted. So no authenticity is claimed.

The author expresses his gratitude to Mr. Wasan and staff of M/s Discovery Publishing House Pvt. Ltd. for their whole hearted co-operation in the publication of this book.

The author tried hard to be accurate and upto date in statement and realises the impossibility of completely avoiding errors therefore, the author will greatly appreciate having his attention called to any questionable statement.

Author

CONTENTS

1

Introduction

In 1866 Gregor Mendel published the results of experiments in which he had investigated inheritance in garden peas. From these findings he discovered the existence of discrete hereditary elements and the rules determining their transmission from parent to offspring. The principles of inheritance that Mendel recognized ultimately became the foundation for genetics and a major factor in the development of modern biology.

Our consideration of genetics will begin with the development of the fundamental concept of the science—namely, that the hereditary determinant deduced by Mendel and now called a *gene* is a unit of inheritance transmitted from parent to progeny during reproduction. The ideas and methods of analysis that were initiated by Mendel are the subject of this chapter.

Mendel and His Experiments

During the period in which Gregor Mendel developed his theory of the basis of heredity, he was a monk and a teacher of mathematics in a local school. However, the study of natural phenomena, especially inheritance, was his main interest. The principal difference between Mendel's approach and that of other scientists who were interested in inheritance is that he thought in quantitative terms. He proceeded by stating simple questions to be answered by experiments and then looking for statistical regularities that might identify general rules.

Mendel selected peas for his experiments for two reasons: (1) he had access to varieties that differed by observable alternative characteristics, and (2) his earlier studies of flower structure indicated that peas usually reproduce by self-pollination (in which pollen produced

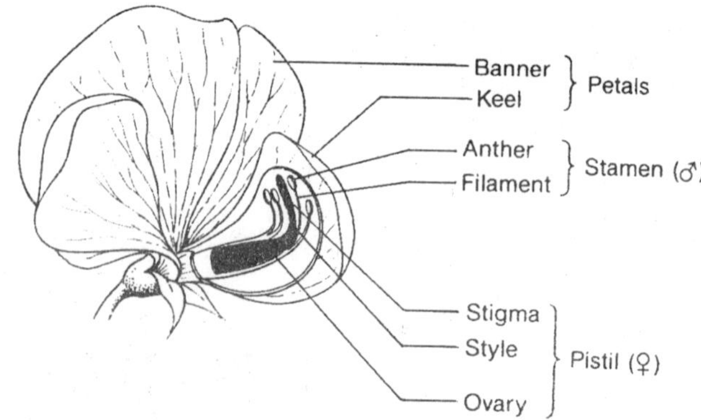

Fig. 1.1. A pea flower from which a section has been removed to show the reproductive structures.

in a flower is transferred to the stigma of the same flower). To produce hybrids by cross-pollination one needed only lo open the keel petal enclosing the reproductive structures, remove the anthers before they had shed pollen, and then dust the stigma with pollen from a flower on a second plant.

Mendel recognized the need for being certain that the characteristics he studied were constant in inheritance and at the beginning of his experimentation he established *true-breeding* lines in which the plants produced only progeny like themselves when allowed to self-pollinate normally. These different lines—which bred true for flower colour, pod shape, or one of the other well-defined characters that Mendel had selected for investigation—provided the parents for hybridization. A *hybrid* is the offspring of a cross between inherently unlike individuals.

In the following we examine a few of Mendel's original experiments; these illustrate the methods he used and how he interpreted his results. One pair of characters that he studied was round versus wrinkled seeds. When pollen from plants of a line with wrinkled seeds was used to cross-pollinate plants from a round-seeded line, all of the hybrid (abbreviated as F_1 for *first filial generation*) seeds produced were round. He also performed the *reciprocal cross*, one in which plants from the round-seeded line were used as the pollen parents and those from the line with wrinkled seeds as female parents; again all of the seeds were round. The F_1, hybrid plants were then allowed to self-pollinate. The progeny plants are called the F_2 (*second filial generation*). Seeds of these plants were like both of the original parental

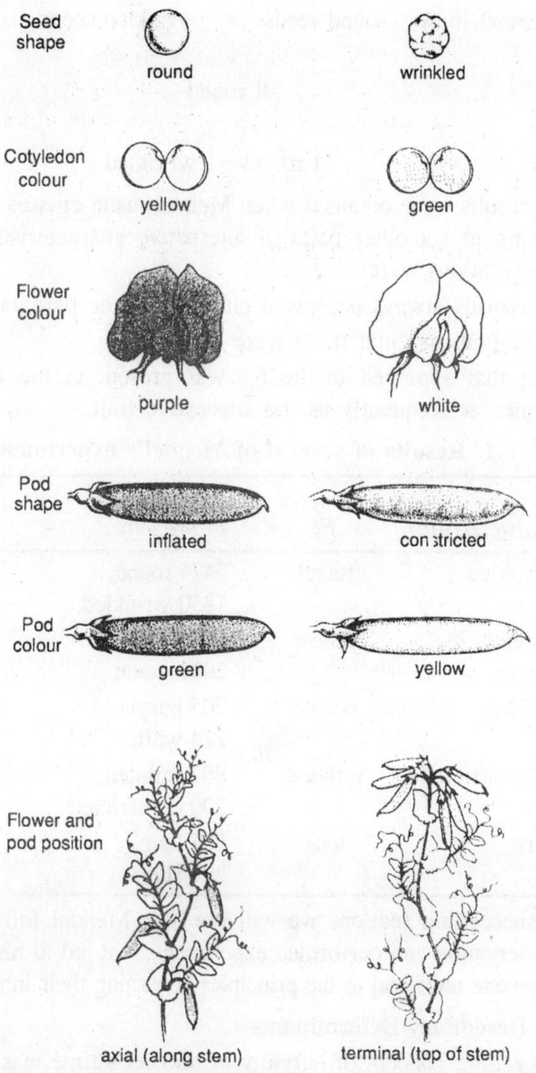

Fig. 1.2. Six of the seven character differences in peas studied by Mendel (the seventh difference was long versus short stems). In each case the characteristic on the left is seen in a hybrid.

types—that is, round and wrinkled. Mendel counted 5474 F_2 seeds that were round and 1850 that were wrinkled and noted that this ratio was approximately 3:1. The results of this experiment can he summarized in the following way:

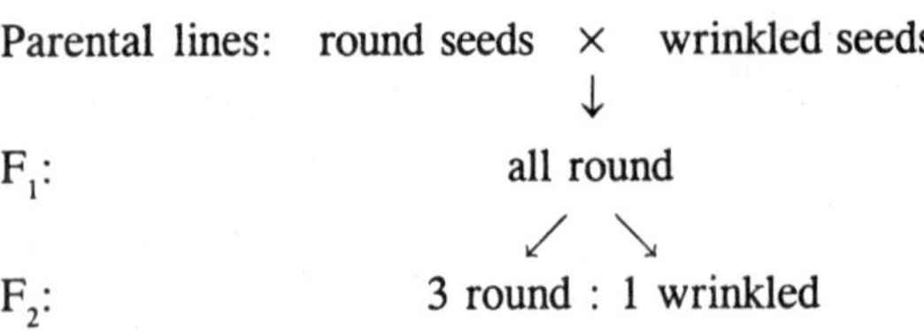

Similar results were obtained when Mendel made crosses between plants differing in six other pairs of alternative characteristics. The principal observations were:

1. The F_1 hybrids always possessed only one of the parental traits.
2. In the F_2, both parental traits were present.
3. The trait that appeared in the F_1, was present in the F_2 about three times as frequently as the alternative trait.

Table 1.1. Results of several of Mendel's experiments

Parental characteristics	F_1	*Numbers of F_2 progeny*	*F_2 ratio*
round × wrinkled (seeds)	round	5474 round, 1850 wrinkled	2.96:1
yellow × green (cotyledons)	yellow	6022 yellow, 2001 green	3.01:1
purple × white (flowers)	purple	705 purple, 224 white	3.15:1
inflated × constricted (pods)	inflated	882 inflated, 299 constricted	2.95:1
long × short (stems)	long	787 long, 277 short	2.84:1

In the succeeding sections we will see how Mendel followed up this basic observation and performed experiments that led to his concept of discrete genetic units and to the principles governing their inheritance.

Particulate Hereditary Determinants

The prevailing concept of heredity in Mendel's time was that the process consisted of a blending of the trails of the parents in a hybrid, as though the hereditary material consisted of fluids that became permanently mixed when combined in the hybrids. However, Mendel's observation that one of the parental characteristics was absent in F_1 hybrids and reappeared in unchanged form in the F_2 was inconsistent with the idea of blending. Thus, Mendel concluded that the traits from the parental lines were transmitted as two different elements *of a particulate nature* that retained their purity in the hybrids. The element associated with the trait seen in the hybrids (round seeds, in the example just used) he called *dominant*, and the other element, associated with the trait not seen in the hybrids but seen in their progeny (wrinkled seeds), he called *recessive*.

Mendel's conclusions were reinforced by the results of experiments in which F_3 progeny produced by the self-pollination of individual F_2 plants were observed. In the experiment with round versus wrinkled seeds, for example, F_2 plants grown from wrinkled seeds produced only wrinkled F_3 seeds. When 565 F_2 plants were grown from round seeds, 193 of them produced round seeds but the other 372 plants produced both round and wrinkled seeds in a proportion very close to 3:1. The results can be diagrammed as follows,

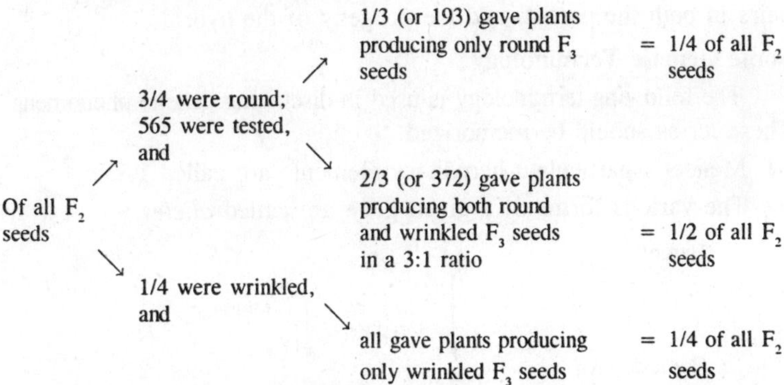

The same 1:2:1 ratio was observed each time progeny from individual F_2 plants were obtained.

Principle of Segregation

From the arithmetical regularities observed in his experimental results and the deduction that the hereditary determinants are distinct paniculate entities, Mendel formulated the following simple explanation of the 1:2:1 ratio in an F_2:

1. A pea plant has two hereditary determinants for each observed trail.
2. Each reproductive cell (*gamete*) of a plant has only one of the two determinants and it may be either member of the pair present in the plant. The two determinants of the pair occur with equal frequencies in the reproductive cells.
3. The union of male and female reproductive cells in the formation of new *zygotes* (fertilized eggs) is a random process.

Application of this explanation to the 1:2:1 ratios observed by Mendel in the F_2 from crosses between plants differing in any pair of alternative characters, using the symbols *A* and *a* to represent the dominant and recessive determinants, respectively.

The essential point in this explanation is the separation, or *segregation*, in unaltered form, of the two hereditary determinants in a hybrid plant during the processes leading to the formation of the reproductive cells. This *principle of segregation* is sometimes called Mendel's first law.

The Principle of Segregation: During the formation of gametes the paired elements separate and segregate randomly such that each gamete receives one or the other element.

Note the assumption that the hereditary elements arc present in pairs in both the parents and the progeny of the hybrids.

Some Genetic Terminology

The following terminology is used in discussing genetic phenomena. These terms should be memorized.

1. Mendel's particulate hereditary elements arc called *genes*.
2. The various forms of a given gene are called *alleles*.

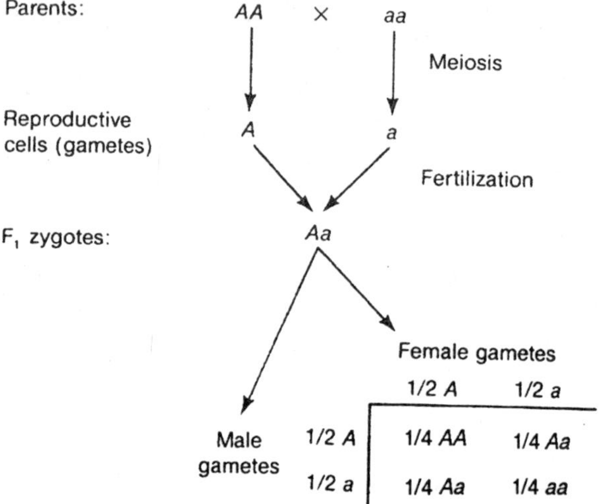

Fig. 1.3. A diagrammatic explanation of the 1:2:1 ratio observed by Mendel in the F_2 progeny from a cross between a homozygous dominant and a homozygous recessive pea plant.

3. Organisms in which the members of a pair alleles are different, as in the *Aa* hybrids, are said to be *heterozygous*, and those in which the two alleles are alike are said to be *homozygous*. An individual may be homozygous for the dominant (*AA*) or for the recessive (*aa*) allele, and in both cases will be true-breeding for the characteristic determined by the particular allele.
4. The *genotype* is the genetic constitution of an organism; *AA*, *Aa*, and *aa* are examples. Since a gamete carries only one allele of a given gene, its genotype will he either *A* or *a*, in the case of an *Aa* organism. The genotype of an individual is usually designated incompletely in that only those pairs of alleles of immediate interest are specified.
5. The *observable* properties of an organism make up its *phenotype*. Dominance results in the expression of the same phenotypic character—for example, round seeds—by both the homozygous dominant (*AA*) and heterozygous (*Aa*) genotypes.

Principle of Independent Assortment

In the experiments described so far, Mendel was concerned with the inheritance of single pairs of alleles. To determine whether the same pattern of inheritance applied to each pair of alleles when more than one pair was present in hybrids, he crossed parental plants that differed in two or three pairs of alleles that affected different characters. For example, plants from a true-breeding line having round seeds that were yellow were crossed with plants from a line having wrinkled green seeds.

The F_1 seeds from this cross were round and yellow; that is, they were hybrid for both characteristics, or *dihybrid*. Assuming that seed shape and colour are independent traits that do not affect one another, this phenotype was expected from the results of the individual *monohybrid* crosses, in which the genes resulting in round seed shape and yellow colour of the seed were dominant over their respective alleles. The F_2 seeds obtained when F_1 plants were grown and allowed to self-pollinate had the four possible combinations of phenotypic characteristics with the following frequencies:

round, yellow	315
wrinkled, yellow	101
round, green	108
wrinkled, green	32
	556

Mendel saw that when the pairs of alternative phenotypes were considered separately, the ratios 423 (315 + 108) round to 133 (101 + 32) wrinkled seeds and 416 (315 + 101) yellow to 140 (108 + 32) green seeds were in each case very close to the 3:1 ratio that he had observed in the F_2 populations from the monohybrid crosses. He also noticed that the four phenotypes in the F_2 from the dihybrid cross occurred approximately in the proportions 9/16 round and yellow, 3/16 wrinkled and yellow, 3/16 round and green, and 1/16 wrinkled and green.

Similar 9:3:3:1 ratios of F_2 phenotypes were found in the progeny of other dihybrid crosses. Mendel recognized that a 9:3:3:1 ratio is the expected result if two independently occurring 3:1 ratios are combined, and formulated the principle of independent assortment, sometimes called his second law.

The Principle of Independent Assortment: Segregation of the members of a pair of alleles is independent of the segregation of other pairs during the processes leading to formation of the reproductive cells.

To illustrate with the dihybrid F_1 we have considered, we can represent the dominant and recessive alleles of the pair affecting seed shape as *W* and *w*, respectively, and the allelic pair affecting seed colour as *G* and *g*. Then, the genotype of the F_1 is

$$\frac{W}{w} \; \frac{G}{g}$$

The result of independent assortment is that *W* is as likely to be included in a gamete with G as it is with *g*, and *w* is equally likely to be included with *G* or *g*. Thus, when two pairs of alleles are segregating, the gametes produced by such a dihybrid are the following:

1/4 *WG*, 1/4 *Wg*, 1/4 *wG*, and 1/4 *wg*

In later chapters we will see that there are important exceptions to the principle of independent assortment.

Mendel's hypothesis for the transmission of inherited characters—that is, alleles segregate and assort independently, and male and female gametes unite at random in the formation of progeny zygotes—explains the 9:3:3:1 ratio F_2 phenotypes in the dihybrid cross. The format used to show which combinations of F_1 female and male gametes produce which F_2 genotypes is called a *Punnett square*. The hypothesis accounted equally well for the more complex ratio of phenotypes that occurred in the F_2 progeny from a trihybrid, in which three pairs of genes were segregating. Mendel tested the predicted genotypes from the crosses by growing plants from the F_2 seeds and obtaining progenies of F_3 seeds by self-pollination.

Round green F_2 seeds would be expected to have the genotype *WW gg,* or, twice as frequently, *Ww gg.* To test this prediction, Mendel grew 102 plants from such seeds and found that 35 of them produced only round green seeds (indicating that they had the genotype *WW gg),* whereas the other 67 produced both round and wrinkled green seeds (indicating that they must have been *Ww gg),* a good agreement with the expected frequencies of the two genotypes. Similar agreement with the predicted relative frequencies of the different genotypes was found when plants were grown from round green and also from wrinkled yellow F_2 seeds. As expected, plants grown from wrinkled green seeds, with the predicted homozygous recessive genotype *ww gg,* produced only wrinkled green seeds.

Testcrosses

A second way in which Mendel tested the hypothesis of independent assortment was by crossing plants of the F_1 dihybrid *Ww Gg* with plants that were homozygous recessive for both genes, *ww gg.* One would predict that the dihybrid plants would produce four types of gametes—*WG, Wg, wG,* and *wg*—in equal frequencies, whereas the *ww gg* plants would produce only *wg* gametes. Thus, the progeny phenotypes are expected to consist of the round yellow, round green, wrinkled yellow, and wrinkled green phenotypes in a 1:1:1:1 ratio; this ratio is a direct reflection of the kinds of gametes produced by the dihybrid because no dominant alleles are contributed by the *ww gg* parent to obscure the results. The progeny Mendel obtained were 55

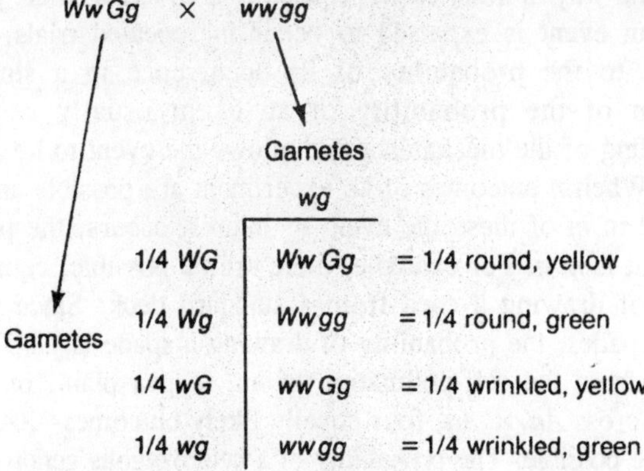

Fig. 1.4. Genotypes and phenotypes resulting from a testcross of a dihybrid.

round yellow, 51 round green, 49 wrinkled yellow, and 53 wrinkled green, in good agreement with the predicted 1:1:1:1 ratio. The results were the same in the reciprocal cross, that is, with the dihybrid as the female parent and the homozygous recessive as the male parent. This observation confirmed Mendel's assumption that in the gametes of the hybrids each possible genotype was present in both female and male gametes in approximately equal proportions.

A cross between a heterozygote, such as the *Ww wg* dihybrid, and an individual homozygous for the recessive alleles of the genes concerned is called a *testcross*. In such a cross both the genotypes and their relative frequencies in the gametes produced by the heterozygote arc known directly from examination of the phenotypes of the progeny, because one parent contributes only recessive alleles. Thus, testcrosses are exceedingly useful in the analysis of genetic processes. Another valuable type of cross is a *backcross*, a cross between a hybrid and an individual with the same genotype as one or the other of its parents. Backcrosses are commonly used by geneticists and by plant and animal breeders.

Mendelian Inheritance and Probability

The proportions of the different types of progeny obtained from a cross are an average result of numerous repeated events. Furthermore, the combinations of dominant and recessive alleles in the zygotes produced by the random union of gametes are subject to chance variation. Thus, some knowledge of the rules of probability for predicting the outcome of chance events is basic to understanding the transmission of hereditary characteristics.

A useful way to think about probability is in terms of the proportion of times an event is expected to occur in repealed trials, which is equivalent to the probability of its occurrence in a single trial. Evaluation of the probability of an event usually requires an understanding of the mechanism that allows the event to he a possible outcome. When n outcomes of an experiment are possible and equally likely, and in m of these the event of interest occurs, the probability of the event is m/n. For example, there are 52 possible, equally likely outcomes of drawing a card from a standard deck. Since 13 of the cards are spades, the probability of drawing a spade is 13/52, or 1/4. Similarly, from the self-pollination of an *Aa* pea plant, or from the equivalent cross *Aa* × *Aa*, four equally likely outcomes—*AA*, *Aa*, *aA*, and *aa*—are possible. The probability of a heterozygous genotype, which occurs in two of the four possible outcomes, is 2/4, or 1/2.

The *addition rule* states that the probability P of the occurrence of either of two events, A or B, is the sum of their individual probabilities minus the probability of their joint occurrence, A and B. That is,

$$P(\text{A or B}) = P(\text{A}) + P(\text{B}) - P(\text{A and B})$$

The rule is applicable, to the probability that a card drawn from a deck will be either an ace or a spade. A deck contains 4 aces and 13 spades, but one of the aces is also a spade; thus, P(ace or spade) = 4/52 (ace) + 13/52 (spade) – 1/52 (ace of spades) = 16/52 = 4/13.

In Mendelian genetics we are usually concerned with events that are *mutually exclusive*. Events are mutually exclusive if the occurrence of one event prevents the occurrence of others of the same set of events in the same trial, so the probability of their joint occurrence P(A and B) is zero. For example, the dominant and recessive phenotypes for a particular trail are mutually exclusive, as are kings and queens in a deck of cards. From the addition rule, *the probability of the occurrence of one or another of a set of mutually exclusive events is the sum of the probabilities of the separate events*. Thus, the probability of a dominant phenotype in the progeny from the cross *Aa* × *Aa* is 1/ 4 + 2/4, or 3/4, which is the sum of the probabilities of a dominant homozygote (from *AA*) and a heterozygote (from *Aa*). Similarly, the probability of drawing a face card—a king, a queen, or a jack—is 4/ 52 + 4/52 + 4/52 = 3/13.

It is sometimes necessary to consider the probability of an event B, when event A has occurred—that is, the probability of B conditional on the occurrence of A, or P(B, given A). For example, assume that a card is drawn and not returned to the deck, and then a second card is drawn. If the first card is an ace, the probability that the second card is an ace is 3/51, because removing the first ace leaves three aces in a deck of 51 cards. By the same reasoning, the conditional probability of drawing a king, if the first two cards drawn are aces, is 4/50.

The *multiplication rule* states that the probability of the joint occurrence of events A and B is the probability of the occurrence of A limes the conditional probability of B given that A has occurred, or

$$P\ (\text{A and B}) = P(\text{A}) \cdot P(\text{B, given A})$$

Using another example of cards drawn from a deck and not replaced, the probability of drawing an ace followed by a second ace is (4/52) · (3/51), or 1/221. The rule can be extended to any number of events. For example, there are four aces in a deck, so the probability of drawing four aces in successive trials is (4/52)·(3/51)·(2/50)·(1/49) = 1/270,725.

In genetics it is more common that the events of interest are independent—that is, the occurrence of the first event has no effect on the probability of occurrence of the second. When this condition applies, the multiplication rule states that *the probability of two or more independent, events occurring together is the product of their individual probabilities*. The application of this rule to determining the probabilities, or expected relative frequencies, of the nine different genotypes among the F_2 progeny produced by self-pollination of a *Ww Gg* dihybrid. The rule provides a simple way to determine the probability of a specific genotype among the progeny from a cross involving numerous pairs of alleles undergoing independent assortment. For example, the probability of the genotype *AaBbCcDd* among the progeny from the cross *AaBbCcDd* × *AaBbCcDd* is (1/2)(1/2)(1/2)(1/2) = $(1/2)^4$, or 1/16.

The reasoning by which the probabilities of the four different phenotypes among the F_2 progeny of a *Ww Gg* dihybrid can be

F_1: *WwGg*

F_2 genotypes:

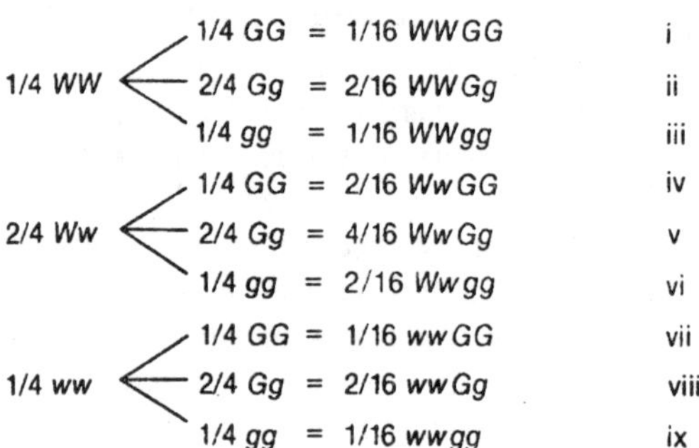

F_2 phenotypes:

3/4 round
- 3/4 yellow = 9/16 round yellow (i + ii + iv + v)
- 1/4 green = 3/16 round green (iii + vi)

1/4 wrinkled
- 3/4 yellow = 3/16 wrinkled yellow (vii + viii)
- 1/4 green = 1/16 wrinkled green ix

Fig. 1.5. An example of the use of the addition and multiplication rules to determine the probabilities of the nine genotypes and four phenotypes in the F_2 produced by self-pollination of a dihybrid F_1.

determined is an example of the use of both the addition and multiplication rules. Recall that the probability of a dominant phenotype for a character is the sum of the probabilities of a homozygote and a heterozygote, or $1/4 + 2/4 = 3/4$, since these are mutually exclusive events. Then, the probability of a dominant phenotype for one character occurring with a dominant phenotype for a second, independent character is the product of their separate probabilities, or $(3/4)(3/4) = 9/16$.

Segregation in Pedigrees

Determination of the genetic basis of a character from the kinds of crosses we have considered requires the production of large numbers of offspring from the mating of selected parents. The analysis of segregation by this method is not possible in humans, whose matings cannot be controlled, and is not usually economically feasible for some traits in large domestic animals. However, the mode of inheritance of a trait can sometimes be determined, by examining the segregation of alleles in several generations of related individuals. This is typically done with a family tree that shows the phenotype of each individual; such a diagram is called a *pedigree*. An important application of probability in genetics is its use in pedigree analysis.

In the construction of a pedigree such as the one for the human family, females and males are by convention represented by circles and squares, respectively, and a diamond is used if the sex of an individual is unknown. Individuals having the phenotype of interest are indicated by shaded symbols (in this case, red). The symbols of parents

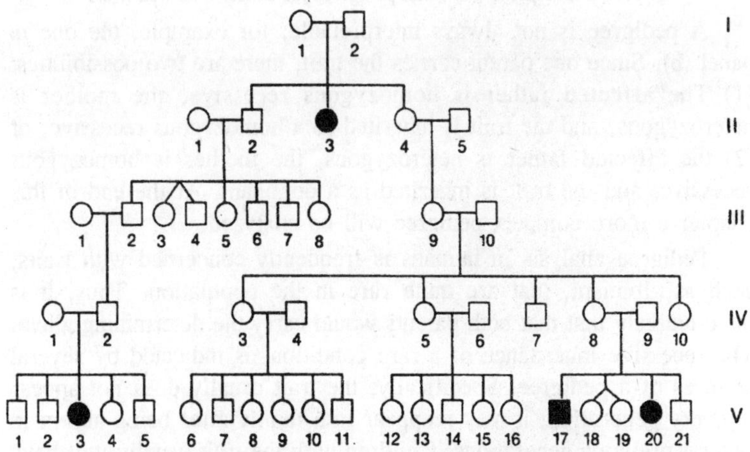

Fig. 1.6. Pedigree of a human family showing the inheritance of albinism. Females and males are denoted by circles and squares, respectively.

are joined by a horizontal line, which is connected vertically to a second horizontal line that extends above the symbols for their offspring. The offspring of two parents are called *siblings*, or *sibs*, regardless of sex, and are represented from left to right in order of their birth. Successive generations in a pedigree are designated by Roman numerals and the individuals in a generation by Arabic numbers. Twins are indicated by diagonal lines, which converge at the horizontal line above the sibship in the case of nonidentical twins or at the end of a short vertical line from the sibship line for identical twins.

Two affected individuals are present among the offspring of unaffected parents. In such a situation a reasonable interpretation is that both parents carry the determining allele (they are both heterozygous) and that the trait of interest is determined by the homozygosity of the recessive allele.

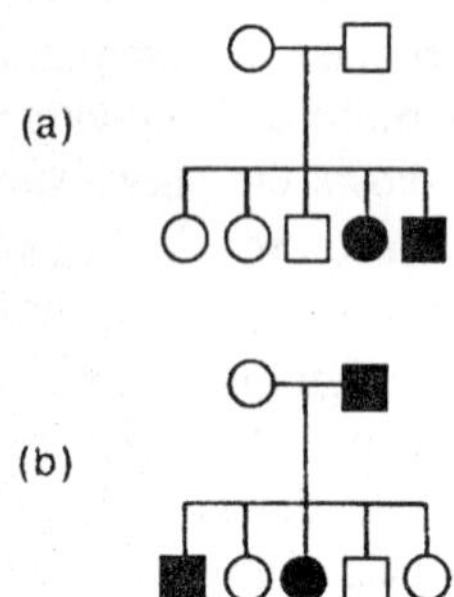

Fig. 1.7. Two hypothetical small pedigrees for simply inherited traits.

A pedigree is not always interpretable, for example, the one in panel (b). Since one parent carries the trait, there are two possibilities: (1) The affected father is homozygous recessive, the mother is heterozygous, and the trait is inherited as a homozygous recessive, or (2) the affected father is heterozygous, the mother is homozygous recessive, and the trait is inherited as a dominant. At the end of this chapter a more complex pedigree will be analyzed.

Pedigree analysis in humans is frequently concerned with traits, such as albinism, that are quite rare in the population. Thus, it is quite unlikely that that both parents would carry the determining allele. The recessive inheritance of a rare condition, is indicated by several features of a pedigree. Specifically, the trait usually does not appear in every generation; it may reappear in a family after being absent in several previous generations. Children with the trait usually will have phenotypically normal parents, who must therefore be heterozygous.

Such a parent is often termed a carrier. As expected from the pedigree, albinism is inherited as a recessive. In the infrequent case in which both parents are affected, all of their offspring will be affected.

If a rare trait is inherited as a dominant, most affected individuals will be heterozygous. Most matings of these individuals will be with homozygous recessive partners and result in about equal numbers of affected and normal offspring. Thus, the trait will appear in every generation, though some lines of descent may lack the trait if by chance only normal offspring occur. In the case of dominant inheritance, the trail will never be seen among the offspring of normal parents.

Gene and Cellular Products

The first suggestion of a relation between genes and specific cellular products was made by Archibald Garrod, an English physician interested in the rare disease *alkaptonuria* and several other human disorders. He proposed that these disorders result from inherited defects in body chemistry and called them *inborn errors of metabolism*. By examining pedigrees of human families in which alkaptonuria occurred, he correctly deduced that alkaptonuria is determined by a single recessive gene. The disease, which is actually quite harmless, is characterized by the accumulation and excretion of an innocuous substance that causes the urine of an affected individual to turn black upon exposure to air. Noting that heterozygous and homozygous individuals had the same phenotype, he suggested (correctly) that the defect in alkaptonuria is the absence of an enzyme required for the breakdown of this compound. The active enzyme would be absent in homozygous recessive (*aa*) alkaptonurics and present in both homozygous dominant (*AA*) and heterozygous (*Aa*) individuals. Since enzymes are catalytic proteins (they increase the rate of chemical reactions) that are unchanged in the reaction and can function repeatedly, a single enzyme molecule may be able to catalyze a particular reaction hundreds (occasionally, millions) of times per second. Thus, a heterozygote with half the number of enzyme molecules possessed by a homozygous dominant individual will, in most cases, not cause phenotypic differences with respect to the trait determined by a particular enzyme. Whereas this is frequently the case, we will see examples in this chapter of phenotypic differences between heterozygous and homozygous dominant individuals.

Variation from Simple Patterns of Dominance

In Mendel's experiments all traits had clear dominant-recessive patterns. This was fortunate since otherwise he might not have made his discoveries. However, lack of strict dominance is widespread in nature. In this section several alternative patterns will be described.

Absence of Dominance of Some Alleles

Absence of dominance of one member of a pair of alleles over the other is quite common in most organisms. For example, in crosses between snapdragon plants from a red-flowered variety and a variety with ivory-coloured flowers, the F_1 plants produce only pink flowers intermediate in colour between those of the parental varieties. In one experiment, the F_2 obtained by self-pollination of the F_1 hybrids consisted of 22 plants with red flowers, 52 with pink flowers, and 23 with ivory flowers. The numbers agree with the Mendelian monohybrid ratio of 1 dominant homozygote:2 heterozygotes:1 recessive homozygote expected in the absence of dominance. In agreement with the predictions from this interpretation, the red-flowered F_2 plants produced only red-flowered progeny, the ivory-flowered plants also were true-breeding, and the pink-flowered plants again produced progeny of all three phenotypes in the proportions 1/4 red, 1/2 pink, and 1/4 ivory.

In this example of flower-colour inheritance the absence of dominance is explained by the mechanism of formation of the red pigment. The pigment is formed by a complex sequence of enzymatic reactions. A critical enzyme is determined by the *I* allele, and a defective enzyme is determined by the *i* allele. In *Ii* heterozygotes, concentrations of the enzyme required for synthesis of the red pigment are reduced. At the reduced enzyme concentration (probably one-half that present in *II* homozygotes), pigment synthesis is also reduced during development of the flower, because the pigment is produced in fixed and limiting amounts per *I* allele. Such an effect does not occur in all systems, since frequently half the amount of an enzyme is still sufficient to make an adequate amount of gene product to yield the dominant phenotype in a heterozygote, owing to the catalytic nature of the enzyme. This is the case for alkaptonuria, as we saw earlier.

Even in cases in which dominance seems unmistakable, it is not unusual to find an effect of a recessive allele evident in heterozygotes. Recall that when Mendel crossed a pea plant having wrinkled seeds with a plant from a round-seeded variety, the F_1 seeds were round—indicating complete dominance of the allele (*W*) from the parent with round seeds. Microscopic examination later revealed differences in the number and form of the starch grains in seeds of the three genotypes. Homozygous *WW* peas contain many large and well-rounded starch grains, with the result that the seeds retain water and shrink uniformly as they ripen, and do not become wrinkled. The grains in wrinkled (*ww*) peas are irregular in shape and much less numerous, so the ripening seeds lose water more rapidly and shrink unevenly. In heterozygous peas, the grains are intermediate in shape and number, but the starch content is high enough to result in uniform shrinking of the seeds and no wrinkling. Thus, the basic physiological phenomenon that determines the shape of pea seeds is the enzyme-mediated synthesis of starch, with the heterozygotes having a capacity for starch synthesis and a starch content intermediate between the two homozygotes. Note that if the phenotypes are considered to be round and wrinkled, *W* is dominant over *w*, but if the phenotypes were determined by microscopic examination of starch grains, dominance would not be evident.

For characters such as flower pigment in snapdragons and the starch content of pea cotyledons (the two halves of the seed), the expression in heterozygotes appears to be almost exactly intermediate between the homozygotes. This is the expected condition if there is *no dominance* of one allele over the other. The expression of other phenotypic characters in heterozygotes, though also intermediate between the respective homozygotes, may be more similar to one than to the other. Phenotypic expression of this type is the result of *partial dominance* of the effects of one of the alleles.

Codominance and Multiple Allelism

Another exception to simple dominance occurs when the two different alleles in a heterozygote are both fully expressed, resulting in a phenotype that is qualitatively different from those of the homozygotes. This is called *codominance*. One of the best examples is the effect of the genes that determine human blood groups, of which the ABO group is the best known. The blood-group genes determine the synthesis of polysaccharides (polymers of sugars) on the surface of red blood cells. Two distinct polysaccharides, A and B, are made, and these are determined by the alleles I^A and I^B respectively. A third allele I^O, which is a recessive, is defective in that it does not determine synthesis of either A or B polysaccharides. The result is that a homozygous recessive I^OI^O individual produces red blood cells lacking both polysaccharides, and such an individual has type O blood. An I^AI^A individual or an I^AI^O heterozygote has type A blood (because the A polysaccharide is present), and an I^BI^B individual or an I^BI^O heterozygote has type B blood. The I^AI^B individual illustrates codominance, for his or her blood cells possess both A and B polysaccharides and hence has type AB blood.

Blood groups are important in medicine because of the frequent need for blood transfusions. An important feature of the ABO system is that most human blood contains antibodies to either the A or B polysaccharide. An *antibody* is a protein made by the immune system, capable of binding to a foreign molecule (called an *antigen*) and inactivating it. Antibodies are specific in that usually only a single foreign molecule is recognized. Inactivation is usually accomplished by formation of a precipitate or at least a large molecular aggregate. For poorly understood reasons, antibodies to a normal body constituent do not form. Thus, type A blood contains red cells with the A surface antigens and only anti-B antibody, and type B blood contains only anti-A antibody. Type O blood, which lacks both A and B antigens, contains both anti-A and anti-B antibodies; and type AB blood lacks both antibodies since both A and B antigens are present. The clinical significance of the blood groups is that a transfusion of type A blood to a type B person will result in clumping of the blood cells and death. Note that type O blood, which lacks both A and B antigens, can be transfused to anyone and a type AB individual can receive any blood, because no antibodies are present. Thus, type O and type AB individuals are called universal donors and universal recipients, respectively.

Note that the ABO system illustrates both codominance (both A and B antigens are produced by an I^AI^B individual) and *multiple allelism* (three alleles—I^A, I^B, I^O—comprise the system and any allelic pair is a possible genotype). Many examples of multiple allelism are known; they do not always exhibit codominance. Also, absence of dominance, as seen with snapdragon colour, produces a blending effect in heterozygotes, but in codominance gene products of both alleles are present.

Effects of Genes on the Expression of Other Genes

In the examples considered so far, distinct traits such as colour and shape have been independent. However, since all organisms are complex biochemical systems and all traits are determined ultimately by a series of chemical reactions, it should not be unexpected that different genes and their particular alleles often influence one another. Several types of mutual influences are possible; for example, the product of one allele might either inhibit or enhance the activity of another gene, or a single trait might require the activity of two or more genes. This phenomenon, which causes departures from Mendelian ratios, is called *epistasis*. It differs from dominance, which always refers to the modification of the expression of one member of a pair of alleles by the other.

A well-studied example of epistasis is comb shape in chickens. There are four alternative shapes—rose, pea, single, and walnut. When the crosses rose × single and pea × single were made, using true-breeding parents of each type, the following results were obtained:

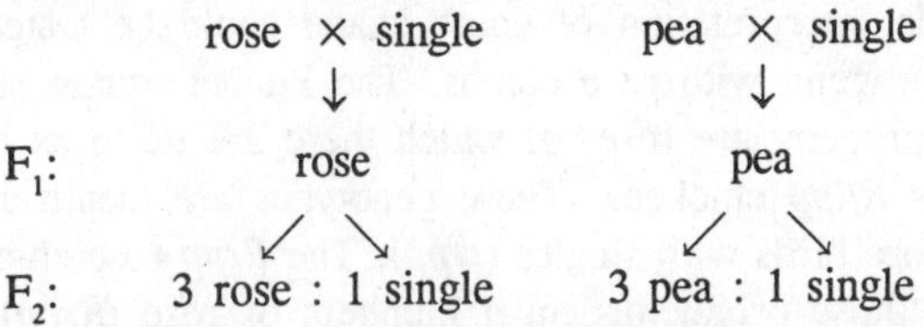

These results are typical of Mendelian segregation, with rose determined by one dominant allele and pea by another allele, single being a homozygous recessive. However, the results of the cross rose × pea were not as straight-forward: the F_1 hybrids were walnut-combed, and all four phenotypes appeared among the F_2, progeny. That the F_2 phenotypes occurred in the approximate proportions 9/16 walnut, 3/16 rose, 3/16 pea, and 1/16 single indicates that walnut comb is the

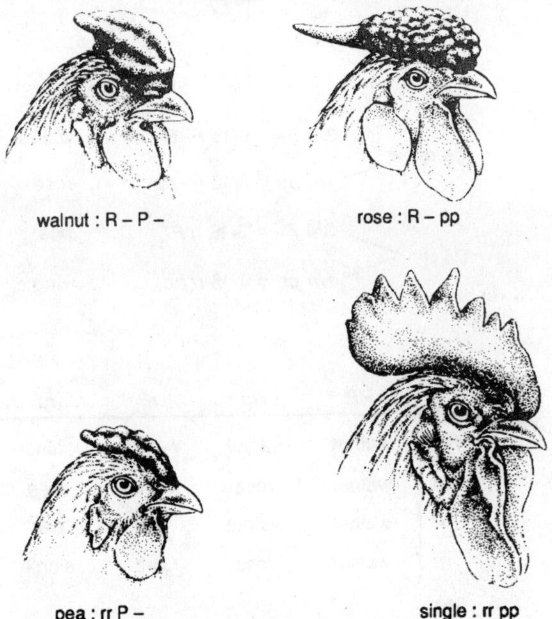

Fig. 1.8. Comb types characteristics of different breeds of chickens and the corresponding genotypes.

product of the combined effects of the alleles of the dominant genes for rose and pea combs. Note that in the grouping of F_2 genotypes into phenotypic classes in the figure, a dash is used to indicate the presence of either a dominant or a recessive allele, since the homozygous dominant and heterozygous genotypes are phenotypically indistinguishable.

The two-gene interpretation of comb shape could be tested by crossing the F_2 progeny with rose combs. The Punnet square shows that 3/16 of the progeny are rose, of which there are twice as many *RrPp* chickens as *RRpp* chickens. These genotypes are identified by testcrossing the rose birds with singles (*rrpp*). The *Rrpp* rose chickens are identified as those producing equal numbers of rose *(Rrpp)* and

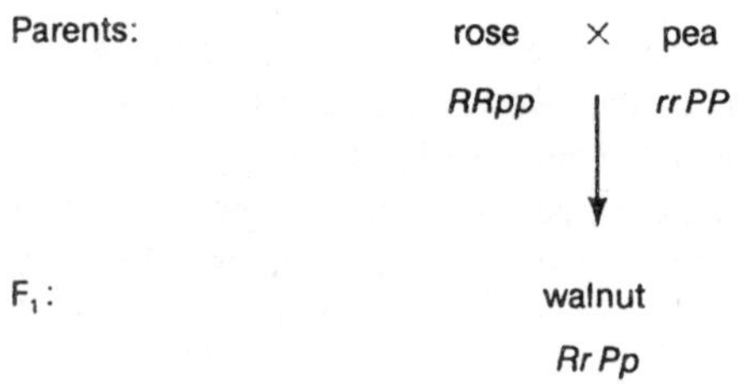

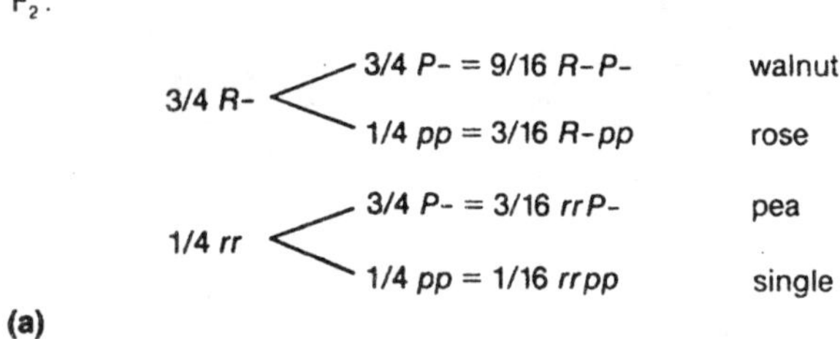

	RP	*Rp*	*rP*	*rp*
RP	walnut	walnut	walnut	walnut
Rp	walnut	rose	walnut	rose
rP	walnut	walnut	pea	pea
rp	walnut	rose	pea	single

(b)

Fig. 1.9. (a) The inheritance of comb type in chickens. (b) Punnett square for a cross between walnut individuals of the F_1 in (a).

single *(rrpp)* offspring; the *RRpp* rose individuals yield only rose *Rrpp* progeny.

A second example of epistasis is the determination of flower colour in sweet peas. When a variety that breeds true for coloured flowers is crossed with either of two different white-flowered varieties, the F_1 plants have coloured flowers in both cases. Self-pollination of the F_1 hybrids from each cross results in an F_2 in which 3/4 of the plants have coloured flowers and 1/4 are white flowered. The simplest explanation for these results is that the two white- flowered varieties are homozygous for a recessive allele of the same gene, in which case they would be expected to produce a white-flowered F_1 when crossed. However, when the two varieties were crossed, the F_1 plants produce coloured flowers. In the F_2 obtained in one experiment by self- pollination of the hybrids, 382 plants with coloured flowers and 269 with while flowers were found—a ratio close to 9:7. The coloured flowers in the F_1 hybrids and the occurrence of a 9:7 ratio in the F_2 can both be explained by the effects of two independently segregating pairs of genes, with the presence of at least one dominant allele of both genes required for the production of flower colour. This interpretation is testable by examining the self-pollinated progeny of individual F_2 plants with coloured flowers. (To demonstrate the predictions for yourself, determine the actual genotypes of the F_2 plants

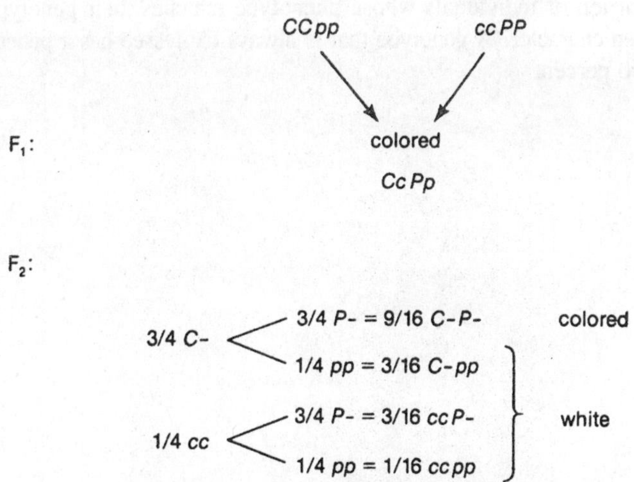

Fig. 1.10. A cross showing epistasis in the determination of flower colour in sweet peas. Colour formation requires at least one dominant allele of each of two genes.

grouped as *C-P*, the expected relative frequencies of these genotypes, and the relative proportions of coloured and white-flowered progeny expected from the self-pollination of plants with each genotype.)

In the absence of gene *C* (that is, in *cc* homozygotes), little or no compound Y would be produced and the pathway would be blocked at that point. In turn, compound Y is the substrate for the gene-*P* enzyme, which converts it into pigment. Therefore, the absence of gene *P* (in *pp* homozygotes) would block the final step in pigment synthesis. The genes are related in that pigment production requires both enzymes, and these are determined by dominant alleles of the genes.

The phenotypic expression of *some* genes is the same in all individuals having the same genotype. However, the phenotypes determined by *most* genes are more variable. This variation may result from the effects of other genes, as just seen, or from sensitivity of the biological processes, which produce the particular phenotype, to environmental conditions. Such genes are said to have *variable expressivity*, meaning that they vary in expression in different individuals. The different degrees of expression often form a continuous series from full expression to no expression of phenotypic characteristics. A second form of variation in the expression of a gene is *variable penetrance*. Examples of this phenomenon include cases of identical human twins in which a genetically determined abnormal character occurs in one twin but not in the other. Penetrance is defined as the proportion of individuals whose phenotype matches their genotype for a given character. A genotype that is always expressed has a penetrance of 100 percent.

2

GENES AND CHROMOSOMES

Mendel's experiments made clear that the units of heredity are stable and particulate. However, at the time, the mechanics of the transmission of genes from one generation to the next were quite mysterious, and both the role of the nucleus in reproduction and the details of cell division were unknown. Once these phenomena became understood and chromosomes were seen by microscopy and recognized to be carriers of genes, new understanding came at a rapid pace. This chapter examines both the relation between chromosomes and genes and the mechanism of chromosome segregation during cell division.

STABILITY OF CHROMOSOME COMPLEMENTS

In the 1870s the importance of the nucleus and its contents was recognized by the observation that the nuclei of two gametes fuse in the process of fertilization. The next major advance was the discovery of *chromosomes*, which had been made visible by light microscopy, stained by basic dyes. Then, chromosomes were found to segregate into both gametes and daughter cells by an orderly process prior to cell division. Finally, three important regularities were observed about the chromosome complements (the complete set of chromosomes) of higher plants and animals:

1. The nucleus of each *somatic cell* (a cell of the body, in contrast with a *germ cell* or gamete) contains a fixed number of chromosomes typical of the particular species. However, the numbers vary tremendously among species and have little relationship to the complexity of the organism.
2. The chromosomes in the nuclei of somatic cells usually occur in pairs. Thus, the 46 chromosomes of humans consist of 7 pairs.

Furthermore, one chromosome of each pair comes from the maternal parent and the other from the paternal parent of the organism. Cells with nuclei of this sort, containing two similar sets of chromosomes are called *diploid*.

3. The germ cells of gametes that unite in fertilization to produce the diploid state of somatic cells have nuclei with only one set of chromosomes, consisting of one member of each pair—these nuclei are *haploid*.

The presence of a constant diploid chromosome number in cells of complex organisms that develop from single cells, and the formation of gametes with the haploid chromosome number indicate that there are two processes of nuclear division, one that maintains chromosome number—mitosis—and another that halves the number—meiosis. These two processes are examined in the following sections.

Mitosis

Mitosis is a precise process of nuclear division that ensures that each of two daughter cells receives a complement of chromosomes identical with the complement of the parent cell. The essential details of the process are the same in all organisms. Moreover, the basic process is remarkably simple: each chromosome, present as a doubled structure at the beginning of nuclear division, divides into identical halves that are separated from each other, and one of them goes into each of the two daughter nuclei that are formed.

In a cell not ready for mitosis chromosomes are not visible. This stage of the cell cycle is called *interphase*. In preparation for mitosis DNA synthesis occurs during a period of late interphase called *S*. DNA synthesis is accompanied by chromosome replication. Before and after S, there are periods, called G_1 and G_2, respectively, in which DNA synthesis does not occur. The *cell cycle*, or the life cycle of a cell, is commonly described in terms of these three interphase periods followed by mitosis, *M*—that is, $G_1 \rightarrow S \rightarrow G_2 \rightarrow M$. This is a somewhat arbitrary representation in which the final event in cell reproduction—The division of the cytoplasm into two approximately equal parts containing the daughter nuclei—is included in the M period.

The length of time required for a complete life cycle varies with cell type. In higher organisms the majority require 18-24 hr. The relative duration of the different periods in the cycle also varies considerably with cell type. Mitosis is usually the shortest period, requiring between 1/2 and 2 hr.

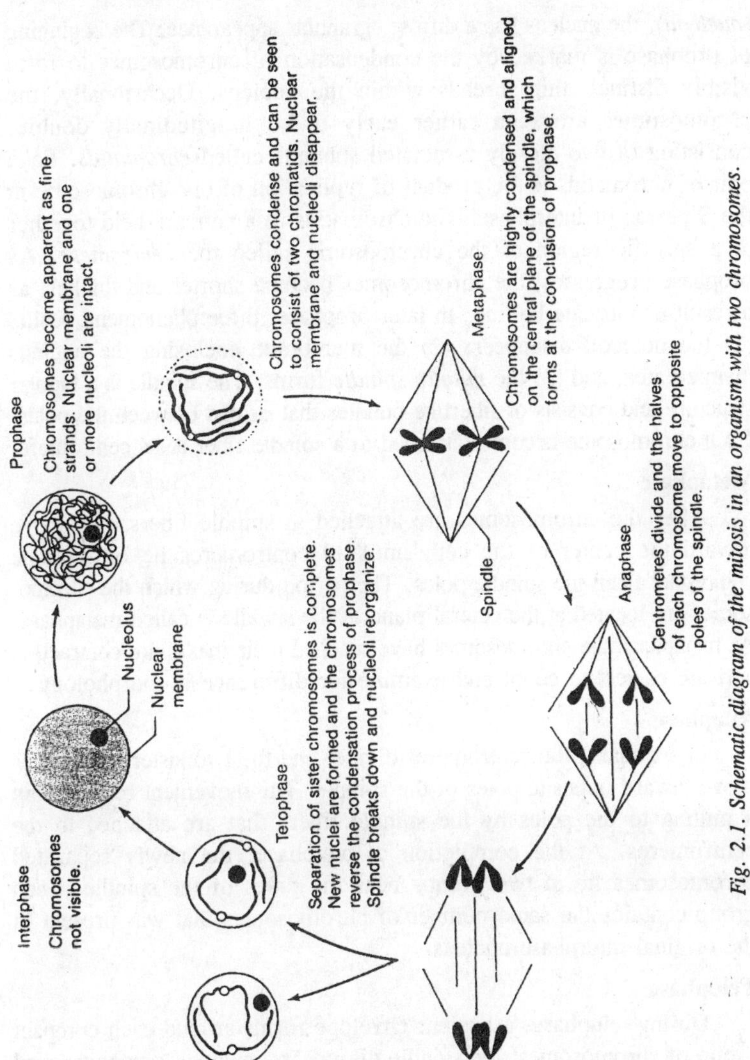

Fig. 2.1. Schematic diagram of the mitosis in an organism with two chromosomes.

The four stages—*prophase*, *metaphase*, *anaphase*, and *telophase*—into which mitosis is conventionally divided have the following characteristics:

Prophase

During interphase, the chromosomes have the form of extended filaments and cannot be seen as discrete bodies with a light microscope. Except for the presence of one or more conspicuous dark bodies (*nucleoli*), the nucleus has a diffuse, granular appearance. The beginning of prophase is marked by the condensation of chromosomes to form visibly distinct, thin threads within the nucleus. Occasionally, the chromosomes are seen rather early to be longitudinally double, consisting of two closely associated subunits called *chromatids*. Each pair of chromatids is the product of replication of one chromosome in the S period of interphase. The chromatids in a pair are held together at a specific region of the chromosome called the *centromere*. As prophase progresses, the chromosomes become shorter and thicker, as a result of intricate boiling. In later prophase, three phenomena occur: (1) the nucleoli disappear; (2) the membrane enclosing the nucleus disintegrates; and (3) the *mitotic spindle* forms. The spindle is a bipolar structure and consists of fiberlike bundles that extend between the poles. Each chromosome becomes attached to a spindle fiber at its centromere.

Metaphase

After the chromosomes are attached to spindle fibers they move toward the center of the cell, until all centromeres lie on a plane equidistant from the spindle poles. The period during which the chromosomes are located at the central plane of the spindle is called metaphase. At metaphase the chromosomes have reached their maximum contraction and are easiest to count and examine for difference in morphology.

Anaphase

In anaphase, the centromeres divide, and the two sister chromatids move toward opposite poles of the spindle. The movement results from a pulling to the poles by the spindle fibers that are attached to the centromeres. At the completion of anaphase, the newly separated chromosomes lie in two groups near the poles of the spindle. Each group contains the same number of chromosomes that was present in the original interphase nucleus.

Telophase

During telophase, a nuclear envelope forms around each compact group of chromosomes, the spindle disappears, nucleoli recognize, and the chromosomes undergo a reversal of the condensation process that occurred in prophase until they are no longer visible as discrete entities. Gradually, the two daughter nuclei assume a typical interphase appearance, and the cell divides.

Meiosis

Meiosis is à mode of cell division in which cells form that have *half* the number of chromosomes present in the premeiotic cell; typically cells with the haploid chromosome number are formed by division of a cell with the diploid number. Meiosis consists of two successive nuclear divisions. During the first division, the two members of each pair of chromosomes, which are said to be *homologous* to each other, become closely associated along their length. The homologous

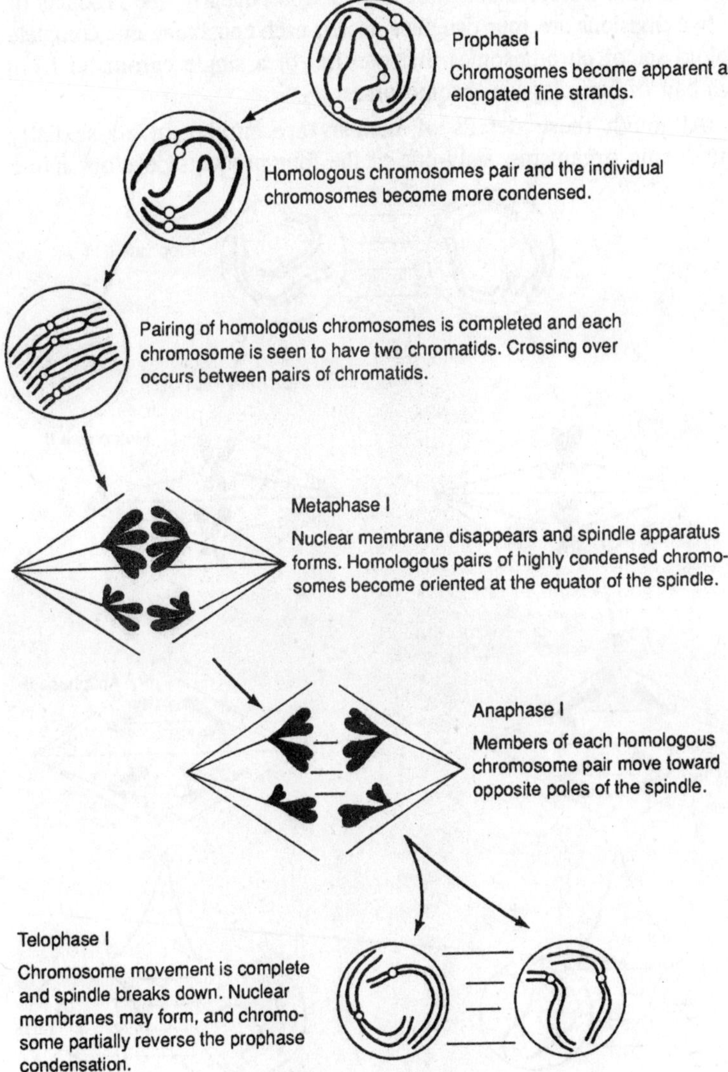

Fig. 2.2. First meiotic division.

chromosomes, each consisting of two sister chromatids that remain joined at the centromere, are then separated from one another into two nuclei, each containing a haploid set of duplex chromosomes. Without chromosome replication, a second division (resembling a mitotic division) occurs in which the chromatids of each chromosome are separated into different daughter nuclei. Consequently, the products of the two divisions are four daughter nuclei, each containing one complete haploid set of chromosomes that consists of a single chromatid from each pair of homologous chromosomes.

Although these details of meiosis are similar in all sexually reproducing organisms, only one of the four products develops into a

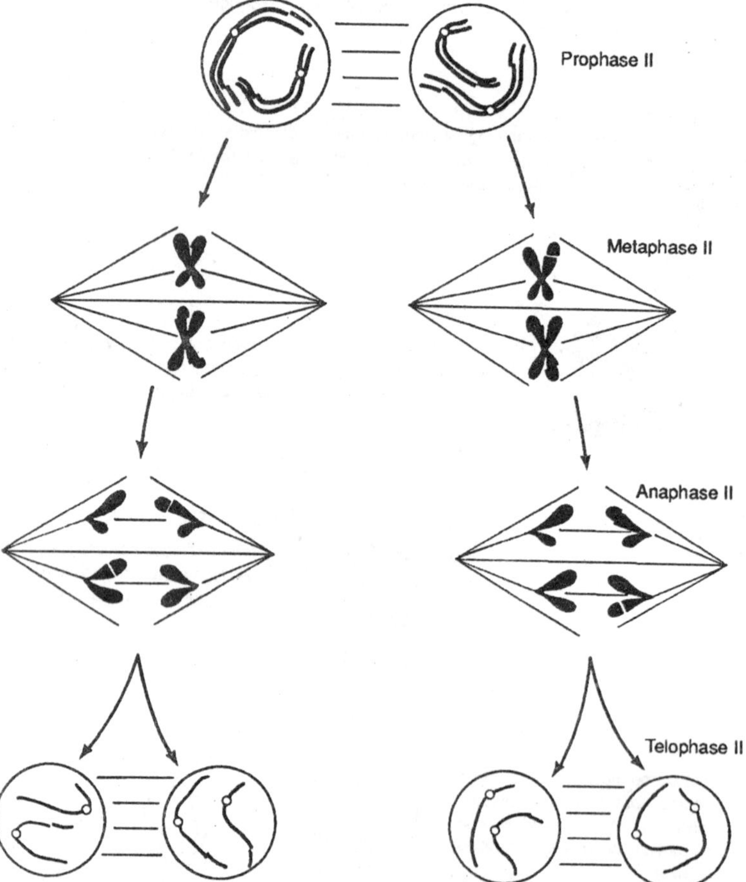

Fig. 2.3. Second meiotic division.

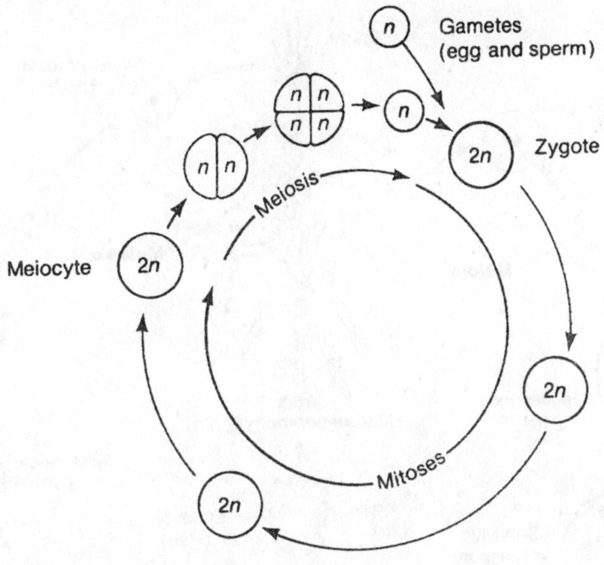

Fig. 2.4. The life cycle of a higher animal; n is the number in the haploid set.

functional cell in females of both animals and plants (the other three disintegrate); meiosis occurs in specific cells called *meiocytes*, a general term for the primary oocytes and spermatocytes in the gamete-forming tissues of animals. In plants the haploid spores produced by meiosis typically undergo one or more mitotic divisions to produce a gametophyte in which gametes are produced by mitotic division of a haploid nucleus. Thus, in animals the products of meiosis are gametes, whereas in plants the products of these nuclear divisions (which occur in the sporophyte generation) are *spores*. These spores develop into gametophytes (the gametophyte generation), in which the gametes are produced by mitosis. In Protista and lower plants haploid spores are produced almost immediately after a diploid zygote is formed by gametic fusion—that is, the sporophyte in these organisms consists only of the zygote.

Meiosis is a more complex and considerably longer process than mitosis and usually requires days or even weeks. The essence of meiosis, which we will now examine in more detail, is that *it consists of two divisions of the nucleus but only one duplication of the chromosomes*. The nuclear divisions—called the *first meiotic division* and the *second meiotic division*—can be separated into a sequence of stages similar

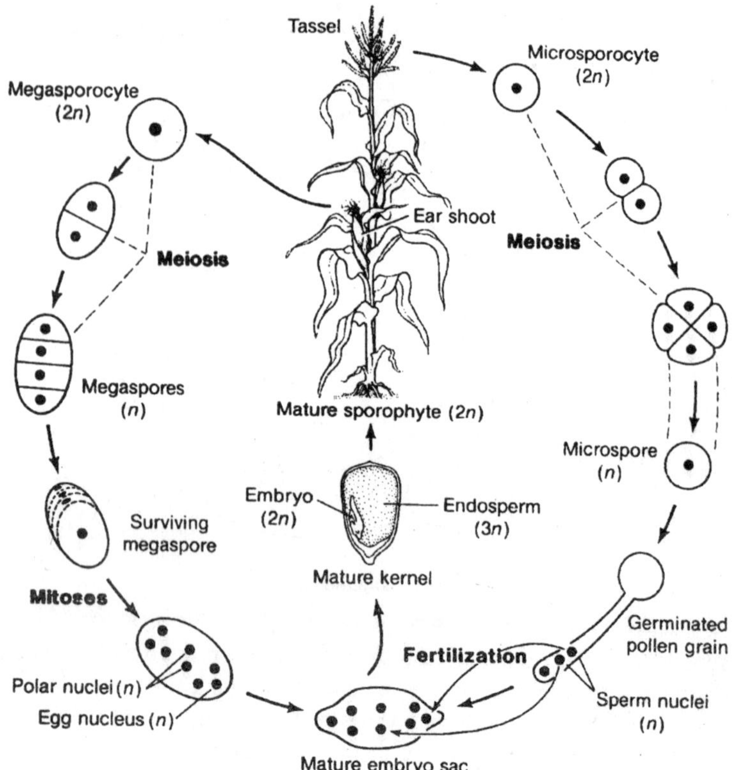

Fig. 2.5. The life cycle of corn Zea mays.

to those used to describe mitosis. The distinctive events of this important process occur during the first division of the nucleus; these events are described in the following section.

First Meiotic Division

The four main stages of the first meiotic division are called *prophase I*, *metaphase I*, *anaphase I*, and *telophase I*. These stages are generally more complex than their counterparts in mitosis.

Prophase I

This is a long stage, lasting several days in most higher organisms and commonly divided into five substages—*leptotene*, *zygotene*, *pachytene*, *diplotene*, and *diakinesis*.

In the *leptotene* substage the chromosomes become visible as long, threadlike structures. The pairs of sister chromatids can be distinguished by electron microscopy. During this initial phase in condensation of the chromosomes numerous dense granules occur at irregular intervals along their length. These localized contractions, called *chromomeres*, have a characteristic number, size, and position in a given chromosome.

The *zygotene* substage is marked by the pairing, or *synapsis*, of homologous chromosomes. This pairing begins at one or more points along the length of the chromosomes and results in a precise chromomere-by-chromomere association. Each pair of synapsed homologous chromosomes is referred to as a *bivalent*.

During the *pachytene* substage condensation of the chromosomes continues, and the chromosome complement is represented by the haploid number of bivalents. Each bivalent consists of a *tetrad* of four chromatids, but the two sister chromatids of each chromosome usually cannot be distinguished. A genetically important event called *crossing over* occurs during pachytene, but it does not become evident until the transition to diplotene, the next substage.

At the onset of *diplotene* the synapsed chromosomes begin to separate. However, they remain held together at regions along their length called *chiasmata* (singular, *chiasma*). A chiasma is the result of breakage and rejoining between nonsister chromatids— that is, *a physical exchange between chromatids of homologous chromosomes*. In normal meiosis each bivalent will have at least one chiasma, and bivalents of long chromosomes often have three or more. During the final substage of prophase I—*diakinesis*—the chromosomes attain their maximum condensation. The homologous chromosomes in a bivalent remain connected by one or two chiasmata, which persist until the first meiotic anaphase. Near the end of diakinesis the formation of a spindle is initiated and the nuclear envelope breaks down.

Metaphase I

There is a general similarity between this stage and a mitotic metaphase. The bivalents become positioned with the centromeres of the two homologous chromosomes on opposite sides of the plane through the middle of the spindle. The co-orientation of the undivided centromeres of each bivalent relative to the two poles of the spindle occurs at *random* and determines the member of each pair of chromosomes that will subsequently move to a particular pole.

Anaphase I

During this stage the homologous chromosomes, each composed of two chromatids joined at an undivided centromere, separate from one another and move to opposite poles of the spindle.

Telophase I

At the completion of anaphase I a haploid set of chromosomes consisting of one homologue from each bivalent is located near each pole of the spindle. During telophase the spindle breaks down and, depending on the species, either a nuclear envelope briefly forms around each group of chromosomes or the chromosomes enter the second meiotic division after only a limited uncoiling.

Second Meiotic Division

In some species the chromosomes pass directly from telophase I to *prophase II* without loss of condensation; in others, there is an interkinesis stage between the two meiotic divisions. *Chromosome replication never occurs between the two divisions*; the chromosomes present at the beginning of the second division are identical to those present at the end of the first division. After a short prophase (prophase II) and the formation of second-division spindles, the centromeres of the chromosomes in each nucleus become aligned on the central plane of the spindle at *metaphase II*. During *anaphase II* the centromeres (replicated in the *first* division) separate and the chromatids of each chromosome move to opposite poles of the spindle. *Telophase II* is marked by a transition to the interphase condition of the chromosomes in the four haploid nuclei accompanied by division of the cytoplasm. Thus, the second meiotic division superficially resembles a mitotic division. However, there is an important difference: *the chromatids of a chromosome are usually not identical sister along their entire length because of the occurrence of crossing over associated with the formation of chiasmata during prophase of the first division.*

CHROMOSOMES AND HEREDITY

The first clear proof that genes are parts of chromosomes was obtained in experiments concerned with the pattern of transmission of the *sex chromosomes*, the chromosomes responsible for the determination of the separate sexes in some plants and in almost all higher animals. These results are examine in this section.

Some Additional Terminology

In this chapter we will be using data from *Drosophila* genetics. We begin by describing the usual notation employed for this organism.

A superscript + (as in a^+) is used to identify the *wildtype* allele of any gene. Wildtype means that the allele is the one found most commonly in natural populations of the organism. A recessive allele is indicated by a small letter, and a dominant allele by a capital letter, so the dominance relations of the allelic forms of the gene are immediately clear. For example, y^+ is the symbol for the wildtype counterpart of recessive allele *y* determining yellow body colour; whereas Cy^+ is the symbols for the wildtype counterpart of another gene for which the dominant allele, *Cy* (Curly), results in wings that are curled. The letters used for gene symbols usually come from a descriptive term for the trait determined by an altered form of the gene. A common practice is to represent the wildtype allele of a gene only with a + sign (omitting the letter), as in the heterozygous genotype *y*/+, when it is clear from the context which gene is being designated. These conventions are also used with many other species, though most plant geneticists elect to represent recessive alleles by small letters and dominant alleles by initial capital letters without designating the wildtype. In this book the notations used will be those in general use for whichever organism is being considered.

Chromosomal Determination of Sex

The sex chromosomes are an exception to the rule that all chromosomes of diploid organisms are present in pairs of morphologically similar homologues. Early microscopic analysis showed that one of the chromosomes in males of some insect species does not have a homologue. This unpaired chromosome, called the *X chromosome*, was found to divide in only one of the meiotic divisions and to be present in only half of the sperm cells produced. The biological significance of these observations become clear when females of the same species were shown to have two X chromosomes. In other species in which the females also have two X chromosomes, it was observed that a morphologically different chromosome, referred to as the *Y chromosome*, is present with the X in males and pairs with it during meiosis. These differences in the chromosomal constitution of males and females were recognized to represent a method for the determination of sex at the time of fertilization. That is, whereas every egg will contain an X chromosome, only half of the sperm will have an X and the other half will, in some organisms, have a Y or, in some organisms, no sex chromosome. Fertilization of an egg by a sperm carrying an X results in an XX zygote, which develops into a female, and fertilization by a sperm having no X produces an XY (if a Y is present) or an X0 zygote (if no Y is present), which develops into a male. The result is a criss-cross pattern of inheritance of the X chromosome, in which a male receives his only X chromosome from his mother and transmits it only to his daughters. In organisms with this type of chromosomal sex determination—which is now known to occur in mammals including humans, many insects and other animals, and some flowering plants—the female is called the *homogametic* sex and the male the *heterogametic* sex because they produce one and two types of gametes, respectively.

Assuming that the union of gametes in fertilization occurs at random, as Mendel had supposed, the inheritance of the sex chromosomes (one X and one Y) nearly explains the 1:1 sex ratio usually observed, However, other genes controlling various processes involved in sexual development occur in the other chromosome pairs. These nonsex chromosomes are collectively called *autosomes*, and they are present equally in the two sexes. Many genes with functions unrelated to sex are also located in the X chromosomes, as will be seen in the next section. In most organisms, including humans, the Y chromosome carries few genes other than those associated with sex determination.

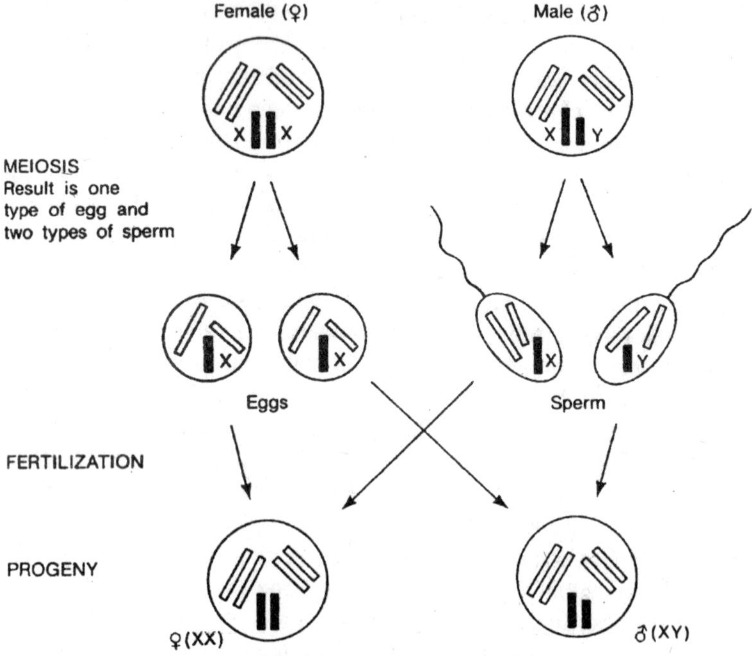

Fig. 2.6. The chromosomal basis of sex determination found in mammals, many insects, and other animals.

X-linked Inheritance

Crosses of the kind considered yield similar progeny when the genotypes of the male and female parents are reversed—this is, in *reciprocal crosses*. One of the earliest observations of an exception to this behaviour was made by Thomas Hunt Morgan in 1910, in an early study of the fruit fly, *Drosophila melanogaster*.

The normal eye colour of the fly is brick red. In a laboratory population that had been maintained for many generations, Morgan found a single male with white eyes. In a mating of this male with red-eyed females, all the F_1 progeny had red eyes, as would be expected if the allele for white is recessive. In the F_2 produced by the mating of F_1 males and females there were 2459 red-eyed females, 1011 red-eyed males, and 782 white-eyed males. These numbers represent a rather poor fit to the expected 3:1 ratio of red- versus white-eyed phenotypes. Note also that all of the white-eyed flies were males, a surprising result. Furthermore, when a white-eyed male was crossed with his red-eyed female offspring, the progeny consisted of both red- and white-eyed males and red- and white-eyed females in approximately equal numbers, indicating that white eyes are not limited to males. Another unexpected result was obtained when white-eyed females were mated with red-eyed males—the *reciprocal* of the cross with the original white-eyed male. In this cross the F_1 females had red eyes and the males again had white eyes.

Morgan summarized the results of these crosses by starting that this trait (not all eye-colour variants) is *sex linked* in inheritance, meaning simply that it is associated with the inheritance of sex. It later became known that *Drosophila* females have two X chromosomes and males have an unequal XY pair, from which the inheritance of the white-eye character could be explained by assuming that the alleles for red (w^+) and white (w) are located on the X chromosome and not present at all on the Y. The chromosomal interpretation of the reciprocal crosses is shown. This diagram accounts for the different phenotypic ratios in the F_1 and F_2 progeny from the two initial crosses. Morgan later discovered other genes that follow this same X-linked pattern of inheritance. Note that in a male only one copy of an X-linked gene is present, because the gene is not also on the Y chromosome. The term *hemizygous* is used to describe this condition.

Let us summarize the signs of sex linked:

1. A heterozygous female will, on the average, transmit the recessive allele to half of her daughters and half of her sons.

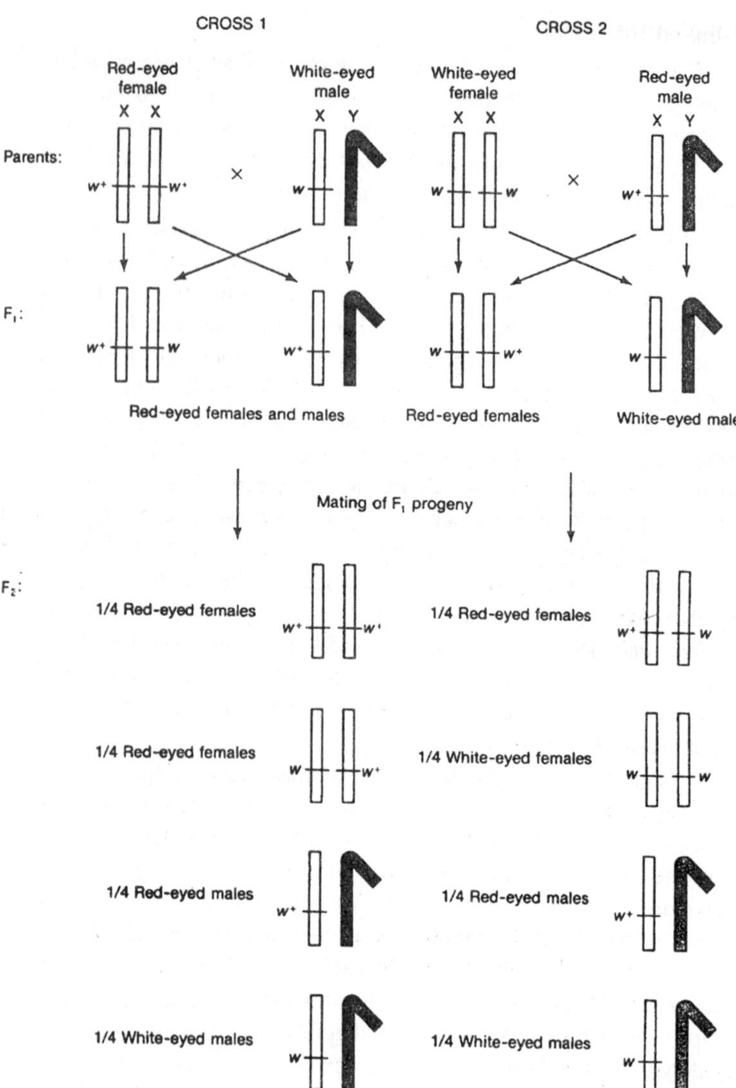

Fig. 2.7. A chromosomal interpretation of the results obtained in F_1 and F_2 progenies when a Drosophila female with red eyes is crossed with a white-eyed male (cross 1) and when the reciprocal cross of white-eyed female with red-eyed male (cross 2) is made.

2. Since a male has only one X chromosome, he will show the defective trait if the recessive allele is present in that chromosome, and will transmit the allele to all of his daughters but none of his

sons. A male who does not show the defective trait does not carry the recessive allele and cannot transmit it to any of his offspring.

3. In general, reciprocal crosses that result in different phenotypic ratios indicate sex linkage.

A famous example of a human trait with an X-linked pattern of inheritance is *hemophilia A*, a severe disorder of blood clotting determined by a recessive allele. Affected individuals are unable to synthesize a blood protein that is required for normal clotting. A famous pedigree of this disease starts with Queen Victoria of England. One of her sons was hemophilic, and two of her daughters were heterozygous carriers of the gene who produced three hemophilic sons and four heterozygous daughters. Through two of these carrier granddaughters the gene was introduced into the royal families of Russia and Spain. The present royal family of England, having descended from a normal son of Victoria, is free of the disease.

A different pattern of sex-linked inheritance occurs in organisms in which the male is homogametic and the female is heterogametic, as in chickens. Some breeds have feathers with alternating transverse bands of light and dark coloured in the nonbarred phenotypes of other breeds. Reciprocal crosses between true-breeding barred and nonbarred types give the following results

Nonbarred ♀ × Barred ♂	Barred ♀ × Nonbarred ♂
↓	↓
Barred ♀♀ and ♂♂	Nonbarred ♀♀ and Barred ♂♂

indicating that the gene determining barring is on the X and is dominant.

Nondisjunction as Proof of the Chromosomal Basis of Heredity

The parallelism between the inheritance of a particular allele and the distribution of the X chromosome carrying it implied that genes must be parts of chromosomes. Other experiments with *Drosophila* provided the definitive proof.

One of Morgan's students discovered rare exceptions to the expected pattern of inheritance in crosses with several X-linked genes. For example, when white-eyed females were mated with red-eyed males, most of the progeny consisted of the expected red-eyed females and white-eyed males. However, about one in every 2000 F_1 flies was an exception, either a white-eyed female or a red-eyed male. It was proposed that these rare exceptional offspring could be accounted for by occasional failure of the two X chromosomes in the mother to

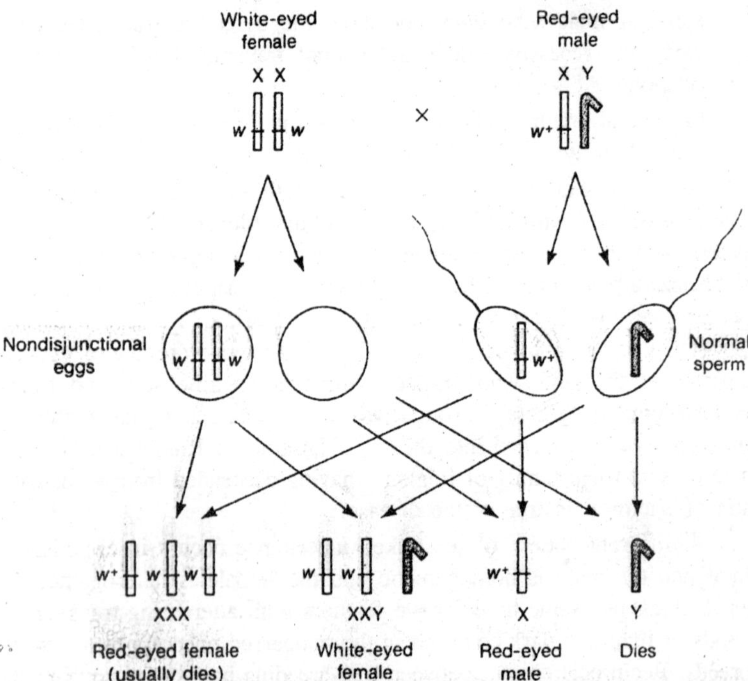

Fig. 2.8. The results of meiotic nondisjunction of the X chromosomes in a Drosophila female.

separate from each other during meiosis—a phenomenon called *nondisjunction*. The consequence of such failure is the formation of some eggs with two X chromosomes and others with none. Four classes of zygotes are expected from the fertilization of these abnormal eggs. Individuals with no X chromosome were not detected because embryos lacking this chromosome are not viable; most progeny with three X chromosomes also die during early development. Examination by microscopy indicated that the exceptional white-eyed females had two X chromosomes and a Y chromosome, and exceptional red-eyed males had a single X but no Y. These X0 males were sterile and could not be used for further genetic analysis.

The results of this and related experiments were of great importance in the development of genetics, because they showed that genes are associated with chromosomes.

Sex Determination in *Drosophila*

The sexual phenotypes resulting from nondisjunction in *D. melanogaster* established that the Y chromosome has no effect on sex determination in this organism. That is, females usually have two X chromosomes and males typically have one X and one Y. Experiments not described showed that unusual females may in addition have a Y (XXY) and rare males may lack a Y (X0) and the organisms will still be female and male, respectively. However, the Y is essential for male fertility, since X0 males are unable to produce normal sperm.

In *D. melanogaster* a complete haploid set of autosomes, represented by A, consists of two large chromosomes with median centromeres and a very small, dotlike chromosome. Studies of the sexual phenotypes of individuals with various combinations of X chromosomes and sets of autosomes provided the evidence that the primary determinant of sex in *Drosophila* is the X:A ratio. Individuals with half as many X chromosomes as sets of autosomes (1X:2A) males and those with equal numbers of chromosomes and complete sets of autosomes (2X:2A, 3X:3A) are females. The genotypes 1X3A (0.33:1.0) and 3X 2A (1.5:1.0) result in normal male and normal female somatic sexual phenotypes, respectively, though these individuals are weak, have underdeveloped reproductive organs, and are sterile.

In some organisms with homogametic females and heterogametic males the Y chromosome is male-determining. An early observation of the flowering plant *Melandrium album* showed that flowers produced by both 2X 2A and 2X 4A plants are pistillate (female), and those of XY 2A and XY 4A plants are invariably staminate (male). When another X chromosome is present, in XXY 2A or XXY 4A plants, most of the flowers are staminate, though an occasional one is bisexual (having both stamens and a functional pistil). This correspondence between the expression of sex and chromosome constitution indicates that in this plant the X is female-determining and, unlike *Drosophila*, the Y is male-determining. A balance between the effects of the two sex chromosomes is approached in XXXXY 4A plants, which produce mostly bisexual flowers, though a few are staminate. Many other variations in the primary sex-determining. The first evidence for this conclusion came from analyses of the chromosome complements associated with two abnormal sexual phenotypes. Males with a condition known as *Klinefelter syndrome* have 47 chromosomes (an extra X) rather than the normal 46 and are XXY. A similar phenotype characterized by underdeveloped testes and sterility has been found to result from XXYY, XXXY, XXXYY, and XXXXY sex-chromosome constitutions. Females with the aberrant condition known as *Turner syndrome* have only 45 chromosomes and are X0. These sexually underdeveloped individuals are sterile.

Humans with an XXX sex-chromosome complement are fertile females, and XYY individuals are fertile males.

The role of the Y chromosome in sex determination in humans and other mammals is to induce a rudimentary embryonic gonad with both male and female potentials to develop into a testis instead of any ovary. A major factor in this induction appears to be related to a substance determined by a gene on the Y chromosome. It is not yet known whether the Y-chromosome gene determines the substance directly or in some way acts to regulate the expression of the gene located on another chromosome. A newly formed testis secretes both a substance that suppresses the development of the primitive oviduct and the hormone testosterone, which is required to induce development of both the genital duct system and secondary sexual characteristics of the male. In the absence of a Y chromosome, the rudimentary gonad differentiates into an ovary and the primitive oviduct into Fallopian tubes and a uterus.

Probability in Genetic Prediction and in Analysis of Genetic Data

Genetic ratios are the result of chance operating in the assortment of genes into gametes and in the combination of gametes into zygotes. Thus, exact predictions are not possible for a particular event. However, it is possible to state in advance that an event has a certain probability of occurring, as we have seen. In this section we consider some of the probability methods used in interpreting genetic data.

Use of the Binomial Distribution in Predicting Genetic Outcomes

The probability that each of three children in a family will be of the same sex is an example of a simple problem that uses both the addition and multiplication rules of probability. The probability that all three will be girls is (1/2) (1/2) (1/2) = 1/8, and the probability that all three will be boys is also 1/8. Since these outcomes are mutually exclusive, the probability of one or the other is the sum of the two probabilities, which is 1/4. The remaining possible outcomes are that two of the children will be girls and the other a boy, or two will be boys and the other a girl. For each of these outcomes only three different orders of birth are possible—for example, GGB, GBG, and BGG—each having a probability of 1/8. Thus, the probability of two girls and a boy, disregarding birth order, is the sum of the probabilities for the three possible orders, or 3/8; likewise, the probability of two boys and a girl is also 3/8. Therefore, the distribution of probabilities for the sex ratio in families with three children is:

GGG	GGB	GBB	BBB
	BGB	BGB	
	BGG	BBG	
$(1/2)^3$	$3(1/2)^2(1/2)$	$3(1/2)(1/2)^2$	$(1/2)^3$

$$1/8 + 3/8 + 3/8 + 1/8 = 1$$

This sex-ratio information can be obtained more directly by expanding the binomial expression $(p + q)^n$, in which p is the probability of the birth of a girl (1/2), q the probability of the birth of a body (1/2), and n is the number of children; in our example,

$$(p + q)^3 = \mathbf{1}p^3 + \mathbf{3}p^2q + \mathbf{3}pq^2 + \mathbf{1}q^3$$

in which the bold numbers can be compared to the numbers above. Similarly, the binomial distribution of probabilities for the sex ratios in families of five children is

$$(p + q)^2 = 1p^5 + 5p^4q + 10p^3q^2 + 10p^2q^3 + 5pq^4 + 1q^5$$

Each term tells us the probability of a particular combination. For example, the third term tells the probability of three girls (p^3) and two boys (q^2) in a family having five children—namely,

$$10(1/2)^2(1/2)^2 = 10/32 = 5/16$$

There are $n + 1$ terms in a binomial expansion. The exponents of p decrease from n in the first term to 0 in the last term, and the exponents of q increase by one from 0 in the first term to n in the last term. The coefficients generated by successive values of n can be arranged in a regular triangle known as *Pascal's triangle*. Note that the horizontal rows of the triangle are symmetrical, and that each number is the sum of the two numbers on either side of it in the row above.

In general, if the probability of event A is p and that of event B is q, and the two events are independent and mutually exclusive, the probability that A will occur four times and B two times—in a specific order—is p^4q^2, by the multiplication rule. However, suppose that we are interested in the occurrence of this combination of events: four of A and two of B, irrespective of order. In that case, we multiply the probability that the combination 4A:2B will occur in any one specific order by the number of possible orders. The number of different combinations of six events, four of one kind and two of another, is

$$\frac{6!}{4\ 2} = \frac{1\times2\times3\times4\times5\times6}{1\times2\times3\times4\times1\times2} = 15$$

(The symbol ! is for factorial, or the product of all positive integers from one through a given number.) This calculation provides the coefficient of the p^4q^2 term in the expansion of the binomial $(p + q)^6$. Therefore, the probability that event A will occur four times and event B two times is $15p^4q^2$.

The general rule for repeated trails of events with constant probabilities is: if the probability of occurrence of event A is p, and the probability of the alternative event B is q, the probability that in n trails event A will occur s times and event B will occur t times is

$$\frac{n}{s!\,t!}p^s p^t$$

in which $s + t = n$, and $p + q = 1$. To use this expression, one must remember that 0! is defined to be 1, and that any number raised to the zero power (e.g., 2^0) also equals 1. Note that each individual term in the expansion of the binomial $(p + q)^n$ is the same as the expression just given.

Let us consider a specific example, in which we calculate the probability of a mating between two heterozygous parents yielding a typical 3:1 ratio of the dominant and recessive traits among families of a particular size. The probability p of one child showing the trait determined by the dominant allele is 3/4, and the probability q of one child showing the trait determined by the recessive allele is 1/4. Suppose that we wanted to know how often in such families with eight children would six of the children have the trait determined by the dominant allele and two children have the trait determined by the recessive allele. In this case, $n = 8$, $s = 6$, $t = 2$, and the probability of this combination of events is

$$\frac{8!}{6!\,2!}(p)^6(q)^2 = \frac{6!\times 7\times 8}{6!\times 2!}(3/4)^6(1/4)^2 = 0.31$$

That is, in 31 percent of the families of eight children the offspring will show the ideal 3:1 phenotypic ratio, the other families will deviate in one direction or the other because of chance variation.

Evaluating the Fit of Observed Results to Theoretical Expectations: The Chi-Squared Method

An important question in dealing with any event whose outcome is subject to the rules of probability is whether an observed result is in agreement with the theoretical expectation based on a particular hypothesis. That is, how far can observed results deviate from those expected before they must be considered an indication of a real difference and not just an accident of sampling? For example, suppose that 100 seedlings from a cross between a green F_1 corn plant and a yellow-green plant of one of the parental strains were grown to test for a 1:1 ratio, and that 65 of the seedling were green and 35 yellow-green. Does this mean the expected ratio is wrong and that the genetic basis for the colour difference is more complex than a single pair of alleles, or might the deviation from the 1:1 ratio merely result from chance? The answer depends on how often, in progeny samples of size 100, a deviation as large or larger would be expected to occur by chance if the expectation were correct.

The probability of obtaining results that differ from an expected 50:50 by 15 individuals or more *in either direction* can be determined from the expansion of the binomial $(p + q)^{100}$. This tedious chore would yield 101 terms, representing the probabilities of all possible outcomes—that is, from 100 green and 0 yellow-green to 0 green and 100 yellow-green. Summing the appropriate terms would tell us that the chance of a deviation as large or larger than 15 is about 1 in 300—a probability so small that we would most likely conclude that the 1:1 expectation is wrong.

There is, of course, still the one chance in 300 that the result is due to chance. Two kinds of mistakes are possible in decisions about the agreement between observed and expected results: (1) a correct hypothesis may sometimes be rejected, or (2) an incorrect hypothesis may sometimes be accepted. In this section a method is described that is commonly used to evaluate the fit of observation and theoretical expectation.

Calculation of exact probabilities for assessing goodness of fit between observed values and those predicted from a specific genetic hypothesis is extremely laborious when the number of observations is large. A particularly useful statistical test is the *chi-square* (χ^2) *method.*

The value of χ^2 is given by the expression

$$\chi^2 = \sum \frac{(\text{Observed} - \text{expected})^2}{\text{Expected}}$$

in which Σ means the summation over all the classes. For each class the difference between the observed number and expected number is squared and then divided by the expected number. To illustrate, suppose we have an F_2 generation consisting of 99 wildtype and 45 mutant individuals, and we wish to know whether this set of observed numbers is in satisfactory agreement with the expected 3:1 ratio resulting from the segregation of a single pair of alleles. Calculation of the value of χ^2 is carried out in table. Note that the sum of the deviations of observed from expected numbers equal zero; when there are only two classes, as in this example, the deviations are always equal in magnitude but opposite in sign. Note also that a deviation of 7 would be a very large one if the expected number were 12, but a relatively small one if the expected number were 120. Since sample size is important, the measure of the size of the deviation from expectation—(observed - expected)^2— is exponents of χ^2, and their summation gives a value of 3,00 in the example.

To make use of the χ^2 value, it must be related to the probability of obtaining, by chance, deviations as large or larger than those observed, if in reality the 3:1 expectation is correct. The larger the difference between expected and observed numbers, the larger χ^2 is for a given sample size. The larger χ^2 is, the less likely it is that the deviations are simply a result of chance. In the interpretation of a χ^2 value the number of classes of data must be taken into account. Every χ^2 test has associated with it a number called its *degree of freedom*, which is used in assessing the significance of the χ^2 value. For the type of χ^2 test, the number of degrees of freedom is simply the number of classes of individuals minus 1.

In general terms, degrees of freedom refers to the number of classes that can vary independently. Two classes of individuals, and since the total sample size is fixed at 144, there is only one degree of freedom. Once the number of individuals in either class has been determined, the number in the other class is automatically set. Similarly, when there are four classes of data, three of them can have frequency, but the frequency of the fourth class must equal the difference between the sum of the three and the total. That is, with four classes of individuals there are three degrees of freedom—the total number of classes minus 1.

When a χ^2 value has been calculated and its degrees of freedom determined, the final step in assessing goodness of fit between expected and observed data is straightforward. One uses either a graph or a table of χ^2 values to determine the approximate probability of obtaining, by chance alone, a deviation as great or greater than that actually observed. In the example, χ^2 = 3.00 with one degree of freedom. The top line corresponds to one degree of freedom, and the probability associated with a χ^2 value of 3.00 is somewhere between 0.05 (χ^2 = 3.841) and 0.20 (χ^2 = 1.642). This range implies that a deviation from the 3:1 ratio at least as great as that observed would be expected to occur by chance in more than 5 percent, but fewer than 20 percent, of similar experiments. Some arbitrary conventions are used to interpret these probability values. If the probability is <5 percent, differences between observed and expected values are considered *significant*, and the hypothesis is rejected. When the probability is >5 percent, differences are considered to be nonsignificant. In this case the agreement between observation and expectation is considered to be satisfactory. This does not mean that the hypothesis is true, but only that it is consistent with observed results.

3

Molecular Organization of Chromosomes

To understand genetic processes requires knowledge of the organization of the genetic material. In this chapter we will see that chromosomes are diverse in size and structural properties and that their DNA differs in the composition and arrangement of nucleotide sequences. The most pronounced differences in structure and genetic organization are between the chromosomes of eukaryotes and those of prokaryotes. Some viral chromosomes are especially noteworthy in that they consist of one single-stranded (rather than double-stranded) DNA molecule and, in a small number of viruses, of RNA instead of DNA. Also, eukaryotic cells contain several chromosomes, each of which contains one intricately coiled DNA molecule, whereas prokaryotes contain a single major chromosome (plus, occasionally, several copies of a small circular DNA molecule called a plasmid). A few RNA-containing animal and plant viruses contain several chromosomes.

The genetic complement of a cell or virus is referred to as a *genome*, though in eukaryotes the term is commonly used to refer to one complete (haploid) set of chromosomes.

Genome Size and Evolutionary Complexity

Measurement of the nucleic acid content of viruses and bacteria, which have a single chromosome, and of the DNA content of the haploid set of chromosomes of eukaryotes had led to the following generalization: *genome size increases roughly with evolutionary complexity*. That is, the single nucleic acid molecule of a typical virus is smaller than the DNA molecule in a bacterial chromosome;

unicellular eukaryotes, such as the yeasts, contain more DNA than a typical bacterium and the DNA is organized in several chromosomes; and multicellular eukaryotes have the greatest amount of DNA. However, among the eukaryotes no correlation exists between evolutionary complexity and the number of chromosomes, because in eukaryotes DNA content is not directly proportional to the number of genes.

Bacteriophage MS2 is one of the smallest viruses. It has only four genes in a single-stranded RNA molecule containing 3569 nucleotides. SV40 virus, which infects monkey and human cells, has a genetic complement of five genes in a circular double-stranded DNA molecule consisting of 5224 nucleotide pairs. The more complex phages and animal viruses have genomes of up to 250 genes in DNA molecules more than 50 times the size of the DNA of the simplest viruses. Bacterial genomes are substantially larger. For example, the chromosome of *E. coli* contains about 1500 genes in a DNA molecule composed of about 4×10^6 nucleotide pairs.

Eukaryotes have a more complex genetic apparatus. Their genomes are packaged in the chromosomes of a haploid set whose number is characteristic of the particular species. In moving up the evolutionary scale of animals or plants, the DNA content per haploid genome generally increases, though the number of chromosomes shows no pattern. One of the smallest genomes in a multicellular animal is that of the nematode worm *Caenorhabditis elegans*, with a DNA content about 20 times that of the *E. coli* genome. The *D. melanogaster* and the human haploid sets of chromosomes have about 40 times and 700 times as much DNA, respectively, as the *E. coli* genome. However, exceptions to the general correspondence between genome size and evolutionary complexity exist; for example, among the amphibia and fish, several species have genomes many times the size of mammalian genomes.

The genomes of higher organisms are extremely large. For example, with an average gene size of a few thousand nucleotide pairs, enough DNA is present in the genomes of *Drosophila melanogaster* and of humans for 60,000 genes and $>10^6$ genes, respectively. However, for a variety of reasons, it is believed that the actual number of genes in these organisms is much less. Furthermore, examples are known of 30-fold differences in DNA content in the genomes of closely related species. The explanation is that in higher eukaryotes most of the DNA has functions other than carrying genetic information.

A remarkable feature of the genetic apparatus of eukaryotes is how the enormous amount of genetic material contained in the nucleus of each cell is precisely divided in each cell division. A haploid human genome, which is contained in a gamete, has a DNA content equivalent to a linear DNA molecule one meter (10^6 μm) in length. The largest of the 23 chromosomes in the genome contains a DNA molecule that is 82 mm (8.2×10^4 μm) long. However, at the metaphase of a mitotic division the DNA molecule is condensed into a compact structure about 10 μm long and less than 1 μm in diameter. The genomes of prokaryotes and viruses, though much smaller than eukaryotic genomes, are also very compact. For example, an *E. coli* chromosome, which contains a DNA molecule about 1300 μm long, is contained in a cell about 2 μm long and 1 μm in diameter.

SUPERCOILING OF DNA

The DNA of prokaryotic and eukaryotic chromosomes is *supercoiled*—that is, double-stranded segments are twisted around one another. The geometry of supercoiling can be illustrated by a simple example. Consider first a linear double-stranded DNA molecule whose ends are joined in such a way that each strand forms a continuous circle. Such a DNA molecule is called a *covalent circle*, and it is

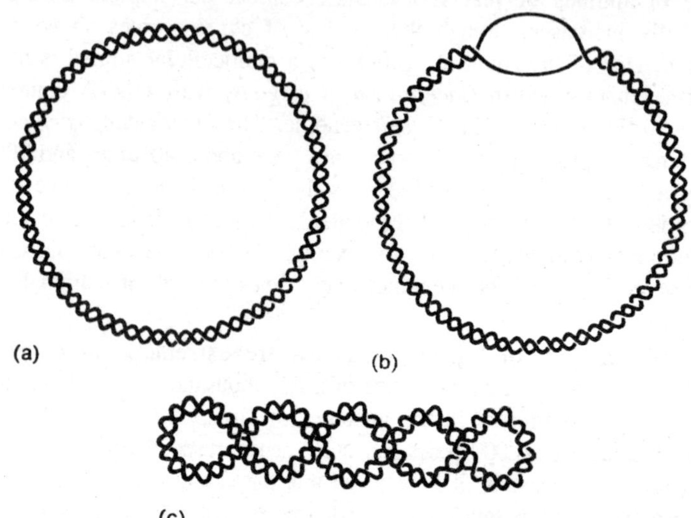

Fig. 3.1. Different states of a covalent circle. (a) A nonsupercoiled relaxed covalent circle having 36 helical turns. (b) An underwound covalent circle having only 32 helical turns. (c) The molecule in (b), but with four twists to eliminate the underwinding.

said to be *relaxed* if no further twisting is present. The individual polynucleotide strands of a relaxed circle form the usual right-handed (positive) helical structure with ten nucleotide pairs per turn of the helix. If, before the ends of the linear molecule are joined, one end is rotated one or more times through 360° with respect to the other end in a direction that produces unwinding to the double helix, then after the ends are joined the molecule will be an underwound circular helix. A DNA molecule has a strong tendency to maintain its standard helical form with ten nucleotide pairs per turn and therefore will respond to the underwinding in one of two ways: (1) by forming regions in which the bases are unpaired, or (2) by twisting the circular molecule in the opposite sense from the direction of underwinding. This twisting is called *supercoiling*, or *superhelicity*, and a molecule with this sense of twisting is *negatively supercoiled*. The two responses to underwinding are not independent, and underwinding is usually accommodated by a combination of the two processes—namely, an underwound molecule contains some unpaired bases and some supercoiling, with the supercoiling predominating. If, instead, the molecule were overwound, supercoiling in the opposite (positive) sense would result. The supercoiling of naturally occurring molecules is always of the negative type.

The supercoiling of natural DNA molecule is not produced by the unwinding of a linear molecule before it is joined into a circle. In bacteria it is the result of the activity of DNA gyrase, one of a general class of enzymes called *topoisomerases*. The DNA of eukaryotic chromosomes from which the proteins have been chemically removed is also supercoiled; the mechanism of supercoiling is more complex than in bacteria and is not clearly known. The introduction of one single-strand break (a nick)—for example, by a *deoxyribonuclease* (*DNase*), an enzyme that breaks sugar-phosphate bonds in DNA strands—into a typical supercoiled DNA molecule eliminates all supercoiling because the constraint of underwinding can be removed by a free rotation of the intact strand about the sugar-phosphate bond opposite the break.

Although supercoiling occasionally plays a role in the expression of some genes, the overall biological function of supercoiling is unknown. Possibly, it has no function and is simply a by-product of the presence of DNA gyrase, which is needed in DNA replication.

Structure of the Bacterial Chromosome

The chromosome of *E. coli* is a condensed unit—called a *nucleoid* or *folded chromosome*—containing a single circular DNA molecule.

The most striking feature of the nucleoid is that the DNA is organized into a set of looped domains, a feature that is also characteristic of eukaryotic chromosomes. As isolated, the nucleoid contains, in addition to DNA, small amounts of several proteins, which are thought to be responsible in some way for the multiply looped arrangement of the DNA. The degree of condensation of the isolated nucleoid (that is, its physical dimensions) is affected by a variety of factors, and some controversy exists about the state of the nucleoid within a cell.

The loops of the DNA of the *E. coli* chromosome are supercoiled. Notice that some loops are not supercoiled; this is a result of the action of several DNases during isolation and indicates that the loops are in some way independent of one another. In the previous, we pointed out that supercoiling is generally eliminated in a DNA molecule by one single-strand break. However, such a break in the *E. coli* chromosome does not eliminate all supercoiling. If nucleoids, all of whose loops are supercoiled, are treated with a DNase and examined at various times after single-strand breaks are introduced, it is observed that a single-strand break removes the supercoiling of only one loop, not all loops. Thus, the loops must be isolated from one another in such a way that rotation in one loop is not transmitted to other loops. However this occurs is unknown.

It is possible experimentally to eliminate all supercoiling (by introduction of many single-strand breaks or by treatment with certain types of topoisomerases). When this is done, the overall looped structure of the chromosome is not lost, when indicates that folding and supercoiling of the DNA are independent phenomena.

Structure of Eukaryotic Chromosome

A eukaryotic chromosome contains a single DNA molecule of enormous length. For example, the largest chromosome in the *D. melanogaster* genome has a DNA content of 6.5×10^7 nucleotide pairs, equivalent to a continuous linear duplex about 18 mm long. The lengths of some of the DNA molecules isolated from *Drosophila* chromosomes.

The DNA of all eukaryotic chromosomes is associated with numerous protein molecules in a stable ordered aggregate called *chromatin*. Some of the proteins present in chromatin determine chromosome structure and the changes in structure that occur during the division cycle of the cell. Other chromatin proteins appear to have important but not well-understood roles in regulating chromosome functions.

Nucleosomes: The Basic Structural Unit of Chromatin

The simplest form of chromatin is that present in nondividing eukaryotic cells in which chromosomes are not sufficiently condensed to be visible by light microscopy. Chromatin isolated from such cells is a complex aggregate of DNA and two classes of protein molecules—a major class, the *histones*, and a minor class, called nonhistone chromosomal proteins, which will not be discussed.

Histones are largely responsible for the structure of chromatin. Five major types—H1, H2A, H2B, H3, and H4—occur in the chromatin of almost all eukaryotes and are present in amounts about equal in mass to that of the DNA. These are small proteins containing 100-200 amino acids and differ from most other proteins in that 20-30 percent of the amino acids are lysine and arginine, both of which have a positive charge. (Only a few percent of the amino acids of a typical protein are lysine and arginine.) The positive charges enable histone molecules to bind to DNA, primarily by electrostatic attraction to the negatively charged phosphate groups in the sugar-phosphate backbone of DNA. Placing chromatin in a solution with a higher salt concentration (for example, 2 *M* NaCl) to eliminate the electrostatic attraction causes the histones to dissociate from the DNA. Histones also bind tightly to each other; both DNA-histone and histone-histone binding are important for chromatin structure.

The histones from different organisms are remarkably similar to one another, with the exception of H1. In fact, the amino acid sequences of H3 molecules from widely different species are almost identical. For example, the sequences of H3 of cow chromatin and pea chromatin differ by only four of 135 amino acids. The H4 proteins of all organisms are also quite similar; again, cow and pea H4 differ by only two of their 102 amino acids. There are few other proteins whose amino acid sequences vary so little from one species to the next. When the variation is very small between organisms, one says that the sequence is highly *conserved*. The extraordinary conservation in histone composition over hundreds of millions of years of evolutionary divergence is consistent with the important role of these proteins in the structural organization of eukaryotic chromosomes.

By electron microscopy chromatin looks like a regularly beaded thread. Brief treatment of chromatin with some DNases yields a collection of small particles of quite uniform size consisting only of histones and DNA. When the histones are removed from these particles, the DNA fragments are found to be of lengths equal to about 200 nucleotide pairs or small multiples of that unit size (the precise size varies with species and tissue).

The beadlike units in chromatin are called *nucleosomes*. Each unit has a definite composition—namely, one molecule of H1, two molecules each of H2A, H2B, H3, and H4, and one segment of DNA containing about 200 nucleotide pairs. Extensive digestion of these units with a nuclease removes some of the DNA and causes the loss of H1. The resulting structure, called a *core particle*, consists of an octamer of pairs of H2A, H2B, H3, and H4, around which the remaining 145-nucleotide-pair length of DNA is wound in about 1-3/4 turns. Thus, a nucleosome is composed of a core particle, additional DNA that links adjacent core particles (the DNA that is removed by nuclease digestion), and one molecule of H1; the H1 binds to the histone octamer and to the linker DNA, causing the linkers extending from both sides of the core particle to cross and draw nearer to the octamer, though some of the linker DNA does not come into contact with any histones. The size of the linker ranges from 20-100 nucleotide pairs for different species and even in different cell types in the same organism (200 - 145 = 55 nucleotide pairs is usually considered an average size). Little is known about the structure of the linker DNA or whether it has a special genetic function, and the cause of the variation in its length is also unknown.

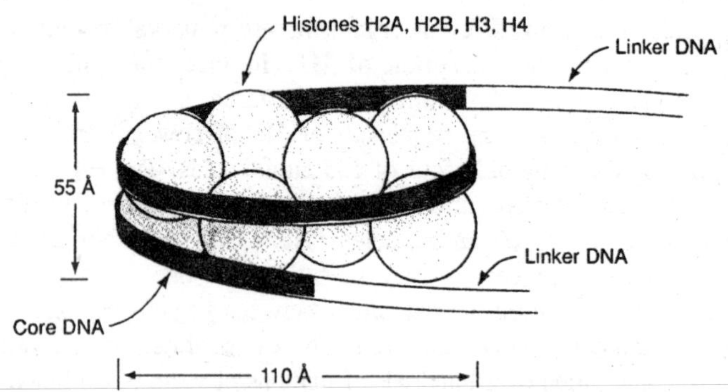

Fig. 3.2. Diagram of a nucleosome core particle.

Arrangement of Chromatin Fibers in a Chromosome

The DNA molecule of a chromosome is folded and refolded in such a way that it is convenient to think of chromosomes as having several levels of organization, each responsible for a particular degree of shortening of the enormously long strand. Assembly of DNA and histones represents the first level—namely, a sevenfold reduction in length of the DNA and the formation of a beaded flexible fiber 100 Å (11 nm) wide, roughly five times the width of free DNA. The structure of chromatin varies with the concentration of salts, and the 110-Å fiber is present only when the salt concentration is quite low. If the salt concentration is increased slightly, the fiber becomes shortened somewhat by forming a zigzag arrangement of closely spaced beads between which the linking DNA is no longer visible in electron micrographs. If the salt concentration is further increased to that present in living cells, a second level of compaction occurs—namely, the organization of the 110-Å nucleosome fiber into a shorter thicker fiber with an average diameter of 300-350 Å, called the 30-nm fiber. In forming this structure the 110-Å fiber apparently coils in a somewhat irregular left-handed superhelix or solenoidal supercoil with six nucleosomes per turn. It is believed that most intracellular chromatin has the solenoidal supercoiled configuration.

The final level of organization is that in which the 30-nm fiber condenses into a chromatid of the compact metaphase chromosome. Little is known about this process other than that it seems to precede in stages. In electron micrographs of isolated metaphase chromosomes from which histones have been removed, the partially unfolded DNA has the form of an enormous number of loops that seen to extend from a central core or *scaffold* composed of nonhistone chromosomal proteins. Electron microscopic studies of chromosome condensation during mitosis and meiosis suggest that the scaffold extends along the chromatid and that the 30-nm fiber becomes arranged into a helix of loops radiating from the scaffold. Details are not known about the additional folding that is required of the fiber in each loop to produce the fully condensed metaphase chromosome.

The compaction of DNA and protein into chromatin and ultimately into the chromosome greatly facilitates the distribution of the genetic material during nuclear division.

Polytene Chromosomes

A typical eukaryotic chromosome contains only a single DNA molecule. However, in the nuclei of cells of the salivary glands and certain other tissues of the larvae of *Drosophila* and other two-winged (dipteran) flies there are giant chromosomes, called *polytene chromosomes*, which contain many DNA molecules. Each of these chromosomes have a volume about 1000 times greater than that of the corresponding chromosome at mitotic metaphase in ordinary somatic cells, and a constant and distinctive pattern of transverse banding. The polytene structures are formed by repeated replication of the DNA in a closely synapsed pair of homologous chromosomes without separation of the replicated chromatin strands or of the two chromosomes. Polytene chromosomes are atypical chromosomes and are formed in "terminal" cells; that is, the larval cells containing them do not divide further during development of the fly and are later discarded during formation of the pupa. However, they have been especially valuable in the genetics of *Drosophila*.

In polytene nuclei of some species, of which *D. melanogaster* is an example, large blocks of heterochromatin (a particular type of chromatin described in the following section) adjacent to the centromeres are aggregated into a single compact mass called the *chromocenter*. Since the two largest chromosomes (numbers 2 and 3) have centrally located centromeres, the chromosomes appear in the configuration: the paired X chromosomes (in a female), the left and right arms of chromosomes 2 and 3, and a short chromosome (4) project from the chromocenter. In a male the Y chromosome, which consists almost entirely of heterochromatin, is incorporated in the chromocenter.

The darkly staining transverse bands in polytene chromosomes have about a tenfold range in width. These bands result from side-by-side alignment of tightly folded regions of the individual chromatin strands that are often visible in mitotic and meiotic prophase chromosomes and are called chromomeres. More DNA is present within the bands than in the identified in the *D. melanogaster* polytene chromosomes. This linear array of bands, which has a pattern that is constant and characteristic for each species, provides a finely detailed *cytological map* of the chromosomes. The banding pattern is such that short regions in any of the chromosomes can be identified.

Because of their large size and finely detailed morphology, polytene chromosomes are exceedingly useful or *in situ* nucleic acid hybridization to determine the location of specific DNA sequences.

ORGANIZATION OF NUCLEOTIDE SEQUENCES IN CHROMOSOMAL DNA

In bacteria the variation of average base composition from one part of the genome to another is quite small. However, in eukaryotes small fractions of DNA can be detected whose base composition can be quite different from the mean (e.g., 3 percent GC for crab DNA). These fractions are called *satellite DNA*. In the mouse, satellite DNA accounts for 10 percent of the genome. A striking feature of satellite

DNA is that it consists of fairly short nucleotide sequences that may be repeated *as many as a million times in a haploid genome.* Other *repetitive sequences* are also present in eukaryotic DNA, but never in prokaryotic DNA. In the first part of this section we examine some of the most significant findings about sequence organization that are revealed by special techniques. Later we will return to the satellite sequences.

Denaturation and Renaturation of DNA

The double-stranded helical structure of DNA is maintained by forces that include hydrogen bonding between the bases of complementary pairs. When solutions of DNA are exposed to temperatures considerably higher than those normally encountered by most living cells or to excessively high pH, the hydrogen bonds break and the paired strands separate. Unwinding of the helix occurs rapidly, the time depending on the length of the molecule. When the ordered structure of DNA is disrupted and the strands are separated, the molecule is said to be *denatured.* A common way to detect denaturation is by measuring the capacity of DNA in solution to absorb ultraviolet light of 260-nm wavelength. The absorbance at 260 nm (A_{260}) of a solution of single-stranded molecules is 37 percent higher than the absorbance of the double-stranded molecules at the same concentration.

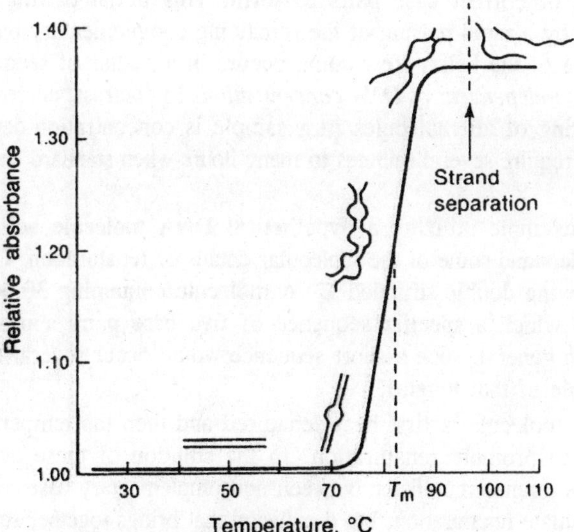

Fig. 3.3. A melting curve of DNA showing T_m and possible shapes of a DNA molecule at various degrees of denaturation.

Thus, when a DNA solution is slowly heated and the value of A_{260} is recorded at various temperatures, a curve called a *melting curve* is obtained. The melting transition is usually described in terms of the temperature at which the increase in the value of A_{260} is half complete. This temperature is called the *melting temperature* and denoted by T_m. The value of T_m increases with G+C content, because GC pairs, joined by three hydrogen bonds, are stronger than AT pairs, which are joined by two hydrogen bonds.

The single strands in a solution of denatured DNA can, under certain conditions, re-form double-stranded DNA. The process is called *renaturation* or *reannealing*. For renaturation to occur, two requirements must be met: (1) The salt concentration must be high enough (>0.25 *M*) to neutralize the negative charges of the phosphate groups, which would otherwise cause the complementary strands to repel one another; and (2) the temperature must be sufficiently high to disrupt hydrogen bonds that form at random between short sequences of bases within the same strand, but not so high that stable base pairs between the complementary strands would be disrupted. A temperature about 20°C below T_m is usually optimal. Renaturation is a fairly slow process and its rate is limited by the initial step in the process—namely, a precise collision between two complementary strands—which permits a short sequence of correct base pairs to form. This initial pairing step is followed by a rapid pairing of the remaining complementary bases and rewinding of the helix. Rewinding occurs in a matter of seconds and *its rate is independent of DNA concentration*. In contrast, correct initial base-pairing of all molecules in a sample is concentration-dependent and may require several minutes to many hours when standard conditions are used.

An example utilizing a hypothetical DNA molecule will enable us to understand some of the molecular details of renaturation. Consider the following double-stranded DNA molecule containing 30,000 base pairs, in which a specific sequence of five base pairs appears only twice. (In general, such a short sequence would occur several times in a molecule of that length).

This molecule is first heat-denatured and then the temperature is lowered to promote renaturation. In the solution of these denatured molecules a random collision between noncomplementary base sequences cannot initiate renaturation, but a collision that brings together sequences I and II′ or II can result in base pairing. However, this pairing will be transient at the elevated temperatures used for renaturation, because the paired region is short and the adjacent bases in the two strands are out of register and unable to pair, as is required to form a double-stranded molecule. However, if a collision results in the pairing of sequence I with I′ or II with II′—or any other short complementary sequences—pairing of the adjacent bases and in fact all other bases in the strands will occur in a zipperlike action. The main point is that only base-pairing that brings the complementary sequences into register will cause renaturation to occur.

Analysis of DNA Sequences by Renaturation Kinetics

Information about the size of repeated sequences and the number of copies of a particular sequence can be obtained by studies of the rate of renaturation. Since the initial step in renaturation is a collision between two complementary single strands, the rate of reassociation increases with DNA concentration. That is, an increase in DNA concentration results in a corresponding increase in the number of potential pairing partners for a given strand. The study of this dependence of renaturation rate on concentration has contributed greatly to our understanding of the organization of the genetic material.

In order to see how the analysis works, we consider the renaturation rates of two solution of DNA molecules, A and B, having no common base sequences and different molecular weights, with A smaller than B. In solutions in which the number of grams of DNA per milliliter is the same, the molar concentration of A is greater than that of B. Thus, if each solution is separately denatured and renatured, the

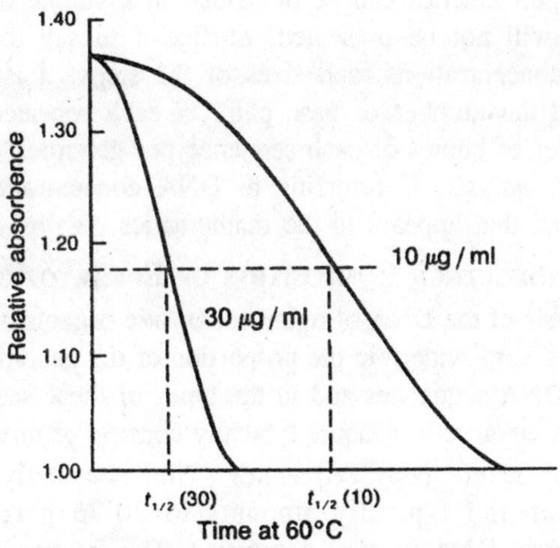

Fig. 3.4. Dependence of renaturation time on the concentration of phage T7 DNA.

molecules in A will renature more rapidly than those in B. If the two solutions are instead mixed, A and B will renature independently of one another (because they are nonhomologous), and a curve will be obtained. Note that the curve consists of two steps, one for the more rapidly renaturing A molecules and the other for the B molecules. Each step accounts for half of the change in A_{260} because the initial concentration (in g/ml, which is proportional to A_{260}) of each type of molecule was the same.

Now consider a molecule containing 50,000 base pairs and consisting of 100 copies of a tandemly repeated sequence of 500 base pairs. The molecules are broken into about 100 fragments of roughly equal size—that is, about 500 base pairs each. A renaturation curve for the fragments will have a single step and a renaturation rate characteristic of molecules 500 nucleotides in length. However, if the molecule contains a unique sequence of 25,000 base pairs and 50 copies of a repetitive sequence of 500 base pairs, the renaturation curve would have two steps, each accounting for half the change in absorbance; one step would have a rate characteristic of a sequence of 25,000 base pairs and the other would be characteristic of a sequence of 500 base pairs. In summary, if a DNA molecule contains only a single nonrepetitive sequence, breakage of the molecule will not yield a renaturation curve consisting of steps. If a molecule that contains both a unique component and several copies of different repeated sequences is fragmented, the renaturation curve will have steps, one step for each repeated sequence.

Renaturation kinetics can be described in a simple mathematical form, which will not be presented. Suffice it to say that from the rates, DNA concentrations, and sizes of the steps, it is possible to calculate both the number of base pairs in each repeated sequence, and the number of copies of each sequence per genome. The analysis is called *Cot analysis*, C referring to DNA concentration and *t* to time, a product that appears in the mathematics.

Nucleotide Sequence Composition of Eukaryotic Genomes

Cot analysis of the DNA of many eukaryotic organisms has shown that eukaryotes vary widely in the proportion of the genome consisting of repetitive DNA sequences and in the types of these sequences that are present. A eukaryotic genome typically consists of three fractions:

1. *Unique* or *single copy sequences*. This is usually the major component and typically amounts to 30-75 percent of the chromosomal DNA in most organisms. The fraction is identified by the most slowly renaturing component of a Cot curve.

2. *Highly repetitive sequences*. The component, which constitutes 5-45 percent of the genome, is the most rapidly renaturing component of a Cot curve. Many of these sequences are the satellite DNA referred to earlier. The sequences in this class are individually repeated more than 10^5 times.
3. *Middle-repetitive sequences*. This component amounts of 1-30 percent of a eukaryotic genome and includes sequences that are repeated from a few times to 10^5 times per genome.

It should be noted that the dividing line between many middle-repetitive sequences and highly repetitive sequences is arbitrary.

Unique Sequences

Most gene sequences and the adjacent nucleotide sequences required for their expression are contained in the unique-sequence fraction. With minor exceptions (for example, the repetition of one or few genes) the genomes of viruses and prokaryotes are composed entirely of single-copy sequences; in contrast, such sequences constitute only 38 percent of the total genome in some sea urchin species, a little more than 50 percent of the human genome, and about 70 percent of the *D. melanogaster* genome.

Highly Repetitive Sequences

The highly repetitive sequences, which are often fairly short, are usually arranged in blocks of tandem repeats. Sequences of this type make up about 6 percent of the human genome and 18 percent of the *D. melanogaster* genome, but 45 percent of the DNA of *D. virilis*. One of the simplest possible repetitive sequences is composed of an alternating ...ATAT... sequence with about 3 percent G+C interspersed that makes up 25 percent of the genomes of three species of land crabs. In the *D. virilis* genome, the major components of the highly repetitive class are three sequences of seven base pairs, which have the following compositions in one of the complementary strands:

5′-ACAAACT-3′
5′-ATAAACT-3′
5′-ACAAATT-3′

Blocks of satellite (highly repetitive) sequences in the genomes of several organisms have been located by *in situ* or *cytological hybridization*, a technique that is a simple extension of the nucleic acid renaturation methods we have described. Cells, some of which are in metaphase, are squashed on a glass cover slip (or simply grown on the glass surface) and treated with an alkaline solution that denatures

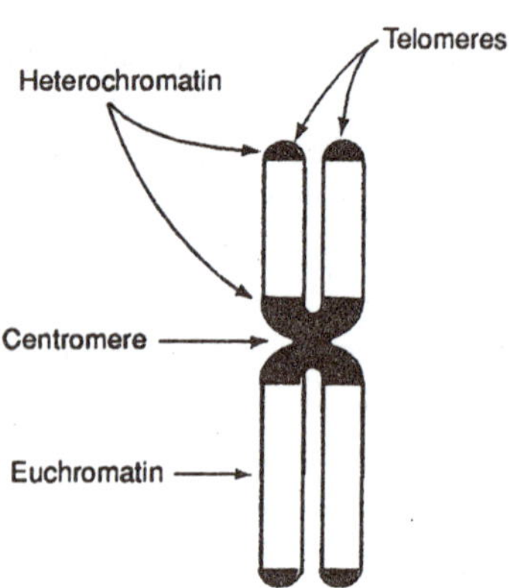

Fig. 3.5. An interpretive drawing of metaphase chromosome.

the cellular DNA. The preparation is then immersed in a solution containing denatured, radioactively labeled copies of a particular repetitive sequence of DNA and subjected to conditions that favour renaturation. The labeled sequences hybridize with complementary sequences in the genome of the cell. After the cells have been washed to remove excess radioactive DNA that has not hybridized, the sites at which hybridization has occurred can be determined by autoradiography. The satellite sequences located by this technique have been found to be in the regions of the chromosomes called *heterochromatin*. These are regions that condense earlier in prophase than the rest of the chromosome and are darkly stainable by many standard dyes used to make chromosomes visible; sometimes the heterochromatin remains highly condensed throughout the cell cycle. *Euchromatin*, when makes up most of the genome, is visible only during the mitotic cycle. The major heterochromatic regions are adjacent to the centromere; smaller blocks occur at the ends of the chromosome arms (the *telomeres*) and interspersed with the euchromatin. In many species an entire chromosome, such as the Y, is almost completely heterochromatic. Different highly repetitive sequences have been purified from *D. melanogaster* and *in situ* hybridization with *Drosophila* cells has shown that each chromosome has its own distinctive types and distribution of these sequences.

Few genes have been located in heterochromatic regions of chromosomes, so this substantial fraction of the chromatin was formerly considered to be genetically inert. However, detailed genetic and cytogenetic experiments have indicated that heterochromatin has well defined, though not well understood, functions in such processes as the pairing and segregation of homologous chromosomes during meiosis, the structural rearrangement of chromosomes, and the regulation of gene expression. The specific DNA sequences that are responsible for these phenomena have not yet been determined.

Middle-Repetitive Sequences

Middle-repetitive sequences constitute about 12 percent of the *D. melanogaster* genome and 40 percent or more of the human and other eukaryotic genomes. These sequences differ greatly in the number of copies and the distribution of these within a genome. They represent many families of related sequences and include several groups of genes. For example, the genes for the RNA components of the ribosomes—the particles on which proteins are synthesized—and the genes for tRNA molecules, which also participate in protein synthesis, are repeated in the genomes of all organisms. Genes for the two major ribosomal RNA molecules occur as a tandem pair that is repeated seven times in the *E. coli* genome, and several hundred times in eukaryotes. The genomes of all eukaryotes also contain multiple copies of the histone genes. Each histone gene is repeated about 10 times per genome in chickens, 20 times in mammals, about 100 times in the *D. melanogaster* genome, and as many as 600 times in some sea urchin species.

The dispersed middle-repetitive-DNA component of the *D. melanogaster* genome consists of at least 40 families of related sequences, each with 20-20 copies that are widely scattered throughout the chromosomes. Many of these sequences are able to move from one location to another in a chromosome and between chromosomes; they are said to be *transposable elements*. Analogous nucleotide sequences are also found in the genomes of yeast, maize, and bacteria (in which they have been extensively studied), and probably occur in all organisms. An important dimension has been added to our understanding of the genome as a structural and functional unit by detection of these mobile elements, for they can in some cases cause chromosome breakage, chromosome rearrangements, modification of the expression of genes, and stable mutations.

Transposable Elements

In the 1940s in a study of the genetics of mottling of maize Barbara McClintock discovered an element that regulated the mottling and also caused breakage of the chromosome that carries the genes for colour and consistency of the kernels. The element was called Dissociation (Ds). Mapping data showed that the chromosome breakage always occurred at or very near the location of Ds. Her critical observation was that Ds did not have a constant location but occasionally moved (*transposition*), causing chromosome breakage at a new site. Furthermore, movement of Ds only occurred if a second element, called Activator (Ac), was also present. In addition, *Ac* itself undergoes movement within the genome and can cause alterations in the expression of genes at or near its insertion site similar to the modifications resulting from the presence of *Ds*.

Additional *transposable elements* with characteristics and genetic effects similar to those of *Ac* and *Ds* are known in maize. Much of the colour variegation seen in kernels of the varieties used for decorative purposes are attributable to the presence of one or more of these elements.

Since McClintock's discovery transposable nucleotide sequences have been observed to be widespread in eukaryotes. In *D. melanogaster* they constitute 5-10 percent of the genome and represent 30-40 distinct families of sequences. One well-studied family of about 30 closely related, but not identical, sequences is called *copia*. These elements contain about 5000 base pairs with two identical sequences of 267 base pairs that are located terminally and in the same orientation (the sequences are called *direct repeats*). The ends of each of these terminal repeats contain two segments of 17 base pairs, whose sequences are also nearly identical. These shorter segments have opposite orientations and are called *inverted repeats*. Other transposable elements have a similar organization of direct and terminal repeats, as do many such elements in other organisms. However, some elements in both prokaryotes and eukaryotes lack the long direct repeats, though a short inverted terminal repeat of 10-35 base pairs seems to be universal.

The molecular processes responsible for the movement of transposable elements are not yet understood. A common feature si

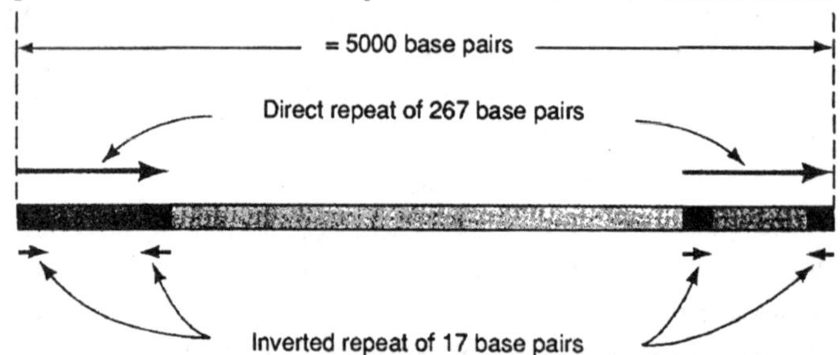

Fig. 3.6. Sequence organization of copia transposable element of Drosophila melanogaster.

that relocation of the element is accompanied by the duplication of 4-12 base pairs originally present at the insertion site, with the result that a copy of this short chromosomal sequence is found immediately adjacent to both ends of the inserted element. This sequence is called the *target sequence*. When a DNA sequence of the region is determined, observation of a pair of inverted-repeat sequences (the terminal segments) separated by a long sequence and flanked by a short direct-repeat sequence (the target sequence) is considered to be the hallmark of a transposable element, even when movement of the element has not been observed. Insertion of a transposable element is not a sequence-specific process, in that at each location the element is flanked by a distinct target sequence; however, the *number* of base pairs in the target sequence is the same at all locations and is characteristic of a particular transposable element. Experimental deletion of part of the base sequences of several different elements has shown that the short terminal inverted repeats are essential for transposition, though the reason is not known. Transposition also requires an enzyme called a *transposase*. Many transposable elements contain a transposase gene, which is located in the central region between the terminal repeats, and hence these elements are able to promote their own transposition. Elements in which the gene has been lost (or inactivated by mutation) are transposable only if a related element is present in the genome to provide this activity. For example, the inability of the maize *Ds* element to transpose without *Ac* results from the absence of a functional transposase gene in *Ds*.

Recognition in recent years that transposable DNA sequences exist in most genomes and are quite numerous has greatly altered our perception of the organization and stability of the genetic material.

Centromere and Telomere Structure

The centromere is a specific region of the eukaryotic chromosome that becomes visible as a distinct morphological entity along the chromosome during condensation. It is responsible for chromosome movement during both mitosis and meiosis, functioning, at least in part, by providing an attachment site for one or more spindle fibers. Electron microscopic analysis has shown that in some organisms—for example, the yeast *Saccharomyces cerevisiae*—a single spindle-protein fiber is attached to centromeric chromatin. The chromatin segment of the centromeres of yeast has a unique structure in that it is exceedingly resistant to the action of various DNases and has been isolated as a protein-DNA complex containing 220-250 base pairs. The nucleosomal constitution and DNA base sequences of four different yeast centromeres have been determined. There are four regions—I-IV; the sequences in regions I, II, and III are nearly identical, but that of region IV varies from one centromere to another. Region II is noteworthy in that 93 percent of the 82-89 base pairs are AT pairs, The centromeric DNA is contained in a structure (the centromeric core particle) that contains more DNA than a typical yeast nucleosome core particle (160 base pairs) and is larger. This structure is responsible for the resistance of centromeric DNA to DNase. It is not known whether histones or other proteins form the centromeric particle. The spindle fiber is believed to be attached directly to this particle.

Whether the base-sequence arrangement of the yeast centromeres is typical or eukaryotic centromeres remains to be determined. In higher eukaryotes the chromosomes are about 100 times larger than yeast chromosomes and several spindle fibers are usually attached to each chromosome; thus, it is possible that the centromeres are larger and more complex than those of yeast. Furthermore, the yeast genome is free of highly repetitive sequences, whereas the centromeric regions of the chromosomes of many higher eukaryotes contain large amounts of heterochromatin, consisting of repetitive satellite DNA.

Telomeres, the complex structures at the ends of eukaryotic chromosomes, are essential for chromosome stability, based on genetic and microscopic observation. For example, in both maize and *Drosophila*, chromosomes that lack telomeres (broken chromosomes) often fuse end to end. Furthermore, if the one end of a single metaphase chromosome is broken away, the chromatids often fuse, forming a chromosome with two centromeres.

Telomeres are thought to be responsible for the completion of the replication of the linear DNA molecule contained in a eukaryotic chromosome. A telomere of the protozoan *Tetrahymena* has been isolated. It has an unusual structure, with between 20 and 70 repeats of the sequence 5′-CCCCAA-3′, a hairpin terminus, and several gaps. Various models have been proposed that show how this structure may enable replication of the chromosome to be completed, but little evidence is available.

4

EUKARYOTIC CHROMOSOME

We have previously discussed the control of gene expression in prokaryotes and bacteriophages. Compared to eukaryotes, bacteriophages and prokaryotes are relatively simple. Of fundamental importance is that, in these lower forms, the operon model of induction and repression of transcription is a unifying theme for control of gene expression. Despite nuances such as catabolite repression and attenuator control, the operon model provides a relatively clear picture of how genes are turned on and off in phages and prokaryotes. This model does not exist for eukaryotes. In attempting to elucidate models for control of gene expression in eukaryotes, we must take one very important factor into account: the complexity of the structure of the eukaryotic chromosome. In this chapter, we cover the current understanding of how these very large structures are organized.

EUKARYOTIC CELL

Eukaryotes and prokaryotes are the two superkingdoms of organisms. The following comparisons, using *E. coli* as a general model for prokaryotes, show how much more complex eukaryotes are:

1. An *E. coli* chromosome contains approximately 4.2×10^6 base pairs of DNA. The haploid human genome contains nearly one thousand times as much DNA.
2. An *E. coli* cell has very little internal structure. Eukaryotes have a number of internal organelles and an extensive lipid membrane system, including the nuclear envelope itself.
3. Eukaryotic DNA is in the form of nucleoprotein, a DNA-histone protein complex. Although a few histonelike proteins have been

found in *E. coli*, its chromosomal DNA is not complexed with protein to anywhere near the same extent.

4. An *E. coli* cell is small (0.5 to 5.0 μm in length for bacteria). Eukaryotic cells are generally larger than prokaryotes (10 to 50 μm in length for animal tissue cells).
5. The messenger RNA of *E. coli* is translated while it is being transcribed. Eukaryotic messenger RNA is modified within the nucleus before it is transported out for translation in the cytoplasm.
6. Almost no messenger RNA isolated from eukaryotic cells, including the messenger RNA of animal viruses, has been found to be polycistronic (containing many genes). Most prokaryotic messenger RNAs are polycistronic.
7. Most *E. coli* genes are parts of inducible or repressible operons; there are almost no operons in eukaryotes.
8. *E. coli* exists as a simple, single cell. Although some prokaryotes do aggregate, sporulate, and show a few other limited forms of differentiation, they are primarily one-celled organisms. And, although some eukaryotes are single-celled (e.g., yeast), the essence of eukaryotes is differentiation. In human beings, a zygote gives rise to every other cell type in the body in a relatively predictable manner.

Eukaryotic Chromosome

DNA Arrangement

Evidence that the eukaryotic chromosome is *uninemic*—that is, contains one double helix of DNA—comes from several sources.The best data are provided by radioactive-labeling studies, first done by J. Taylor and his colleagues in 1957. If a eukaryote is allowed to undergo one DNA replication in the presence of tritiated (^{3}H-) thymidine, each of the daughter chromatids would be expected to contain a double helix with one unlabeled DNA template strand and one labeled strand of newly synthesized bases. This configuration is expected on the basis of semiconservative replication, with each chromatid containing one double helix. A second round of DNA replication, in the absence of ^{3}H-thymidine, should produce chromosomes in which one chromatid would have unlabeled DNA and one would have labeled DNA. As expected, one chromatid of every pair is labeled and one is not.

In another kind of experiment, R. Kavenoff, L. Klotz, and B. Zimm demonstrated that *Drosophila* nuclei contained pieces of DNA of the size predicted from their DNA content, based on the premise

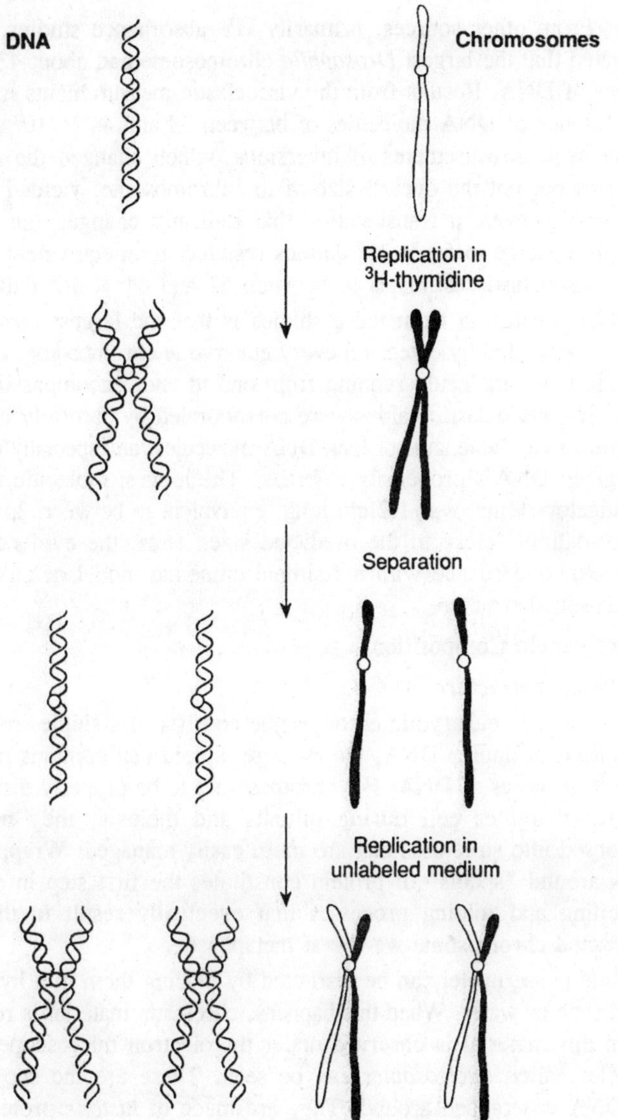

Fig. 4.1. Radioactive labeling of a uninemic eukaryotic chromosome following semiconservative replication.

that each chromosome contains one DNA molecule. They isolated the DNA and measured the size of the largest DNA molecules using the *viscoelastic* property of DNA, the rate at which stretched molecules relax. From other sources, primarily UV absorbance studies, it was estimated that the largest *Drosophila* chromosome had about 43 $\times$ 10^9 daltons of DNA. Results from the viscoelastic measurements indicated the presence of DNA molecules of between 38 and 44 $\times$ 10^9 daltons. Viscoelastic measurements of inversions, which changed the ratio of the arms but not the overall size of the chromosome, yielded similar results. However, a translocation that radically changed the size of the chromosome to 59 $\times$ 10^9 daltons resulted in an equivalent change in the viscoelastic estimates to between 52 and 64 $\times$ 10^9 daltons.

The conclusion from these studies is that the largest *Drosophila* chromosome, and by extension every eukaryotic chromosome, contains a single DNA molecule running from end to end, encompassing both arms. The viscoelastic values were corroborated by carefully isolating and measuring the lengths of long DNA molecules, an especially difficult task given DNA's propensity to break. The longest molecule that the investigators found was 1.2 cm long, equivalent to between 24 and 32 $\times$ 10^9 daltons, close to the predicted size. Thus, the evidence is in complete concordance with the simple uninemic model of eukaryotic chromosomal structure.

Nucleoprotein Composition

Nucleosome structure

Since each eukaryotic chromosome consists of a single, relatively long piece of duplex DNA, the average diploid cell contains many of these long pieces of DNA. For chromosomes to be properly distributed to each daughter cell during mitosis and meiosis, they must be condensed into structures that are more easily managed. Wrapping the DNA around "spools" of protein constitutes the first step in a series of coiling and folding processes that eventually result in the fully compacted chromosome we see at metaphase.

Interphase nuclei can be disrupted by placing them in a hypotonic liquid such as water. When this happens, chromatin material is released. When this material is observed under the electron microscope, small particles called *nucleosomes* can be seen. These are the spools that the DNA is wrapped around. They are made of *histone* proteins and associated DNA. The histones, a group of arginine- and lysine-rich basic proteins, have been well characterized. They are especially well suited to bind to the negatively charged DNA.

When chromatin is treated with micrococcal nuclease, individual nucleosomes can be isolated, indicating that the DNA between nucleosomes is accessible to digestion. The results of these studies

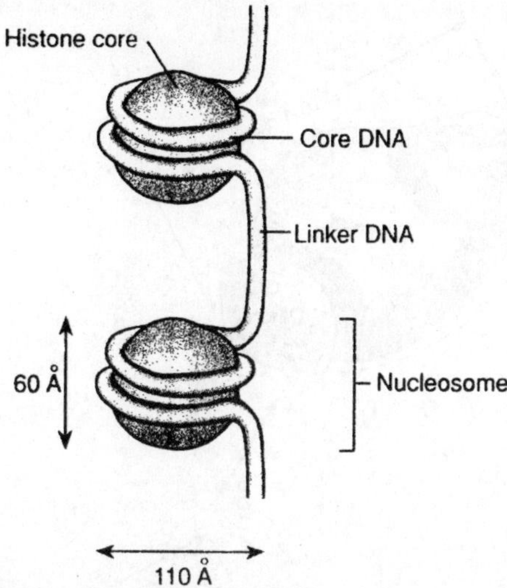

Fig. 4.2. The eukaryotic chromosome is associated with histone proteins to form nucleosomes.

indicate that a length of 168 base pairs (bp) of DNA, the core DNA, is intimately associated with the nucleosome, and another 50 to 75 base pairs, depending on species, connects the nucleosomes (linker DNA). When the quantities of the various histones were measured, there were two each of histones H2A, H2B, H3, and H4 per nucleosome and only one molecule of histone H1. Reconstitution and degradation studies have indicated that histone H1 is not a necessary component in the formation of nucleosomes. We believe that histone H1 is associated with the linker DNA as it enters and emerges from the nucleosome, although its exact position is not known with certainty. Histone H1 may be more off center and internally located than illustrated. The term *chromatosome* has been suggested for the core nucleosome plus the H1 protein, a unit that includes approximately 168 base pairs of DNA. Nucleosomes, then, are a first-order packaging of DNA; they reduce its length and undoubtedly make the coiling and contraction required during mitosis and meiosis more efficient.

When DNA is replicated, twice as many nucleosomes are needed since one double helix becomes two. Recent studies indicate that a parental nucleosome is partly disassembled during DNA replication and reassembled on one or the other daughter strand, apparently randomly. The other DNA strand has a new nucleosome constructed of histones from the cellular pool with the help of proteins called *chromatin assembly factors*; at least three of these factors are known.

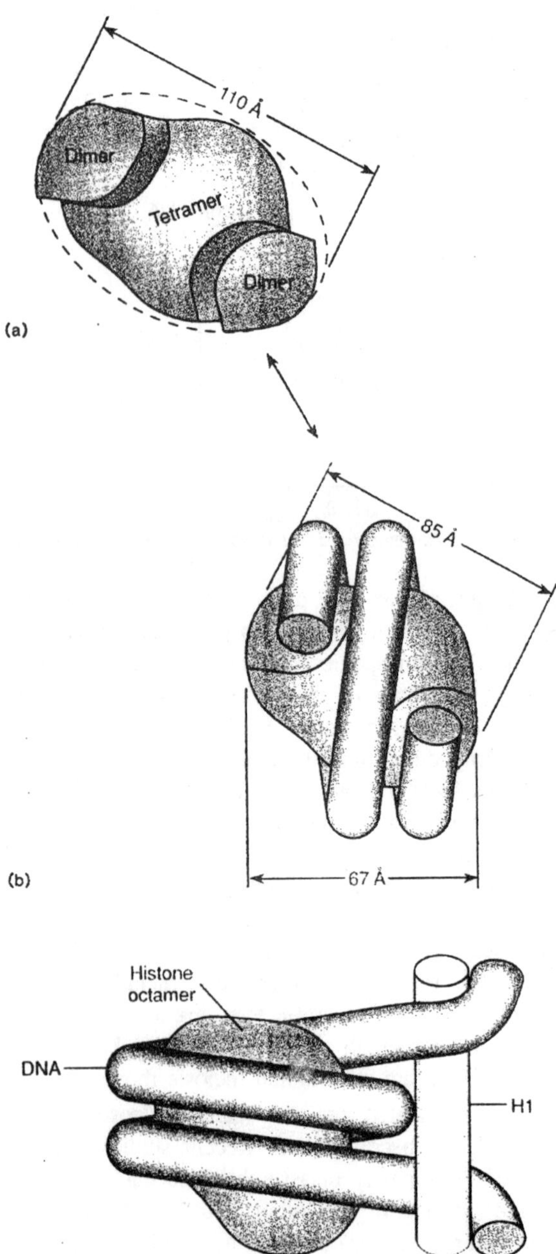

Fig. 4.3. Nucleosome structure.

Table 4.1. The constituency of calf thymus chromatin

Constituent	*Relative Weight*
DNA	100
Histone proteins	114
Nonhistone proteins	33
RNA	1

For example, in fruit flies, a protein complex called the *replication-coupling assembly factor* assembles new nucleosomes. In addition, a protein complex called *condensin* is needed for the condensation of interphasechromosomes to mitotic chromosomes. This complex includes two *SMC proteins* (for structural maintenance of chromosomes) and two non-SMC proteins. SMC proteins also aid other chromosomal activities, such as mitotic segregation, sister-chromatid adhesion, dosage compensation, and recombination. Thus, a diverse array of proteins is involved in creating nucleosomes and chromatosomes, condensing interphase chromosomes, and performing numerous other activities of chromosomes.

Dosage compensation has recently been associated with a change in nucleosome structure. The inactivated X chromosome appears to have a different type of histone present. Histone H2A is replaced by a variant called mH2A. The details of this mechanism are under study.

Nucleosomes apparently play a major role in controlling gene expression; DNA with nucleosomes has a much lower transcription rate than DNA without nucleosomes. It makes sense that the positions of nucleosomes can provide or prevent access to promoters. There are regions of the DNA, known as *nuclease-hypersensitive sites*, that appear to be nucleosome free. These sites, usually mutiples of a nucleosomal region of about two hundred base pairs, are particularly sensitive to digestion by different nucleases. When these regions are isolated, they usually have sequences that control functions in replication, transcription, or other activities of DNA. For example, numerous promoter regions in *Drosophila*, mouse, and human DNA are in nuclease-hypersensitive sites. Hence, some specific DNA sequences are kept free of nucleosomes, and these sequences appear to be recognized by various enzymes such as RNA polymerase. In many other cases, however, nucleosomes do appear to cover promoters and repress transcription. For transcription to occur in these cases, some form of *chromatin remodeling* must take place.

Two general classes of proteins are involved in chromatin remodeling. First are proteins that acetylate the N-terminal tails of the histones, a process that may cause the nucleosomes to bind the DNA less tightly and thus make it available for attachment of transcription factors. These enzymes are called *histone acetyl transferases* (HATs). Deacetylating enzymes have the reverse effect: They act to repress transcription. Second, a class of ATP-dependent proteins such as the SWI/SNF complex in yeast also affect chromatin remodeling. (Some workers called the proteins SWI because they were involved in mating type switching, and others called them SNF for sucrose nonfermenting.) The SWI/SNF complex is a group of eleven proteins involved in transcription activation in many genes, presumably allowing transcription factors to access promoters by remodeling chromatin. These proteins are able to reposition a nucleosome on DNA by sliding the nucleosome down the DNA.

We thus conclude that although nucleosomes serve as a general, first-order packing mechanism in eukaryotic DNA, they can be positioned precisely and can attenuate transcription. It is interesting to note that once transcription begins, RNA polymerase apparently moves along nucleosomed DNA by translocation of the histones by 75 to 80 base pairs without disrupting the nucleosome itself. This seems to be accomplished by the RNA polymerase moving the DNA and then re-forming the nucleosome in its wake.

Higher-order structure of chromatin

Since the nucleosome has a width of only 110 Å, and metaphase chromosomes appear to be constructed of a fiber having a diameter of about 2,400 Å, several additional levels of chromatin compaction lead to the metaphase chromosome. Various experiments, which change the ionic strength the chromatin is subjected to, indicate that the 110 Å DNA spontaneously forms a 300 Å, solenoidlike fiber with increased ionic strength. It seems that this fiber results from the coiling of the nucleosomal DNA. This 300 Å fiber is not, however, the final form of the DNA. We can account for the contraction of the 300 Å fiber to the 2,400 Å fiber found in metaphase chromosomes by the formation of a second solenoidlike structure from the winding of the 300 Å fiber.

If the histones are removed from a chromosome, the DNA billows out, leaving a proteinaceous structure termed a *scaffold*. This scaffold structure is formed from *nonhistone proteins*; two of them predominate, namely SC1 and SC2. SC1 has been identified as topoisomerase II. It

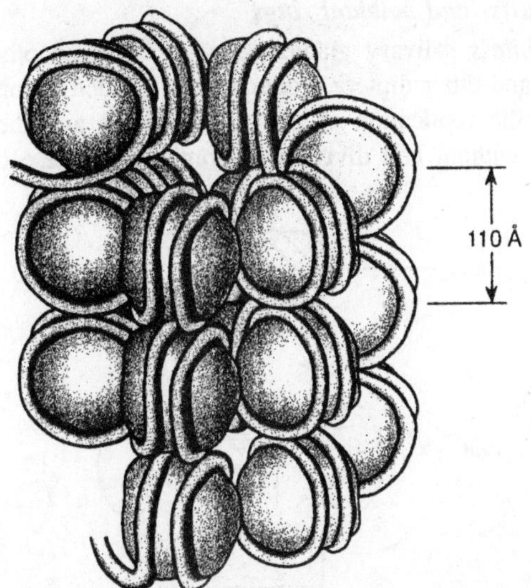

Fig. 4.4. Solenoid model for the formation of the 300-Å chromatin fiber.

would not be unreasonable to expect several hundred different proteins, many in minute quantities, to be associated with the chromosome and involved in replication, repair, and transcription.

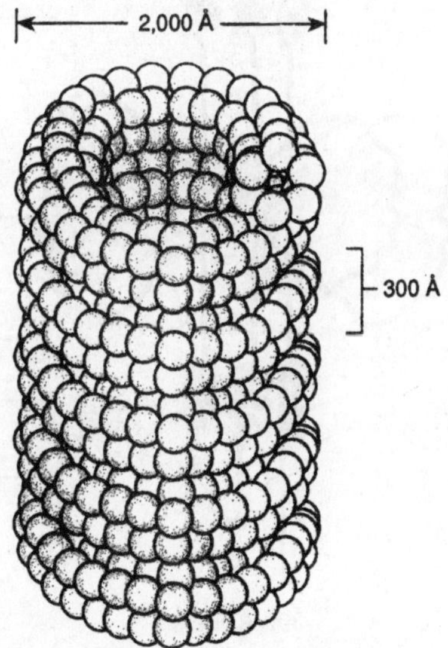

Fig. 4.5. The 2,000-Å fiber of the eukaryotic chromosome is a solenoidlike structure formed by the coiling of the 300-Å fiber, which itself is a solenoid.

Polyteny, puffs, and balbiani rings

Drosophila's salivary glands, as well as some other tissues of *Drosophila* and other diptera, contain giant banded chromosomes that result from the replication of the chromosomes and the synapsis of homologues without cell division (endomitosis). These chromosomes

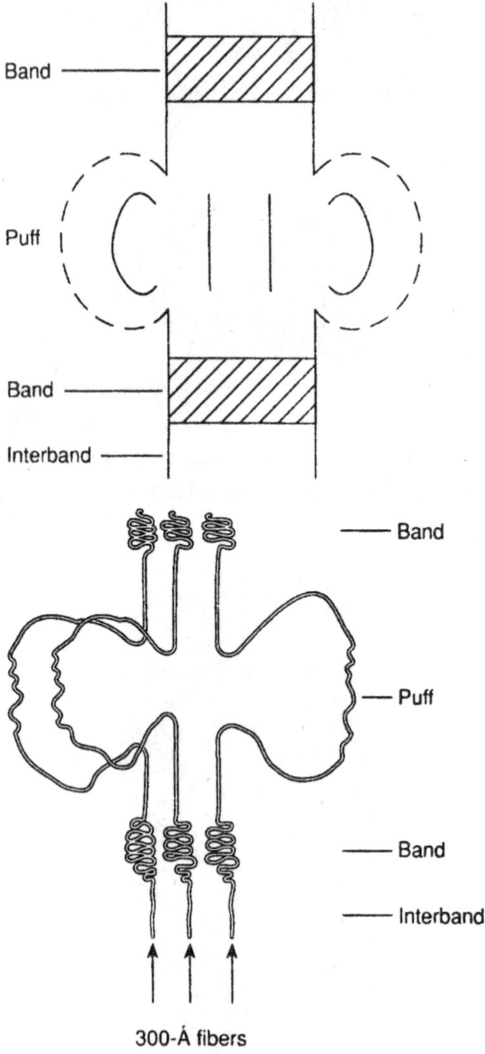

Fig. 4.6. Polytene chromosome with bands and a puff. Three of the approximately one thousand synapsed chromatids are shown diagrammatically on the below.

consist of more than one thousand copies of the same chromatid and appear as alternating dark bands and lighter interband regions. The dark bands are referred to as chromomeres. Also seen are diffuse areas called *chromosome puffs*. Chromosome puffs are also referred to as *Balbiani rings*. These rings were originally defined as puffs in the midge, *Chironomus*, whose polytene chromosomes were discovered by E. G. Balbiani in 1881. Currently, the term applies to all puffs, or at least the larger puffs, in all species with polytene chromosomes.

The structure of the polytene chromosome can be explained by the diagram. Dark bands (chromomeres) are due to tight coiling of the 300 Å fiber; light interband regions are due to looser coiling. The figure also shows how chromosome puffs would come about as fibers unfold in regions of active transcription.

Staining with reagents specific for RNA, such as toluidine blue, or autoradiography with tritiated (^{3}H) uridine, have been used to demonstrate that active transcription is going on in the puffs but not in neighbouring regions of the polytene chromosomes. The messenger RNA isolated from cells with puffs has also been shown to hybridize only to the puffed regions of the chromosomes. Thus, these regions of the DNA are complementary to the messenger RNA and represent areas of active transcription. Modern recombinant DNA techniques have also shown that many puffs probably represent the transcription of only one gene, although there are exceptions.

Puffs generally fall into four categories. *Stage-specific puffs* appear during a certain stage of development, such as molting. *Tissue-specific puffs* are active in one tissue but not another. (In dipteran larvae, tissues other than the salivary glands, such as the midgut and Malpighian tubules, have polytene chromosomes.) *Constitutive puffs* are active almost all the time in a specific tissue. And *environmentally induced puffs* appear after some environmental change, such as heat shock. In *Drosophila*, about 80% of the puffs are stage specific; in *Chironomus*, only about 20% are. For example, at the time of molt in insects, the hormone ecdysone is secreted by the prothoracic gland. At the same time, many puff patterns change. Similar changes in puff patterns can be induced by the injection of ecdysone. Hence, molting, a stage-specific developmental sequence, is related to a sequential transcription sequence in the chromosomes.

Lampbrush chromosomes

Lampbrush chromosomes, which occur in amphibian oocytes, are so named because their looped-out configuration has the appearance of a brush for cleaning lamps, now a relatively uncommon household item. The loops of the lampbrush chromosomes are covered by an RNA matrix and are the sites of active transcription. Presumably, the loops are unwindings of the single chromosome, similar to the unwindings in the polytene chromosome. Thus, under certain circumstances, such as in polytene chromosomal puffs and in lampbrush chromosomes, active transcription can be seen in the light microscope. Since only certain bands puff at any one moment in polytene chromosomes, and since the loops of lampbrush chromosomes are of various sizes (with some regions not looped at all), we have evidence of specific transcription. However, we have no indication, so far, of the nature of the control of that transcription.

Chromosomal Banding

Several chromosomal staining techniques reveal consistent banding patterns. By means of these patterns, all of the human chromosomes can be differentiated. Of possibly greater importance is the fact that these staining techniques have provided some insight into the structure of the chromosome. The techniques for staining the C, G, and R chromosomal bands will serve as an illustration.

G-bands are obtained with *Giemsa stain*, a complex of stains specific for the phosphate groups of DNA. Treatment of fixed chromatin with trypsin or hot salts brings out the G-bands. Giemsa stain enhances banding that is already visible in mitotic chromosomes. The banding pattern is caused by the arrangement of chromomeres. Under careful observation, the major G-bands prove to consist of many smaller chromomeres. This banding appearance has led D.

C-bands are Giemsa-stained bands after the chromosomes are treated with NaOH. The *C* is for "centromere," because these bands represent constitutive heterochromatin surrounding the centromeres. The DNA is also usually satellite rich. *Satellite DNA* differs in *buoyant density* from the major portion of cellular DNA. When eukaryotic DNA is isolated and centrifuged in CsCl, forming a density gradient, the majority of the DNA forms one band in the gradient at a single buoyant density. The buoyancy is determined by the G-C content of the DNA. However, smaller secondary bands are also usually present, indicating regions of DNA having sequences different from the majority of the cell's DNA. DNA isolated this way is referred to as *satellite DNA* because of the secondary, or satellite, bands formed in the density gradient. As we will see, this DNA is found primarily around centromeres and consists of numerous repetitions of a short sequence.

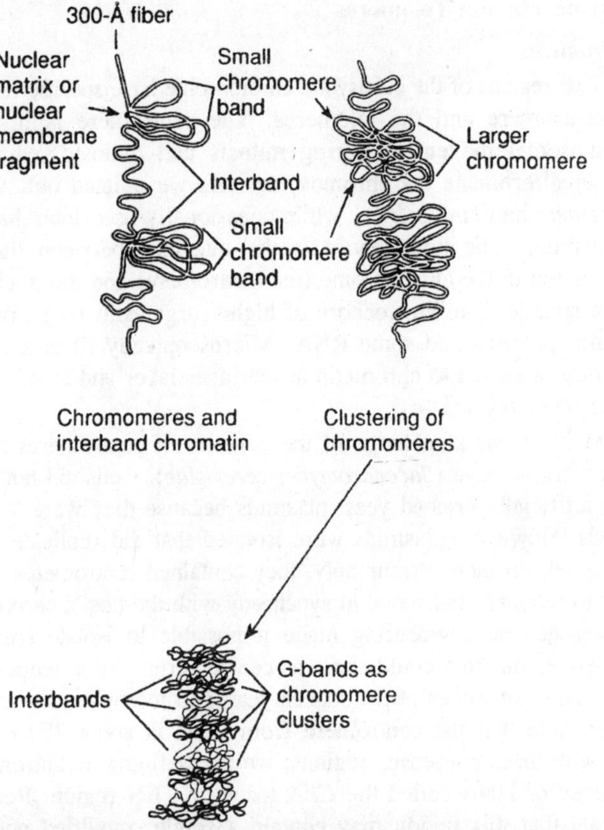

Fig. 4.7. Model of eukaryotic (mammalian) chromosomal banding.

R-bands are visible with a technique that stains the regions between G-bands. The chromosomes are fixed, stained with Giemsa, and then viewed with a phase contrast microscope. Since the dark-light pattern is the opposite of the G-band pattern, these bands are called *reverse bands*.

From the information gleaned from these staining techniques, D. Comings distinguished between three basic chromatin types: euchromatin, constitutive heterochromatin, and intercalary heterochromatin. Presumably, the only chromatin involved in transcription is *euchromatin*. *Constitutive heterochromatin* surrounds the centromere and is rich in satellite DNA. *Intercalary heterochromatin* is found throughout the chromosome. Thus, it becomes apparent that the eukaryotic chromosome is a relatively complex structure.

Centromeres and Telomeres

Centromeres

Two regions of the eukaryotic chromosome have specific functions—the centromere and the telomeres. The centromere is involved in chromosomal movement during mitosis and meiosis, whereas the telomeres terminate the chromosomes. As we pointed out, the terms *centromere* and *kinetochore*, while occasionally used interchangeably, are distinct. The kinetochore is the interface between the visible constriction in the chromosome (the centromere) and the microtubules of the spindle. The kinetochore of higher organisms (e.g., mammals) contains proteins and some RNA. Microscopically, it is a trilaminar structure, attached to chromatin at the inner layer and to microtubules at the outer layer.

Most of our knowledge of the genetics of centromeres has come from work in yeast (*Saccharomyces cerevisiae*). Cells did not maintain most artificially created yeast plasmids because they were lost during mitosis. However, plasmids were isolated that did replicate normally during cell division. Presumably, they contained centromeres, allowing them to replicate and move in synchrony with the host's chromosomes. Further genetic engineering made it possible to isolate smaller and smaller regions that could serve as centromeres. After sequencing the centromeres of fifteen of the sixteen yeast chromosomes, it was possible to conclude that the centromere from yeast is about 250 base pairs long with three consensus regions; we are defining a centromere as a sequence of DNA called the *CEN* locus or CEN region. Recent data indicate that this region may contain a single, modified nucleosome associated with region II. The 250 base-pair length of the CEN regions of yeast chromosomes is about 200 Å, the same as the diameter of a microtubule, indicating that only one micro-tubule attaches to each centromere during mitosis or meiosis in a yeast cell. This region is called a *point centromere*. Higher eukaryotes have larger centromeric regions that attach more microtubules. These regions are referred to as *regional centromeres*. Regional centromeres range from nineteen to one hundred kilobases (kb; 19,000–100,000 bases) with unique and satellite (repeated sequence) DNA that is heterochromatic and may include expressed genes. We know much less about regional centromeres than we do about point centromeres.

Telomeres

Since eukaryotic chromosomes are linear, each has two ends, referred to as *telomeres*, that not only mark the termination of the linear chromosome but also have several specific functions. Telomeres must prevent the chromosomal ends from acting in a "sticky" fashion, the way that broken chromosomal ends act. In other words, chromosomal ends must not elicit a DNA repair response. Telomeres must also prevent the ends of chromosomes from being degraded by exonucleases and must allow chromosomal ends to be properly replicated.

Most telomeres isolated so far are repetitions of sequences of five to eight bases. In human beings, the telomeric sequence is TTAGGG, repeated 300 to 5,000 times at the end of each chromosome. The human telomere was discovered by R. Moyzis and his colleagues when they probed the highly repetitive segment of human DNA. (Highly repetitive DNA, as its name implies, consists of numerous copies of a single sequence and usually comprises the satellite components of the cell's DNA; see next section.) When a probe for this sequence was applied to human chromosomes, the sequence was found at the tip of each chromosome in roughly the same quantity.This is a highly conserved sequence, found in all vertebrates studied as well as in unicellular trypanosomes. Similar sequences are found in various other eukaryotes; the first sequence was isolated by E. Blackburn and J. Gall in 1978.

When a linear DNA molecule is replicated, the 3' → 5' strand can be replicated to the end. The 5' → 3' strand, however, is replicated with RNA primers that are then degraded, leaving a short gap on the progeny strand. It is always the G-rich strand of telomeric DNA that ends up single-stranded, forming a 3' overhang of twelve to sixteen nucleotides. Thus, the normal replication process of a linear DNA molecule leaves an incomplete terminus. Hence, scientists suspected that there would be a unique mechanism for the replication of telomeres.

Telomeric sequences appear to be added de novo without, DNA template assistance by an enzyme called *telomerase*, discovered by E. Blackburn and her colleagues. This was seen when telomeres from another species were engineered into yeast cells. After a cell cycle, the yeast telomeric sequence had been added on at the ends of the foreign chromosome, the result, presumably, of the telomerase enzyme.

When Blackburn and her colleagues isolated telomerase, they discovered that a segment of RNA, about 160 base pairs, is an integral part of the enzyme. That RNA has a region that is complementary to the G-rich repeat of the telomeric DNA sequence of the species. After careful experimentation, including modifying the gene for the

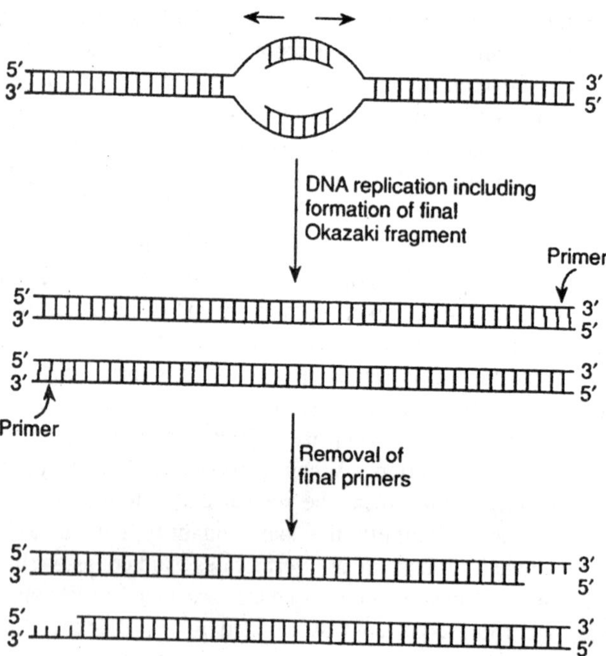

Fig. 4.8. Removal of final primers after the replication of linear DNA creates single-stranded ends.

telomerase RNA, Blackburn and her colleagues concluded that telomerase uses its RNA as a template for adding telomeric repeats to the ends of chromosomes. Telomerase is thus a reverse transcriptase, using RNA nucleotides as a template to polymerize DNA nucleotides.

Blackburn and her colleagues proposed that the first step in telomere extension is hybridization of the 3' end of the telomere with the RNA component of telomerase. Then, with the telomerase RNA as a template, the 3' end of the telomere is extended. Finally, a translocation step takes place that displaces the telomere in respect to the RNA, returning to the configuration at the beginning of the process. The single-stranded C-rich strand is then synthesized with DNA polymerase and DNA ligase.

Once telomeres have been added to the ends of eukaryotic chromosomes, different organisms use any of three different methods known to protect the ends of the chromosomes. First, the guanine-rich DNA can form complex structures. Biochemists have discovered that four guanines can form a planar *G-tetraplex*, with the four bases hydrogen bonded to each other. Several structures have been hypothesized

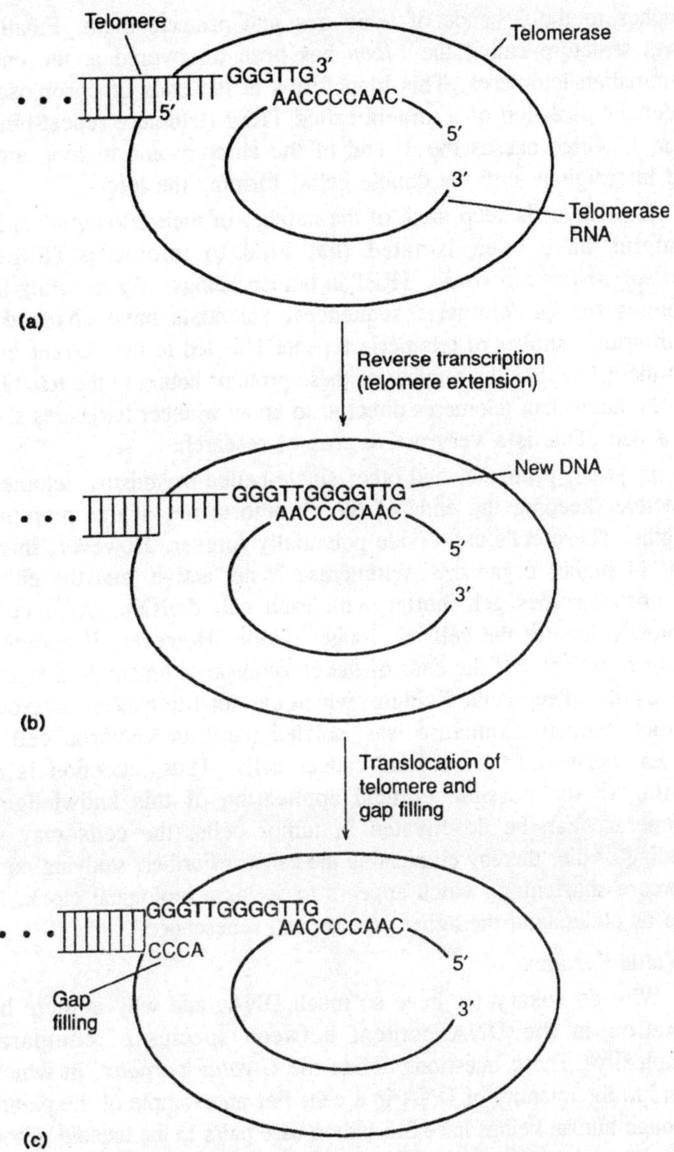

Fig. 4.9. Telomerase extends telomeres using telomerase RNA as a template Gap filling by DNA polymerase I and ligase complete the double helix.

to explain the novel ends of these chromosomes. Second, proteins have been discovered that bind to the 3' ends of telomeres. In the ciliate *Oxytricha nova*, a protein called the telomere end-binding protein (TEBP) attaches to the 3' ends of telomeres and protects them. Finally, a novel structure called the *t-loop* has been discovered at the end of mammalian telomeres. This loop forms at the ends of chromosomes under the direction of a protein called TRF2 (telomere repeat-binding factor), which causes the 3' end of the chromosome to loop around and interdigitate into the double helix, forming the loop.

How do cells keep track of the number of their telomeric repeats? Proteins have been isolated that bind to telomeres (Rap1 in *Saccharomyces cerevisiae*, TRF1 in human beings). By mutating these proteins or the telomeric sequences, scientists have changed the equilibrium number of telomeric repeats.This led to the current model that the cell counts the number of these proteins bound to the telomeres, not the number of telomeres directly, to know whether telomeres should be added. This is a very active area of research.

In yeast, protozoa, and other single-celled organisms, telomerase is active, keeping the ends of the chromo somes at the appropriate lengths. These cells can divide potentially forever. However, in most cells of higher organisms, telomerase is not active, and the ends of the chromosomes get shorter with each cell division. At a certain telomeric length, the cells no longer divide. However, if telomerase becomes active, and the ends of the chromosomes lengthen, a signal is conveyed to keep cells dividing, which can lead to cancerous growth. In fact, human telomerase was isolated from an immortal cell line (HeLa) derived from cervical cancer cells. Thus, attention is now turning to the possible clinical application of this knowledge: If telomerase can be deactivated in tumor cells, the cells may stop dividing or die, thereby eliminating the cancer. Further, studying normal telomere shortening, which appears to act as a biological clock, may help us understand the aging process and senescence.

C-Value Paradox

Why do eukaryotes have so much DNA, and why is there huge variation in the DNA content between species of comparable complexity? These questions define the *C-value paradox*, in which *C* refers to the quantity of DNA in a cell. For an example of the paradox, although human beings have 3.3 billion base pairs in the haploid genome, an amoeba has more than 200 billion base pairs. And although an average bony fish has over 300 billion base pairs of DNA in its haploid genome, the Japanese puffer fish has less than half a billion base pairs. If the basic bony fish pattern can be created with less than half a billion base pairs, why does the average bony fish have over 600 times that much DNA? What is this excess DNA doing? To explain the C-value paradox, researchers examined the repetitiveness of DNA, and more recently, probed and sequenced DNA to understand its properties.

DNA-DNA Hybridization

R. Britten and his colleagues, using the technique of *DNA-DNA hybridization*, first systematically analyzed the repetitiveness of the DNA within eukaryotes. When DNA is heated, it denatures or unwinds into single strands; when it cools, it renatures. The rate of renaturation depends on the DNA sequences. If the sample contains DNA with repeated sequences, it will hybridize faster than DNA that does not have repeated sequences. From these studies, Britten and his colleagues found that eukaryotic chromosomes contain regions of unique, moderately repetitive, and highly repetitive DNA. *Unique DNA* is, as its name implies, DNA with unrepeated sequences. *Repetitive DNA* is DNA whose sequences are repeated in the genome.

Satellite DNA, found around centromeres, is highly repetitive DNA with a unique repeat length of about two hundred base pairs. Given the quantity of satellite DNA per cell, there must be more than one million repetitions of this two-hundrednucleotide sequence in higher eukaryotes. At the other end of the spectrum is unique DNA, which makes up most of the transcribed genes of an organism. The rest of the DNA is repetitive DNA in a few to several hundred thousand copies. This repetitive DNA comprises at least three categories. One is "junk" DNA, DNA that is not useful to the organism, made up of untranscribed and parasitic sequences (selfish DNA). Another category is transcribed genes in many copies that have diverged from each other, such as antibody, collagen, and globin genes. We use the term *gene family* to refer to genes that have arisen by duplication, with or without divergence, from an ancestral gene. And finally, transcribed genes in many copies that are virtually identical, such as ribosomal RNA and histone genes, make up a third category of repetitive DNA.

Junk DNA

We saw that transposons in prokaryotes are generally viewed as selfish or parasitic: They serve no purpose to the cell. The transposons replicate on their own, increasing in number. Eukaryotic transposons are mostly *retrotransposons*, transposable elements that move by way of an RNA intermediate. That is, the retrotransposon is transcribed into RNA and then, by reverse transcription, converted to a cDNA that is then inserted into the genome. These elements can make up

50% of the eukaryotic genome, existing in hundreds of thousands of copies. They generally fall into two categories: LINES and SINES. *Long interspersed elements* (LINES), are up to seven thousand base pairs each and contain genes for reverse transcription, RNA binding, and endonuclease activity. They thus have the ability to jump by way of an RNA intermediate. Human DNA is believed to be composed of about 15% LINES.

Short interspersed elements (SINES) are generally derivatives of transfer RNA genes and do not have the ability to retrotranspose on their own. That is, in the past, their transcripts were modified, converted to cDNA by reverse transcription, and then reinserted into the host's genome. They rely on the reverse transcriptase provided by the genes of LINES or retroviruses. One group of SINEs not derived from transfer RNA is derived from the RNA of the signal recognition particle; members of this group occur in human beings in about five-hundred thousand copies of a three-hundred-basepair sequence. Because these sequences are cleaved by the restriction endonuclease *Alu*I, they are called the *Alu family*. The human genome is also permeated by remnants of at least a dozen distinct families of ancient retroviruses scattered throughout our chromosomes.

At this point, we can see some potential explanations for the C-value paradox. Much eukaryotic DNA is junk, apparently doing no harm. In some cases, 97% of the host genome is composed of junk DNA. Recent work seems to indicate that gross differences in DNA content between higher organisms may be due to the differing abilities of different species to rid themselves of this parasitic DNA. If it builds up without being removed, the DNA content of the species can soar. Thus, the wide differences in DNA content among higher eukaryotes mentioned at the beginning of this section have little to do with the complexity of the organism, but rather with the ability of the organism to remove junk DNA as it forms.

Expressed genes in many copies

Several types of genes create a product that is needed in such large quantity that one copy of the gene could not fulfill the cell's needs. We are familiar with the nucleolus, the site of the ribosomal RNA genes. Human beings have about two hundred copies of the major ribosomal RNA gene and about two thousand copies of the 5S ribosomal RNA gene. Fruit flies have about two hundred and one hundred copies, respectively, of the two genes. In some cases, the normal number of multiple copies of a gene is still not enough. The cell must then resort to *gene amplification*, a process whereby the cell increases the number of copies of the gene. For example, during oogenesis, ribosomal RNA genes (rDNA) are often amplified. In *Xenopus*, rDNA is amplified about one thousand times, which allows an oocyte to accumulate about 10^{12} ribosomes. The amplified DNA is in the form of small, circular, extrachromosomal molecules of DNA. Several models have been proposed as to how cells actually amplify their DNA. One model relies on unequal crossing over (as in *Bar* eye in *Drosophila*), whereas another model is based on unscheduled extra DNA replication in a region, followed by recombinational events that generate linear and circular forms of the excess DNA. It is not presently clear which model is correct.

In addition to ribosomal RNA genes, other genes are repeated, ensuring adequate gene products. The number and location of repeated genes are usually discovered by hybridization studies using probes, similar to the way that telomeric DNA was shown to be at the tips of the chromosomes. Repeated genes include the genes for transfer RNAs and histones. The average transfer RNA is repeated about a dozen times in *Drosophila*. Human beings have over thirteen hundred copies of transfer RNA genes in the haploid genome. In many species, the five histone genes form a repeated cluster, although each gene is transcribed independently, while prokaryotic operons are transcribed as a unit. The arrangement of histone genes may be more complex in higher forms. There are indications that in mammals, histone genes may lie in small groups or even as individual genes.

Several types of genes occur in similar but not identical forms—that is, an original gene was duplicated but, unlike histone or ribosomal RNA genes, the copies diverged in function. These gene families include globin genes, immunoglobulin genes, chorion protein (insect eggshell) genes, and *Drosophila* heat shock genes.

Globin gene family

Globins are oxygen-transporting and storage molecules found in animals, some plants, and microorganisms. In higher vertebrates, there are two types of globins: myoglobin, which stores oxygen in muscles, and hemoglobin, found in red blood cells. Myoglobins function as single molecules, whereas hemoglobins occur as tetramers, two each of two protein chains. Evolution in the globin gene family can be traced by comparative studies of globins in different species as well as molecular studies of globins within a species. Studying hemoglobins has provided a great deal of information on gene expression and evolution. We turn our attention to the globin gene family in human beings. During human development, four major hemoglobins appear: embryonic hemoglobin, Hb F, Hb A, and Hb A_2. Structurally, the ζ (Greek, zeta) subunit (a component of embryonic hemoglobin) is α-like, whereas the rest are β-like. Fetal hemoglobin has a higher affinity for oxygen than does adult hemoglobin, thus allowing fetuses to draw oxygen from their mother's blood. From a comparative study of the DNA sequences, the evolution of the various hemoglobin genes has been inferred.

The α genes are located in a cluster on chromosome 16; the β genes are located in a cluster on chromosome 11. These two clusters provide a clear case history of gene duplication, presumably by unequal crossing over, followed by divergence. Having a second or third copy of a gene allows one of the duplicates to diverge (and perhaps to become nonfunctional in the process), whereas the original still performs the required function.

Many diseases of genetic interest involve the hemoglobins. In fact, hemoglobinopathies, including sickle-cell anemia and the thalassemias, are the most common genetic disorders in the world population. The best-known mutation of a hemoglobin gene itself is the one that causes sickle-cell anemia, a mutation of the sixth amino acid of the β chain. In the homozygous state, the disease is usually fatal. However, heterozygotes show an increased resistance to malaria. One of the ramifications is that the sickle-cell allele is maintained at relatively high frequencies in malarial regions.

The *thalassemias* are a group of diseases that affect the regulation of the α and β hemoglobin genes. (*Thalassemia* comes from the Greek for "sea blood," because the disease is best known in individuals living around the Mediterranean Sea.) In α and β thalassemias, the α or β subunit, respectively, is present in very low quantities or entirely absent. Many of the genetic defects are deletions, possibly due to unequal crossing over within the globin gene complexes. T. Maniatis showed that β thalassemia is caused by a mutation in the β-globin gene that disrupts RNA splicing. The body compensates by forming γ_4 or β_4 hemoglobin in a thalassemias, or $\alpha_2\gamma_2$ or $\alpha_2\delta_2$ in β thalassemias. These are relatively unsuitable or inefficient responses; the diseases range from very mild to very severe and frequently fatal. More information is needed regarding the control of hemoglobin production in the thalassemias.

5

Chromosome Theory of Inheritance

Dolores Becker was 37 years old and decided that if she was ever going to have a child, she should not wait any longer. She soon became pregnant and happily anticipated the arrival of her child. However, the birth of her daughter touched off legal battles that still reverberate through the staid halls of New York's court houses. Mrs. Becker's daughter was born with a genetic defect known as *Down syndrome*. This condition is caused by an extra *chromosome*, a carrier of the genetic information we inherit from our parents. Mrs. Becker's physician did not warn her that, at her age, she ran a substantial risk (about 1 in 250) of giving birth to a child with Down syndrome. He could have analyzed the fetus's chromosomes to see if it had the correct number, but he did not. The Beckers sued the physician for the damages they sustained as a result of his failure to inform them of the risks and to offer diagnostic tests. In this "wrongful birth" suit, the Beckers claimed that they were denied the opportunity to make an informed decision to continue the pregnancy or terminate it. The child, through her parents, also sued the physician. It was her contention that she should never have been allowed to be born with the severe mental and physical abnormalities that characterize Down syndrome. This is called a "wrongful life" suit.

On the first go-around, the court dismissed the case, stating that it did not recognize a cause of action for "wrongful birth," as the parents claimed, or for "wrong full life," as the child claimed. The Beckers appealed the ruling to a higher court, and it was reversed.

The physician then appealed to New York's highest court of appeals. This court supported the concept of "wrongful birth," but rejected the notion of "wrongful life." So to this day in the state of New York, parents can sue a physician for a "wrongful birth," but a child cannot sue for being born in a defective condition. In the court's words:

Whether it is better never to have been born at all than to have been born with even gross deficiencies is a mystery more properly left to the philosophers and theologians.

Though New York does not recognize "wrong full life" suits, other states do. In California, a young girl was born with Tay-Sachs disease because the laboratory that tested the parents said that they were not carriers. The laboratory was negligent. The parents successfully sued the laboratory on behalf of their child (the suit was based on emotional stress and deprivation of 72.6 years of life).

The foundation on which the Becker story rests is the chromosome, a linear array of genes found in cell nuclei. Down syndrome is caused by a mistake in cell division that leads to an extra copy of chromosome number 21.

When Mendel formulated the laws governing inheritance, he knew nothing about chromosomes. Nobody did. People knew about cells, and toward the latter part of the nineteenth century they knew that the nucleus was the key to inheritance. But what entities inside the cell's nucleus provided a physical basis for the laws of inheritance? Soon after biologists discovered the pioneering experiments carried out by Mendel and the principles of inheritance that emerged from those experiments, chromosomes were identified a the cellular entities responsible for inheritance.

CELL DIVISION AND THE TRANSMISSION OF CHROMOSOMES

Identifying Chromosomes as the Carriers of Heredity

Biologists' knowledge of internal cell structure was greatly enhanced by improvements in the microscope and by the development of staining techniques during the 1840s. Because various parts of the cell were found to react with specific stains, or dyes, it became possible to see structures previously not visible. Biologists soon discovered that the cell nucleus contains a threadlike substance that stains darkly with certain stains. This substance they called *chromatin* (from the Greek *chromos*, colour). Over the next few decades, many observers noticed that just before a cell divides, the *chromatin* condenses and forms dark-staining bodies called *chromosomes* ("colour bodies").

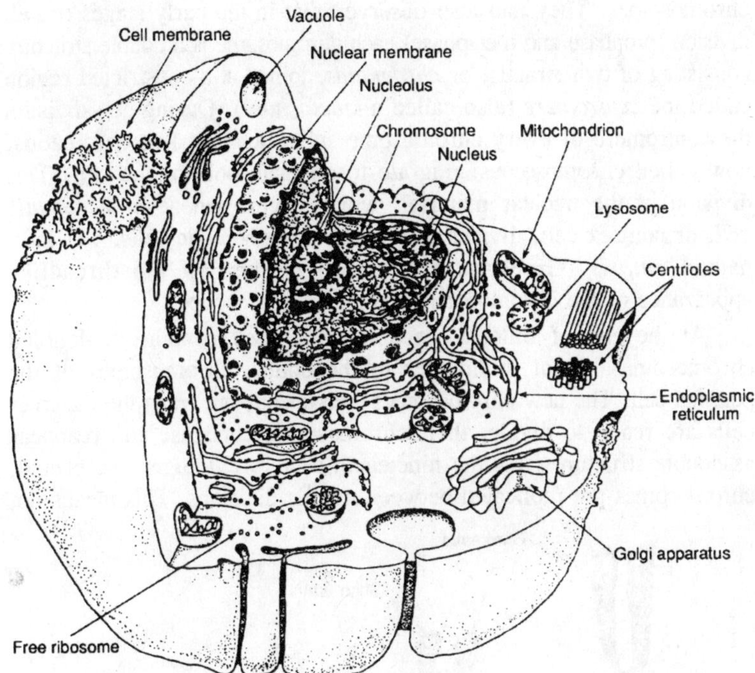

Fig. 5.1. A centralized animal cell showing some of the structures commonly found.

Mitosis: Duplication of nuclear material

By the mid-1870s cytologists realized that chromatin did not actually disappear before cell division, but condensed to form the

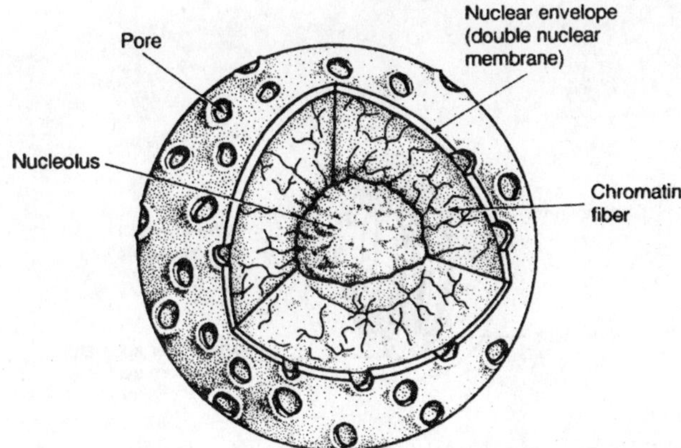

Fig. 5.2. A cell nucleus showing a nucleolus, the nuclear pores in the membrane, and the uncoiled chromatin that condenses into chromosomes during cell division.

chromosomes. They had also observed that in the early stages of cell division (prophase and metaphase) each chromosome is a double structure consisting of two strands, or *chromatids*, joined at a constricted region called the *centromere* (also called a *kinetochore*). During cell division the centromere of every chromosome splits, and the two chromatids, now called chromosomes, migrate to opposite pole of the cell. This division of the nuclear material, which occurs whenever a *somatic cell*, or non-sex cell, divides to produce other somatic cells, was later named *mitosis* (Greek *mitos*, thread) because of the threadlike appearance of the chromosomes under the microscope.

At the end of mitosis, each *daughter cell* contains undoubled chromosomes, equal in number to the double chromosomes of the parental cell. The new chromosomes then uncoil, but when the daughter cells are ready to divide, their chromosomes condense and reappear as double structures. As the nineteenth-century cytologists suspected, chromosomes are replicated between mitotic divisions. This means not

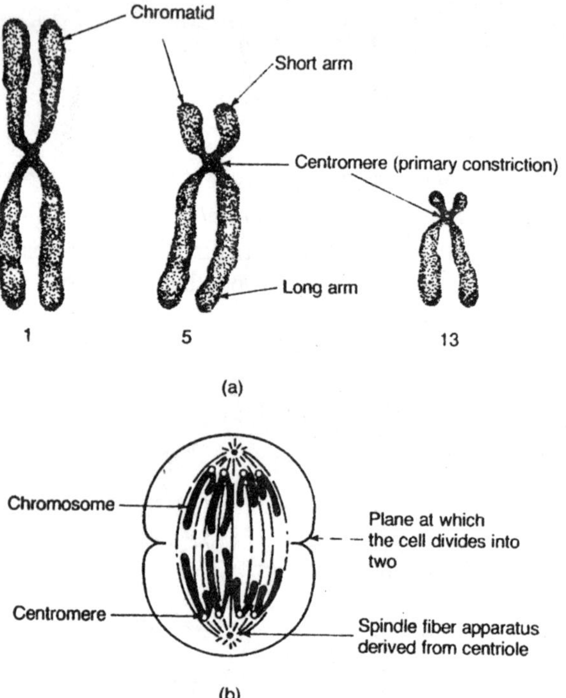

Fig. 5.3. (a) Human chromosomes, 1, 5, and 13. (b) In cell division, the centromere divides and the chromosomes move to opposite poles of the spindle.

only that the amount of genetic material is doubled but also that every gene is replicated exactly. Each of a chromosome's chromatids is identical to the other.

We will examine mitosis in more detail later in the chapter, but its essential features are simple. As a cell divides, its replicated chromosomes move apart so that each new cell has a representative of that particular chromosome. Daughter cells are genetically identical to each other and to the parental cell.

The discovery of mitosis strongly supported the idea that nuclear material is continuous from one cell generation to the next and that it influences the characteristics of cells. Still, the nucleus was not clearly implicated in inheritance—that is, in the contribution of parents to their offspring via gametes—until the cellular events involved in fertilization were described in the late 1870s.

Fertilization: Combining two sets of chromosomes

Even before fertilization was described, biologists had reason to suppose the nucleus was involved. Beginning in the middle of the eighteenth century, plant breeders had noted that in the inheritance of alternative traits, such as red or white flower colour, the sex of the parents did not usually influence the outcome of a cross. *Reciprocal crosses*—for example, a white male crossed with a red female and a white female crossed with a red male—produced identical results. Yet the egg in all species is much larger than the sperm; the volume of *cytoplasm*, or material outside the nucleus, is up to 1000 times greater in the egg. If the cytoplasm were responsible for inheritance, one would expect the genetic contribution of the female to be much greater than that of the male. All this remained rather speculative, however, as long as the mechanism of fertilization was unknown. Since many nineteenth-century researchers believed that more than one sperm is required to fertilize an egg, the argument about relative cytoplasmic volumes was not entirely convincing.

Working with the gametes, or sex cells, of plants and of sea urchins, researchers in the late 1870s observed that fertilization involves the union of a single egg with a single sperm and that the nuclei of the two gametes fuse shortly after the cells unite. They concluded correctly that fusion of the nuclei is the critical event in fertilization and that the fertilized egg's nucleus is composed of nuclear material from both parents. There was now impressive evidence that the chromatin is continuous not only from one cell generation to the next but also from one generation of multicellular organism to the next.

Such continuity made chromatin a promising candidate for the role of hereditary substance.

Chromosome pairs: A consequence of fertilization

A consequence of fertilization is that the zygote contains two sets of chromosomes, one from each parent. In animals, this means that every somatic cell also contains two sets of chromosomes, since every somatic cell is ultimately derived from the zygote by mitotic divisions, which reproduce the chromosomes exactly. (The situation in many plants and a few animals is more complicated.) We refer to a cell with two chromosome sets as a *diploid* cell and to its chromosome number as the diploid number, or 2n. Each chromosome in a diploid cell, with an exception we will discuss later, has a *homologous chromosome*, or *homolog*, very much like itself in appearance and genetic information, but derived from the other parent. However, this situation is not particularly evident in the mitotic nucleus, where the chromosomes are mixed together randomly and homologs may be far apart. Though cytologists realized after observing the fusion of sex cell nuclei that fertilized eggs contain chromosomes from both parents, they did not know that chromosomes come in pairs until they observed a special kind of cell division in which homologous chromosomes pair up with each other.

Meiosis: Halving the nuclear material

The fusion of gametes presents a logistical problem. If the nuclear material of two somatic cells is combined in the zygote, one would expect the quantity of nuclear material—the number of chromosomes—to double in every generation. It is clear that this does not happen, for every species has a characteristic chromosome number. Humans, for example, have a diploid number of 46 chromosomes, meaning that they have 46 chromosomes in most somatic cells. Cytologists therefore suspected that gametes must contain only half the amount of nuclear material found in somatic cells, and this idea was confirmed when *meiosis* (Greek *meion*, "smaller") was described in 1883.

Meiosis is the type of cell division that produces the gametes. (Again, we are speaking primarily of animals, for in plants meiosis may occur at a different stage in the life cycle.) In meiosis, a diploid cell undergoes two nuclear divisions after chromosome replication to produce four cells, each with half the usual number of chromosomes. Such cells are called *haploid*, and the haploid number of chromosomes is designated n, indicating a single set. Thus $n = 23$ in humans, and the diploid number, 46, $= 2n$.

In the first meiotic division, called meiosis I, the chromosomes are arranged in pairs, each alongside its homolog. Each chromosome is composed of two chromatids, having replicated prior to cell division. As the cell divides, one member of each chromosome pair goes to one of the newly forming nuclei and its homolog goes to the other, without any splitting of the centromeres Early cytologists suggested that all the chromosomes of maternal origin go to one nucleus and all those of paternal origin to the other, but, infact, it is purely a matter of chance which member of a given chromosome pair ends up in which nucleus: the chromosome pairs assort independently. At the end of meiosis I, each new nucleus contains half the original chromosomes—one of each pair— although the chromosomes still contain two identical chromatids. Thus, meiosis I is a *reduction division*.

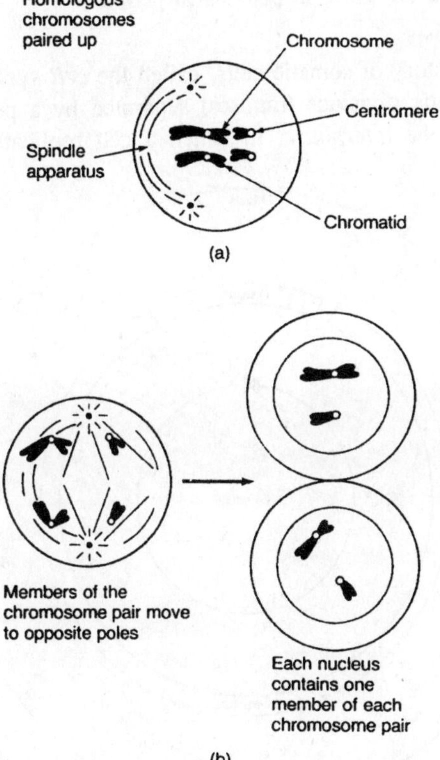

Fig. 5.4. A key feature of meiotic cell division is (a) the synthesis, or pairing, of homologous chromosomes and (b) the segregation of the pair members into different nuclei.

In meiosis II the nuclei divide again, but this time the centromere of each chromosome divides, and the two chromatids pull away from each other, each going to a new nucleus. Meiosis II is superficially like mitosis. At the end of meiosis, there are four haploid nuclei containing single-stranded chromosomes.

Whereas mitosis preserves the number of chromosomes in each cell, meiosis reduces the number to half the original. Fertilization then restores an organism's full chromosome complement the major differences between mitosis and meiosis, and illustrates the preservation of the chromosome number in a human life cycle. (Recognize that though the life cycle of plants is much more complex than that of animals, the critical event is the same: haploid gametes unite to form a diploid zygote. This means that the principles of chromosome transmission are the same in peas as in people.)

Details of Mitosis

The life history of somatic cells, called the *cell cycle*, consists of successive mitotic divisions (mitoses) separated by a period of non-division called the *interphase*, in which a cell replicates its genetic

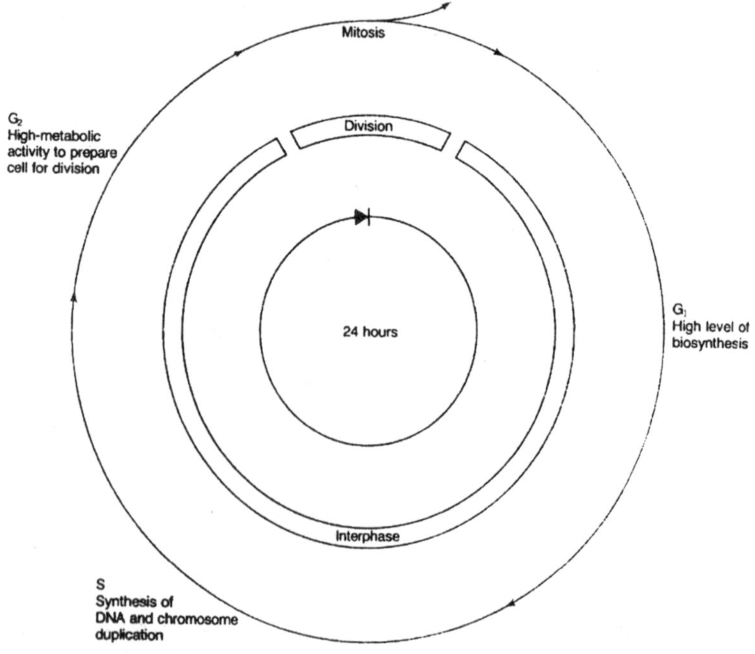

Fig. 5.5. The cell cycle.

material. Each interphase, then, is preceded and followed by a mitosis phase, sometimes called the *M phase*. The proportion of time the cell spends in each of these stages.

Interphase

The chromatin in the interphase nucleus is visible in high-magnification electron micrographs as long strands, jumbled together like strands of spaghetti in a bowl. Each chromatin strand is a highly uncoiled chromosome during mitosis it will coil tightly and condense into the chromosome form visible under the light microscope. The *nucleolus*, a nuclear entity whose constituents function in protein synthesis, is clearly visible through a light microscope during interphase.

Early cytologists sometimes called interphase the 'resting phase," but the term is quite inaccurate. The interphase cell is constantly engaged in its normal metabolic activities of molecular synthesis and energy production. During the interphase, the cell grows to approximately twice its original size. The chromatin, or rather, that part of the chromatin called DNA, directs the synthesis of proteins and is thus directly or indirectly responsible for all the cell's growth and activity.

Replication of the chromosomes also occurs in interphase. The period during which this takes place is designated the S (for synthesis) phase, and the periods preceding and following it are called G_1 and G_2 (for gap) phases. The length of G_1 is extremely variable. It may last anywhere from a few minutes to the lifetime of the organism, depending on how often the particular kind of cell divides. The G_2 is generally quite short. During the G_2 the chromosomes are still in the form of lengthy strands, but each strand is now double.

Mitotic division

Mitosis is divided into four main phases. These are somewhat artificial, since the process of nuclear division is actually continuous, but biologists have long divided the process into phases for convenience in description.

The first stage of division, called *prophase*, begins when the chromosomes start to coil and condense into structures visible through the light microscope. At the same time, a *spindle apparatus* begins to form in the cytoplasm. This structure consists of slender protein fibers called *spindle fibers* attached to two cytoplasmic bodies called *centrioles*; the spindle fibers will contract and move the chromosomes to opposite poles of the cell. By mid-prophase the chromosomes are

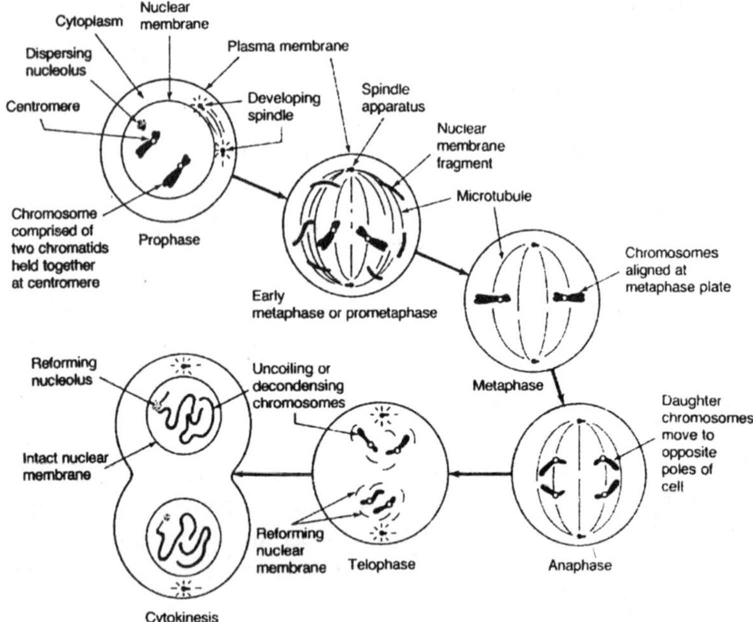

Fig. 5.6. The stages of mitotic cell division.

distinct and obviously double. The material of the nucleolus disperses throughout the nuclear region during prophase and is not visible through the light microscope for the rest of the cell division.

The second stages, *prometaphase* and *metaphase*, begin when the nuclear membrane breakdown and the nucleolus is completely dispersed. The chromosomes continue to coil and thicken, and become aligned randomly at the cell's equatorial region, or *metaphase plate*. Some of the spindle fibers are now seen to extend from the centrioles to the centromeres of the chromosomes, though others still extend from one centriole to the other.

The third stage, *anaphase*, begins when the centromeres separate as the *sister chromatids* of each chromosome move to opposite ends of the cell. After separation, sister chromatids are referred to as *daughter chromosomes*.

The final stage, *telophase*, occurs when the chromosomes have completed their movement toward the poles. It is marked by the formation of two daughter nuclei and two cells. Nuclear membranes form around the two groups of chromosomes; the chromosomes uncoil; the spindle apparatus disappears, and *cytokinesis*, or division of the cytoplasm, occurs. Narrowly, the term *mitosis* refers only to the division of the nuclear material, but it is often used broadly to mean the entire process of cell division, including cytokinesis. The end result of mitosis is two genetically identical daughter cells, each containing the diploid number of chromosomes.

Mitotic Cell Division and Cancer

Cancer cells do not respond properly to the regulatory signals that control mitotic cell division. Consequently, they divide in an uncontrolled fashion. These cells can invade other tissues and organs, disrupting normal functions and ultimately causing death.

Cancer cells are mature somatic cells that behave as if they were embryonic cells, dividing over and over again. There are indications that some cancer cells carry regulatory protein molecules in their membranes that are normally found only in embryonic cells. These regulatory molecules allow embryonic cells to divide rapidly for specific periods of time. In the absence of these regulators, cell division is controlled by a different regulatory scheme. The regulatory proteins that trigger the rapid cell division are normal structurally, but they are being synthesized in the cell at an inappropriate time. Cancer cells are normal in most respects, except that some of their genes are acting in the wrong place at the wrong time to alter the regulatory scheme of mitosis.

What causes a normal cell, undergoing a normal mitotic cycle, to become cancerous? We shall explore this question in more detail later, but one cause of cancer may lie with certain types of viruses. These viruses may be able to change the pattern of gene activity in a mature cell so that a gene normally active only in the embryo becomes activated. Transforming the cell into a cancer cell.

Details of Meiosis

Meiosis is a lengthy process in which the chromosomes duplicate once and the nucleus divides twice, thus reducing the chromosome number by half. Like the term *mitosis*, the term *meiosis* may refer to the nuclear division alone, or to nuclear division an the accompanying cytokinesis. Meiosis result in the formation of four haploid cells from one diploid cell.

Each of the two nuclear divisions of meiosis has phases with the same names as those of mitosis. However, the phases of meiosis I and the corresponding phases of mitosis bear only a superficial resemblance to each other.

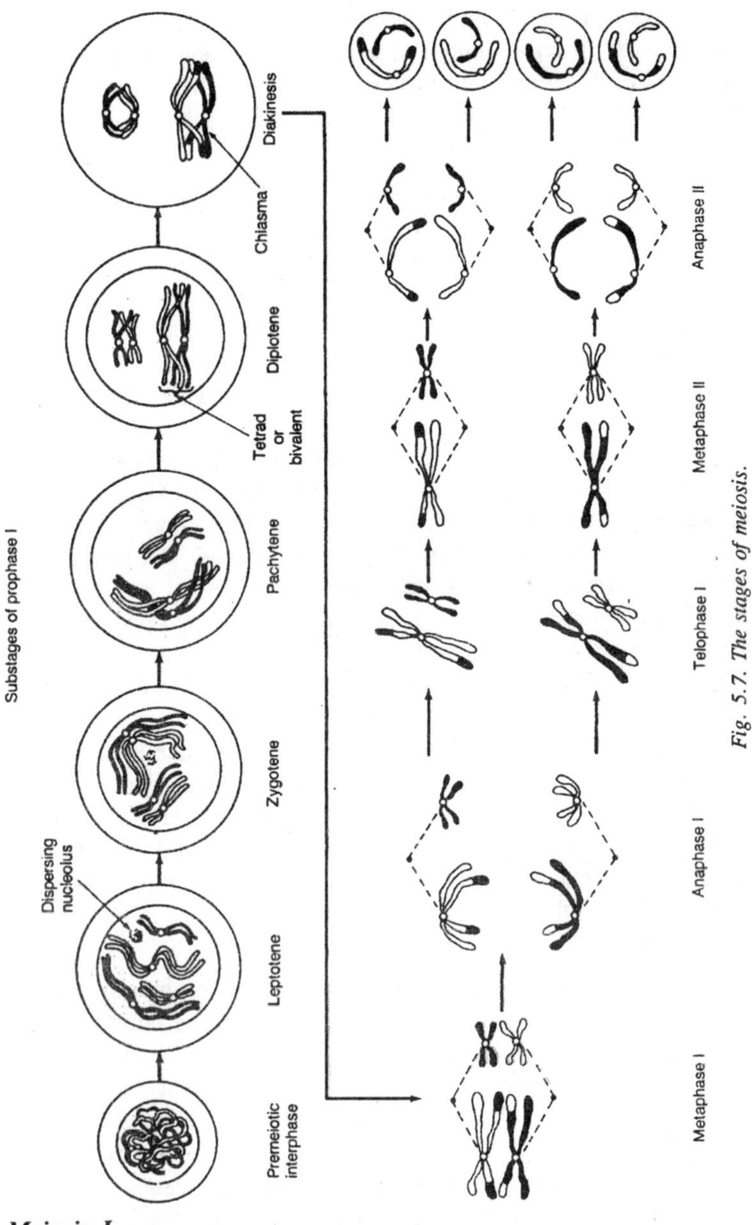

Fig. 5.7. The stages of meiosis.

Meiosis I

The chromosomes replicate during the interphase preceding meiosis I. In *prophase I*, the first stage of meiosis I, each double-stranded chromosome comes to lie alongside its homolog and then intertwines with it in a process called *synapsis*. At the start of synapsis, each chromosome pair looks like a single structure, but as the homologs pull away from each other slightly, it becomes obvious that there are two of them and that each consists of two sister chromatids. Each intertwined pair is called a *bivalent* (for the two chromosomes) or a *tetrad* (for the four chromatids).

As the lengthy and complex prophase I continues, the homologous chromosomes seem to repel each other, but they remain attached at some points, forming X-shaped regions called *chiasmata* (singular: *chiasma*). The chiasmata apparently indicate where *crossing over*, or exchange of homologous chromosome parts, is occurring. Crossing over is extremely important genetically be cause it provides a basis for generating new combinations of alleles. Toward the end of prophase I, the bivalents start moving toward the metaphase plate, the nucleolus begins to disperse, and a spindle apparatus starts to form in the cytoplasm.

Meiotic metaphase I begins with the disassembly of the nuclear membrane. During metaphase I, the bivalents, their members still attached at the chiasmata, are aligned at the metaphase plate. The members of each pair point toward opposite poles of the cell, and each centromere is attached to a spindle fiber. During *anaphase I*, the homologs are pulled toward opposite poles. The centromeres do not divide, so each chromosome still consists of two chromatids.

When the chromosomes have reached opposite ends of the spindle apparatus, *telophase I* begins. This phase is usually very short, with the chromosomes uncoiling only partially and incomplete nuclear membranes forming. In some species, including humans, cytokinesis occurs during telophase I, producing two cells. In any case, there are now two separate sets of chromosomes, each with half the number in the parental cell, but each chromosome still contains twice the usual amount of genetic material. There is only a very short interphase, or none at all, after meiosis I, and there is no duplication of chromosomes.

Meiosis II

Meiosis II superficially resembles a normal mitosis. In *prophase II*, the first phase of meiosis II, the chromosomes in each group recondense and start moving toward the new equatorial regions. At *metaphase II*, the chromosomes are aligned at the metaphase plates, with spindle fibers attached to their centromeres. During *anaphase II*, sister chromatids are pulled apart (the centromeres split), and the daughter chromosomes move to opposite poles. *Telophase II* begins when the chromosomes reach the poles and cease movement. Nuclear membranes now form around each haploid complement of chromosomes, and cytokinesis occurs. The second division completed, we have four haploid cells with a single set of chromosomes.

Autosomes and Sex Chromosomes

We mentioned earlier that there is an exception to the rule that every chromosome in a human somatic cell has a similar homolog. This exception is found in the cells of males. In 22 of a male's chromosome pairs the homologs are indeed very like each other, but the twenty-third pair consists of one chromosome called X and one very small one called Y. The X and Y chromosomes are not homologous and are not paired along their lengths in meiosis, but have an end-to-end association. The corresponding pair of chromosomes in a female consists of two homologous X chromosomes. The X and Y chromosomes are called *sex chromosomes*, and the other 44 chromosomes, which are the same in both sexes, are called *autosomes*.

It has been known for a long time that the X and Y chromosomes determine a person's sex. When gametes are formed by meiosis, the two sex chromosomes go to different cells, just like the members of every other chromosome pair. This means that each of a female's eggs will have an X chromosome, but half of a male's sperm cells

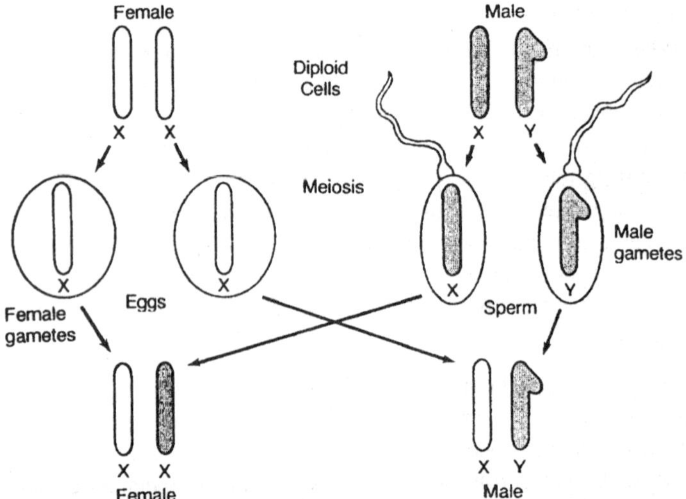

Fig. 5.8. Segregation of the sex chromosomes at meiosis results in a single kind of egg but two classes of sperm.

will contain an X and the other half a Y. At fertilization, a zygote normally receives an X chromosome from the mother and either an X or a Y from the father and will develop accordingly as a female or a male. The formation of equal numbers of X- and Y-bearing sperm is the reason for the approximately equal number of female and male births.

Gamete Formation arid Fertilization in Humans

In humans and other mammals, meiosis occurs in the gonads—the male testes and the female ovaries—and produces sperm and ova, or eggs. The process of gamete formation is called *spermatogenesis* in the male and *oogenesis* (oh-oh-genesis) in the female. We will consider spermatogenesis first, since it is the simpler of the two processes.

Spermatogenesis

In sexually mature human males, sperm cells from continuously in the seminiferous tubules of the testes. The cells that line these tubules and ultimately give rise to the sperm are called *spermatogonia*. Spermatogonia go through several mitotic divisions over a period of three to four weeks, the final division producing cells called *primary*

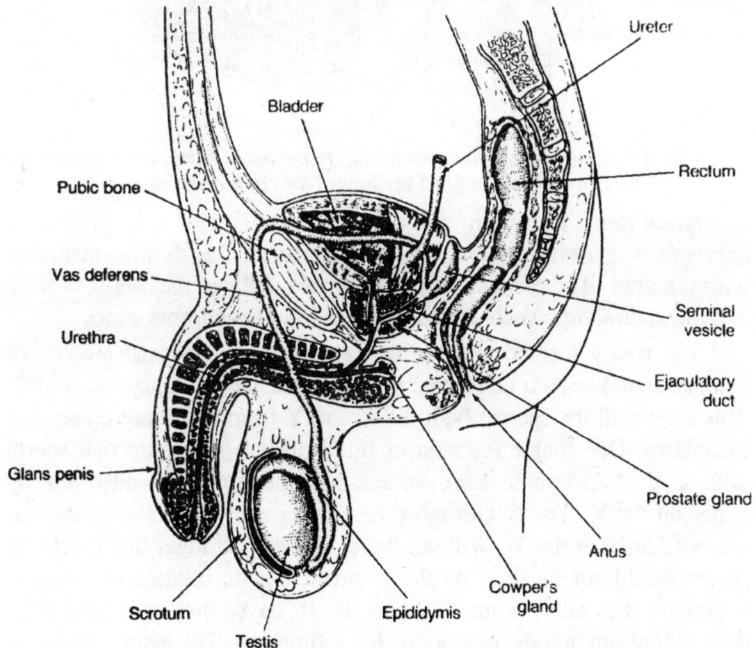

Fig. 5.9. Male reproductive system.

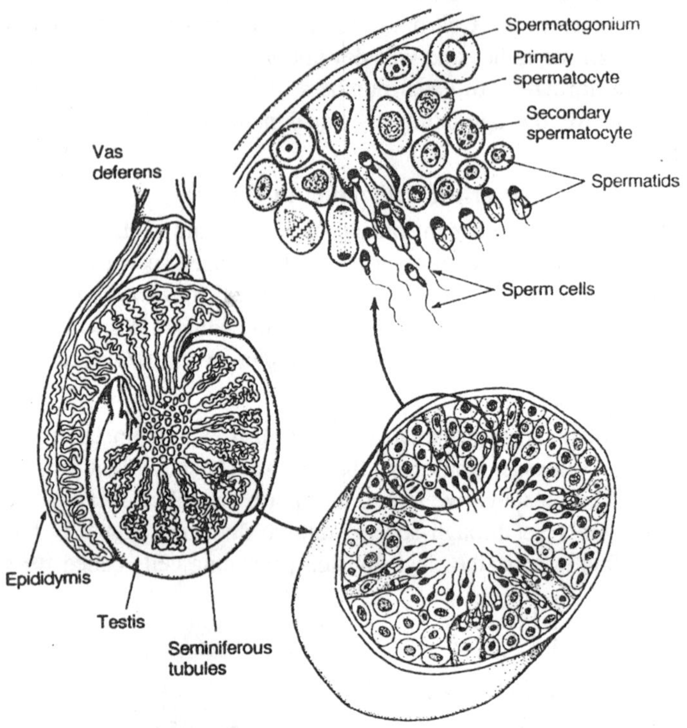

Fig. 5.10. Arrangement of seminiferous tubules in the testes, with a cross section of a seminiferous tubule and a closer view of the cell undergoing spermatogenesis.

spermatocytes. These diploid cells undergo meiosis I, producing *secondary spermatocytes*, each containing 23 double-stranded chromosomes. The secondary spermatocytes undergo meiosis II to form haploid *spermatids*, each with 23 single-stranded chromosomes.

The newly formed spermatids have an almost normal amount of cytoplasm and remain connected to each other by a cytoplasmic bridge. This allows all the sperm, both the X and Y forms, to share a common cytoplasm. One major function of this bridge is to ensure that sperm with a Y chromosome have access to gene products coded for by genes on the X. The X chromosome carries many essential genes that are not found on the Y. Without the cytoplasmic bridge, the Y-bearing sperm would not survive. As the spermatids mature into spermatozoa, a process that takes from 10 hours to 16 days, they lose nearly all their cytoplasm and develop a tail for swimming. The *mature sperm* is essentially a nucleus with a tail—a packet of genetic material capable of moving about.

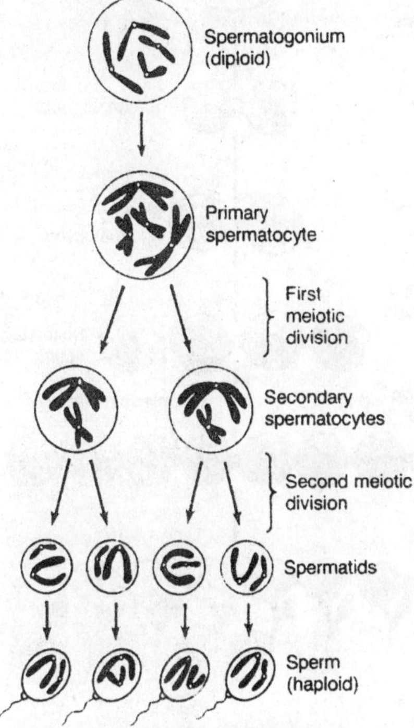

Fig. 5.11. The meiosis of spermatogenesis.

Mature sperm are stored in the epididymis (a cordlike structure at the back of the testis) until ejaculation, when they mix with secretions of the seminal vesicles and prostate gland to form *semen*. This mixing takes place in the latter portions of the vas deferens, or sperm duct, and the semen is ejected via the urethra. Three hundred million sperm cells may be present in a single ejaculate, about 100 million per cubic centimeter of fluid. When these sperm are deposited in the vagina, they move quickly into the cervical canal, but only a few dozen of them manage to make the long trip to the upper part of the fallopian tube, or oviduct, where an egg may be waiting. Sperm are viable for 48 hours or so after ejaculation, so if an egg is released into the fallopian tube within roughly two days after intercourse, fertilization may still occur. Once a sperm and egg unite, all other sperm are excluded.

Even though only one sperm is needed to fertilize an ovum, large numbers of active sperm are required to produce the enzymes that allow a sperm cell to fertilize the ovum. If a man's sperm count falls

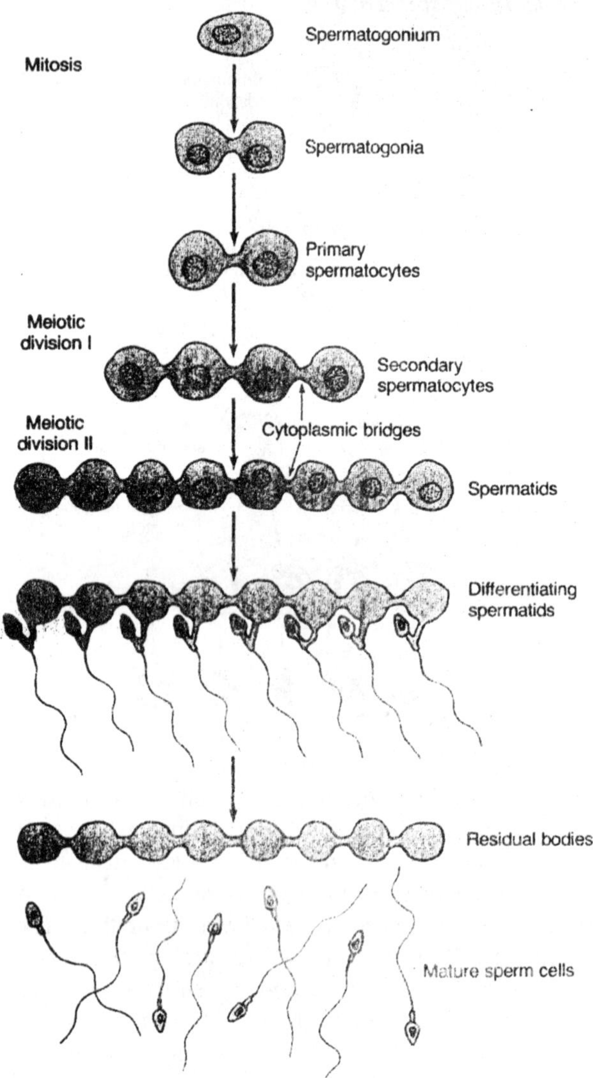

Fig. 5.12. ***Diagram** showing how the **progeny** of a **single** spermatogonium remain **connected** to **each other by** cytoplasmic bridges **throughout** their differentiation **into mature** sperm.*

much below 20 million per ejaculation, he will probably be sterile. A number of factors can interfere with sperm development, resulting in infertility or even birth defects. Cell metabolism in the male reproductive tract is very high, and this causes chemicals to be concentrated in the semen. The seminal fluid is a very sensitive indicator of toxins. Lead, tobacco products, THC from marijuana, large amounts of alcohol, and many pesticides may be concentrated in semifinal fluid and result in lower sperm counts.

Oogenesis and fertilization

Oogenesis in humans begins early in embryonic life, between the eighth and twentieth weeks of development. Cells destined to become female gametes, the *primordial germ cells*, migrate to the developing ovary, where they become *oogonia*. These oogonia divide rapidly by mitosis to form the many *primary oocytes* of the female fetus. Each oocyte is surrounded by a layer of specialized secretory cells called *granulosa cells*. The primary oocyte and its surrounding granulosa cells constitute the *primary follicle* of the fetus.

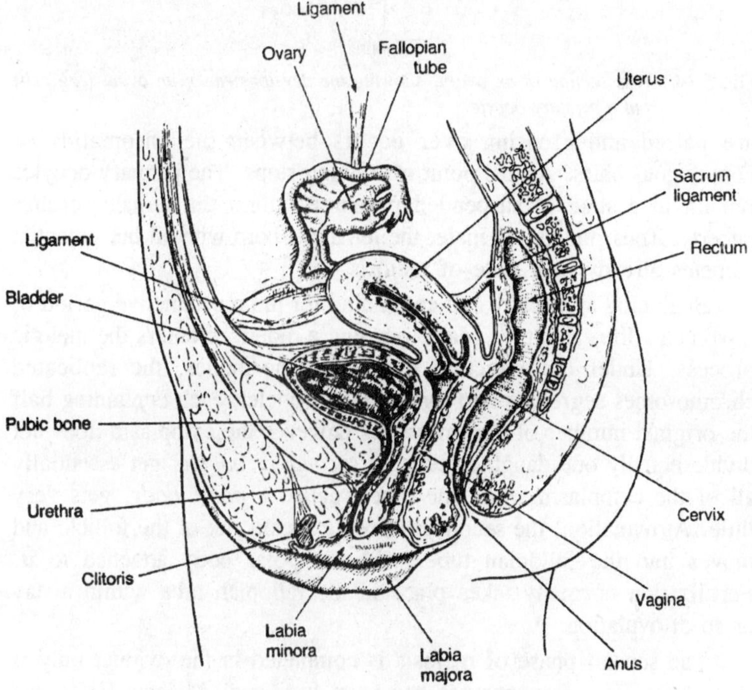

Fig. 5.13. Female reproductive system.

Unlike meiosis in males, meiosis in females begins in the third month of intrauterine life. The primary oocytes enter the long prophase of the first meiotic division. The DNA has replicated so that each chromosome consist of two chormatids; the homologous chromosome

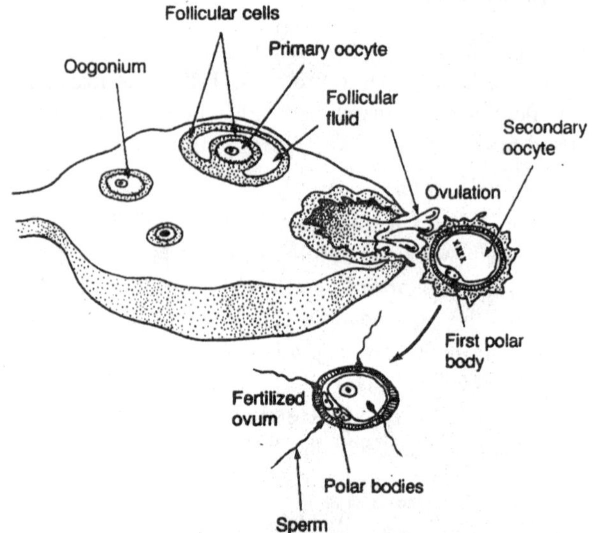

Fig. 5.14. Cross section of an ovary, showing the development of an ovum (egg cell) from a primary oocyte.

are paired and crossing over occurs between the chromatids or homologous pairs. At this point everything stops. The primary oocytes remain in a state of suspended prophase I until the female reaches puberty. Thus, unlike the male, the female is born with all her potential gametes already in a state of meiosis.

Beginning at puberty and continuing for the reproductive period of a woman's life, about 40 years, one egg a month re-enters the meiotic process. Under the direction of specific hormones, the replicated chromosomes segregate into two daughter nuclei; each containing half the original number of chromosomes however the cytoplasm does not divide equally one daughter cell the *secondary oocyte*, get essentially all of the cytoplasm while the other, called a *polar body*, gets very little. At ovulation, the secondary oocyte breaks out of the follicle and moves into the fallopian tube, with the polar body attached to it. Fertilization normally takes place in the fallopian tube within a day or so of ovulation.

The second phase of meiosis is completed in the oviduct only if the ovum (secondary oocyte) has been fertilized. Meiosis II is very rapid. The centromeres separate and daughter cells appear, but again there is an Unequal distribution of cytoplasm. The secondary oocyte divides into a *mature ovum* and a second polar body. The first polar body also completes meiosis II by producing two very small polar

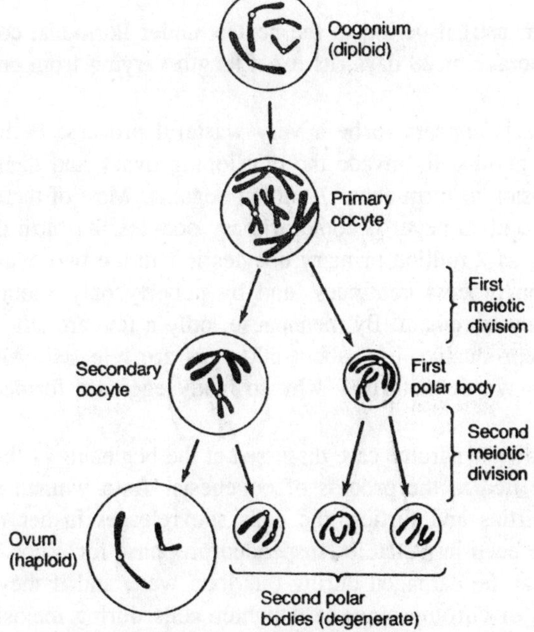

Fig. 5.15. The meiosis of oogenesis.

bodies. The mature ovum is about 1000 times the volume of a polar body (or a sperm, for that matter).

In contrast to meiosis in the male, which results in four functional sperm, the result of meiosis in the female is four haploid cells, but only one of them is a functional gamete. The three polar bodies are never fertilized, as far as we know, and simply disintegrate within the fallopian tube.

The nucleus of the mature ovum fuses with the sperm nucleus about one hour after fertilization to form the diploid *zygote*. As the zygote travels through the fallopian tube, it undergoes repeated mitotic divisions to form an embryo. Arriving in the uterus about five days after ovulation, the embryo becomes implanted in the thickened uterine lining, which supplies it with nourishment.

If an egg is not fertilized within about 24 hours of ovulation, meiosis does not go to completion, and the egg degenerates. After the egg has been released, if it has not been fertilized, the menstrual period occurs. This bleeding is caused by the sloughing off of the thickened uterine lining. A new lining starts to form as another primary follicle begins to mature. The *menstrual cycle*—the reproductive events from one menstrual period to the next is under hormonal control and takes an average of 28 days, its exact length varying from one woman to another.

Oogenesis appears to be a very wasteful process. Perhaps 1500 primordial germ cells invade the developing ovary and then undergo mitotic division to form about 7 million oogonia. Most of these oogonia degenerate and so never become primary oocytes. At birth there may be as many as 2 million primary oocytes left in the two ovaries. This degeneration process continues, and by puberty only about 250,000 primary oocytes remain. By menopause, only a few are left. During a woman's reproductive life, about 500 eggs are released. All the rest degenerate. We do not know why so many eggs are formed only to degenerate.

The Down syndrome case discussed at the beginning of this chapter is probably tied to the process of oogenesis. As a woman ages, say into her thirties and forties, the eggs she releases in her menstrual cycles have been in a state of suspended prophase for 30 or 40 years. The eggs can be damaged during this long wait, and if they are, the distribution of chromosomes to daughter cells during meiosis can be disrupted. This may explain why a 40-year-old woman has a 1% chance of having a child with Down syndrome, whereas a 20-year-old has only a 0.04% chance, a 25-fold difference.

Mating game: Sperm meets egg

The primary function of the mating game is to promote the union of gametes, which creates a new individual with a unique combination of genes. Many unicellular organisms reproduce by an asexual act of simple fission or mitosis, but in asexual reproduction the offspring are identical to the parents except when a *mutation*, or change in the structure of a gene, arises. It is the segregation and independent assortment of chromosomes during meiosis, followed by the random combination of sperm and egg that gives us our biologic variability. This scrambling of genetic material in every generation is called *genetic recombination*. The endless variation generated by recombination has provided an enormous evolutionary advantage to sexually reproducing species, since it allows for faster adaptation to a variety of conditions.

Human Chromosome

Viewing Human Chromosomes

Most early knowledge about chromosomes was derived from studies of nonhuman cells. Geneticists struggled for decades to develop techniques that would give them a reliable view of human chromosomes, but they encountered enormous difficulties. It was not easy to obtain human tissue to study; fixing and staining procedures produced erratic results; and it was not at all unusual to get contradictory data from seemingly identical experiments. You can appreciate the magnitude of the problems involved if you realize that until the mid-1950s geneticists did not even know the exact number of human chromosomes. Early investigators reported human chromosome complements ranging from 8 to 73, but in 1923 an authoritative study seemed to show that the normal diploid number is 48. This became the generally accepted number until 1956, when Joe-Hin Tjio and Albert Levan announced their use of new techniques to show that the correct number is 46. In retrospect, it seems amazing that the answer to so simple a question as How many chromosomes does a person have?" was not known until three years, after the structure of DNA was announced.

Tjio and Levan are to human cytogenetics what Mendel was to genetics. Their brilliant and painstaking improvements of existing methods for studying cells include two techniques that were particularly important to the success of their chromosome-counting work and that have since had widespread application in the study of human chromosomes. The first of these is the technique of placing dividing cells in hypotonic solutions (a technique that Levan learned from T. C. Hsu)—salt solutions of lower concentration than that of the cell contents. One reason for the earlier discrepancies in chromosome counts was the tendency of the chromosomes to overlap and stick together. Placing a cell in hypotonic solution causes water to flow inward, so that the cell swells up and the chromosomes separate from each other, becoming more easily distinguishable. The second technique that Tijo and Levan perfected was that of culturing mammalian cells. They grew lung fibroblast cells (immature connective-tissue cells) in a culture medium to obtain their material for chromosome study.

For their study of human cells. Tjio and Levan also adapted important techniques used in cytologic studies of other organisms. One such technique is the use of a stain called *orcein*, which stains chromosomes in a very distinct fashion, so that they are visible in more detail than with older staining procedures. An other was the arresting of dividing cells at metaphase by means of a drug called colchicine, derived from the autumn crocus. Colchicine interferes with the attachment of spindle fibers to the centromere, so that when chromosomes are arranged at the metaphase plate they cannot migrate

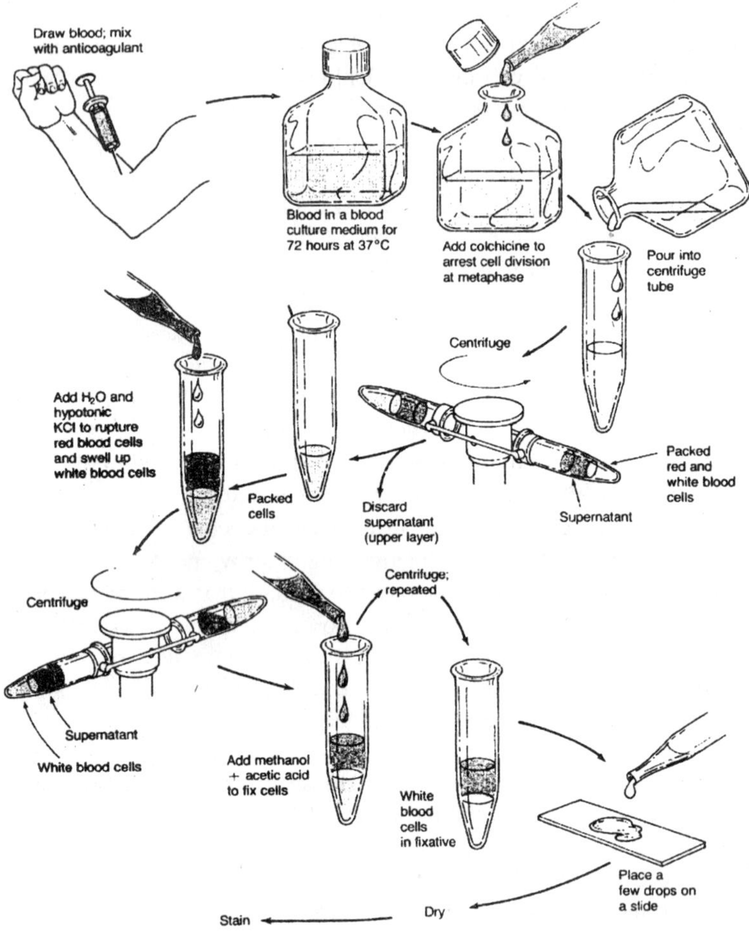

Fig. 5.16. The most common method of harvesting human chromosomes from lymphocytes.

to opposite poles of the cell. The use of colchicine stops mitosis and allows a large number of dividing cells to accumulate for observation.

Another great advance in human cytogenetics occurred when Moorehead developed a method of culturing lymphocytes (a class of white blood cells) taken from the circulating peripheral blood (i.e., blood near the surface of the body). Obtaining blood samples is vastly easier than obtaining samples of other human tissues, so the problem of material for study was at least partially solved by this technique, which is now standard laboratory procedure. The most common method of harvesting human chromosomes from lymphocytes is outlined.

Identifying Human Chromosomes

Chromosome classification

In recent years, cytogeneticists have devoted major efforts to establishing uniform standards and nomenclature (names) for the classification of human chromosomes. Toward this end they have held a series of international conferences beginning in 1960. They have agreed that the 22 pairs of autosomes (non sex chromosomes) should be numbered in descending order of length—the longest has the lowest number, 1—and that if two pairs are essentially the same length, the pair with the centromeres most centrally located would get the lower number. They have further decided that chromosomes should be organized into seven groups according to their size and centromere position. A schematic of a human male's *karyotype*, or chromosome makeup, arranged according to these rules of classification.

Table 5.1. A general classification of the human chromosomes

Group	*Chromosomes*	*Characteristic*
A	1, 2, 3	Large, metacentric chromosomes'; approximately median centromere.
B	4, 5	Large, submetacentric chromosomes"; submedian centromeres.
C	6 through 12 and X (sex chromosome)	Medium-sized, submetacentric chromosomes.
D	13, 14, 15	Medium-sized, acrocentric" chromosomes with nearly terminal centromeres. Each chromosome in this group has a small appendage, or "satellite," attached to the end of the short arm, observable in good preparations
E	16, 17, 18	Shorter than group D; metacentric or submetacensric
F	19, 20	Short; metacentric
G	21, 22, Y (sex chromosome)	Very short, acrocentric chromosomes; 21 and 22 have small satellites. Again, these satellites are observed only in better preparations

In 1960, when these classifications were being worked out, only a few chromosome pairs (1, 3, and 16) could be identified unambiguously on the basis of length and centromere position. The discovery of additional physical landmarks, such as secondary constrictions (the primary constriction is the one at the centromere), enabled

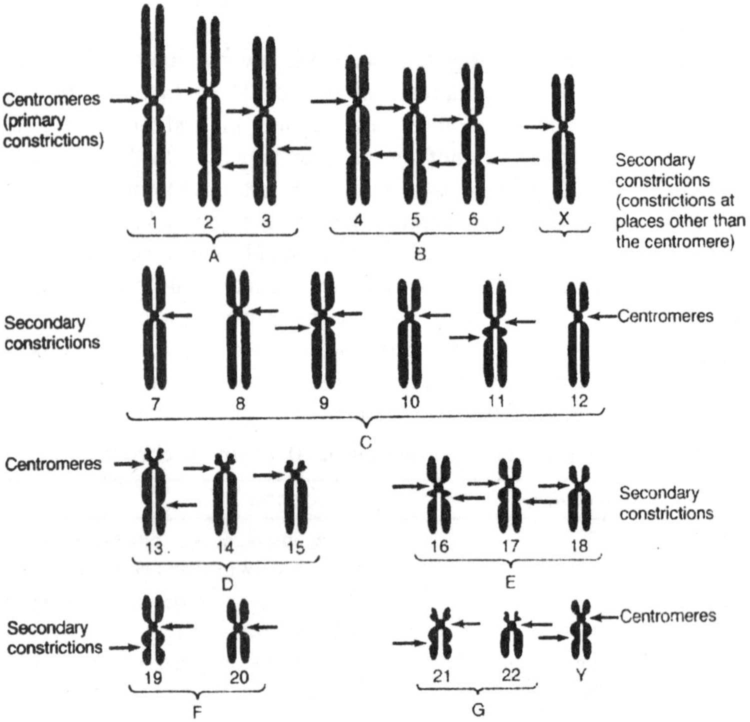

Fig. 5.17. Schematic of the normal male karyotype (chromosome makeup).

cytogeneticists to identify other chromosomes. However, a true revolution in human cytogenetics occurred when banding techniques were developed.

Chromosome banding

During the late 1960s and early 1970s, several new staining procedures were discovered that gave the chromosomes truly distinctive appearances. These procedures caused various regions of the chromosomes to stain differently, prompting the appearance of light and dark *bands*. Banding patterns are the most powerful tool now available for chromosome identification, because the pattern for every chromosome pair is unique. Furthermore, different regions of the same chromosome can be consistently identified by their banding patterns.

The first of the major banding techniques to be discovered uses quinacrine mustard, a fluorescing dye that preferentially binds to specific regions of chromosomes. When chromosomes treated with this dye are viewed under ultraviolet light, fluorescent bands of varying intensity appear. The pattern is characteristic for each chromosome. These are called *Q bands* (Q for quinacrine). The most brilliantly fluorescing chromosome is the Y, which makes Q-banding an especially valuable technique for identifying the Y chromosome.

A second technique, C-banding, uses a dye mixture called Giemsa stain, which stains the region around the centromere of each chromosome much more deeply than the rest. The dark bands are called *C bands* (C for centromeric). These bands are especially prominent in chromosomes 1, 9, and 16.

After the development of C-banding, cytologists found that by modifying the procedure, they could use Giemsa stain to show a banding pattern similar to the Q bands, but more detailed. The bands produced by the modified procedure are called Giemsa bands, or *G bands*. The G-banding technique is most successful if the chromosomes are pretreated with a protein-digesting enzyme called trypsin before the stain is applied. G banding is more common than Q-banding be cause it is less expensive, yields a permanent slide record, and does not require a fluorescence microscope.

The last of the important banding procedures is called "*reverse Giemsa*," or R-banding. This technique produces bands that are in reverse contrast to the Q and G bands. That is, a dark *R band* appears where a light Q or G band would be, and vice versa. This technique is especially valuable for observing the ends of chromosomes, which come out very dark.

Banding revealed such intricate details of each chromosome that new standards had to be set. So at the Paris conference of 1971, cytogeneticists established a system of classification for the chromosome bands and regions. This logical system uses numbers and letters to enable us to pinpoint any band in which we might be interested. The short arm of each chromosome is called the *p arm* ("p" for French *petite*, "small"), and the long arm is the *q arm*. Regions and bands are numbered from the centromere out. To identify a band, a sequence of four items is used: chromosome number, arm, region, and band number. For example, 9q34 refers to chromosome 9 the long arm, region 3, band 4. This band is indicated with an arrow in. For the sex chromosomes, an X or a Y is used instead of the first number.

Chromosome Structure

As soon as the chromosome was identified as the carrier of genetic information, scientists began to seek in its chemistry and structure an answer to the question "What is a gene?" Interestingly enough, they had a satisfactory answer to the question before they had a completely satisfactory picture of a chromosome for the answer lay in the molecular structure of one constituent of chromosomes—the *DNA*.

In the early years of this century, chemical analysis showed that chromosomes contain DNA (deoxyribonucleic acid) and protein. In the 1940s, Avery, MacLeod and McCarty performed experiments in which bacteria were genetically transformed by assimilation of DNA isolated from different strains. This demonstrated that the DNA, not the protein, was the genetically significant part of the chromatin strand. This was confirmed in 1952 when Hershey and Chase showed that in T4 bacterial viruses, DNA, not protein, was the genetic material. With the exception of certain viruses, DNA is confirmed as the genetic material in all living things. In 1953, Watson and Crick published their famous paper on the molecular structure of DNA, and their model, which has remained virtually unchanged for 30 years, quickly proved to hold the key to the genetic code. Only in the 1970s, however, did a clear picture begin to emerge of how DNA and protein are organized in the chromosome.

Genes are DNA

Shortly after the turn of the century, some biologists proposed that the chromosome is an inert "home" structure for genes, which journey away and perform their functions in other parts of the cell. But we now know that genes are segments of chromosomal DNA, and that they direct the synthesis of proteins by means of intermediary molecules (called *ribonucleic acid*, or RNA) that are copied from DNA templates and then move into the cytoplasm through the pores of the nuclear membrane. A later view portrayed chromosomes as consisting of genes strung together like beads on a string. In some ways, the beads-on-a-string model is not entirely in accurate. We find that chromosomes consist of DNA and protein elaborately wound together in a complex three-dimensional structure with genes arranged linearly. This linear view of gene organization was useful, for it allowed geneticists to work out the sequence of specific genes on chromosomes long before they understood the structure or functioning of genes.

Nucleosome model

the current view of mammalian chromosome structure. The basic molecular components of the chromatin strand are DNA and several varieties of a class of protein called *histories*. The DNA molecule consists of two spiral strands, linked together at intervals by hydrogen bonds to form a double helix. The chemical structure of the DNA double helix is the basis of the genetic code. A chromosome contains a continuous length of DNA, wound around individual structures made up of histones, rather like a continuous thread winding around a series of spools. Each DNA-histone unit is called a *nucleosome*. The nucleosomes coil and condense into units that appear as bands or chromomeres when they are appropriately stained. Further coiling and condensation produce the chromosome we are able to view with the electron microscope.

6

Change in Chromosome Structure

It has already been stated that chromosomes occasionally break and that the rate of breakage can be increased by the use of various mutagens such as ionizing radiation(s), ultraviolet light, and certain chemicals. When a chromosome breaks, the two broken ends usually undergo *restitution* or healing, and everything is as before. But this does not always happens, and the result can be the formation of (1) deficiencies, (2) duplications, (3) inversions, or (4) translocations. The first three of these ordinarily involve a single chromosome, while the fourth involves two or more chromosomes.

There is very strong evidence the DNA in chromosomes that extends as a double helical thread throughout the entire length of the structure. Furthermore, we know that the genes are linearly arranged in the DNA and that at least in some instances groups of genes under the control of common regulatory units are grouped together. It is of great interest then to ask about the genetic consequences of breaks in specific regions of chromosomes. One interesting observation made by George Lefevre on Drosophila chromosomes is that perhaps as many as 70 percent of chromosome break points that have successfully reunited with new neighbouring genes have no detectable genetic effect at all. In other words, only about 30 percent of healed breaks points have mutant effects associated with them. This could mean that only a portion of the DNA of chromosomes is informational, and breaks within the regions without information are inconsequential. It could also means that these regions may be more susceptible to breakage and rejoining than others. We do not yet know, but C. S. Lee has suggested that those break points that manage to reunite are likely to be in regions of the DNA that are represented repeatedly in the genome. The reasoning behind this suggestion has to do with the healing process itself rather than with a differential fragility of chromosome regions. The union of broken ends may involve some degree of base pairing at the joint in order for the DNA strands to be properly positioned and stabilized for ligase to be effective in forming covalent bonds between the two chains. It is of course possible that unions can be formed without a perfect match between the bases of the two strands. Experiments, with a λ phage by Wu and Taylor have shown that the ends of the λ chromosome in its linear form have complementary sequences of nucleotides at the protruding cohesive ends. The λ chromosome goes from the linear to the circular form by the formation of hydrogen bonds between the complementary bases as shown in the figure. The same sort of protruding single strand ends with complementary or mostly complementary sequences may cause the joining of broken ends of eukaryotic chromosomes. Broken chromosome ends have been described for many years by cytogeneticists as being sticky. This sickness may be nothing more than the complementarily that exists between repeated DNA sequences.

It is known that in some tissues of many organisms, such as the endosperm of maize kernels, where the broken end soft chromosomes remain unhealed at the time of chromosome replication, that there is often a fusion of the broken ends of the sister chromatids. The results in a dicentric chromosome that will produce a chromosome bridge at the anaphase of the next mitotic division. In plant cells, such a bridge will often break as the cell wall is laid down between newly formed daughter cells. This produces another broken end in each of the nuclei, and the cycle may begin again. This breakage-fusion-bridge cycle may be carried on for several cell generations, and it can be used to great advantage for manipulating gene dosage in such cells. As the bridge breaks, it may not do so at the original fusion point and the result will be a duplication of some genes in one cell and their deletion in the other. McClintock used such a scheme to study chromosome organization and gene regulation in the endosperm of maize.

For most cells, however, the rule is that aberrations that persist are those that result from rejoined ends. This is because a broken chromosome, unrejoined, will generally not persist through the zygote stage. The segment without the centromere, called the acentric fragment, will be lost. The segment that has the centromere may act as a dominant lethal, depending on how much and what is lost in the acentric fragment.

Deletions

Deletions are also referred to as *deficiencies*. Some geneticists, following the historical origins of the terms, use deletion to describe an intercalary (involving two breaks in the chromosome) loss of chromatin and deficiency to describe a terminal loss. But here we use the terms deficiency and deletion as synonyms, because in either case an acentric fragment is lost. A spindle fiber cannot attach to an acentri fragment during mitosis or meiosis and guide it to one of the poles.

Two pairs of chromosomes	1 2 3 4 5 6 1 2 3 4 5 6	7 8 9 10 11 12 7 8 9 10 11 12
Translocation heterozygote	7 8 3 4 5 6 1 2 3 4 5 6	1 2 9 10 11 12 7 8 9 10 11 12
Translocation homozygoyte	7 8 3 4 5 6 7 8 3 4 5 6	1 2 9 10 11 12 1 2 9 10 11 12

Fig. 6.1. Chromosome constitution of a translocation heterozygote and a translocation homozygote.

If the DNA in the chromatin that is lost is crucial for viability, sterile gametes or nonfunctional somatic cells may result. Some deficiencies are known that are viable even when homozygous. For example, in *D. melanogaster*, a deficiency that removes the *white* locus produces, when homozygous, fully developed flies that appear normal except for their white eye colour. Most deficiencies, however, are lethal when homozygous, and these may involve no more loss of chromatin than in the example of white locus. A loss of a large segment of a chromosome may result in a dominant lethal effect even if a normal homologue is present with it in the heterozygote. If the dominant effect of a deletion is not lethal, it may result in an abnormal phenotype.

Genetic Significance of Deficiencies

The chromosomal deficiencies have following genetic effects :

(i) Lethal effect

Organisms with homozygous deficiency usually do not survive to an adult stage because a complete set of genes is lacking.

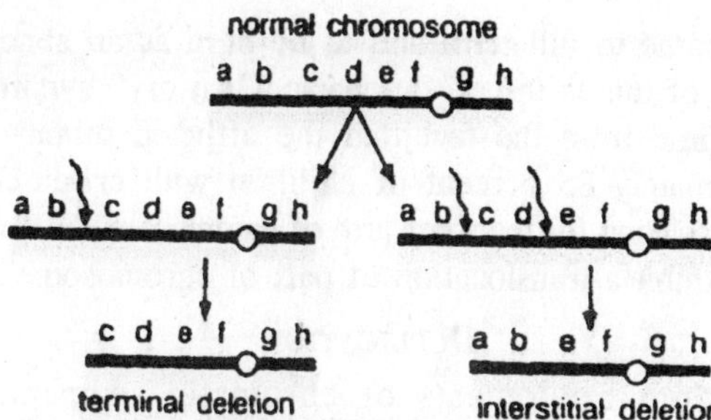

Fig. 6.2. Production of terminal and interstitial deletion. Chromosomes can be broken when struck by ionizing radiation (wavy arrows).

Examples

A mutant sex-linked condition called "notch" is lethal in *Drosophila* when hemizygous in males or when homozygous in females. This "notch phenotype is a sex-linked deletion (deficiency) which acts like a dominant mutation ; a deletion at another sex-lined locus behaves as recessive mutation, producing yellow body colour when homozygous.

(ii) Pseudodominance

When an organism heterozygous for a pair of alleles, A and a, loses a small portion of the chromosome bearing the dominant allele (A), the recessive allele (a) on the other chromosome being hemizygous will become expressed phylogenetically. The phenotypic expression of recessive allele (a) due to deficiency of dominant allele (A) called *pseudodominance.*

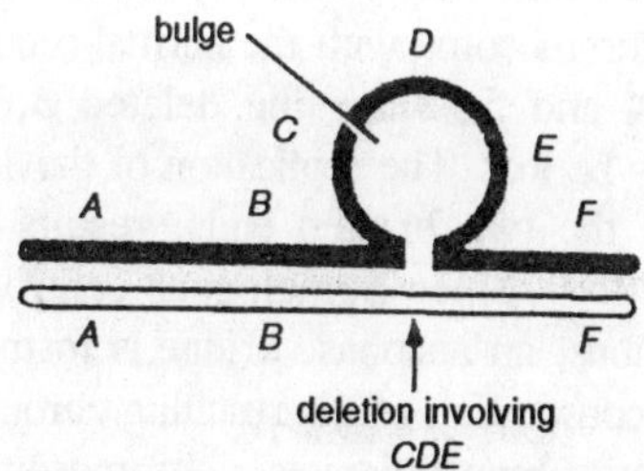

Fig. 6.3. Formation of a deletion loop during synapsis in a deletion heterozygote.

With a deficiency exchange (crossing over) becomes impossible. Disturbance of pairing causes a reduction of exchange in a segmen around the deficiency.

Occurrence of Deletions in Human Beings

Deletions are expected to occur in all organisms including humans. Some do not cause early spontaneous abortions, but unfortunately allow the fetus to come to full term and to be born as an abnormal child. One example of this is the cri-du-chat or "cat cry" syndrome, which derives its name from the fact that the afflicted infant cries like a cat. Approximately 85 percent of children with cri-du-chat show a heterozygous deletion for the short arm of chromosome 5. The remaining 15 percent exhibit a translocation of part of chromosome 5.

Duplication

Duplications are repeats of chromatin segments within a chromosome. Chromosome containing a duplication therefore possess more than the normal amount of DNA. There are several possible mechanisms for generating duplicate DNA segments in chromosomes.

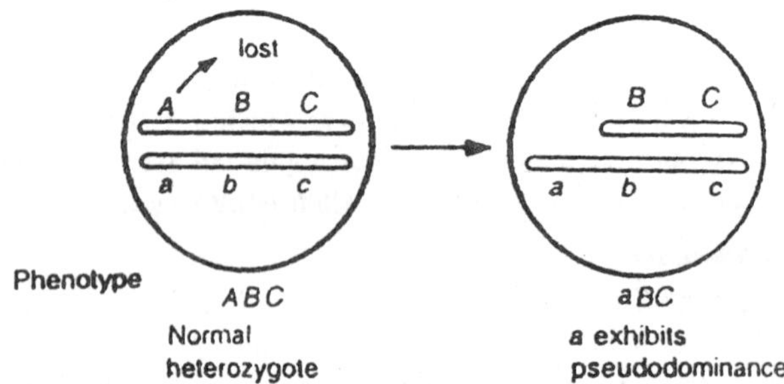

Fig. 6.4. Pseudodominance. A deficiency in the segment of chromosome bearing the dominant gene A allows the recessive allele a to become phenotypically expressed.

Duplications and deletions may also be generated by the breakage-fusion-bridge cycle. A chromosome with the normal sequence of 1.23456 has a break between 4 and 5. Since the deleted 5,6 is an acentric fragment it will probably be lost. The replication of the 1.2 3 4 fragment, followed by joining of the two broken ends, results in the dicentric chromosome 1. 234-432. 1. Since homologous centromeres generally move in opposite directions, an anaphase bridge is formed and breakage will occur. The genetic constitution of the resulting chromosomes depends on where the break occurs. Figure depicts a chromosome with deletions of regions 4,5 and 6. Also it shows a chromosome with both deleted (5,6) and duplicated (3,4) regions.

The breakage-fusion-bridge cycle that has been found in maize results in a wide variety of duplications and deletions. Note that duplications and deletions. Note that duplications created in this manner often are displaced, that is, duplicated segments are not positioned side by side on the chromosome. Duplications play an important role in the regulation of gene activity because the multiple copies of a

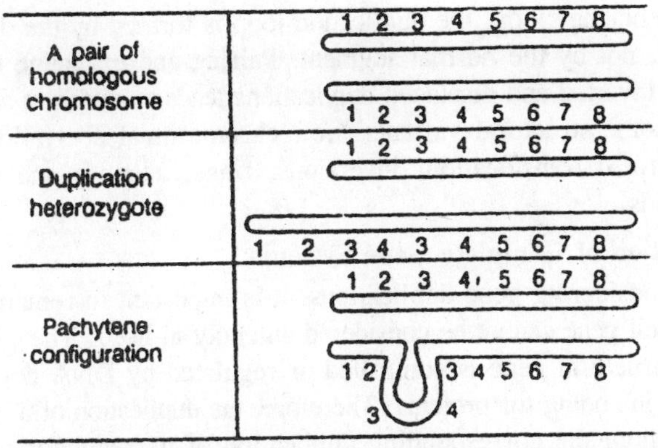

Fig. 6.5. Loop formation during chromosome pairing in a duplication heterozygote.

gene allow large quantities of RNA to be generated quickly. Examples of this type of reiteration are the cistrons coding for the ribosomal RNA's and those coding for histones. Table 6.1. gives some examples of proteins and RNA's thought to be coded by repetitive DNA sequences.

Table 6.1. Examples of repetitive DNA sequences

Group	*No repetitive DNA sequences*	*Degree of DNA or protein homology, %*
Satellite DNA	103–106	80–100
18S-28S Ribosomal RNA	100–600	97–100
5S Ribosomal RNA	100–200	97–100
tRNA	6–400	
Histones	10–1200	87–99
Hemoglobins	=10	<75–100

Satellite DNA's contain large numbers of repeating sequences which apparently are never transcribed. The nature of the mechanism(s) that generate large numbers of DNA segments in tandem linkage is unknown but it may well be by unequal crossing over. Also unknown are the factors that protect the repeated sequences from mutational changes.

Duplication occurs when a segment of the chromosome is represented two or more times in a chromosome of a homologous pair. This extra-chromosomal segment may be a free fragment with a centromere or chromosomal segment of the normal complement. During meiotic pairing the chromosome bearing the duplicated segment forms a loop to maximize the juxtraposition of homologous regions. In contrast to the deficiency loop, the duplication loop is formed by the duplicated segment, not by the normal segment. Pairing and exchange (crossing over) is inverted and displaced duplications leads to different secondary chromosome structural variants (i.e., chromosomal aberrations) such as reciprocal translocation, inversions, rings, acentric and dicentric chromatids.

Duplication of Complete Gene System

In considering gene duplications, it is important to remember that a structural gene cannot be considered an entity in itself. The expression of any structural gene is controlled or regulated by DNA not directly involved in coding for proteins. Therefore, the duplication of a structural gene without the corresponding duplication of its regulator may lead to a large array of new phenotypes including lethality.

Gene Duplication as a source of New Genetic Material

In addition to permitting a cell or organism to vary its genetic capabilities through gene dosage effects, duplications may also provide a cell with a reservoir of extra DNA. The duplicated genes could be considered as spare parts in the sense that one gene is sufficient to enable normal cell function. With one gene functioning in the normal manner, the duplicate would be free to undergo mutation, since its gene product could no longer be essential to maintain normal function.

By taking this reasoning a step further, it may be postulated that the duplicate gene may mutate and eventually evolve into a different gene coding for a protein with a new function. If so, gene duplications offer a mechanism for the evolution of new genes. There are many examples in nature that appear to fit the hypothesis that gene duplication is followed by gene changes through point mutation. Base nucleotide additions or deletions and frameshift mutations may result in genes coding for new phenotypes. The following two examples illustrate this concept.

Some of the most extensively studied human proteins that are thought to have arisen through gene duplications are the multiple hemoglobins of vertebrates. Hemoglobins are tetramers composed of two different polypeptide chains. Adult humans possess hemoglobins A and A_2. These two hemoglobins, represented by the formulas $\alpha_2\beta_2$ and $\alpha_2\delta_2$, respectively, share a common α-chain, but have distinct β and δ-chains. Thus, the hemoglobins found in the red blood cells of adults are coded by three distinct genes. Hemoglobin studies in certain families with α-chain mutants indicate that there is probably more than one α-chain gene per haploid genome. In addition, during development, embryonic hemoglobins and fetal hemoglobins occur. The Gγ, Aγ, δ and β genes have been shown to be closely linked. As we have shown the amino acid sequences of the beta and delta chains are very similar, suggesting that the genes coding for these chains arose by means of gene duplication of a common ancestral gene. Furthermore, the gene that codes for the α polypeptide is structurally related to the other hemoglobin genes, but is not linked to them. The genes coding for the δ, γ, and β chains probably arose through gene duplications from the original a gene and subsequently moved to a different linkage group by means of translocation.

Since the myoglobin chain is also structurally related to the hemoglobin polypeptides, it is thought that its genes and all the hemoglobin genes are derived from a common ancestral gene by a series of duplications over a long period of time.

Haptoglobin, one of the iron-binding proteins in vertebrate serum, is another example of a protein that probably arose by gene duplication. Haptoglobin, like hemoglobin, is a tetramer. Apparently, two genes α and β are involved. The α locus has two alleles, α_1 and α_2. Three phenotypes occur in the population Hp1, Hp2, and Hp1-2. The sera of humans exhibit either the Hp1 type (α, β) or the Hp2 type (α_2,β_n), or the Hp–2 type (α, α_2, β_n). The Hp2 haptoglobin is unique to humans, suggesting that a recent gene duplication gave rise to the Hp2. Studies of amino acid sequences clearly show that a partial gene duplication (intracistronic duplication) us have arisen resulting in a large polypeptide chain, different from the original α gene product in size and ability to combine with several beta chains to yield the polymeric haptoglobin Hp1–2.

These two examples—hemoglobin and haptoglobin–clearly indicate that gene duplication has probably played an important role in evolution.

Inversions

Inversions result when two breaks occur within a chromosome and the broken fragment is rejoined to the original chromosome in a reversed order. In this example, a chromosome with a normal sequence of 12345678910 undergoes breakage where the arms are in the contact while folded over on itself, say between 3 and 4 and 8 and 9. An inversion takes place when the 3 end fuses with the 8 end and the 4 end fuses with the 9 end to give the order 12387654910. Inversions are of two types, pericentric, with breaks flanking the centromere, and paracentric, with both breaks on the same side of the centromere. Remember that the same polarity must be maintained along a strand of DNA. Proper integration of an inverted segment could never occur in a single strand of DNA. The proper integration of a double-stranded segment of DNA occurs if the inverted segment undergoes a 180° rotation.

Types of Inversions

The inversions are of following types :

(i) Pericentric Inversion

When the inverted segment of chromosome includes or contains centromere, then such inversions are called heterobranchial or pericentric inversions. If crossing over occurs within the loop of a pericentric inversion, the resulted chromatids include half of the chromatids with duplications and deficiencies forming nonfunction. The other half of the chromatids form functional gametes : 1/4 gametes have normal chromosome order, 1/4 gametes have the inverted arrangement.

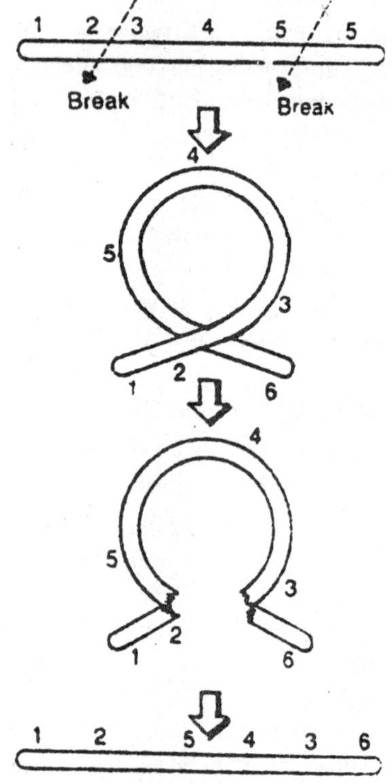

Fig. 6.6. Origin of an inversion in a chromosome.

(ii) Paracentric Inversions

When the inverted segment includes no centromere and the centromere remains located outside the segment, then such type of inversion is called homobranchial or paracentric inversion. Crossing over within the inverted segment of a paracentric inversion, produces a dicentric and an acentric chromosome. The dicentric chromosome contains two centromeres and forms a bridge from one pole to the other during first meiotic anaphase. When anaphase chromosomes separate towards poles, this bridge breaks somewhere along its length and the resulting fragments contain duplications and/or deficiencies. The acentric chromosome because lacks in centromere and fails to move to either pole and so, is not included in the meiotic products. Such, breakage-fusion bridge cycles of crossing over of paracentric inversions are most common in maize. The meiotic products includes half non-function, 1/4 functional normal and 1/4 functional inverted chromosomes.

Cytological and Genetical Methods for Detection and Identification of Inversions

Since the banding patterns of polytene chromosomes are visible, is an obvious way of detecting inversions. Figure shows a polytene chromosome in Drosophila with an inversion paired with a normal chromosome. The development of techniques that differentially stain metaphase chromosomes has also made the cytological characterization of inversions possible in species other than Drosophila.

The detection of inversions also involves the study of pairing relationships between a chromosome containing inverted DNA and its noninverted homologue during the prophase stage of meiosis. Pairing would homologous chromosomes on a point-by-point basis. However, homologous pairing between an inverted arrangement and its normal arrangement is difficult because they cannot line up properly. Therefore, in order for pairing to occur, an inversion loop must be formed.

Inversions have been dubbed crossover suppressors. The results of recombination within paracentric and pericentric inversions will clearly illustrate the reason for this name, which is, in fact, not entirely appropriate. Keeping in mind that crossing over occurs at the four-strand stage, it is probable that only two of the nonsister chromatids will be involved in the crossover while the other two remain unaffected. Let us consider two chromosomes that pair, one chromosome containing the normal gene sequence, ABCD and the other chromosome containing an inverted segment, ABCD. After replication and pairing occur, and while they are still in the four-strand stage, a single crossover occurs between nonhomologous chromatids within the inversion loop (e.g,. between genes C and B). Such crossing over results in the formation of a dicentric chromosome ABCD and an acentric fragment, DCBD, both of which contain duplications and deficiencies. Dicentric chromosomes undergo anaphase bridge formation which, in some types of cells, may be followed by breakage. The result will be chromosomes with deletions and duplications. The acentric treatment probably will remain at the metaphase plate and subsequently be lost. All of the recombination products that result from crossovers that occur within a paracentric inversion will form deficient gametes. Crossing over within the inversion loop region of a pericentric inversion also produces duplication and deficiency products.

Inversions are crossover suppressors, not because crossovers fail to occur within them in heterozygotes, but because the recombinant chromosome resulting from a crossover does not permit the offspring receiving it to survive if the crossover occurs within the inversion.

As crossover suppressors, inversion. Provide useful tools for geneticists. Inversions maintain particular seta of alleles of different loci within linkage groups by preventing recombinant offspring from surviving. Therefore, as for example in the isolation of sex-linked genes in Drosophila with the Basic stock. Inversions have also proved useful in the detection of linkage groups. A reduced number of recombinant types in a particular cross indicate that the genes are located within or near an inverted segment. And, conversely, a normal number of recombinant types indicate that the genes are located outside the inversion.

The number and type of inversions and the effects that they have in humans have not been extensively investigated until recently. Investigation has been limited by the difficulties in detecting inverted segments in human chromosomes. However, improved chromosome staining procedures now allow geneticists to detect paracentric and pericentric inversions in humans, but much work remains to be done in the field. One target area involves investigating the role of inversions in certain diseased states, such as heritable cancerous conditions.

TRANSLOCATIONS

Translocation is a broad term including all types of unilateral or bilateral transfer of chromosome segments from one chromosome to another. An important class of translocation having evolutionary significance is known as reciprocal translocations or segmental interchanges, which involve mutual exchange of chromosome segments between non-homologous chromosomes.

Cytology of a Translocation Heterozygote

If a translocation is present in one of the two sets of chromosomes, this will be a translocation heterozygote. In such a plant, the normal pairing into bivalents will not be possible among the chromosomes involved in translocation. Due to pairing between homologous segments of chromosomes, a cross-shaped (+) figure involving four chromosomes will be observed at pachytene. These four chromosomes at metaphase I can have one of the following three orientations:

1. *Alternate*. In alternate orientation, the alternate chromosomes will be oriented towards the same pole. In other words, the adjacent chromosome will orient towards opposite poles. This will be possible by the formation of a figure of eight.
2. *Adjacent I*. In adjacent I orientation, adjacent chromosomes having non-homologous centromeres will orient toward the same pole. In other words the chromosomes having homologous centromeres will orient towards opposite poles. A ring of four chromosomes will be observed.
3. *Adjacent II*. In adjacent II orientation, the adjacent chromosomes having homologous centromeres will orient towards the same pole. A ring of four chromosomes will be observed.

The alternate disjunction will give functional gametes. Adjacent I and adjacent II disjunctions will form gametes, which would carry duplications or deficiencies and as a result would be non-functional or sterile. Therefore, in a plant having translocation in heterozygous condition, there will be considerable pollen sterility.

A ring of four chromosomes as described above is found under conditions when a single interchange is found. If two interchanges are involving three non-homologous chromosomes, a ring of six chromosomes is found, and the size of the ring can increase with additional interchanges. More than one rings can also be found if two or more interchanges are independently found, each involving two different non-homologous chromosomes.

The first case of translocation was found in *Oenothera*, which was originally described as mutation by de Varies while working for his Mutation Theory. Oenothera, *Tradescantia* and *Rhoeo* are such cases, where translocations in the heterozygous condition are frequently found in nature. In many other crop plants they have been artificially induced.

Breeding Behaviour of a Translocation Heterozygote

The presence of translocation heterozygosity can be detected by the presence of semi-sterility and low seed set. This can then be confirmed at meiosis by quadrivalent formation. As shown above only two types of functional gametes are forced which result from alternate disjunction.

The functional gametes will give rise to three kinds of progeny namely (i) normal (ii) translocation heterozygote and (iii) translocation homozygote. These three types would be obtained in 1 : 2 : 1 ratio.

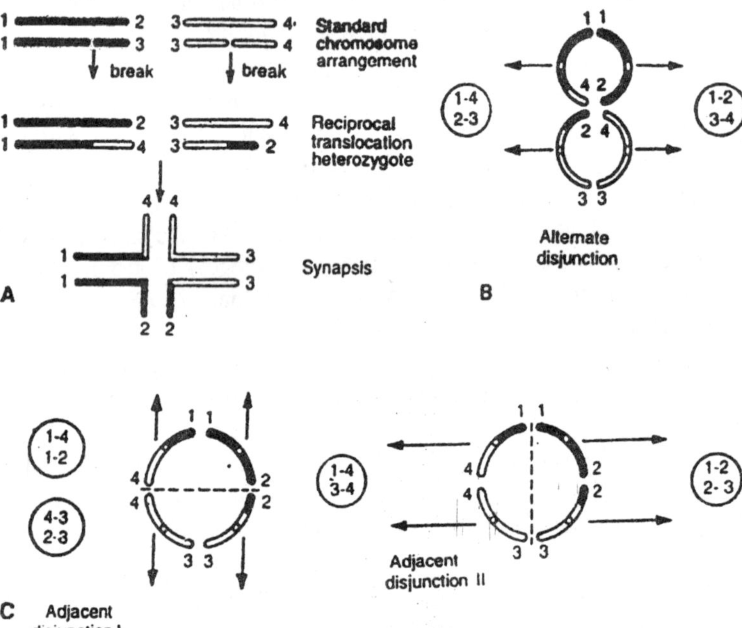

Fig. 6.7. A—Cross shaped figure formation during heterozygous reciprocal translocation; B—Alternate disjunction; C—Adjacent I and II disjunctions.

Interchange Heterozygosity in Oenothera

Subgenus *Euoenothera* of the genus *Oenothera* has been studied during 1920-1930 and cytogenetic structure leading to evolution in this group was examined. This group has 2 n = 14 and all 7 chromosomes of haploid complement have median chromosomes. There are three classes. (i) First is represented with species showing bivalents or small rings at meiosis (e.g. *O. hookeri*, *O. grandiflora*, *O. argillicola*). (ii) Second class is represented by species forming rings of various sizes at meiosis indicating the presence of interchanges. These rings are not permanent but are maintained due to their superiority in adaptive value (e.g., *O. irrigua*). (ii) The third class is represented by those having permanent translocation heterozygosity involving all chromosomes, so that a ring of 14 chromosomes is regularly formed (e.g., *O. biennis*, *O. strigosa*, *O. parviflora*).

The three classes described above also differ in phenotypes like flower size etc. and can be identified. The members of third category behave like pure lines and are actually permanent heterozygotes.

Balanced lethals and gametic complex-permanent hybridity in Oenothera. Permanent hybridity is maintained due to operation of a balanced lethal system, which may function due to gametic lethality or zygotic lethality. Since complete rings are formed and alternate disjunction is a rule, only two types of gametes are formed showing complete linkage between chromosomes. The gametic and zygotic lethality leads to survival of only heterozygotes.

Chromosome Aberrations in Humans

Chromosome deletions are usually lethal even as heterozygotes, resulting in zygotic loss, stillbirths, or infant deaths. Sometimes infants with small chromosome deficiencies, however, survive long enough to permit observation of some of the abnormal phenotypes they express. Lejeune and his colleagues, for example, discovered a chromosome deficiency in humans that has been associated with the *cri-du-chat* (cat cry) *syndrome*. The name of this syndrome came from a plaintive catlike mewing cry from small weak infants with the disorder. Other characteristics microcephaly (small head), broad face and saddle nose, widely spaced eyes with epicanthic folds, unique facial features and physical and mental retardation IQs of cri-du-chat children studied are in the range of 20–40. The chromosome deficiency is in the short arm of chromosome 5 and is designated 5p.

Cri-du-chat patients die in infancy or early childhood and do not transfer the chromosome deletion to offspring. This chromosome deficiency, however, has been shown by Lejeune and others to become involved sometimes in a reciprocal translocation and thus to be transmitted. When the short arm of chromosome 5 became translocated to chromosome 15, the heterozygous translocation was carried in a normal healthy parent. Some gametes, however, carried only the deficient member of the translocation pair. Children inheriting the 5p chromosome expressed the cri-du-chat syndrome.

Another human disorder that is associated with a chromosome abnormality is chronic myelocytic (myelogenous) leukemia. A deletion of chromosome 22 was first described by Nowell and Hungerford and was called the Philadelphia (Ph) chromosome after the city in which the discovery was made. It was observed consistently in bone marrow preparations of patients with chronic myelocytic leukemia. Later, a translocation discovered by J. Rowley in a leukemia patient provided the correct chromosome rearrangement. A part of the long arm of chromosome 22 was translocated to another chromosome, usually chromosome 9 (46,XX.9q + 22q–), leaving a deficiency in the long arm of No.22.

More chromosomal anomalies are now being associated with malignancy. New staining methods permit more precise comparisons of (1) chromosome arms and (2) differentially stained sister chromatids. With balanced chromosomes, Burkitt lymphoma was related to a translocation of chromosome 14 [t(8q–; 14q+) (q24;q32). A deletion in chromosome 13q (band 14.1) is associated with the human embryonic tumor retinoblastoma. Williams tumor, an embryonic kidney tumor, is associated with a deletion in band 11p13. Sister chromatid exchanges, exchanges occurring between sister chromatids, occur with high frequency in somatic cells of patients with Bloom syndrome, indicating chromosome instability. Most people with this syndrome die with some form of cancer before age 30. Irregular chromosome numbers are also observed in malignant cells, particularly in later stages of cancer.

Like deficiencies, chromosome duplications are usually lethal even as heterozygotes, but sometimes they are sufficiently viable to permit observations of the abnormalities they produce. Like deficiencies, they may be associated with translocations and thus transmitted by normal healthy parents. Remember that a translocation is an exchange of parts between nonhomologous chromosomes or a transfer from one chromosome to a nonhomolog. Broken parts may be further divided and some may be lost or gained in a transfer. Thus, deficiencies and duplications may accompany a translocation carried in a parent. Such a parent may be a translocation heterozygote, with the long arm of one chromosome 21 attached at the centromere to the long arm of chromosome 14 along with normal chromosomes 14 and 21. Some gametes will contain a normal 21 and translocation 14q21q. When such a gamete is fertilized with a gamete from a normal individual, a translocated 21, along with two normal chromosomes 21, results in a viable infant with trisomy-21 and the Down syndrome.

With fluorescene microscope techniques, I.A. Uchida and C.C. Lin discovered a partial trisomy-12 that could not be identified by conventional methods. A body with some clinical features resembling the Down syndrome had been studied with conventional chromosome techniques. Because of continued lack of motor development at seven months age, further chromosomal investigations were carried out on lymphocyte cultures and slides stained with quinacrine dihydrochloride. With this technique, an additional band was identified in the short arm of chromosome 8. The mother's chromosomes were normal; but in the father, the short arm of No. 21 had become translocated to the short arm of No. 8 [46,XY, (8p+,12p–)]. The same chromosomal rearrangement was found in his daughter, an older sister of the patient. Since both father and daughter were clinically normal, the translocation was presumed to be reciprocal. The patients's No. 8 pair consisted of one normal and one translocation chromosome, similar to that of his father and sister, but both of his No. 12 chromosomes were normal. Thus, the boy had a duplication of part of the short arm of No. 12 and a deficiency of the tip of No. 8. Many translocations, addition to those cited above, have been detected in studies of human chromosomes, but most were apparently reciprocal and produced no phenotypic anomalies. At the Yale-New Haven Hospital, for example, cytological studies were conducted on 4500 infants born consecutively during one year. Lymphocytes from umbilical cord blood of each infant were grown in vitro and prepared for microscopic observation of chromosomes. Six translocations were detected. None of these was associated with a distinctive phenotypic anomaly. It is not the translocation process per se that produces abnormalities, but the imbalance of genetic material reflected in chromosome deficiencies and duplications that are produced by segregation of translocated chromosomes.

P. W. Allerdice et al. described a syndrome called the *chromosome 3 duplication-deletion syndrome*. Phenotypically, this syndrome includes a group of morbid symptoms; stillbirths, neonatal deaths, and spontaneous abortions. Most pregnancies are lost, but two children survived and became probands for the investigation. He cannot sit up, turn over, or eat solid food. Facial malformation of the living children includes a distorted head shape; thick, low eyebrows; low hair-line; long eyelashes; persistent lanugo; distended veins on scalp; hypertelorism; oblique palpebral fissures; a very short nose with a broad, depressed bridge and anteverted nares; protruding maxilla; thin upper lip; micrognathia; low-set ears; and short, webbed neck. Port-wine stains, congenital glaucoma, cloudy corneas, cleft palate, and harelip also occur frequently. Each infant had difficulty sucking and swallowing. Internal physical abnormalities were noted in infants who died neonatally.

Giemsa- and quinacrine-banded karyotypes from a parent of an affected child revealed an inversion [inv(3)(p25q21). Fetal cells cultured for prenatal diagnosis from a subsequent pregnancy of this couple carried a recombinant chromosome 3, with the long arm described as rec (3) del p, dup q, inv(3)(p25q21). With a banded chromosome 3, the inversion was analyzed. The inverted segment included the centromere (pericentric). Breaks had occurred in the short arm (p) at band 25 and in the long arm (q) at band 21. The central part of the chromosome including the centromere had rotated 180° .and become reinserted into chromosome 3. Inv 3(p25q21) had been carried in the kindred for at least four generations and 35 kindered members were presumed to carry it. Karyotype of Case 1 is 46,XYrec(3), dup q, inv(3) (p25q21). He was the second child born to a 23-year-old carrier mother with karyotype 46,XX, inv(3)(p25q21) and a 26-year-old father, karyotype 46,XY.

Crossing over within the inversion loop is presumed to produce the imbalance of genetic material associated with duplications and deficiencies and to cause the symptoms of the syndrome. Odd numbers of crossovers within the inverted are of a chromosome 3 would be expected to result in genetic imbalance. Earlier in this chapter, crossing over in *Drosophila* inverted chromosomes was shown to create irregular combinations resulting in lethals. This, in turn, resulted in "suppressing" crossing over. In humans, unbalanced zygotes from inverted chromosome crossovers sometimes survive. Some infants carrying unbalanced chromosomes are kept alive, but with varying degrees of birth defect handicaps. The degree of imbalance of genetic material may be determining factor for life or death and degree of abnormality.

7

CHANGE IN CHROMOSOME NUMBER

Somatic cells of higher plants and animals usually have chromosomes in pairs (2n); that is, two of each kind of chromosome are present in each cell. Mature germ cells, having undergone reduction division, normally have one number of each pair (n). Many individual plants and animals, however, have local areas of somatic tissue characterized by a multiple of the basic chromosome number. A doubling process in cell division is the usual explanation for these deviations.

With the exception of sex differences, somatic doubling, and minor variations that occur in natural and experimental populations, all members of a species of plants or animals have the same basic chromosome number. Chromosome number can be overemphasized as a criterion for species identification, but it represents a valid characteristic to be used along with others for distinguishing species. The range or reported chromosome numbers in animals extends from 2 pair in a rhabdocoel Gyratrix hermaphroditus and some mites, midges, and scale insects, to more than 100 in some butterflies and Crustacea. The Crustacean, *Paralithodes camtschatica*, for example, has 208 chromosomes or 104 pairs. The reported range in plants is from 2 pairs in the small composite plant Haplopappus gracilis to several hundred in some ferns. A species of fern-like plants of the genus Ophioglossum is reported to have 768 chromosomes.

Where all individuals within a species, with the exceptions noted above, have the same chromosome number, different species within a genus often have different numbers. Cytological investigations of chromosomes help to unravel problems of species formation. The evolutionary path of a certain species can be followed in some cases by comparing numerical and structural relations of its chromosomes with those of other species within the genus. The essential genetic material is a major factor in determining evolutionary patterns, but chromosome number itself represents merely the number of packages into which the genetic material is divided. Chromosome number is probably more constant, however, than any other single morphological characteristic that is available for species identification.

Table 7.1. Chromosome number of some common animals and plants

Species	*Number of chromosomes pair*
Plants	
Garden pea, *Pisum sativum*	7
Sorghum, *Sorghum vulgare*	10
Maize, *Zea mays*	10
Johnson Grass, *Sorghum halepense*	20
Alfalfa, *Medicago sativa*	16
Barley, *Hordeum vulgare*	7
Oats, *Avena sativa*	21
Tomato, *Lycopersicon esculentum*	12
Tobacco, *Nicotiana tabacum*	24
Trillium, *Trillium erectum*	5
Animals	
Gypsy moth, *Lymantria dispar*	31
Mouse, *Mus musculus*	20
Rabbit, *Oryctolagus cuniculus*	22
Cow, *Boss tarus*	30
Horse, *Equus caballus*	32
Donkey, (ass) *Equus asinus*	31
Dog, *Canis familaris*	39
Monkey, *Macaca rhesus*	21
Chimpanzee, *Pan troglodytes*	24

Changes in the number of chromosomes may be reflected in phenotypic variations, which constitute a useful tool for identifying the influence of individual chromosomes. If, for example, phenotypically distinguishable individuals with different chromosome numbers can be identified in natural populations or produced experimentally, it is sometimes possible to determine the effect of adding or removing certain chromosomes. Some plants with increased chromosome numbers have phenotypic changes in morphological or physiological characteristics which are of practical importance to man. Grape and tomato plants with chromosome numbers above 2n are larger and produce more desirable fruit than do corresponding varieties with the usual 2n number.

Classifications of chromosome changes are arbitrary and superficial because these changes are necessarily interpreted in terms of obvious additions or eliminations of parts of chromosomes, whole chromo-somes, or whole chromosome sets. The presently accepted classification system, therefore, is merely a working tool. Two main classes are euploidy and aneuploidy ("ploid," Greek for unit; "eu," true or even; and "aneu," uneven). Euploids have chromosome complements consisting of whole sets or genomes. The chromosome number of euploid organisms is basically represented by the monoploid (n). Euploids with chromosome numbers above the monoploid level may be diploid (2n), triploid (3n), tetraploid (4n), or have some other "polyploid" number.

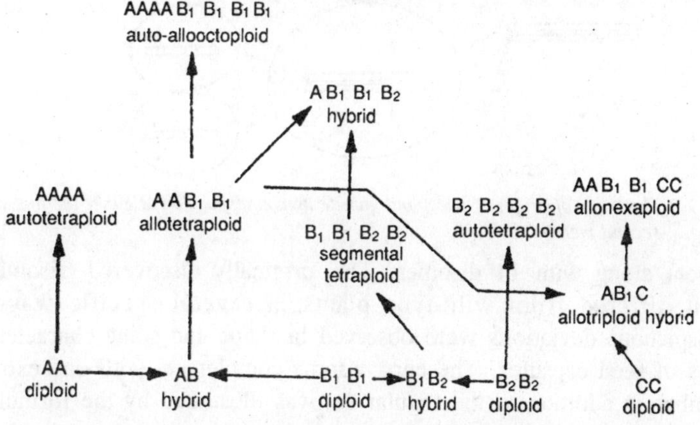

Fig. 7.1. Mode of formation of different kinds of ployploid.

ANEUPLOIDY

The first critical study of aneuploid plants was made by Blakeslee and Bellingusing the common Jimson weed Datura stramonium, which normally has 12 pairs of chromosomes in the somatic cells. In 1924, these investigators announced the discovery of a "mutant type" having 25 rather than 24 chromosomes. At the meiotic metaphase, one of the 12 pairs was found to have an extra member; that is, one trisome was

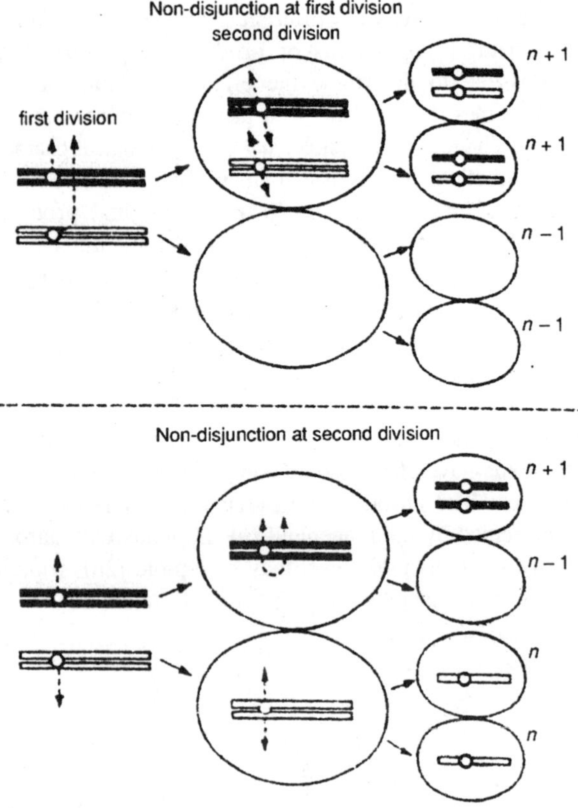

Fig. 7.2. The mode of origin of aneuploid gamete by non-disjunction at either the first or second meiotic division.

present along with 11 disomes. This originally discovered trisomic plant differed from wild-type plants in several specific ways. Conspicuous deviations were observed in shape and spine characteristics of seed capsules. The chromosome complement with one extra member in addition to the regular set was illustrated by the formula 2n + 1. Theoretically, because the some have, however, been divided successfully into 7 groups identified with letters A to G. Numbers 1 to 22 are associated with the autosomes in descending order by length. All autosomes can be placed satisfactorily within a group but the numbering within the groups is more or less tentative. The X chromosome is difficult to distinguish from members of the C group and the Y chromosome shows considerable variability in different preparations.

Nullisomics (2n – 2)

Although nullisomy is a lethal condition in regular diploids, an organism like wheat (which "pretends" to be diploid but is fundamentally hexaploid) can tolerate nullisomy. In fact, all of the possible 21 wheat nullisomics have been produced. Their appearances are different from normal wheat; furthermore, most of them show less vigorous growth.

Monosomics (2n – 1)

Monosomic chromosome complements are generally deleterious for two main reasons. First, the balance of chromosomes that is necessary for a finely tuned cellular homeostasis, carefully put together during evolution, is grossly disturbed. For example, if a genome consisting of two of each of chromosomes, a, b, and c becomes monosomic for c (that is 2a + 2b + 1c), the ratio of these chromosomes is changed from 1c:1 (a+b) to 1c : 2(a + b). Second, any deleterious recessive on the single remaining chromosome becomes hemizygous and may be directly expressed phenotypically. (Note that these are the same effects as those produced by deletions.)

Monosomics, trisomics (2n +1), and other chromosome aneuploids are probably produced by nondisjunction during mitosis or meiosis. In meiosis it can happen at either the first or the second division. If an n – 1 gamete is fertilized by an n gamete, a monosomic (2n – 1) zygote is produced; an n + 1 and an n gamete give a trisomic 2n +1; and an n + 1 and n + 1 give a tetrasomic if the same chromosome is involved or a double trisomic if different chromosomes are involved, and so on.

In Neurospora (a haploid), the n – 1 meiotic products abort, and do not darken like the normal ascospore; so MI and MII nondisjunctions are detected as asci with 4:4 and 6:2 ratios of normal to aborted spores. For loci on the aneuploid chromosomes, what ascus genotypes are produced?

In humans, the sex-chromosome monosomic (44 autosomes + 1X) produces a phenotype known as Turner's syndrome. Affected people have a characteristic, easily recognizable, phenotype: they are sterile females, are short in stature, and often have a web of skin extending between the neck and shoulders. Their intelligence is near-normal, although some specific cognitive functions are defective. Their frequency is about 1 in 5000 female births. Monosomics for all autosomes die in utero.

If viable, nullisomics and monosomics are useful in locating newly found recessive genes on specific chromosomes in plants. In one such method, different monosomic lines lacking a different chromosome in each line are obtained. Homozygotes for the new gene are crossed with each monosomic line, and the progeny of each cross are inspected for expression of the recessive phenotype. The cross in which the phenotype appears identifies its chromosomal location. In nullisomics and monosomics, of course, n - 1 gametes are produced. In general, these gametes tend to be more viable in a female parent than in a male. It is the union of these n – 1 gametes within n gametes, bearing the new mutation, that provides the crucial progeny types for the linkage test.

A similar approach can be used in humans. For example, two people whose vision is normal may produce a daughter who has Turner's syndrome and is also red-green colour-blind. This shows that the allele for red-green colour blindness is recessive, that it was on the X chromosome of the mother, and the nondisjunction must have occurred in the father.

Trisomics (2n + 1)

In trisomics, trivalents are regularly seen. For genes that are tightly linked to the centromere of a trisomic chromosome set, the random segregations can be represented a trisomic Aaa. All types occur equally frequently, and a gametic ratio of 1A:2Aa:2a:1aa is produced. Trisomics are sometimes recongnised by these ratios, which are also useful in locating genes on chromosomes. We have already observed a complete set of trisomic lines in Datura. Once again, note that chromosome imbalance produces highly chromosome-specific deviations from the normal appearance.

In humans there are several examples of viable trisomics. The combination XXX (1/1000 male births) results in Klinefelter's syndrome, producing males that have lanky builds, are mentally retarded, and sterile. Another combination, XYY, also occurs in about in 1000 male births. A lot of excitement was aroused when an attempt was made to link the XYY condition with a predisposition toward violence. This is still hotly debated, although it is now clear that an XYY condition in no way guarantees such behaviour. Nevertheless, several enterprising lawyers have attempted to use the XYY genotype as grounds for acquittal or compassion in crimes of violence. The XYY males are usually fertile. We have already looked at the generation of Down's syndrome through adjacent segregation in translocation heterozygotes.

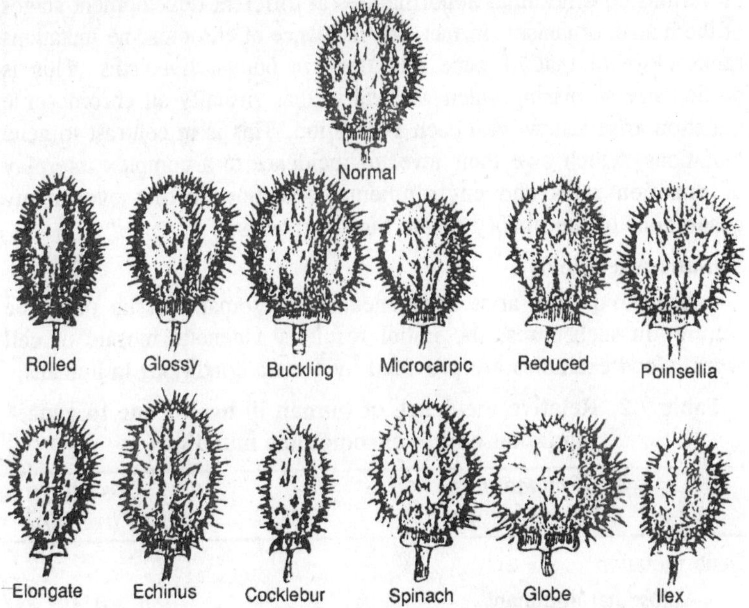

Fig. 7.3. Fruit capsules of the 12 primary trisomics of Datura stramonium, each with its particular phenotype.

Down's syndrome also occurs much more commonly as a result of nondisjunction during meiosis, and it is then called trisomy 21. In this form of Down's syndrome, there is generally no family history of the phenotype; however, the frequency of this form is dramatically higher among children born to older mothers. The overall incidence of this abnormality is about 0.15 percent of births.

Down's syndrome is a severely incapacitating condition. Affected individuals are mentally retarded, and about one-third die by the age of 10 years. Recent advances in mapping the human genome will allow the identification of precisely those genes on the long arm of chromosome 21 that must be trisomic to produce this syndrome; these advances offer some hope of a more precise understanding of its chemical nature and possible therapy. In humans, the only other two autosomal trisomics known to survive past birth are individuals with trisomy 13 and trisomy 18. Affected children are even more severely handicapped, both mentally and physically, and rarely survive to 1 year of age.

Chromosome mutation in general plays a prominent role in determining genetic ill health in humans. The surprisingly high levels of various chromosomal abnormalities at different development stages of the human organism. In fact, the incidence of chromosome mutations ranks close to that of gene mutations in human livebirths. This is particularly surprising when we realize that virtually all chromosome mutation arise a new with each generation. This is in contrast to gene mutations, which owe their level of incidence to a complex interplay of mutation rates and environmental selection, acting over many generations of the history of the human species.

Somatic Aneuploids

Aneuploids can arise spontaneously in somatic tissue or tissue culture. In such cases, the initial result is a genetic mosaic of cell types. Good examples are provided by certain conditions in humans.

Table 7.2. Relative incidence of human ill health due to gene mutation and to chromosome mutation

Type of mutation	*Percentage of live birth*
Gene mutation	
Autosomal dominant	0.90
Autosomal recessive	0.25
X-linked	0.05
Total gene mutation	1.20
Chromosome mutation	
Autosomal trisomies (mainly Down's syndrome)	0.14
Other unbalanced autosomal aberrations	0.06
Balanced autosomal aberrations	0.19
Sex chromosomes	
XYY, XXY, and other YY	0.17
XO, XXX, and other MM	0.05
Total chromosome mutation	0.61

Sexual mosaics provide the first example. These are people whose bodies are a mixture of male and female tissue. One type of sexual mosaic is XO/XYY. This mosaic can be explained by postulating an XY zygote in which an early mitotic division involved a nondisjunction of the Y chromosomes, so that both went to one pole:

The phenotypic sex of such individuals depends upon where in the body the male and female sectors end up. In this case, if nondisjunction occurred at a later mitotic division, there would be a three-way XY/XO/XYY.

Aneuploidy in Man

More recent studies on individuals have related chromosome numbers below and above 46 with intersex conditions and other irregularities manifesting physical, reproductive, and mental abnormalities. Participants in the Chicago Conference agreed on a system of nomenclature for identifying numerical and structural chromosome alterations. In a description of a karyotype, the first item to be recorded is the total number of chromosomes, including the sex chromosomes, followed by the sex chromosome constitution and any autosomal aberrations. A complement of 44 autosomes and one X, for example, is symbolized 45, X. This monosomic chromosome complement has been associated with an abnormal female condition known for many years as Turner's syndrome and which occurs in one of about 5000 people in the general population.

The Turner Syndrome (45,X)

This monosomic has a chromosome complement of 44 autosomes and one X chromosome. The chromosome anomaly is associated with an abnormal female phenotype described in 1938 by H. H. Turner and associates and known as the Turner syndrome. It occurs in about 1 per 2500 live female births. More than 90 percent abort spontaneously. A rough estimate for 45,X adults in the general population is in 1 in 5000. These adults have virtually no ovaries, have limited secondary sexual characteristics, and are sterile. Microscopic sections of the ovaries show fibrous streaks of tissue representing remnants of ovaries. Affected females have short stature, low-set ears, webbed neck, and shieldlike chest. Mental deficiency is not usually associated with this syndrome. Epithelial cells of 45,X patients are X chromatin negative, as expected when only X chromosome is present.

X monosomic probably originate from exceptional eggs or sperm with no sex chromosome or from the loss of a sex chromosome in mitosis during early cleavage stages, after an XX or XY zygote has been formed. This latter probability is supported by the high frequency of mosaics that result from postzygotic events in patients with the Turner syndrome. Mosaics with X/XX sex chromosomes show symptoms of the Turner syndrome but are usually taller than X and have fewer anomalies that nonmosaic 45,X females. They show more feminization, more normal menstruation, and may be fertile. Many cases of the somatic Turner phenotype without the typical 45,X chromosome constitution are now known. Most of these have one normal X chromosome and a fragment of a second X chromosome. Both arms of the second X chromosome are apparently necessary for normal ovarian differentiation. Individuals with only the long arm of the second X are short in stature and show other somatic symptoms of the Turner syndrome, whereas those with only the short arm of the second X have normal stature and do not show as many signs of the Turner syndrome. This indicates that the Turner phenotype is mostly controlled by genes on the short arm of the X chromosome.

Patients with partial deletion of one X chromosome are X chromatin positive and therefore may be misdiagnosed if a buccal smear is the only test used. The deficient X chromosome always forms the X chromatin body. A Y chromosome also occurs in some individuals with the Turner phenotype. These patients are usually mosaic for 45,X/46,XY, with a normal Y. People with one X and a Y fragment, not including the Y short arm, have only streak ovaries but are normal in phenotype. This suggests that male-determining genes are in the short arm of the Y chromosome, and those that prevent Turner phenotype are in the Y long arm as well as the X short arm. Major features of the Turner phenotype occur in some males as well as in females. The male Turner syndrome is characterized by defective development of the testes, sterility, and limited male secondary sexual characteristics, along with somatic features of the Turner phenotype. These people have normal male karyotypes.

The Klinefelter Syndrome (47,XXY)

An extra X chromosome in addition to the usual male (XY) chromosome complement (47,XXY) has been associated with the abnormal male syndrome described (in 1942) by H.F. Klinefelter and known as the *Klinefelter syndrome*. It is estimated to occur in 1 per 500 live male births. Individuals with this syndrome are phenotypically males but with some tendency toward femaleness, particularly in secondary sex characteristics. Such features as enlarged breasts, underdeveloped body hair, small testes, and small prostate glands are a part of the syndrome. Presumably, the XXY constitution originates either by fertilization of an exceptional orginates either by fertilization of an exceptional XX egg by a Y sperm or of an X egg by an exceptional XY sperm. Studies of Klinefelter syndrome and Turner syndrome indicate that the Y chromosome in human beings, unlike that in *Drosophila*, determines male sex.

The most common karyotype (about three-quarters of the cases) for the Klinefelter syndrome is 47,XXY, but the symptoms of the syndrome will usually occur whenever more than one X chromosome is present along with a Y chromosome. More complex karyotypes associated with the Klinefelter syndrome include: XXYY, XXXY, XXXYY, XXXXY, XXXXYY, and XXXXXY. All patients with the Klinefelter syndrome have one or more X chromatin bodies in the their cells. Mental retardation is usually found when there are more than two X chromosomes. The XY/XXY mosaicism in patients with Klinefelter syndrome is associated with less severe physical and reproductive anomalies.

Aneuploidy of X Chromosomes and Mental Deficiency

Other irregular combination of X chromosomes have also been recognized among females with X chromosome aberrations. About 1 percent of all mentally defective women in institutions have been shown to have one or more extra X chromosomes. This chromosome abnormality occurs in about 1 in 700 live births in the general population. Individuals with the "triple X syndrome" are comparable in some ways with Drosophila metafemales (XXX). In Drosophila, however, such individuals are usually lethal, and those that survive are strikingly abnormal and sterile. Human XXX individuals are sometimes visibly undistinguished from normal XX females, but there is considerable range in phenotypic expression. They may be mentally abnormal.

The best-known symptoms in this syndrome are abnormalities associated with functional processes such as menstruation. One patient cited by P. A. Jacobs was a 37-year-old female who reported that the first suggestion of an abnormality was highly irregular menstruation. When the abdominal wall was opened, the ovaries appeared as if they were postmensopausal. Microscopically, they showed deficient ovarian follicle formation. Of 63 cells observed, 51 had 47 chromosomes; the extra chromosome was an X. Nondisjunction in the production of the egg from which this woman developed was postulated as the mechanism for the occurrence of extra chromosome. Buccal smears showed two sex chromatin bodies in the epithelial cells as expected when three X chromosomes are present. Individuals with tetrasomic X chromosomes (48,XXXX) are all mentally defective. The degree of mental deficiency increases with the number of X chromosomes present.

47,XYY and Behaviour

P. A. Jacobs and her associates reported in 1965 that seven XYY males were detected in a population of 197 male, mentally subnormal inmates of a penal institution in Scotland. The XYY men were unusually tall, with an average height of 73.1 inches, compared with 64 inches for XY men in the same prison. Numerous other studies, mostly in institutionalized populations, have since confirmed that a high proportion of XYY individuals are tall, subnormal in intelligence (with IQs individuals are tall, subnormal in intelligence (with IQs ranging from 80 to 95), and antisocial. The aggressive behaviour that brought them into conflict with the law was usually against property rather than people.

XYY trisomy occurs about once in 1000 live male births in the general European population. Only a few of these can be accounted for in the criminal population. Furthermore, most XYY men have been described as perfectly normal in behaviour. Hook has shown that only 3.6 percent of all XYY men are institutionalized for any reason.

Environmental factors are presumed to be involved in the development of aggressiveness. Since some XYY men are subnormal in intelligence and excessively tall in stature, particular environmental situations in childhood or adulthoood may lead to withdrawal from society or aggressive behaviour. Unfavourable social conditions such as frustration in personal accomplishment and taunting from associates may encourage physical aggression as a means of adaptation. Males with this sex trisomy have not been found to transmit the extra Y chromosome to their sons. This extra chromosome seems to be weeded out in gametogenesis. A wide range of physical and mental abnormalities has been detected in institutionalized XYY men, but most of these are irregular in occurrence and do not form a syndrome. Tallness of stature and mental dullness, however, are fairly constant characteristics among institutionalized XYY men.

Chromosomal Mosaics

Individuals who have at least two cell lines, with different karyotypes derived from one zygote, originate from nondisjunction in a cleavage division after fertilization. One daughter cell would thus receive one too many and the other would be one deficient. Each cell would give rise to cell line with its irregular chromosome number. Proportions of cells representing the different cell lines would vary in different tissues, making the extent of the mosaicism and the effect on the organism difficult to predict.

Many sex chromosome mosaics have been detected in human beings. The main phenotypic characteristic is extreme variability. Some sex chromosome mosaics have been reported —X/XX, X/XY, XX/XY, XXY/XX, XX/XXX, XXX/X XXX/XXXXY—and several other combinations reflecting two or three cell lines. Mid to severe phenotypic symptoms have been associated with these sex chromosome mosaics.

Abnormal Euploidy

Monoploids

In this section we shall consider monoploidy as an unusual condition. Monoploid individuals can arise spontaneously in natural populations as rare aberrations, but in several forms (such as bees, wasps, and ants) the males are normally monoploid, having derived from unfertilized eggs.

In the germ cells of a monoploid, meiosis cannot occur normally because the chromosomes having no pairing partners. Thus monoploids are characteristically sterile. (However, meiosis can be bypassed in some monoploid animals, such as male honeybees, which produce gametes essentially by mitotic division). If meiosis occurs and the single chromosomes segregate randomly, then the probability of their all going to one pole is $(1/2)^{x-1}$, where x is the number of chromosomes. This will determine the frequency of viable (whole-set) gametes, obviously a vanishingly small number if x is large.

Monoploids have a major role in modern approaches to plant breeding. Diploidy is an inherent nuisance in the induction and selection of new favourable plant mutations and of new selection of new favourable plant mutations and of new combinations of genes already present. Monoploids provide a way around some of these problems. In some plants, monoploids may be artificially derived from the products of meiosis in the plant's anthers. A cell destined to become a pollen grain may be induced by cold treatment to grow instead into an embryoid, a small dividing mass of cells. The embryoid may be grown on agar to form a monoploid planter, which can then be potted in soil to mature.

Monoploids may be exploited in several ways. In one method, they are first examined for favourable traits or gene combinations. These may arise from heterozygosity already present in the parent or induced in the parent by mutagens. The monoploid can then be subjected to chromosome doubling to achieve a completely homozygous diploid with a normal meiosis, capable of providing seed. How is this achieved? Quite simply, by the application of a compound called colchicine to meristematic tissue. Colchicine, an alkaloid drug extracted from the autumn crocus, inhibits the mitotic spindle, so that cells with two chromosomes sets are produced. These may proliferate to form a sector of diploid tissue that can be identified cytologically.

Another way the monoploid may be used is to treat its cells, basically like a population of haploid organisms, in a mutagenesis-and-selection procedure. The cells are isolated, their walls are removed by enzyme treatment, and they are treated with mutagen. They are then plated on selective medium— perhaps a toxic compound normally produced by one of the plant's parasites, or an insecticide— to select resistant cells. Resistant plantlets grow eventually into haploid plants, which can then be doubled (using colchicine) into a pure-breeding resistant type. These are potentially powerful techniques that can circumvent the normally'slow process of what is basically meiotic plant breeding. The techniques have been successfully applied in several important crop plants, such as soybeans and tobacco. This is, of course, another aspect of somatic-cell genetics in higher organisms.

The another technique of or producing monoploids does not work in all organism or in all genotypes of an organism. Another useful technique has been developed in barley, an important crop plant. When diploid barley, Hordeum vulgare, is pollinated using a diploid wild relative called Hordeum bulbosum, fertilization occurs, but during the ensuing somatic cell divisions, the chromosomes of H. Bulbosum are preferentially eliminated from the zygote, resulting in a haploid embryo. (The haploidization process appears to be caused by a genetic incompatibility between the chromosomes of the different species.) The resulting haploids can be doubled with colchicine. This approach has led to the rapid production and widespread planting of several new barley varieties. It is being used successfully in other species too.

Polyploids

Once into the realm of polyploids, we must distinguish between autopolyploids and allopolyploids. *Autopolyploids* are composed of multiple sets from within one species, whereas *allopolyploids* are composed of sets from different species. Allopolyploids form only between closely related species; however, the different chromosome sets are homeologous (only partially homologous), not fully homologous as they are in autopolyploids.

Triploids

Triploids are usually autopolyploids. They are constructed from the cross of a 4x (tetraploid) and a 2x (diploid). the 2x and the x gametes unite to form a 3x triploid.

Triploids also are characteristically sterile. The problem again involves pairing at meiosis. Although pairing can take place in several ways, it usually occurs between only two chromosomes at a time. The

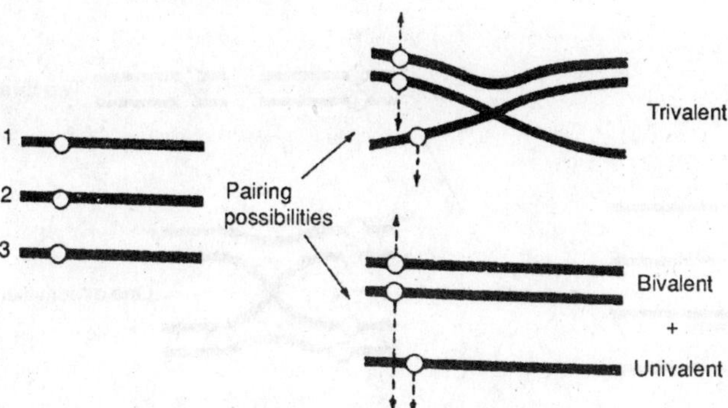

Fig. 7.4. Meiotic pairing possibilities in a triploid.

net result is always the same, an unbalanced segregation of one of the following types:

$$\frac{1+2}{3} \text{ or } \frac{1+3}{2} \text{ or } \frac{2+3}{1}$$

This happens for every chromosome threesome, and the probability of obtaining either a 2 x or x gamete is $(½)^{x-1}$, where x is the number of chromosomes in a set. The other will be unbalanced gametes, having two of one chromosome type, one of another, two of another, and so on, and most will be nonfunctional. Even if the gametes are functional, the resulting zygotes will be unbalanced. A practical application of the sterility associated with triploidy lies in the production of seedless varieties of watermelons and bananas.

Autotetraploids

Autotetraploids occur either naturally, by the spontaneous accidental doubling of a 2x genome to 4x, or artificially, through the use of colchicine. Autotetraploids are evident in many commercially important crop plants because, as with other polyploids, the larger number of chromosome sets is often associated with increased size of the plant. This is manifested in increased cell size, fruit size, stomata size, and so on. Because 4 is an even number, autotetraploids can have a regular meiosis, although this is by no means always the case. The crucial factor is how the four chromosomes of one type pair and segregate. The two bivalent and the quadrivalent pairing modes tend to be most regular in segregation, but even here there is no guarantee of a 2 → 2 segregation. If a regular 2 → 2 segregation is achieved at each chromosome type, as is the case in some species, than a formal genetic analysis can be developed for autotetraploids.

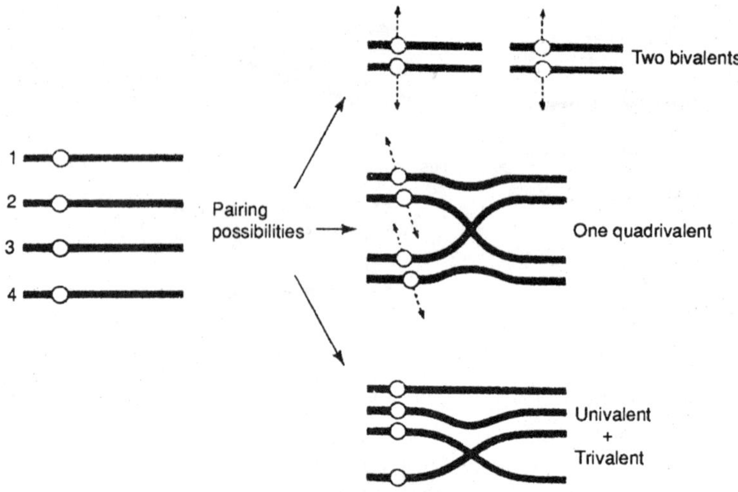

Fig. 7.5. Meiotic pairing possibilities in tetraploids.

Let's hypothesize an experiment in which colchicine is used to double the chromosomes of an *Aa* plant into an *AAaa* autotetraploid, which we will assume shows 2 → 2 segregation. We now have a further worry because autotetraploids give different genetic results in their progeny, depending on whether or not the locus concerned is tightly linked to the centromere. First we consider a centromeric gene. The three possible pairing and segregation patterns are presented in Figures, these occur by chance and with equal frequency. As the figure shows, the 2x gametes will be *Aa, AA, or aa,* and these will be produced in a ratio of 8:2:2, or 4:1:1. If such a plant is offspring is obviously 1/6 × 1/6 = 1/36. In other words, a 35:1 phenotypic ratio will be observed if *A* is fully dominant over three *a* alleles.

If, in the same kind of plant, a genetic locus *B/b* is very far removed from the centromere, crossing-over must be considered. This forces us to think in terms of chromatids instead of chromosomes, and we have for *B* chromatids and for *b* chromatids. Because the number of crossovers in a such a long region will be large, the genes will become effectively unlinked from their original centromeres, and the packaging of genes two at a time into gametes is very much like grabbing two balls at random from a bag of eight balls, four of one kind and four of another. The probability of picking two *b* genes is then

4/8 (the first one) × 3/7 (the second one) = 12/56
= 3/14

So, in a selfing, the probability of a *bbbb* phenotype will be equal 3/14 × 3/14 = 9/196 = 1/22. Hence there will be a 21:1 phenotype ratio of *B - - -:bbbb*. For genetic loci of intermediate position, intermediate ratios will, of course, result.

Allopolyploids

The "classical" allopolyploid was synthesized by G. Karpechenko in 1928. He wanted to make a fertile hybrid between the cabbage (*Brassica*) and the radish (*Raphanus*) that would have the leaves of the former and roots of the latter. Each of these species has 18 chromosomes, and they are related closely enough to allow intercrossing. A variable hybrid progeny individual was produced from seed. However, this hybrid was functionally sterile because the nine chromosomes from the cabbage parent were different enough from the radish chromosomes that homology was insufficient for normal synapsis and disjunction.

However, one day a few seeds were in fact produced by this (almost) sterile hybrid. On planting, these seeds produced fertile individuals with 36 chromosomes. These individuals were allopolyploids. They had apparently been derived from spontaneous accidental chromosome doubling in the sterile hybrid, presumably in tissue that eventually became germinal and underwent meiosis. Thus, in $2n_1 + 2n_2$ tissue, there is a pairing partner for each chromosome, and balanced gametes of the type $n_1 + n_2$ are produced. These fuse to given $2n_1 + 2n_2$ allopolyploid progeny, which are in turn fertile also. This kind of allopolyploid is sometimes called an amphidiploid. (Unfortunately for Karpechenko, his amphidiploid had the roots of a cabbage and the leaves of a radish.)

If the allopolyploid is crossed to either parent species, sterile offspring result. In the case of the cross to radish, these offspring would be $2n_1 + n_2$, constituted from an $n_1 + n_2$ gamete from the allopolyploid, and an n_1 gamete from the radish. Obviously, the n_2 chromosomes will have no pairing partners, so sterility will result. Consequently, Karpechenko had effectively created a new species, with no possibility of gene exchange with its parents. He called his new species *Raphanobrassica*.

Nowadays, allopolyploids are routinely synthesized as a major tool in plant breeding. The goal obviously is to combine some of the worthwhile features of both parental species into one type. This kind of endeavor is very uncertain, as Karpechenko found out. In fact, only one amphidiploid has ever been intentionally produced that is of potentially widespread use. This is *Triticale*, an amphidiploid between wheat (*Triticum, 2n = 6x = 42*) and rye (*Secale*, 2n = 2x = 14). *Tricale* combines the high yields of wheat with the ruggedness of rye. A massive international *Triticale* testing program is now under way, and many breeders have great hopes for the future of this artificial amphidiploid.

In mature, allopolyploidy seems to have been a major force in speciation of plants. There are many different examples. One particularly satisfying one is shown by the genus *Brassica*. Here three different parent species have been hybridized in all possible pair combinations to form new amphidiploid species. This has all taken place in nature, but *Brassica* amphidiploids also have been artificially synthesized.

A particularly interesting natural allopolyploid is bread wheat, *Triticum aestivum* (2n = 6x = 42). By a study of various wild relatives, it has been possible to reconstruct a probable evolutionary history of breat wheat. In a wheat meiosis, there are always 21 pairs of chromosomes. Furthermore, it has been possible to establish that any given chromosome has only one specific pairing partner (homologous pairing)—not five other potential ones (homologous pairing). The suppression of such homeologous pairing (which would lead to much reduced stability of the species) is maintained by a gene *Ph* ensures a diploid-like genetics for this basically hexaploid species. Without *Ph*, bread wheat could probably never have arisen. It is interesting to speculate on whether Western civilization could have arisen or progressed without this species—in other words, without *Ph*.

Somatic Allopolyploids from Cell Hybridization

Another innovative approach to plant breeding is to try to make allopolyploid-like hybrids by asexual methods. Theoretically, such a technique would permit combination of widely differing parental species. The technique does indeed work, but so far the only allopolyploids that have been produced are those that can also be made by the sexual methods we have considered already. The procedure is as follows. Cell suspensions of the two parental species are prepared and stripped of their cell walls by special enzyme treatments. The stripped cells are called *protoplasts*. The two suspensions (protoplast suspensions) are combined with polyethylene glycol, which enhances protoplast fusion. The parental cells and the fused cells will proliferate to form colonies (in much the same way as microbes) on agar medium. If these colonies, or calluses, are examined, a fair percentage of them are found to be allopolyploid-like hybrids with chromosome number equal to the sum of the parental types. Thus, not only do the protoplast cell membranes fuse to form a kind of heterokaryon, but the nuclei fuse too.

A good example of an allopolyploid-like hybrid is commercial tobacco, *Nicotiana tabacum*, which has 48 chromosomes. This species of tobacco was originally found in nature as a spontaneously occurring amphidiploid. The two probable parents are N. Sylves and N. Tomentosiformis, each of which has 24 chromosomes. A sexual cross between N. Tabacum and either of the other two gives a 36-chromosome hybrid n which there are 12 chromosome pairs plus 12 unpaired chromosomes. A cross between N. Sylvestris and N. Tomentosiformis gives a 24-chromosome hybrid n which there is no pairing at all. Hence, it appears that part of the N. Tabacum genome is from N. Sylvestris and part from N. Tomentosiformis. This amphidiploid can be re-created either sexually, by processing involving colchicine as described previously, or somatically by cell fusion. When cells or the prospective parental species are fused, a 48-chromosome hybrid cell line is produced from which may be grown plants whose behaviour is identical to that of N. Tabacum. (Note that in the latter method, colchicine is not required, since the fusion product is already amphidiploid.) The recovery of somatic hybrids may be enhanced if a selective system is available. For example, two different monoploid lines of *N. Tabacum* had light-sensitive yellowish and light-resistant, as a result of complementation between the parental genotypes. The calluses can be grown into plantlets, which then either are grafted onto a mature plant to develop or are themselves potted.

Application of Polyploidy

Among the cultivated varieties of wheat, three different chromosome numbers are represented: 14, 28, and 42 (x = 7). For example, the primitive small-grained einkorn type of Europe and Asia, Triticum monococcum, has 14 chromosomes in its vegetative cells. Its yield is low and it is of comparatively little value. An emmer wheat (durum), T. dicoccum, grown chiefly in southern Europe but also in the United States, has 28 chromosomes. It has thick heads with large hard kernels and issued mainly for macaroni, spaghetti, and stock feed. The bread wheats, T. aestivum, with 42 chromosomes, were postulated by J. Percival in England to have come from a cross between emmer wheat and goat grass (Aegilops), both of which are native to the Babylonian region where bread wheat originated.

When techniques for artificial chromosome doubling became established, investigations of the origin of bread wheat confirmed

Percival's theory. Experimental evidence obtained by E. S. McFadden and E. R. Sears and separately by H. Kihara traced the pathway for the origin of one type of bread wheat, T. Spelta.

Aegilops squarrosa (n = 7) was found to carry a group of major characteristics that distinguish the hexaploid (n=21) T. Spelta from the tetraploids (n = 1) T. dicoccum and T. dicoccoides. Hybrids between these tetraploid species of wheat and A. squarrosa proved to have all of the major taxonomic characters of T. spelta but the hybrids were completely or nearly sterile. When the F_1 hybrids of T. dicoccoides × A. squarrosa were treated with colchicine, highly fertile allopolyploids with 42 chromosomes were obtained. These synthetic hexaploids closely resembled the cultivated. T. spelta, and they produced highly fertile hybrids with that species and with T. vulgare, known to be in the ancestry of the bread wheats. This demonstrated that the genome of the hexaploid wheats corresponded to one chromosome set of A. squarrosa. It was postulated that T. spelta is the ancestral hexaploid wheat of Europe, having arisen, possibly in fairly recent times, in southeastern Europe or southwestern Asia following chromosome doubling of natural hybrids of T. dicoccoides (or its cultivated close relative, T. dicoccum) × A. squarrosa. T. spelta is believed to have been carried over the northerly route into central and western Europe. Experiments of McFadden, Sears, and Kihara reconstructed the pathway through which a moderately useful wheat and a goat grass hybridized in nature and produced forerunners of a most valuable crop, bread wheat.

New World Cotton

Crosses can be made between distinct species of cotton, members of the benes Gossypium. The hybrids show a wide range of vigor and fertility, making the material favourable for studies of origins. Three cytological groups have been found to correspond with the major world distributional areas. Old World cotton had 13 pairs of large chromosomes. American cotton, which originated in Central or South America, has 13 pairs of small chromosomes. New world cotton (the cultivated long-staple type) has 26 pairs, 13 large and 13 small. Evidently, hybridization and chromosome duplication occurred somewhere in the ancestry of the New World Cotton.

J. O. Beasley used the colchicine technique and succeeding in doubling the chromosomes of a hybrid between the Old World and American cotton. The resulting hybrids, with four set of chromosomes (amphidiploids), crossed readily among themselves and produced fertile plants resembling New World cotton. The process by which the valuable polyploid cotton may have originated in nature was thus duplicated in the laboratory.

Primrose Hybridization

The primrose, Primula kewensis, is an allotetraploid with 36 (2n) chromosomes. It was derived from a cross between two diploids, P. floribunda (x= 9) and P. verticillata (x= 9). Plants from these two species crossed readily, producing hybrids with 18 chromosomes in their vegetative cells. 9 from P. floribunda and 9 from P. verticillata, but the hybrids were sterile. Eventually, however, a branch on a hybrid plant developed from a cell in which the chromosome number was doubled (36), so that each chromosome had a homologous partner. This branch was propagated and gave rise to a fertile primrose plant with cells containing 36 chromosomes of the two diploid parents, the sterile diploid hybrid, and the fertile allotetraploid are shown.

Tobacco Resistance

Induced polyploidy has been exploited to a great extent. Practical applications may become more common as additional data are accumulated. By artificially induced polyploidy, disease resistance and other desirable qualities have been incorporated into some commercial crop plants. Tobacco, Nicotiana tabacum, for example, is susceptible to the tobacco mosaic virus (TMV), whereas N. glutinosa appeared at first observation to be resistant. Further investigation, however, showed that in N. glutinosa the virus killed the cells that were invaded and the virus particles became isolated in the dead cell. The apparent resistance thus was attributable to hypersensitivity. When the two tobacco species were crossed, the hybrid was found to be "resistant" to the virus, but totally sterile. When the chromosomes were doubled, it was possible to secure a fertile polyploid "resistant" to the virus.

Polyploid Fruits, Flowers, and Wheat

Some varieties of plants that serve human needs more effectively than others have now been identified as polyploids. Many polyploids were selected and cultivated because of their large size, vigor, and ornamental values, before their chromosome numbers were known. Giant "sports" from twings of McIntosh apple trees that were found to be tetraploid (4n) were propagated into whole trees, which produce extra-large fruit. The texture of the giant apples is as fine as that of diploids, but the yield is inferior. Mass selection of seedlings may overcome this difficulty. Bartlett pears, several varieties of grapes, and cranberries have also produced sports with giant fruits. Some of these show promise of practical usefulness. With colchicine treatment, a number of polyploids have been developed artificially. This technique has provided a way to explore the mechanism involved in polyploid formation and to make use of the good qualities of polyploids. Tetraploid (4n) maize is more vigorous than the ordinary diploid and produces some 20 percent more vitamin A. Its fertility is somewhat reduced, but this drawback responds to selection. Polyploid watermelons have been developed from colchicine treatment by Kihara and others. The tetraploid with 44 chromosomes is large and has practical value. Triploid watermelons with 33 chromosomes are especially desirable because they are sterile and have no seeds. Among the flower garden varieties, 4n marigolds and snapdragons are widely cultivated.

Polyploid plants respond to artificial selection and hybridization, as do diploid species. The recent history of plant breeding has been characterized by a marked improvement in many polyploid plant crops. The yield of wheat, for example, has increased appreciably. This has been accomplished by developing disease-resistant strains and breeding for increased hardiness and greater efficiency so that crops may survive under the various environmental conditions found in wheat-growing areas. A constant threat to the wheat crop is rust—a fungus that attacks the stems and leaves of the growing plants and destroys the ripening grain. Spores are borne by wind and, when conditions are right, they spread like fire through wheat fields. The disease can be combated by developing rust-resistant strains and by eradicating barberry bushes, which are hosts to the spores during the spring months. But new varieties of rust that destroy previously resistant grain keep evolving, thus perpetuating the job of plant breeders. The larger kernels at the left are from a new strain of rust-resistant spring wheat. At the right are shown kernels of wheat, similar in other respects but not resistant, that are dwarfed from infection with stem rust. The number of kernels of grain per plant as well as the size of the kernels is decreased by rust infection. Investigators in agricultural experiment stations are constantly alert for new rusts. When a new one is found, the standard wheat varieties are tested against it. If they are not resistant, breeding programs are initiated immediately to develop new strains resistant to that particular rust.

Chromosome Anomalies in Spontaneous Abortions in Humans

A wide variety of chromosome numbers and chromosome structural aberrations is found in spontaneoulsy aborted human fetuses. The types of aberrations found vary according to differences in the age of the fetus at the time of abortion. For example, 40 percent of spontaneously aborted fetuses under 90 days of gestational age (i.e., length of time since the last menstrual period of the mother) exhibit chromosome anomalies. For 91-to 120-day-old fetuses, 25 percent show chromosomal anomalies, and only 5 percent of fetuses over 120 days old exhibit chromosome anomalies. Thus, chromosomal anomalies cause most fetuses to die and be aborted in early developmental stages.

Before the percentage of spontaneous abortions resulting from chromosomal anomalies can be calculated, one must first define what constitutes an aborted fetus. Apparently a large number of conceptions occur in humans, and the rechronic myelogenous leukemia possess two cell lines; one cell line has a normal chromosome complement, whereas the other appears to be missing the long arm of chromosome 2. This condition was originally thought to be a monosomy; however, using band staining techniques to identify the long arm, it was learned that the long arm was translocated to one of the larger chromosomes, usually chromosome 9 (referred to as the Philadelphia chromosome). The role of this chromosomal aberration in the induction, development, and progression of cancer is unknown.

Inherited autosomal recessive disorders, such as Bloom's syndrome, Fanconi's anemia, ataxia-telangiectasia, and xeroderma pigmentosum, have been associated with chromosomal instability and or deficiency in mutation repair mechanisms that result in chromosomal aberrations. These individuals have a high incidence of cancer.

8

LINKAGE AND GENETIC MAPPING IN EUKARYOTES

According to Mendel, we expect that two different genes will segregate and independently assort themselves during gamete formation. After Mendel's work was re-discovered at the turn of the 20th century, chromosomes were identified as the cellular structures that carry genes. The chromosome theory of inheritance explained how the transmission of chromosomes is responsible for the passage of genes from parent to offspring.

When geneticists first realized that chromosomes contain the genetic material, they began to suspect that a conflict may sometimes occur between Mendel's law of independent assortment of genes and the behaviour of chromosomes during meiosis. In particular, geneticists assumed that each species of organism must contain thousands of different genes, yet cytological studies revealed that most species have at most a few dozen chromosomes. Therefore, it seemed likely (and turned out to be true) that each chromosome would carry many hundreds or even thousands of different genes. In 1911, Thomas Hunt Morgan conducted experiments showing that the transmission of genes located on the same chromosome violates the law of independent assortment.

In this chapter, we will consider the pattern of inheritance that occurs when different genes are situated on the same chromosome. We will also explore how the data from genetic crosses used to construct genetic maps that describe the order of genes along a chromosome. This chapter ends with a discussion of the eukaryotic microorganisms collectively known as fungi. This group includes yeast, such as *Saccharomyces cerevisiae* (baker's yeast), and molds, such as *Neurospora crassa* (red bread mold) and *Aspergillus nidulans* (green bread mold). We will consider the unique features of sexual reproduction that occur in certain fungal species. These features have provided the basis for distinctive genetic mapping approaches.

LINKAGE AND CROSSING OVER

In eukaryotic species, each linear chromosome contains a very long piece of DNA. As we have mentioned, a chromosome contains many individual functional units—called genes—that influence an organism's traits. A typical chromosome is expected to contain many hundreds or perhaps a few thousand different genes. The term *linkage* refers to the phenomenon that two or more genes can be located on the same chromosome. The genes are physically linked to each other, because each eukaryotic chromosome contains a single, continuous, linear piece of DNA.

As an example of linkage, let's consider a human karyotype that contains 46 chromosomes .All of the genes on each chromosome are linked to each other. Chromosomes thus are sometimes called *linkage groups*, because a chromosome contains a group of genes that are linked together. In a particular Species, there are as many linkage groups as there are types of chromosomes. For example, humans have 46 chromosomes, which are composed of 22 types of autosomes that come in pairs and one pair of sex chromosomes. There are two types of sex chromosomes, the X and Y. Therefore, humans have 22 autosomal link age groups, an X-chromosome linkage group, and a Y-chromosome linkage group.

Geneticists are often interested in the transmission of two or more traits in a genetic cross. 'When a geneticist follows two traits in a cross, this is called a *dihybrid cross*; when three traits are followed, it is a *trihybrid cross*; and so forth. The outcomes of dihybrid and trihybrid crosses depend on whether or not the genes are linked to each other along the same chromosome. In this section, we will examine how linkage affects the transmission patterns of two or more traits.

Crossing Over may Occur During the Tetrad Stage of Meiosis; When it Does, It Produces Recombinant Chromosomes and Ultimately Recombinant Phenotypes

Even though the alleles for different genes may be linked along the same chromo some, the linkage can be altered during the process of gamete formation. In diploid eukaryotic species, homologous chromosomes can exchange pieces with each other by crossing over. This event occurs frequently during prophase I of meiosis. The replicated chromosomes, known as sister chromatids, associate with the homologous sister chromatids to form a structure known as a *bivalent* or a *tetrad.* A tetrad is composed of two pairs of sister chromatids. In prophase I, a sister chromatid of one pair commonly will cross over with a sister chromatid from the homologous pair.

One of the parental chromosomes carries the *A* and *B* alleles, while the homologue carries the *a* and *b* alleles. Therefore, the gametes contain the same combination of alleles as the original chromosomes. In this case, two gametes carry the *A* and *B* alleles, and the other two gametes carry the recessive *a* and *b* alleles. The arrangement of linked alleles has not been altered.

In contrast, what can happen when crossing over occurs. Two of the gametes contain combinations of alleles (namely, *A* and *b*, *a* and *B*) that differ from those in the original chromosomes. In these two gametes, the grouping of linked alleles has been changed. An event such as this, leading to a new combination of alleles, is known as *genetic recombination*. The gametes carrying the *A* and *b*, or the *a* and *B*, alleles are called *non-parental* or *recombinant* gametes. Like wise, if these gametes participate in fertilization, the resulting offspring are called non-parental or recombinant offspring. These offspring can display combinations of traits that are different from those of either parent. In contrast, offspring that have inherited the same combination of alleles as their parents are known as *parental* or *non-recombinant* offspring.

Bateson and Punnett Discovered Two Traits that did not Assort Independently

The earliest study indicating that some traits may not assort independently was carried out by William Bateson and Reginald Punnett in 1905. As mentioned already, they were interested in the pattern of inheritance of genes in several organisms, including the chicken and the sweet pea. According to Mendel's law of in dependent assortment, a dihybrid cross between two individuals, heterozygous for two genes, should yield a 9:3:3:1 phenotypic ratio among the offspring. However, a surprising result occurred when Bateson and Punnett conducted a cross in the sweet pea involving two different traits, flower colour and pollen shape.

As seen here, they began by crossing a true-breeding strain with purple flowers (*PP*) and long pollen (*LL*) to a strain with red flowers (*pp*) and round pollen (*ll*). This yielded an F generation of plants that all had purple flowers and long pollen (*PpL1*). The unexpected result came from the F_2 generation. Even though there were four different phenotypic categories among the F_2 generation, the observed numbers of offspring did not conform to a 9:3:3:1 ratio. Bateson and Punnett found that the F_2 generation had a much greater proportion of the two parental types: purple flowers with long pollen, and red flowers with round pollen. Therefore, they suggested that the transmission of these two traits from the parental generation to the F_2 generation was somehow coupled and not easily assorted in an independent manner. However, Bateson and Punnett did not realize that this coupling was due to the linkage of the flower colour gene and the pollen shape gene on the same chromosome.

Morgan Provided Evidence for the Linkage of Several X-linked Genes and Proposed that Crossing Over between X-chromosomes can Occur

The first direct evidence that different genes can be physically located on the same chromosome came from the studies of Thomas Hunt Morgan. The earlier studies provided the groundwork to demonstrate that the genes governing X linked traits are physically linked on the X-chromosome.

Morgan investigated the inheritance pattern of many different traits that had been shown to follow an X-linked pattern of inheritance. His parental crosses were normal male fruit flies to females that had yellow bodies (*yy*), white eyes (*ww*), and miniature wings (*mm*). The wild-type alleles for these three genes are designated y^+ (gray body), w^+ (red eyes), and m^+ (normal wings). As expected, the phenotypes of the F_1 generation were wild-type females and males with yellow bodies, white eyes, and miniature wings. The linkage of these genes was revealed when the F_1 flies were mated to each other and the F_2, generation examined.

Instead of equal proportions of the eight possible phenotypes, Morgan ob served a much higher proportion of the parental combinations of traits. There were 758 flies with gray bodies, red eyes, and normal wings, and 700 flies with yellow bodies, white eyes, and miniature wings. The former combination (gray body, red eyes, and normal wings) was found in the males of the parental generation, the latter combination (yellow body, white eyes, and miniature wings) in the females of the parental generation. Morgan's proposed explanation for this higher proportion of parental combinations was that all three genes are located on the X-chromosome and, therefore, tend to be transmitted together as a unit.

However, to fully account for the data, Morgan needed to interpret two other key observations. First, he needed to explain why a significant proportion of the F_2 generation had non-parental combinations of alleles. Along with the two parental phenotypes, there were six other phenotypic combinations that were not found in the parental generation. Second, he needed to explain why there was a quantitative difference between non-parental combinations involving body colour and eye colour versus eye colour and wing length. This quantitative difference is revealed by reorganizing the data from Morgan's cross by pairs of genes:

	Total	
Gray body, red eyes	1159	
Yellow body, white eyes	1017	
Gray body, white eyes	17	Nonparental offspring
Yellow body, red eyes	12	
	2205	

	Total	
Red eyes, normal wings	770	
White-eyes, miniature wings	716	
Red eyes, miniature wings	401	Non-parental offspring
White-eyes, normal wings	318	
	2205	

We see that there were substantial differences between the numbers of non-parental offspring when pairs of genes were considered separately. It was fairly common for non-parental combinations to occur when just eye colour and wing shape were examined (401 + 318 non-parental offspring). In sharp contrast, it was rare to obtain non-parental combinations when looking at body colour and eye colour (17 + 12 non-parental offspring).

To explain these data, Morgan considered the previous studies of the French cytologist, F.A. Janssens. In 1909, Janssens proposed that crossing over involves a with his data. Overall, he made three important hypotheses to explain his results:

1. The genes for body colour, eye colour, and wing length are all located on the same chromosome (the X-chromosome), Therefore, it is most likely for all three traits to be inherited together.

2. Due to crossing over, the homologous X-chromosomes (in the female) can exchange pieces of chromosomes and create new (non-parental) combinations of alleles.
3. The likelihood of crossing over depends on the distance between two genes. If two genes are far apart from each other, it is more likely that crossing over will occur between them.

With these ideas in mind, the possible events that occurred in the F_1 female flies of Morgan's experiment. One of the X-chromosomes contained all three dominant alleles, the other all three recessive alleles. During oogenesis in the F_1 female flies, crossing over may or may not have occurred in this region of the X-chromosome. If no crossing over occurred, the parental phenotypes were produced in the F_2 offspring. Alternatively, a crossover sometimes occurred between the eye-colour gene and the wing-length gene to create non-parental offspring (namely, gray body, red eyes, and miniature wings; or yellow body, white eyes, and normal wings). According to Morgan's proposal, this is a fairly likely event, because these two genes are far apart from each other on the X-chromosome. Because of the long distance, it was fairly likely for a crossover to occur in this region. In contrast, he proposed that the body colour and eye colour genes are very close together, which makes crossing over between them an unlikely event. Nevertheless, it occasionally occurred, yielding off spring with gray bodies, white eyes, and miniature wings, or with yellow bodies, red eyes, and normal wings. Finally, it was also possible for two homologous chromosomes to cross over twice. This double crossing over is expected to be a very unlikely event. Among the 2205 offspring Morgan examined, he only found 1 fly (gray body, white eyes, normal wings) that could be explained by this phenomenon.

Chi Square Analysis can be Used to Distinguish between Linkage and Independent Assortment

Now that we have an appreciation for linkage and the production of recombinant offspring, let's consider how an experimenter can objectively decide whether two genes are linked or assort independently. Chi square analysis was introduced to evaluate the goodness of fit between a genetic hypothesis and ob served experimental data, This method is frequently used to determine if the outcome of a dihybrid cross is consistent with linkage or independent assortment.

To conduct a chi square analysis, we must first propose a hypothesis. In a dihybrid cross, the standard hypothesis is that the two genes are not linked. This hypothesis is chosen even if the observed

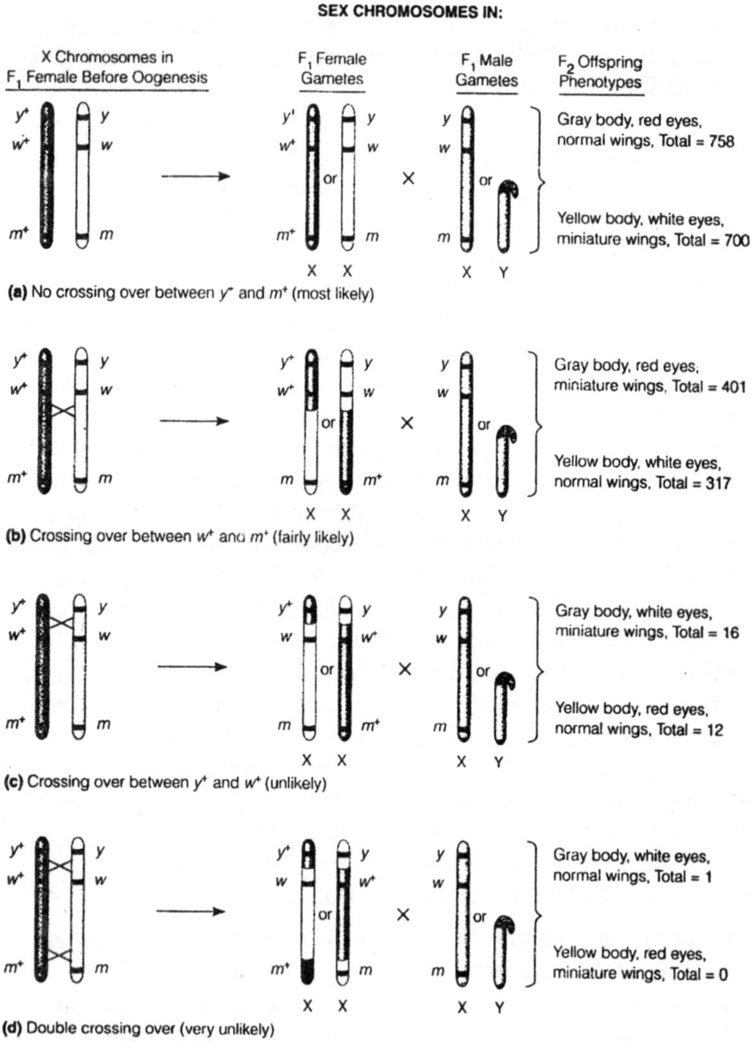

SEX CHROMOSOMES IN:

X Chromosomes in F_1 Female Before Oogenesis | F_1 Female Gametes | F_1 Male Gametes | F_2 Offspring Phenotypes

Gray body, red eyes, normal wings, Total = 758

Yellow body, white eyes, miniature wings, Total = 700

(a) No crossing over between y^+ and m^+ (most likely)

Gray body, red eyes, miniature wings, Total = 401

Yellow body, white eyes, normal wings, Total = 317

(b) Crossing over between w^+ and m^+ (fairly likely)

Gray body, white eyes, miniature wings, Total = 16

Yellow body, red eyes, normal wings, Total = 12

(c) Crossing over between y^+ and w^+ (unlikely)

Gray body, white eyes, normal wings, Total = 1

Yellow body, red eyes, miniature wings, Total = 0

(d) Double crossing over (very unlikely)

Fig. 8.1. The likelihood of crossing over provides an explanation of Morgan's trihybrid cross.

data suggest linkage, because an independent assortment hypothesis allows us to calculate the expected number of offspring based on the genotypes of the parents and the law of independent assortment. In contrast, for two linked genes that have not been previously mapped, we cannot calculate the expected number of offspring from a genetic cross, because we do not know how likely it is for a crossover to occur between the two genes. Without expected numbers of recombinant and parental offspring, we cannot use a chi square test. Therefore, we begin with the hypothesis that the genes are not linked; then, we determine whether or not our data fit this hypothesis. If the chi square value is low and we cannot reject our hypothesis, we infer that the genes assort independently. On the other hand, if the chi square value is so high that our hypothesis is rejected, we will conclude that a linkage hypothesis is correct.

As an example, let's consider the data shown on page 104 concerning body colour and eye colour. This cross produced the following offspring: 1159 gray body, red eyes; 1017 yellow body, white eyes; 17 gray body, white eyes; and 12 yellow body, red eyes. However, when a heterozygous female ($y^+y\ w^+w$) is crossed to a hemizygous male (ywY), an independent assortment hypothesis predicts the following outcome:

	F$_1$ male gametes →	X^{yw}	Y	
F$_1$ female gametes	$X^{y^+w^+}$	$X^{yw}X^{y^+w^+}$	$X^{y^+w^+}Y$	= Gray body, red eyes
	X^{y^+w}	$X^{yw}X^{y^+w}$	$X^{y^+w}Y$	= Gray body, white eyes
	X^{yw^+}	$X^{yw}X^{yw^+}$	$X^{yw^+}Y$	= Yellow body, red eyes
	X^{yw}	$X^{yw}X^{yw}$	$X^{yw}Y$	= Yellow body, white eyes

The independent assortment hypothesis predicts a 1:1:1:1 ratio among the four phenotypes. The observed data mentioned above obviously seem to conflict with this hypothesis. Nevertheless, we stick to the strategy just discussed. First, we pro pose that the two genes are not linked, and then we use a chi square analysis to see if the data fit this hypothesis. If the data do not fit, we will reject the idea that the genes assort independently and conclude that the genes are linked.

An example of a chi square approach to determine linkage is shown here:

Step 1. *Propose a hypothesis*. Even though the observed data appear inconsistent with this hypothesis, we propose that the two genes for eye colour and body colour are X-linked but somehow are able to obey Mendel's law of independent assortment. This hypothesis will allow us to calculate expected values. We actually anticipate that the chi square analysis will allow us to reject the independent assortment hypothesis in favour of a linkage hypothesis.

Step 2. *Based on the hypothesis, calculate the expected values of each of the four phenotypes.* Each phenotype has an equal probability of occurring. Therefore, the probability of each genotype is 1/4. The observed F_2 generation contained a total of 2205 individuals. Our next step is to calculate the expected numbers of offspring with each phenotype when the total equals 2205; 1/4 of the offspring should be each of the four phenotypes:

1/4 × 2205 = 551 (expected number of each phenotype)

Step 3. *Apply the chi square formula, using the data for the observed values (0) and the expected values (E) that have been calculated in step 2.* In this case, there are four categories within the population:

$$\chi^2 = \frac{(O_1 - E_1)^2}{E_1} + \frac{(O_2 - E_2)^2}{E_2} + \frac{(O_3 + E_3)^2}{E_3} + \frac{(O_4 - E_4)^2}{E_4}$$

$$= \frac{(1159 - 551)^2}{551} + \frac{(17 - 551)^2}{551} + \frac{(12 - 551)^2}{551} + \frac{(1017 - 551)^2}{551}$$

$$= 670.9 + 517.5 + 527.3 + 394.1$$

$$= 2109.8$$

Step 4. *Interpret the calculated chi square value.* This is done with a chi square. Since there are four experimental categories (n = 4), the degrees of freedom is $n - 1 = 3$.

The calculated chi square value is enormous! Thus, the deviation between served and expected values is very large. Such a large deviation is expected to occur by chance alone less than 1% of time. Therefore, we reject the hypothesis that the two genes assort independently. In other words, we conclude that the genes are linked.

Creighton and McClintock Correlated Crossing Over that Produced new Combinations of Alleles with the Exchange of Homologous Chromosomes

As we have seen, Morgan's studies were consistent with the hypothesis that crossing over occurs between homologous chromosomes to produce new combination of alleles. In the experiment described here, which was published two years after the work of Morgan, Harriet Creighton and Barbara McClintock an interesting strategy involving parallel observations. First, they made crosses involving two linked genes to produce parental and recombinant offspring. Second, they used a microscope to view the structures of the chromosomes in the par and in the offspring. Because the parental chromosomes had some unusual structural features, they could microscopically distinguish the two homologous chromosomes within a pair. As we will see, this enabled them to correlate the occurrence of recombinant offspring with microscopically observable exchanges in segment of homologous chromosomes.

While working in the botany department at Cornell University, Creighton and McClintock focused much of their attention on the pattern of inheritance traits in corn. In previous cytological examinations of corn chromosomes, some strains were found to have an unusual chromosome (#9) with a darkly stair knob at one end. McClintock also identified an abnormal version of this chromosome that had an extra piece of a different chromosome (#8) at the other (called an *interchange* or a *translocation*). As, this unusual version of chromosome 9 had changes at both ends that could be distinguish under the microscope.

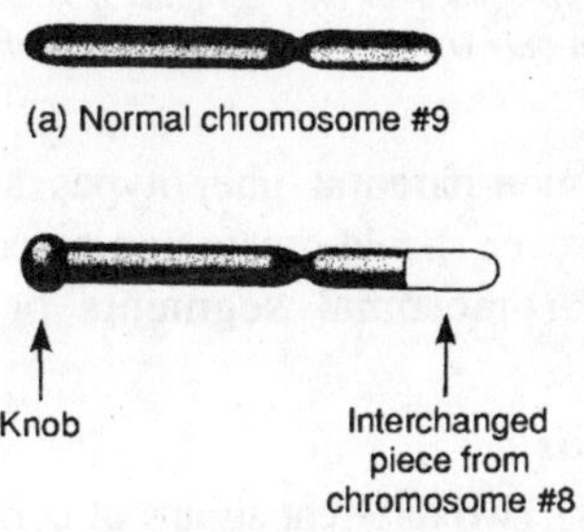

Fig. 8.2. Normal and abnormal chromosome 9 in corn used by Creghton and McClintock. A normal chromosome 9 (a) is compared with an abnormal chromosome 9 (b) that contains a knob at one end and a translocation at the opposite end.

Creighton and McClintock insightfully realized that this abnormal chromosome could be used to demonstrate that two homologous chromosomes physically exchange segments as a result of crossing over. They knew that a gene located near the knobbed end of chromosome 9 that provided colour to corn kernels. It existed in two alleles, the dominant allele *C* (coloured) and the recessive allele c (colourless). Toward the other end of the chromosome was located a second gene that affected the texture of the kernel endosperm. The dominant allele *Wx* caused starchy endosperm, while the recessive *wx* allele caused waxy endosperm Creighton and McClintock reasoned that a crossover involving a normal chromosome 9 and a knobbed/ translocated chromosome 9 would produce a chromosome that had either a knob or a translocation but not both. This chromosome would be distinctly different from either of the parental chromosomes

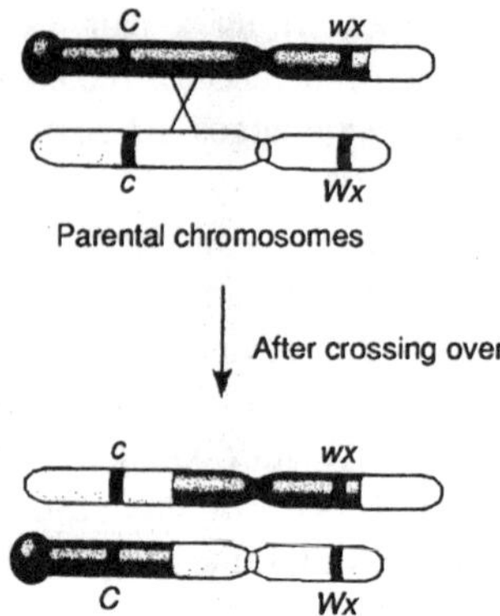

Fig. 8.3. Crossing over between normal and abnormal chromosome 9s in corn. A crossover produces a chromosome that only contains a knob at one end, and another chromosome that only contains a translocation at the other end.

Hypothesis

Offspring with non-parental phenotypes are the product of a crossover. This crossover should create non-parental chromosomes via an exchange of chromosomal segments between homologous chromosomes.

Testing the hypothesis

Starting materials: Two different strains of corn. One strain (referred to as parent A) has an abnormal #9 (knobbed/translocation) with a dominant *C* allele and a recessive *wx* allele. It also contains a cytologically normal copy of chromosome #9 that carries the recessive c allele, and the dominant *Wx* allele. Its genotype is *Cc Wxwx*. The other strain (referred to as parent B) has two normal versions of chromosome #9. The genotype of this strain is *cc Wxwx*.

1. Cross the two strains described. The tassel is the pollen-bearing structure and the silk (equivalent to the stigma and style) is connected to the ovary. After fertilization, the ovary will develop into an ear of corn.
2. Observe the kernels from this cross.
3. Microscopically examine chromosome #9 in the kernels.

Interpreting the data

In interpreting these results, we must note that Creighton and McClintock did not carry out this experiment like a standard cross, because neither of the parents were homozygous recessive for both genes. This adds some ambiguity in the relationship between the phenotypic categories and genetic recombination. In this experiment, we are interested in whether or not crossing over has occurred in parent A, which is heterozygous for both genes. This parent can produce four types of gametes, while parent B can only produce two types of gametes:

Parent A	*Parent B*
C wx (non-recombinant)	*c Wx*
c Wx (non-recombinant)	*c wx*
C Wx (recombinant)	
c wx (recombinant)	

The following types of offspring can be produced:

	c Wx	*c wx*	
C Wx	*CcWxwx* coloured/starchy	*Ccwxwx* coloured/way	Nonrecombinant
C Wx	*CcWxwx* coloured/starchy	*ccWxwx* coloured/way	Nonrecombinant
C Wx	*CcWxWx* coloured/starchy	*CcWxwx* coloured/starchy	Recombinant
c wx	*ccWxwx* coloured/starchy	*ccwxwx* coloured/way	Recombinant

Two cf the phenotypic categories are ambiguous: coloured/starchy (*Cc Wxwx*) and colourless/starchy (*cc WxWx*). These phenotypes can be produced whether or not recombination occurs in parent A. Therefore, let's begin by considering the two unambiguous phenotypic categories: coloured/waxy (*Cc wxwx*) and colour less/waxy (cc wxwx). The coloured/waxy phenotype can occur only if recombination did not occur in parent A and if parent A passed the knobbed/ translocated chromosome to its offspring. As shown in the data table, three kernels were obtained with this phenotype, and all of them contained the knobbed/translocated chromosome. By comparison, the colourless/waxy phenotype can only be obtained if gen^tic recombination did occur in parent A and this parent passed a chromosome 9 that had a translocation but was knobless. Two kernels were obtained with this phenotype, and both of them contained the expected chromosome that had a translocation but was knobless.

Taken together, these results show a perfect correlation between genetic re combination of alleles and the cytological presence of a chromosome displaying a genetic exchange of chromosomal pieces in parent A. The other two phenotypic categories are ambiguous, because either a colourless/starchy or a coloured/starchy phenotype can be produced in the presence or the absence of genetic recombination in parent A. Nevertheless, the results agree with the hypothesis that genetic re combination is correlated with an exchange of chromosome pieces.

Overall, the observations described in this experiment are consistent with the idea that a crossover occurred, in the region between the *C* and *wx* genes, involving an exchange of segments between two homologous chromosomes. As stated by the authors, "Pairing chromosomes, heteromorphic in two regions, have been shown to exchange parts at the same time they exchange genes assigned to these regions." These results support the view that genetic recombination involves a physical exchange between homologous chromosomes. This microscopic evidence helped to convince geneticists that recombinant offspring arise from the physical exchange of segments of homologous chromosomes.

Crossing Over Occasionally Occurs During Mitosis

In multicellular organisms, the union of egg and sperm is followed by many cellular divisions, which occur in conjunction with mitotic divisions of the cell nuclei. Mitosis normally does not invoke the homologous pairing of chromosomes to form a tetrad. Therefore, crossing over during mitosis is expected to be much less likely than during meiosis. Nevertheless, it does occur on rare occasions. When it happens, mitotic crossing over may produce a pair of recombinant chromosomes that have a new combination of alleles. This is known as *mitotic recombination*. If it occurs during an early stage of embryonic development, the daughter cells containing the recombinant chromosomes will continue to divide many times to produce a patch of tissue in the adult. This may result in a portion of tissue with characteristics different from those of the rest of the organism.

In 1936, while working at the University of Rochester, Curt Stern proposed that unusual patches on the bodies of certain *Drosophila* strains were due to mitotic recombination, he was working with strains carrying X-linked alleles affecting body colour and bristle morphology. The recessive *y* allele confers yellow body colour, and the recessive *sn* allele confers shorter body bristles that look singed. The corresponding wild-type alleles confer gray body colour (y^+) and normal bristles (sn^+). Females that are y^+y sn^+sn are expected to have gray body colour and normal bristles. This was generally the case. However, when Stern carefully observed the bodies of these female flies under a low-power microscope, he occasionally noticed places in which two adjacent regions were different from the rest of the body. This is called a *twin spot*. He concluded that twin spotting was too frequent to be explained by the random positioning of two independent single spots that happened to occur close together. Instead, Stern proposed that twin spots were due to a single mitotic recombination within one cell during embryonic development.

As shown here, the X-chromosomes of the female fly are y^+ *sn* and *y* sn^+ Rarely, though, a crossover can occur during mitosis to produce two adjacent daughter cells that are y^+y^+ *snsn* and *yy* sn^+ sn^+. As embryonic development proceeds, the cell on the left will continue to divide to produce many cells, eventually producing a patch on the body that has gray colour with singed bristles. The daughter cell next to it will produce a patch of yellow body colour with normal bristles. These two adjacent patches (a twin spot) will be surrounded by cells that are y^+y sn^+sn and, thus, have gray colour and normal bristles. These infrequent twin spots provide evidence that mitotic recombination occasionally occurs.

Genetic Mapping in Diploid Eukaryotes

The purpose of *genetic mapping* (also known as gene mapping or chromosome mapping) is to determine the linear order of genes that are linked to each other along the same chromosome. Simplified genetic map of *Drosophila melanogaster* depicting the locations (i.e., loci) of many different genes along the individual chromosomes. As shown here, each gene has its own unique locus at a particular site within a chromosome. For example, the gene designated vg, which affects wing length, is located on chromosome 2. The gene designated *b*, which affects body colour, is found a moderate distance away on the same chromosome.

Even though it is an enormous amount of work, the construction of a genetic map is useful in many ways. First, it allows geneticists to understand the overall complexity and genetic organization of a particular species. The genetic map of a species portrays the underlying basis for the inherited traits that an organism displays. In some cases, the known locus of a gene within a genetic map can help molecular geneticists to clone that gene and thereby obtain greater information about its molecular features. In addition, genetic maps are useful from a evolutionary point of view. A comparison of the genetic maps among different species can improve our understanding of the evolutionary relationships among these species.

Along with these scientific uses, genetic maps have many practical benefits. For example, many human genes that play a role in human

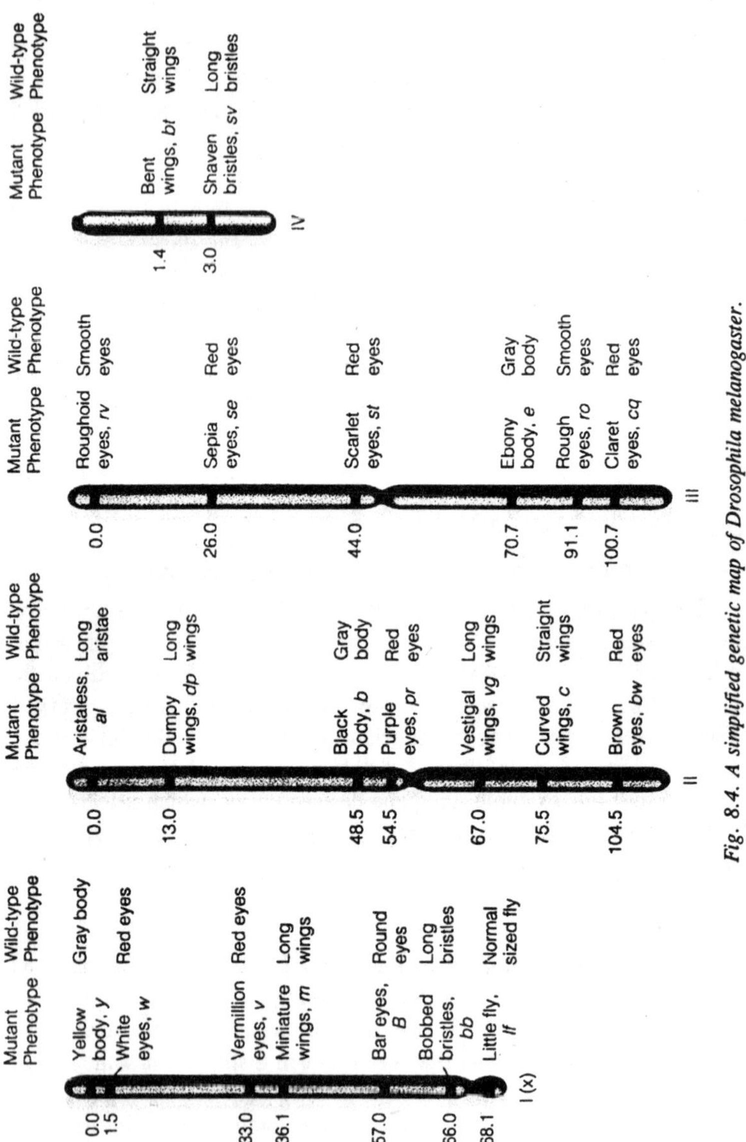

Fig. 8.4. A simplified genetic map of Drosophila melanogaster.

disease have been genetically mapped. This information can be used to diagnose and perhaps someday to treat inherited human diseases. It can also help genetic counselors predict the like hood that a couple will produce children with certain inherited diseases. In addition, genetic maps are gaining increasing importance in agriculture. A genetic map can provide plant and animal breeders with helpful information for improving agriculturally important strains through selective breeding programs.

In this section, we will begin by discussing conventional mapping techniques. These methods analyze crosses involving individuals heterozygous for two or more genes. The frequency of non-parental offspring provides a way to deduce the linear order of genes along a chromosome. This linear arrangement of genes is shown in a chart known as a *genetic linkage map*. This approach is particularly useful for analyzing organisms that are easily crossed and produce a large number of offspring in a short period of time. It has successfully mapped the genes of several plant species (with an annual generation time) and certain species of animals, such as *Drosophila*. For many organisms, however, conventional mapping approaches are difficult due to long generation times or the inability to carry out crosses (e.g., humans). Fortunately, many alternative methods of gene mapping have been developed in the past few decades. Cytological and molecular approaches also can be used to map genes.

Frequency of Recombination between Two Genes can be Correlated with their Map Distance along a Chromosome

Genetic mapping allows us to estimate the relative distances between linked genes, based on the likelihood that a crossover will occur between them. If two genes are very close together on the same chromosome, a crossover is unlikely to begin in the region between them. However, if two genes are very far apart, a crossover is more likely to be initiated in this region and thereby recombine the alleles of the two genes. Experimentally, the basis for genetic mapping is that the percentage of recombinant offspring is correlated with the distance between two genes. If two genes are far apart, many recombinant offspring will be produced. However, if two genes are close together, very few recombinant offspring will be observed.

To interpret a genetic mapping experiment, the experimenter must know if the characteristics of an offspring are due to crossing over during gamete formation in a parent. This is accomplished by conducting a *test cross*. Most test crosses are between an individual who is heterozygous for two or more genes and an individual who is recessive and homozygous for these same genes. The goal of the test cross is to determine if recombination has occurred during gamete formation in the heterozygous parent. New combinations of alleles cannot occur in the other parent, who is homozygous for these genes.

A test cross provides an experimental strategy to distinguish between recombinant and non-recombinant offspring. This cross concerns two linked genes affecting bristle length and body colour in fruit flies. The recessive alleles are *s* (short bristles) and *e* (ebony body), and the dominant (wild-type) alleles are s^+ (normal bristles) and e^+ (gray body). One parent displays both recessive traits. Therefore, we know that this parent is homozygous for the recessive alleles of the two genes (i.e., *ss ee*). The other parent is heterozygous for the linked genes affecting bristle length and body colour. This parent was produced from a cross involving a true-breeding wild-type fly and a true-breeding fly with short bristles and an ebony body. Therefore, in this heterozygous parent, we know that the *s* and *e* alleles are linked on one chromosome and the corresponding s^+ and e^+ alleles are linked on the homologous chromosome.

Now let's take a look at the four possible types of offspring these parents can produce. The offspring's phenotypes are normal bristles/gray body, short bristles/ebony body, short bristles/gray body, and normal bristles/ebony body. All four types of offspring have inherited a chromosome carrying the s and e alleles from their homozygous parent (shown on the right in each pair). Focus your attention on the other chromosome. The offspring with short bristles and ebony bodies have also inherited a second chromosome carrying the *s* and *e* alleles from their other parent. This chromosome is not the product of a crossover in the heterozygous parent. The offspring with normal bristles and gray bodies have inherited a chromosome carrying the s^+ and e^+ alleles from the heterozygous parent. Again, this chromosome is not the product of a crossover.

The other two types of offspring, however, can only be produced if crossing over has occurred. Those with normal bristles and ebony bodies or short bristle and gray bodies have inherited a chromosome that is the product of a crossover during gamete formation in the heterozygous parent. As noted in, the recombinant offspring are fewer in number than are the non-recombinant offspring

The data shown at the bottom of can be used to estimate the distance between the two genes. The map distance is defined as the number of recombinant offspring divided by the total number of offspring, multiplied by 100. With the data, we can calculate the map distance between the *s* and *e* alleles using this formula:

$$\text{Map distance} = \frac{\text{Number of recombinant offspring}}{\text{Total number of offspring}} \times 100$$

$$= \frac{76 + 75}{542 + 537 + 76 + 75} \times 100$$

$$= 12.3 \text{ map units}$$

The units of distance are called *map units* (mu) or sometimes *centimorgans* (cM) in honor of Thomas Hunt Morgan. In this example, we would say that the s and e alleles are 12.3 map units apart from each other along the same chromosome.

Alfred Sturtevant Used the Frequency of Crossing Over between Two Genes to Produce the First Genetic Map in 1911

The first individual to construct a (very small) genetic map was Alfred Sturtevant, an undergraduate who spent time in the laboratory of Thomas Hunt Morgan. In 1965, more than fifty years after he constructed the first genetic map, Sturtevant wrote: In the latter part of 1911, in conversation with Morgan . . . I suddenly realized that the variations in the strength of linkage, already attributed by Morgan to differences in the spatial separation of the genes, offered the possibility of determining sequences [different genes] in the linear dimension of a chromosome. I went home and spent most of the night (to the neglect of my undergraduate homework) in producing the first chromosome map, which included the sex-linked genes, y, w, v, m, and r, in the order and approximately the relative spacing that they still appear on the standard maps.

In the experiment described here, Sturtevant considered the outcome of crosses he conducted involving six different mutant alleles that altered the phenotype of normal flies. All of these alleles were known to be recessive and X-linked. They are *y* (yellow body colour), *w* (white eye colour), *w-e* (eosin eye colour), *v* (vermilion eye colour), *m* (miniature wings), and *r* (rudimentary wings). The *w* and *w-e* alleles are alleles of the same gene. In contrast, the *v* allele (vermillion eye colour) is an allele of a different gene that also affects eye colour. The two alleles that affect wing length, *m* and *r*, are also in different genes. Therefore, Sturtevant studied the inheritance of six recessive alleles, but since *w* and *w-e* are alleles of the same gene, his genetic map only contained five genes. The corresponding wild-type alleles are y^+ (gray body), w^+ (red eyes), v^+ (red eyes), m^+ (normal wings), and r^+ (normal wings).

Hypothesis

When genes are located on the same chromosome, the distance between the genes can be estimated from the proportion of recombinant offspring. This provides a way to map the order of genes along a chromosome.

Testing the hypothesis

Starting materials: Sturtevant began with several different strains of *Drosophila* that contained the six alleles already described.

1. Cross a female that is heterozygous for two different genes to a male that is hemizygous recessive for the same two genes. In this example, cross a female that is $X^{y+w+}X^{yw}$ to a male that is $X^{yw}Y$. This strategy was employed for many dihybrid combinations of the six alleles already described.
2. Observe the outcome of the crosses.
3. Calculate the percentage of offspring that are the result of crossing over (# of non parental/total).

Data

Alleles concerned	*Number recombinant/ total number*	*Percent recombinant offspring*
y and *w/w-e*	214/21,736	1.0
y and *v*	1,464/4,551	32.2
y and *r*	115/324	35.5
y and *m*	260/693	37.5
w/w-e and *v*	471/1,584	29.7
w/w-e and *r*	2,0632/6,116	33.7
w/w-e and *m*	406/898	45.2
v and *r*	17/573	3.0
v and *m*	109/405	26.9

Interpreting the data

Let's begin by contrasting the results between particular pairs of genes. In some dihybrid crosses, the percentage of non-parental offspring was rather low. For example, dihybrid crosses involving the *y* allele and the *w* or *w-e* allele yielded 1% recombinant offspring. This result suggests that these two genes are very close together. By comparison, other dihybrid crosses showed a higher percentage of non-parental offspring. Crosses involving the *v* and *m* alleles produced 26.9% recombinant offspring. These two genes are expected to be farther apart.

To construct his map, Sturtevant began with the assumption that the map distances would be more accurate between genes that are closely linked. Therefore, his map is based on the distance between *y* and *w* (1.0), *w* and *v* (29.7), *v* and *r* (3.0), and *v* and *m* (26.9). He also considered other features of the data to deduce the order of the genes. For example, the percentage of crossovers between *w* and *r* was 33.7. The percentage of crossovers between *w* and *v* was only 29.7, suggesting that *v* is between *w* and *r*, but closer to *r*. The proximity of *v* and *r* is confirmed by the low percentage of crossovers between *v* and *r* (3.0). Sturtevant collectively considered all these data and proposed the genetic map shown here:

In this genetic map, Sturtevant began at they allele and mapped the genes from left to right. For example, the *y* and *v* alleles are 30.7 map units apart, and the *v* and *r* alleles are 3.0 (mu) apart. This study by Sturtevant was a major breakthrough, since it showed how to map the locations of genes along chromosomes by making the appropriate crosses.

If you look carefully at Sturtevant's data, you will notice that there were two observations that do not agree very well with his genetic map. The percentage of recombinant offspring for the *y* and *m* dihybrid cross was 37.5 (but the map distance is 57.6), and the crossover percentage between *w* and *m* was 45.2 (but the map distance is 56.6). As the percentage of recombinant off spring approaches a value of 50%, this value becomes a progressively more inaccurate measure of map distance. When the distance between two genes is large, the likelihood of multiple crossovers in the region between them causes the observed number of recombinant offspring to underestimate this distance. In addition, multiple crossovers set a quantitative limit on the relationship between map distance and the percentage of recombinant offspring. Even though two different genes can be on the same chromosome and more than 50 map units apart, a test cross is only expected to yield a maximum of 50% recombinant offspring.

Trihybrid Crosses can be Used to Determine the Order of and Distance between Linked Genes

Until now, we have been considering the construction of genetic maps using dihybrid test crosses to compute map distance. The data from trihybrid crosses can also yield information about map distance and gene order. In a trihybrid cross, the experimenter crosses two individuals that differ in three traits. The following experiment follows a common strategy for using trihybrid crosses to map genes. In this experiment, the parental generation consists of fruit flies that differ in body colour, eye colour, and wing shape. We must begin with true-breeding lines so that we know which alleles are initially linked to each other on the same chromosome. In this ex ample, all the dominant alleles are linked on the same chromosome.

Step 1. *Cross two true-breeding strains that differ with regard to three alleles*. In this example, we will cross a fly that has a black body (*bb*), purple eyes (*prpr*), and vestigial wings (*vgvg*) to a homozygous wild-type fly ($b^+b^+pr^+pr^+vg^+vg^+$): The goal in this step is to obtain F_1 individuals that are heterozygous for all three alleles. In the F_1 heterozygotes, all the dominant alleles are located on one chromosome, all the recessive alleles on the other homologous chromosome.

Step 2. *Perform a test cross by mating F_1 female heterozygotes to male flies that are homozygous recessive for all three alleles (bb prpr vgvg)*: During gametogenesis in the heterozygous female F_1 flies, crossing over may occur to produce new combinations of the three alleles.

Step 3. *Collect data for the F_2 generation*. There are eight possible phenotypic combinations:

Phenotype	*Number of observed offspring*
Gray body, red eyes, normal wings	411
Black body, purple eyes, vestigial wings	412
Gray body, purple eyes, vestigial wings	30
Black body, red eyes, normal wings	28
Gray body, red eyes, vestigial wings	61
Black body, purple eyes, normal wings	60
Gray body, purple eyes, normal wings	2
Black body, red eyes, vestigial wings	1

Analysis of the F_2 generation flies will allow us to map these three genes. Since the three genes exist as two alleles each, there are $2^3 = 8$ possible combinations of offspring. If these alleles assorted independently, all eight combinations would occur in equal proportions. However, we see that the proportions of the eight phenotypes are far from equal.

The genotypes of the parental generation correspond to the phenotypes gray body, red eyes, and normal wings and black body, purple eyes, and vestigial wings. In crosses involving linked genes, the parental phenotypes occur most frequently in the offspring. The remaining six phenotypes are due to crossing over.

Two of the phenotypes (namely, gray body, purple eyes, and normal wings; and black body, red eyes, and vestigial wings) arise from a double crossover between two combinations of genes. The double crossover is always expected to be the least frequent category of offspring. Also, the combination of traits in the double crossover tells us which gene is in the middle. When a chromatid undergoes a double crossover, it separates the gene in the middle from the other two genes at either end. In the double crossover categories, the recessive purple-eye allele is separated from the other two recessive alleles. When mated to a homozygous recessive fly in the test cross, this yields flies with gray bodies, purple eyes, and normal wings, or with black bodies, red eyes, and vestigial wings. This observation indicates that the gene for eye colour lies between the genes for body colour and wing shape.

Step 4. *Calculate the map distance between pairs of genes.* To do this, we must regroup the data according to pairs of genes. From the parental generation, we know that the dominant alleles are initially linked to each other, as are the recessive alleles. This allows us to group pairs of genes into parental and non-parental combinations. The parental combinations are composed of a pair of dominant or a pair of recessive genes, whereas non-parental combinations have one dominant and one recessive gene. After we have regrouped the data in this way, the map distance between two genes can be calculated:

Parental offspring	*Total*	*Non-parental offspring*	*Total*
Gray body, red eyes, (411 + 61)	472	Gray body, purple eyes, (30+2)	32
Black body, purple eyes, (412 + 60)	472	Black body, red eyes (28+1)	29
	944		61
Gray body, normal wings (411 + 1)	413	Gray bodies, vestigial (30+61)	91
Black body, vestigial wings (412 + 28)	413	Black body, normal wings (28+60)	88
	826		179
Red eyes, normal wings (411 + 28)	439	Red eyes, vestigial wings (61 + 1)	62
Purple eyes, vestigial wings (412 + 30)	442	Purple eyes, normal wings (60 + 2)	62
	881		124

Map distance between body colour and eye colour:

$$\text{Map distance} = \frac{61}{944 + 61} \times 100 = 6.1 \text{ mu}$$

Map distance between body colour and wing shape :

$$\text{Map distance} = \frac{179}{826 + 179} \times 100 = 17.8 \text{ mu}$$

Map distance between eye colour and wing shape :

$$\text{Map distance} = \frac{124}{881 + 124} \times 100 = 12.3 \text{ mu}$$

Step 5. *Construct the map*. Based on the map unit calculation, the body colour and wing shape genes are farthest apart. The eye colour gene must lie in the middle. As mentioned earlier, this order of genes is also confirmed by the pattern of traits found in the double crossovers. To construct the map, we use the distances between the genes that are closest together.

In our example, we have placed the body colour gene first and the wing shape gene last. Our data also are consistent with a map in which the wing shape gene comes first and the body colour gene comes last. In detailed genetic maps, the locations of genes are mapped relative to the centromere.

Interference can Influence the Number of Double Crossovers that Occur in a Short Region

The product rule allows us to predict the expected likelihood of a double crossover provided we know the individual probabilities of each single crossover. Let's reconsider the data of the trihybrid test cross just described to see if the frequency of double crossovers is what we would expect based on the product rule. If we multiply the likelihood of a single crossover between *b* and *pr* (6.1%) times the likelihood of a single crossover between *pr* and *vg* (12.3%), then the product rule predicts

Expected likelihood of a double crossover = 0.061 × 0.123 = 0.0075 = 0.75%

Based on a total of 1005 offspring produced,

Expected number of offspring due to a double crossover = 1005 × 0.0075 = 7.5

In other words, we would expect about 7 or 8 offspring to be produced as a result of a double crossover. The observed number of offspring was only 3 (namely, 2 with gray bodies, purple eyes, and normal wings, and 1 with a black body, red eyes, and vestigial wings).

This lower than expected value is not due to random sampling error. Instead, it is due to a common genetic phenomenon known as *positive interference*. When a crossover occurs in one region of a chromosome, it often decreases the probability that another crossover will occur nearby. In other words, the first crossover interferes with the ability to form a second crossover in the immediate vicinity. To provide interference with a quantitative value, we first calculate the *coefficient of coincidence* (C):

$$C = \frac{\text{Observed number of double crossover}}{\text{Expected number of double corssover}}$$

Interference (I) is expressed as

$$I = 1 - C$$

For the data of the trihybrid test cross, the observed number of crossovers is 3 and the expected number is 7.5, and so the coefficient of coincidence equals 3/7.5 = 0.40. In other words, only 40% of the expected number of double crossovers were actually observed. The value for interference equals 1 - 0.4 = 0.60 or 60%. This means that 60% of the expected number of crossovers were prevented from occurring. Since *I* has a positive value, this is positive interference. Rarely, the out come of a test cross yields a negative value for interference. A negative interference value suggests that a first crossover enhances the rate of a second crossover in a nearby region. Although the molecular mechanisms that cause interference are not entirely understood, most organisms regulate the number of crossovers so that very few occur per chromosome. The reasons for positive and negative interference will require further research.

GENETIC MAPPING IN HAPLOID EUKARYOTES

Before ending our discussion of genetic mapping, it is interesting to consider some pioneering studies that involved the genetic mapping of haploid organisms. It may be surprising to you that certain species of lower eukaryotes, particularly unicellular algae and fungi, which spend the greatest part of their life cycle in the haploid state, have also been used in mapping studies. The sac fungi (ascomycetes) have been particularly useful to geneticists because of their unique style of sexual reproduction. In fact, much of our earliest understanding of genetic recombination came from the genetic analyses of fungi.

Fungi may be unicellular or multicellular organisms. Fungal cells are typically haploid ($1n$) and can reproduce asexually. In addition, fungi can also reproduce sexually by the fusion of two haploid cells to create a diploid zygote (2*n*). The diploid zygote can then proceed through meiosis to produce four haploid cells, which are called *spores*. This group of four spores is known as a *tetrad* (not to be confused with a tetrad of four sister chromatids). In some species, meiosis is followed by a mitotic division to produce eight cells, known as an *octad*. The cells of a tetrad or octad are contained within a sac known as an *ascus* (plural, asci). In other words, the products of a single meiotic division are contained within one sac. This is a key feature that is useful to geneticists, and it dramatically differs from sexual reproduction in animals and plants. For example, in animals, oogenesis produces a single functional egg, and spermatogenesis occurs in the testes, where the resulting sperm become mixed with millions of other sperm.

Using a microscope, researchers can dissect asci and study the traits of each haploid spore. In this way, these organisms offer a unique opportunity for geneticists to identify and study all of the cells that are derived from a single meiotic division. In this section, we will consider how the analysis of asci can be used to map genes in fungi.

In Fungal Asci, Tetrads and Octads of Spores can be Ordered or Unordered

The arrangement of spores within an ascus varies from species to species. In some cases, the ascus provides enough space for the tetrads or octads of spores to randomly mix together. This is known as an *unordered tetrad* or *octad*. These occur in fungal species such as *S. cerevisiae* and *A. nidulans* and also in certain unicellular algae (*Chlamydomonas rheinhardii*). By comparison, other species of fungi produce a very tight ascus that prevents spores from randomly moving around. This can create a *linear tetrad* or *octad*. In this example, spores which carry the A allele have orange pigmentation, while spores having the a (albino) allele are white.

A key feature of linear tetrads or octads is that the position and order of spores within the ascus reflects their relationship to each other as they were produced by meiosis and mitosis. After the original diploid cell has undergone chromosome replication, the first meiotic division produces two cells that are arranged next to each other within the sac. The second meiotic division then produces four cells that are also arranged in a straight row. Due to the tight enclosure of the sac around the cells, each pair of daughter cells is forced to lie next to each other in a linear fashion. Likewise, when each of these four cells divides by mitosis, each pair of daughter cells is located next to each other.

Linear Tetrad Analysis can be Used to Map the Distance between a Gene and the Centromere

In the case of species that make linear tetrads and octads, experimenters can analyze the phenotypes of the spores within the asci and map the distance between a single gene and the centromere. Since the location of the centromere can be seen under the microscope, the mapping of a gene relative to the centromere provides a way to correlate a gene's location with the cytological characteristics of a chromosome. This approach has been extensively exploited in *N. crassa*.

The arrangement of cells within a *Neurospora* ascus depending on whether or not a crossover has occurred between two homologues that differ at a gene with alleles *A* (orange pigmentation) and *a* (albino, which results in a white phenotype). The octad contains a linear arrangement of four haploid cells carrying the *A* allele, which are adjacent to four haploid cells that contain the *a* allele. This 4:4 arrangement of spores within the ascus is called a *first-division segregation* (FDS) *pattern* or an *M1 pattern*.

In contrast, if a crossover occurs between the centromere and the gene of interest, the linear octad will deviate from the 4:4 patter Depending on the relative locations of the two chromatids that participated in the crossover, the ascus will contain a 2:2:2:2 or 2:4:2 pattern. These are called *second-division segregation* (SDS) *patterns* or *M2 patterns*.

Since a pattern of second division segregation is a result of crossing over, the percentage of M2 asci can be used to calculate the map distance between the centromere and the gene of interest. To understand why this is possible, let's consider the pattern of movement of a crossover site, or *chiasma* (plural, *chiasmata*). A., a chiasma forms at a particular site on a chromosome and then moves away from the centromere and toward the terminal end of the chromosome. As shown here, a crossover will only separate a gene from its original centromere if it begins in the region between the centromere and that gene. Therefore the chances of getting a 2:2:2:2 or 2:4:2 pattern depend on the distance between the gene of interest and the centromere.

To determine the map distance between the centromere and a gene, the experimenter must count the number of SDS asci and the total number of asci. In SDS asci, only half of the spores are actually

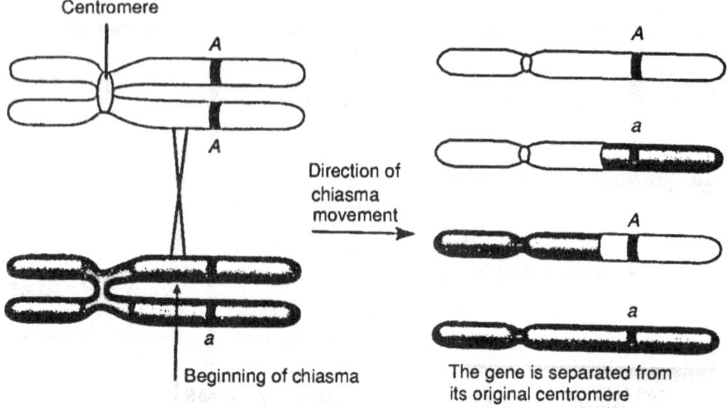

(a) Chiasma begins between centromere and gene of interest

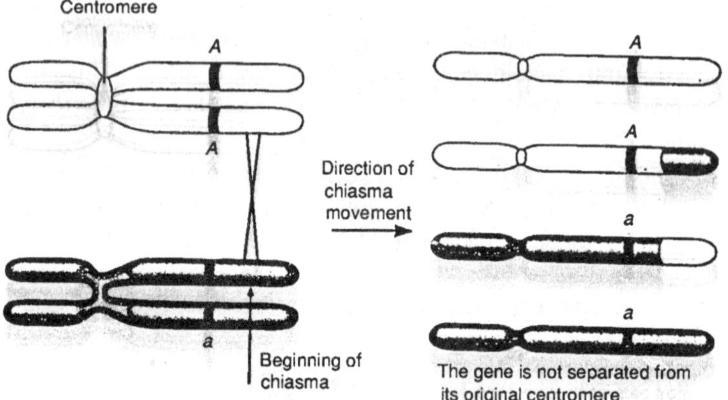

(b) Chiasma does not begin between centromere and gene of interest

Fig. 8.5. The movement of chiasmata during crossing over.

the product of a crossover. Therefore the map distance is calculated as

$$\text{Map distance} = \frac{(1/2)\ (\text{Number of SDS asci})}{\text{Total number of asci}} \times 100$$

Unordered Tetrad Analysis can be Used to Map Genes in Dihybrid Crosses

Unordered tetrads contain a group of spores that are randomly arranged and the product of meiosis. An experimenter can conduct a dihybrid cross, remove the spores from each asci, and determine the phenotypes of the spores. This analysis can determine if two genes are linked or assort independently. If two genes are linked, a tetrad analysis can also be used to compute map distance.

The possible outcomes starting with a diploid yeast zygote that has the genotype *ura*$^+$*ura*-2 *arg*$^+$*arg*-3. *Ura*$^+$ and *arg*$^+$ are normal alleles required for uracil and arginine biosynthesis. *Ura*-2 and *arg*-3 are defective alleles that result in yeast strains that require uracil and arginine in the growth medium. This diploid cell was produced from the fusion of two haploid cells that were *ura*$^+$*arg*$^+$ and *ura*-2 *arg*-3. After the diploid cell has completed meiosis, there are three distinct possible combinations of four haploid cells. One possibility is that the tetrad will contain four spores with the parental combinations of alleles. This ascus is said to have the *parental ditype* (PD). Alternatively, an ascus with a *non-parental ditype* (NPD) contains four cells with non-parental genotypes. Finally, it is possible to have a ascus that has two parental cells and two non-parental cells. This is called a *tetratype* (T).

When two genes assort independently, the number of asci having a parental ditype is expected to equal the number having a non-parental ditype, thus yielding 50% recombinant spores. For linked genes, the relationship between crossing over and the type of ascus that will result. If no crossing over occurs in the region between the two genes, then the parental ditype will be created. A single crossover event will produce a tetratype. Double crossovers can yield either a parental ditype, tetratype, or non-parental ditype depending on the combination of chromatids that are involved. A non-parental ditype is produced when a double crossover involves all four chromatids. A tetratype will result from a three chromatid crossover. Finally, a double crossover between the same two chromosomes will produce the parental ditype.

The data from a tetrad analysis can be used to calculate the map distance between two linked genes. As in conventional mapping, the map distance is calculated the percentage of offspring that carry recombinant chromosomes. As mentioned, a tetratype contains 50% recombinant chromosomes, a non-parental ditype 100%. Therefore, the map distance is computed as

$$\text{Map distance} = \frac{\text{Nonparental ditypes} + (1/2)\ (\text{Tetratypes})}{\text{Total number of asci}} \times 100$$

Over short map distances, this calculation provides a fairly reliable measure of distance. However, it does not adequately account for double crossovers. When two genes are far apart on the same chromosome, the calculated map distance using this equation underestimates the actual map distance due to multiple crossing over. Fortunately, a particular strength of tetrad analysis is that we can derive another equation that accounts for double crossovers and thereby provides a more accurate value for map distance. To begin this derivation, let's consider a more precise way to calculate map distance:

$$\text{Map distance} = \frac{\text{Single crossover tetrad} + (2)\,(\text{Double crossover tetrad})}{\text{Total number of asci}} \times 0.5 \times 100$$

This equation includes the number of single and double crossovers in the computation of map distance. The total number of crossovers equals the number of single crossovers plus two times the number of double crossovers. Overall, the tetrads that contain single and double crossovers also contain 50% non-recombinant chromosomes. To calculate map distance, therefore, we divide the total number of crossovers by the total number of asci and multiply by 50%.

Next, we need to relate this equation to the number of parental ditypes, non-parental ditypes, and tetratypes that are obtained by experimentation. To derive this relationship, we must consider the types of tetrads that are produced from no crossing over, a single crossover, and double crossovers. As shown there, the parental ditype and tetratype are ambiguous. The parental ditype can be derived from no crossovers or a double crossover; the tetratype can be derived from a single crossover or a double crossover. However, the non-parental ditype is unambiguous, since it can only be produced from a double crossover. We can use this observation as a way to determine the actual number of single and double crossovers. Therefore, the total number of double crossovers equals 4 times the number of NPD.

Next, we need to know the number of single crossovers. A single crossover will yield a tetratype, but double crossovers can also yield a tetratype. Therefore, the total number of tetratypes overestimates the true number of single crossovers. Fortunately, we can compensate for this overestimation. Since there are two types of tetratypes that are due to a double crossover, the actual number of tetratypes arising from a double crossover should equal 2NPD. Therefore, the true number of single crossovers is calculated as T – 2NPD.

Now we have accurate measures of both single and double crossovers. The number of single crossovers equals T – 2NPD, and the number of double crossovers equals 4NPD. We can substitute these values into our previous equation:

$$\text{Map distance} = \frac{(\text{T} - 2\ \text{NPD}) + (2)\,(4\ \text{NPD})}{\text{Total number of asci}} \times 0.5 \times 100$$

$$= \frac{T - 6\ NPD}{\text{Total number of asci}} \times 0.5 \times 100$$

This equation provides a more accurate measure of map distance, since it considers both single and double crossovers.

Linkage refers to the phenomenon that many different genes may be located the same chromosome. Chromosomes are sometimes called *linkage groups* because they contain a group of linked genes. Linkage affects the pattern of inheritance, because closely linked genes do not assort independently during gamete formation. This produces a greater percentage of offspring that display parental phenotypes. Nevertheless, non-parental offspring can be produced as result of *crossing over*.

The likelihood of crossing ovcr depends on the *distance* between two genes. If two genes are far apart from each other on the same chromosome, it is more likely that crossing over will occur between them. Therefore, when two genes are widely separated, a substantial percentage of recombinant offspring will be obtained fro a *test cross*. However, the percentage of recombinant offspring cannot exceed value of 50%, even when two genes are more that 50 map units apart on the same chromosome. The relationship between the percentage of recombinant offspring and the linear distance between genes is the basis for *genetic mapping*.

Experimentally, the phenomenon of linkage was deduced from genetic crosses. Bateson and Punnett were the first scientists to notice that certain genes do not as sort independently. Morgan conducted crosses involving X-linked traits in fruit flue and correctly proposed that linkage is due to the location of particular genes on the same chromosome. He also hypothesized that recombinant phenotypes occur be cause of crossing over during meiosis. Morgan realized that the likelihood of crossing over depends on the distance between two genes. The proposal that genetic recombination is due to crossing over was confirmed cytologically by the studies of Creighton and McClintock, which showed that the production of recombination offspring correlates with the production of recombinant chromosomes.

Genetic mapping is the determination of gene order and distance along chromosomes. In this chapter, we have considered how test crosses are conducted as method to map genes. Sturtevant was the first person to understand that the percentage of recombinant offspring in a test cross could be used as a measure of the relative distance between two genes. Map distance is computed as the number of recombinant offspring divided by the total number of offspring. This approach can be readily applied to map genes using dihybrid and trihybrid test crosses. Genetic mapping is most accurate when map distances are calculated between closely linked genes. As the map distance approaches 50 map units (mu) and above, the percent age of recombinant offspring is not a reliable measure of map distance.

This chapter ended with a discussion of gene mapping methods in fungi. I group of fungi known as the ascomycetes have been extensively used in genetic studies, because they produce all the products of a single meiosis within an ascus For fungi such as *Neurospora* that make a linear ascus, the spores are arranged in manner that reflects their relationship to each other during meiosis (and mitosis) Linear asci can be analyzed to map the location of a single gene relative to the centromere. Fungal species that produce unordered asci have also been used in map ping studies. In this case, dihybrid crosses are made, and the distance between the two genes can be computed by determining the proportions of parental ditypes tetratypes, and non-parental ditypes. Although bacteria normally reproduce asexually, they still can transfer genetic material by various different mechanisms. As we will see, these mechanisms also provide a way to map genes along the bacterial chromosome.

9

MAPPING IN PROKARYOTES

Thus far, our attention in Part II of this text has focused mostly on genetic analyses of eukaryotic species such as fungi, plants, and animals. As we have seen, these organisms are amenable to genetic studies for two reasons. First, allelic differences, such as white versus red eyes in *Drosophila* and tall versus dwarf pea plants, provide readily discernable traits among different individuals. Second, since eukaryotic species reproduce sexually, crosses can be made, and the pattern of transmission of traits from parent to offspring can be analyzed. The ability to follow allelic differences in a genetic cross is a basic tool in genetic examination of eukaryotic species.

In this chapter, we will turn our attention to the genetic analysis of bacteria. Like their eukaryotic counterparts, bacteria often possess allelic differences that affect their cellular traits. Common allelic variations among bacteria that are readily discernable involve traits such as sensitivity to antibiotics and varying nutrient requirements. Throughout this chapter, we will consider interesting experiments that genetically examine bacterial strains with allelic differences affecting such traits. However, compared with eukaryotes, one striking difference in prokaryotic species is their mode of reproduction. Since bacteria reproduce asexually, crosses are not used in genetic analyses of bacterial species. Instead, researchers rely on a similar phenomenon called *genetic transfer*. In this process, a segment of bacterial chromosomal DNA is transferred from one bacterium to another. As we will learn, there are several ways that bacterial species can transfer genetic material. Researchers have used genetic transfer to map the locations of genes along the single, circular bacterial chromosome.

In the second part of this chapter, we will examine *bacteriophages* (also known as *phages*), which are viruses that infect bacteria. Bacteriophages contain their own genetic material, which governs the traits of the phage. As we will see, the genetic analysis of phages can yield a highly detailed genetic map of a small chromosomal region. These types of analyses have provided researchers with insights regarding the structure and function of genes.

Genetic Transfer and Mapping in Bacteria

Genetic transfer is a process whereby genetic material from one bacterium is transferred to another bacterium. Like sexual reproduction in eukaryotes, genetic transfer in bacteria is thought to enhance the genetic diversity of bacterial species. For example, a bacterial cell carrying a gene that provides antibiotic resistance may transfer this gene to another bacterial cell, allowing that bacterial cell to survive exposure to the antibiotic.

There are three naturally occurring ways that bacteria can transfer genetic material. The first route, known as *conjugation*, involves direct physical interaction between two bacterial cells. One bacterium acts as donor and transfers genetic material to a recipient cell. A second means of transfer is called *transduction*. In this situation, a virus that infects bacteria, a bacteriophage, transfers bacterial genetic material from one bacterium to another. The last mode of genetic transfer is *transformation*. In this case, genetic material is released into the environment when a bacterial cell dies. This material then binds to a living bacterial cell, which can take it up. In this section, we will describe these three systems of genetic transfer in greater detail. We will also learn how genetic transfer between bacterial cells has provided unique ways to accurately map bacterial genes.

Bacteria can Transfer Genetic Material during Conjugation

The natural ability of some bacteria to transfer genetic material between each other was first recognized by Joshua Lederberg and Edward Tatum while working at Yale University in 1946. They were studying strains of *Escherichia coli* (*E. coli*) that had different nutritional requirements for growth. The general methods for growing bacteria in a laboratory are described in the appendix. As shown in the experiment, they studied one strain, designated $B^-M^-P^+T^+$, which required one vitamin, biotin (*B*), and one amino acid, methionine (*M*), in order to grow. This strain did not require the amino acids phenylalanine (*P*) or threonine (*T*) for growth. An other strain, designated $B^+M^+P^-T^-$, had just the opposite requirements. It needed phenylalanine and threonine for growth, but not biotin and methionine. These differences in nutritional requirements correspond to variations in the genetic material of the two strains. The first strain had two defective genes encoding enzymes necessary for biotin and methionine synthesis. The second strain contained two defective genes required to make phenylalanine and threonine.

The two strains were mixed together and when they were not mixed. Without mixing, about one billion (10^9) $B^-M^-P^+T^+$ cells were applied to plates, and no colonies were observed to grow. This result is expected, since the plates do not contain biotin and methionine. Likewise, when 10^9 $B^+M^+P^-T^-$ cells were plated, no colonies were observed, because phenylalanine and threonine were also missing from this growth medium. However, when $B^-M^-P^+T^+$ and $B^+M^+P^-T^-$ cell were mixed together and then 10^9 cells plated, approximately 100 cells were observed to grow and divide to form visible bacterial colonies. Since growth occurred, the genotype of the cells within these colonies must have been $B^+M^+P^+T^+$. To explain these results, Lederberg and Tatum hypothesized that some genetic material was being transferred between the two strains. One possibility is that the genetic

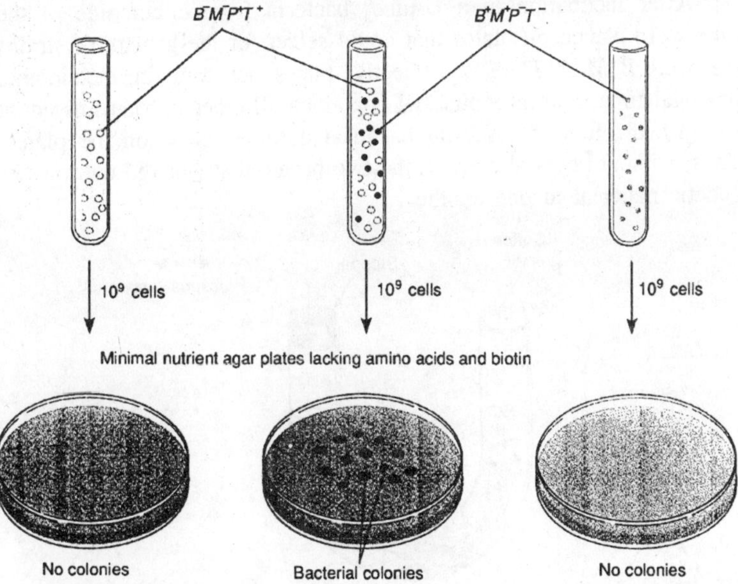

Fig. 9.1. Experiment of Ledgerberg and Tatum demonstrating genetic transfer during conjugation in E. coli.

material providing the ability to synthesize phenylalanine and threonine (P^+T^+) was transferred to the $B^+M^+P^-T^-$ strain. Alternatively, the ability to synthesize biotin and methionine (B^-M^+) may have been transferred to the $B^-M^-P^+T^+$ cells. The results of this experiment cannot distinguish between these two possibilities.

Bernard Davis at Cornell subsequently conducted experiments showing that the two strains of bacteria must make physical contact with each other to transfer genetic material. The apparatus he used, known as a *U-tube*. At the bottom of the U-tube is a filter with pores small enough to allow the passage of genetic material (i.e., DNA molecules), but too small to permit the passage of bacterial cells. On one side of the filter, Davis added a bacterial strain with a certain combination of nutritional requirements (the $B^-M^-P^+T^+$ strain), on the other side a different bacterial strain (the $B^+M^+P^-T^-$ strain). The application of pressure or suction promoted the movement of liquid through the filter. Since the bacteria were too large to fit through the pores, the movement of liquid did not allow the two types of bacterial strains to mix with each other. However, genetic material (which could have been released from a bacterium) could pass through the filter.

After incubation in a U-tube, bacteria from either side of the tube were placed on plates that could select for the growth of strains that were $B^+M^+P^+T^+$. These selective plates lacked biotin, methionine, phenylalanine, and threonine but contained all other nutrients essential for growth. In this case, no bacterial colonies grew on the plates. Thus, without physical contact, the two bacterial strains did not transfer genetic material to one another.

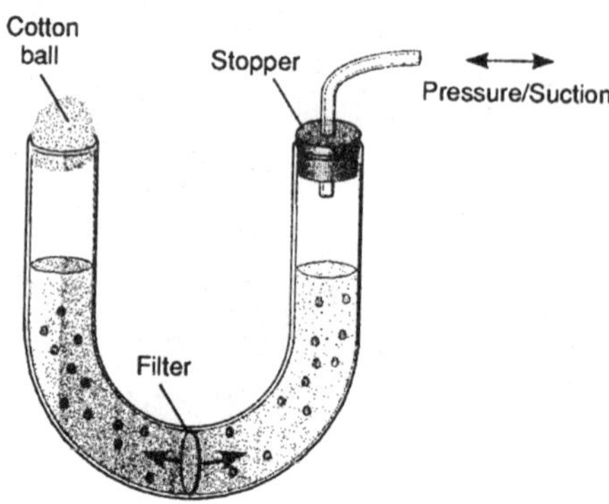

Fig. 9.2. A U-tube apparatus like that used by Bernard Davis. A conceptual diagram of the U-tube.

The term *conjugation* is now used to describe the natural process of genetic transfer between bacterial cells that requires direct cell-to-cell contact. Many, but not all, species of bacteria can conjugate. During the late 1940s and the 1950s, scientists continued to explore this phenomenon of genetic transfer between bacterial cells. Working independently, Joshua and Esther Lederberg, William Hayes, and Luca Cavalli Sforza discovered that only certain bacterial strains can act as donors of genetic material. For example, only about 5% of natural isolates of *E. coli* can act as donor strains. Research studies showed that a strain incapable of acting as a donor could subsequently be converted to a donor strain after being mixed with another donor strain. Hayes correctly proposed that donor strains contain a fertility factor that can be transferred to conjugation-defective strains to make them conjugation proficient.

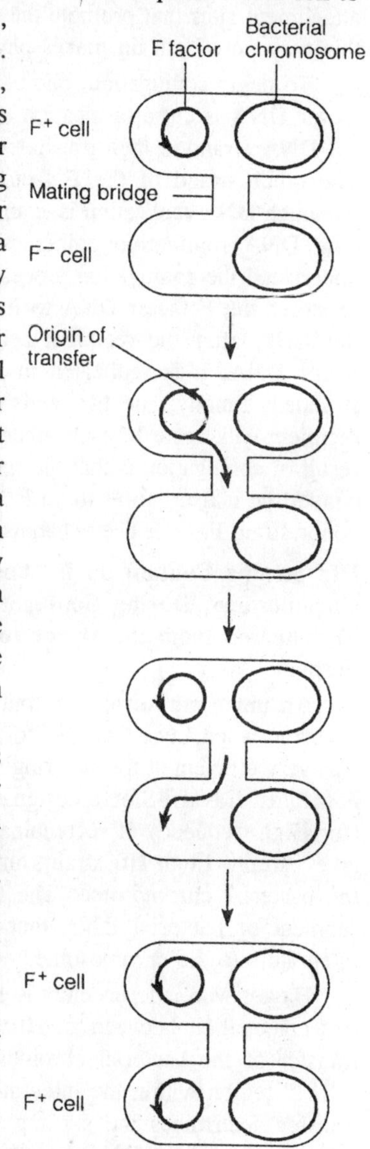

Fig. 9.3. The transfer of a fertility factor during bacterial conjugation.

We now know that donor strains usually contain a small circular segment of genetic material known as an *F factor* (for Fertility factor) in addition to their circular chromosome. Strains of bacteria that contain an *F* factor are designated F^+, strains without *F* factors are F^-. The more general term *plasmid* is used to describe circular pieces of DNA that exist independently of the chromosome.

The process of bacterial conjugation has been extensively studied in many bacterial species, particularly *E. coli*. F^+ strains of *E. coli* produce structures on their cell surface known as *sex pili* (singular, *pilus*). The pili act as attachment sites that promote the binding of bacteria to each other. In this way, an F^+ strain makes physical contact with an F^- strain.

To begin conjugation, one of the strands in the double-stranded F factor DNA is cut at a location known as the *origin of transfer*. This cut DNA strand is then transferred in a linear manner to the F^- cell. The other strand of the F factor DNA remains in the donor cell. Although DNA replication is examined elsewhere, let's briefly consider how DNA replication coincides with conjugation so that we can understand the conjugation process. DNA replication in the donor cell re stores the F factor DNA to its original double-stranded condition. Similarly, after the recipient cell receives a single strand of the F factor DNA, it is replicated in the recipient cell to become double stranded. Finally, the two ends of the linear F factor DNA in the recipient cell ligate to each other to become a circular F factor. The result of conjugation is that the recipient cell has acquired an F factor, converting it from an F^- to an F^+ cell. The genetic composition of the donor strain has not been changed.

Hfr Strains Contain an F⁺ Factor Integrated into the Bacterial Chromosome; During Conjugation, the Bacterial Chromosome is Transferred from the Donor to the Recipient Strain in a Linear Fashion

An important advance in our understanding of bacterial genetics occurred when Luca Cavalli Sforza discovered a strain of *E. coli* that was very efficient at transfer ring many chromosomal genes to recipient F^- strains. Cavaffi-Sforza designated this bacterial strain an *Hfr strain* (for High frequency of recombination). It was originally derived from an F^+ strain. In an Hfr strain, an F factor has become integrated into the bacterial chromosome. The term *episome* is used to describe a segment of bacterial DNA that can exist as an F factor and also integrate into the chromosome.

Hayes, who independently isolated another Hfr strain, demonstrated that conjugation between an Hfr strain and an F^- strain involves the transfer of the bacterial chromosome from the Hfr strain to the F^- cell. A region within the integrated F^+ factor known as the origin of transfer determines the starting point and direction of this transfer process. One of the DNA strands is cut at the origin of transfer. This cut, or nicked, site is the starting point that will enter the F^- recipient cell. Behind this starting point, the rest of the bacterial chromosome enters the F^- cell in a linear manner. This transfer process occurs in conjunction with chromosomal replication, so that the Hfr cell retains its original chromosomal composition. It generally takes about 1.5 to 2 hours for the entire Hfr chromosome to be passed into the F^- cell. Since most matings do not last that long, usually only a portion of the Hfr chromosome is transmitted to the F^- cell.

Once inside the F^- cell, the chromosomal material from the Hfr cell can swap, or recombine, with the homologous region of the recipient cell's chromosome. The net result is that thc recipient cell has received a new segment of chromosomal DNA from the Hfr cell. This recombination may provide the recipient cell with a new combination of alleles. Prior to mating, the recipient strain was *lac*$^-$ (unable to metabolize lactose) and *pro*$^-$ (unable to synthesize pro line). If mating occurred for a short time, the recipient cell received a short segment of chromosomal DNA from the donor. In this case, the recipient cell has become *lac*$^+$ but remains *pro*$^-$. If the mating is prolonged, the recipient cell will receive a longer segment of chromosomal DNA from the donor. After a longer mating, the recipient becomes *lac*$^+$ and *pro*$^+$. As noted, an important feature of Hfr mating is that the bacterial chromosome is transferred linearly to the recipient strain. In this example, *lac*$^+$ is always transferred first and *pro*$^+$ is transferred later.

In any particular Hfr strain, the origin of transfer has a specific orientation that either promotes a counterclockwise or clockwise transfer of genes. Also, among different Hfr strains, the origin of transfer may he located in different regions of the chromosome. Therefore, the order of gene transfer depends on the location and orientation of the origin of transfer. For example, another Hfr strain could have its origin of transfer next to *pro*$^+$ and transfer *pro*$^+$ first and then *lac*$^+$.

Wollman and Jacob used Hfr Matings to Map Genes along the *E. coil* Chromosome in the 1950s

The first genetic mapping experiments in bacteria were carried out by Elie Wollman and Francois Jacob during the 1950s while working at the Pasteur Institute in Paris. At the time of their studies, there was not much information about the organization of bacterial genes along the chromosome. A few key advances during the 1940s and early 1950s made Wollman and Jacob realize that the process of genetic transfer could be used to map the order of genes in *E. coli*. Most importantly, the discovery of conjugation by Lederberg and Tatum, and the identification of Hfr strains by Cavaffi Sforza and Hayes, made it clear that bacteria can transfer genes from donor to recipient cells in a linear fashion. In addition, Wollman and Jacob were aware of previous microbiological studies concerning bacteriophages that bind to *E. coli* cells and subsequently infect them. These studies showed that bacteriophages can be sheared from the surface of *E. coli* cells if they are spun in a blender. In this treatment, the bacteriophages are detached from the surface of the bacterial cells, but the bacteria them selves remain healthy and viable. Wollman and Jacob reasoned that a blender treatment could also be used to separate bacterial cells that were in the act of conjugation without killing them. This technique is known as an *interrupted mating*.

The rationale behind Wollman and Jacob's mapping strategy is that the time it takes for genes to enter a donor cell is directly related to their order along the bacterial chromosome. Because the Hfr chromosome is transferred linearly, they realized that interruptions of mating at different times would lead to various lengths of the Hfr chromosome being transferred to the F^- recipient cell. If two bacterial cells had mated for a short period of time, only a small segment of the Hfr chromosome would be transferred to the recipient bacterium. However, if the bacterial cells were allowed to mate for a longer period of time before being interrupted, a longer segment of the Hfr chromosome could be transferred. By determining which genes were transferred during short matings and which required longer mating times, Wollman and Jacob were able to deduce the order of particular genes along the *E. coli* chromosome.

For this experiment, Wollman and Jacob began with two *E. coli* strains. The donor (Hfr) strain had the following genetic composition:

T^+: able to synthesize threonine, an essential amino acid for growth

L^+: able to synthesize leucine, an essential amino acid for growth

Az^s: sensitive to killing by azide (a toxic chemical)

$T1^s$: sensitive to infection (i.e., a plaque formation) by bacteriophage T1

lac^+: able to metabolize lactose, and use it for growth

gal^+: able to metabolize galactose, and use it for growth

str^s: sensitive to killing by streptomycin (an antibiotic)

The recipient (F^- strain had the opposite genotype: T^- L^- Az^r $T1^r$ lac^- gal^- str^r (r = resistant). Before the experiment, Wollman and Jacob already knew that the T^+ gene was transferred first, followed by the L^+ gene, and both were transferred relatively soon (5-10 minutes) after mating. Their main goal in this experiment was to determine the times at which the other genes (Az^s $T1^{s}$' lac^+ gal^+) were transferred to the recipient strain. The transfer of the str' gene was not examined because streptomycin was used to kill the donor strain following conjugation.

Hypothesis

The chromosome of the donor strain in an Hfr mating is transferred in a linear manner to the recipient strain. The order of genes along the chromosome can be deduced by determining the time various genes take to enter the recipient strain.

Testing the hypothesis

Starting materials: The two *E. coli* strains already described, one Hfr strain ($T^+ L^+ Az^sT1^slac^+gal^+Str^s$) and one F⁻ ($T^-L^-Az^rT1^rlac^-gal^- Str^r$).

1. Mix together a large number of Hfr donor and F^- recipient cells.
2. After different periods of time, take a sample of cells and interrupt conjuction in a blender.
3. Plate the cells on minimal media lacking threonine and leucine, but containing streptomycin. Note: The general method for growing bacteria in a laboratory are decided in the appendix.
4. Pick each surviving colony ,which would have to be $T^+L^+Str^r$, and test to see if it is sensitive to killed by azide, sensitive to infection by T1 bacteriophage, and if it is able to metabolize lactose or galactose.

Data

Minute that bacterial cells were allowed to mate before Blender treatment	*percent of surviving bacterial colonies with the following genotypes:*				
	T^+L^+	Az^s	$T1^s$	lac^+	gal^+
5	—	—	—	—	—
10	100	12	3	0	0
15	100	70	31	0	0
20	100	88	71	12	0
25	100	92	80	28	0.6
30	100	90	75	36	5
40	100	90	75	38	20
50	100	91	78	42	27
60	100	91	78	42	27

Interpreting the data

Before discussing the conclusions of this experiment, it is helpful to describe how Wollman and Jacob monitored gene transfer. To determine if particular genes had been transferred after mating, they took the mated cells and first plated them on growth media that lacked threonine and leucine but contained streptomycin. On these plates, the original donor and recipient strains could not grow, because the donor strain was streptomycin sensitive and the recipient strain required threonine and leucine. However, mated cells in which the donor transferred chromosomal DNA carrying the T^+ and L^+ genes would be able to grow.

To determine the order of gene transfer of the Az^s, $T1^s$, lac^+, and gal$^+$ genes, Wollman and Jacob picked colonies from the first plates and re-streaked them on plates that contained azide or bacteriophage T1, or on minimal plates that contained lactose or galactose as the sole source of energy for growth. The plates were incubated overnight to observe the formation of visible bacterial growth. Whether or not the bacteria could grow depended on their genotypes. For example, a cell that is Az^s cannot grow on plates containing azide, and a cell that is lac^- cannot grow on minimal plates containing lactose as the carbon source for growth. By comparison, a cell that is Az^r and lac^+ can grow on both types of plates.

Now let's discuss the data. After the first plating, all survivors would be cells in which the T^+ and L^+ alleles had been transferred to the F^- recipient strain (which is already streptomycin resistant). As seen in the data, five minutes was not sufficient time to transfer the T^+ and L^+ alleles, since no surviving colonies were observed. After 10 minutes or longer, however, surviving bacterial colonies with the T^+ L^+ genotype were obtained. To determine the order of the remaining genes (Az^s, $T1^s$, lac^+, and gal^+), each surviving colony was tested to see if it was sensitive to killing by azide, sensitive to infection by T1 bacteriophage, able to utilize lactose for growth, or able to utilize galactose for growth. A consistent pattern emerged from the data. The gene that conferred sensitivity to azide (Az^s) was transferred first, followed by $T1^s$, lac^+ and finally gal^+. From these data, as well as those from other experiments, Wollman and Jacob constructed a genetic map that described the order of these genes along the *E. coli* chromosome.

This work provided the first method for bacterial geneticists to map the order of genes along the bacterial chromosome. Throughout the course of their studies, Wollman and Jacob identified several different Hfr strains in which the origin of transfer had been integrated at different places along the bacterial chromosome. When they compared the order of genes among different Hfr strains, their results were consistent with the idea that the *E. coli* chromosome is circular.

Detailed Genetic Map of the *E. coli* Chromosome has been Obtained from many Conjugation Studies

Conjugation experiments have been used to map more than 1000 genes along the circular *E. coli* chromosome. This simplified map only shows the locations of 12 genes. Since the chromosome is circular, we must arbitrarily assign a starting point on the map. The gene *thrA* is at the location of 0 minutes. The *E. coli* genetic map is 100 minutes long, which is approximately the time that it takes to transfer the complete chromosome during an Hfr mating.

We scale genetic maps from bacterial conjugation studies in units of *minutes*. This unit refers to the relative time it takes for genes to first enter an F recipient strain during a conjugation experiment. The

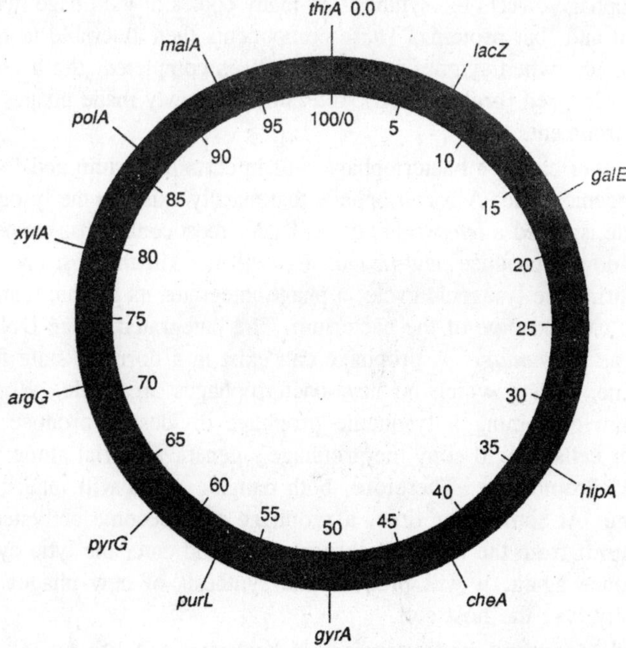

Fig. 9.4. A simplified genetic map of the E. coli chromosome indicating the position of several genes.

distance between two genes is determined by comparing their times of entry during a conjugation experiment. The time of entry is found by conducting mating experiments at different time intervals before interruption. We compute the time of entry by extrapolating the time back to the origin. In this experiment, the time of entry of the *lacZ* gene was approximately 16 minutes, and that of the *galE* gene was 25 minutes. Therefore, these two genes are approximately 9 minutes apart from each other along the *E. coli* chromosome.

Bacteriophages can also Transfer Genetic Material from one Bacterial Cell to Another in the Process of Transduction

Before we discuss the ability of bacteriophages to transfer genetic material between bacterial cells, let's consider some general features of a phage's life cycle. Bacteriophages are composed of genetic material that is surrounded by a protein coat. Certain types of bacteriophages can bind to the surface of a bacterium and inject their genetic material into the bacterial cytoplasm. Depending on its type and the growth conditions, the phage may follow a *lytic cycle* or a *lysogenic cycle*. Some phages can follow both cycles. During the lytic cycle the bacteriophage directs the synthesis of many copies of the phage genetic material and 'bat proteins. These components then assemble to make new phages, when synthesis and assembly is completed, the bacterial host cell is lysed (broken apart), releasing the newly made phages into the environment.

In other cases, a bacteriophage will infect a bacterium and follow the lysogenic cycle. A bacteriophage that usually exists in the lysogenic life cycle is called a *temperate phage*. Under most conditions, temperate phages do not produce new phages and will not kill the host bacterial cell. During the lysogenic cycle, a phage integrates its genetic material into the chromosome of the bacterium. This integrated phage DNA is known as a *prophage*. A prophage can exist in a dormant state for a long time, during which no new bacteriophages are made. When a bacterium containing a lysogenic prophage divides to produce two daughter cells, it will copy the prophage's genetic material along with its own chromosome. Therefore, both daughter cells will inherit the prophage. At some later time, a prophage may become activated to excise itself from the bacterial chromo some and enter the lytic cycle. Then, once again, it will promote the synthesis of new phages and eventually lyse the host cell.

With a general understanding of bacteriophage life cycles, we will now examine the ability of phages to transfer genetic material between bacteria. This process is called *transduction*. Examples of phages that can transfer bacterial chromosomal DNA from one bacterium to another are the P22 and P1 phages that infect the bacterial species *Salmonella typhimurium* and *E. coli*, respectively. The P22 and P1 phages can follow either the lytic or lysogenic cycle. While in the lytic cycle, the phage directs the synthesis of phage DNA and coat proteins, which then assemble to make new phages. During this process, the bacterial chromosome becomes fragmented into small pieces of DNA.

Occasionally, a mistake can happen in which a piece of bacterial DNA assembles with the coat proteins. This creates a phage that contains bacterial chromosomal DNA. When phage synthesis is completed, the bacterial cell is lysed and releases the newly made phage into the environment. Following release, this abnormal phage can still bind to a living bacterial cell and introduce its genetic material into the bacterium. This DNA fragment (which was derived from the bacterial chromosomal DNA) can then recombine with the bacterial chromo some inside the infected cell. In the example any piece of the bacterial chromosomal DNA can be incorporated into the phage. This type of trans-

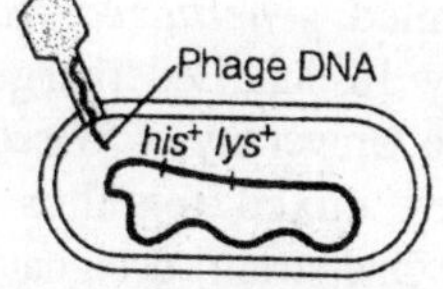

Phage infects bacterial cell.

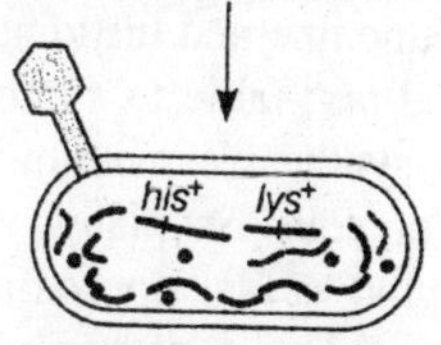

Host DNA is hydrolyzed into pieces, and phage DNA and proteins are made.

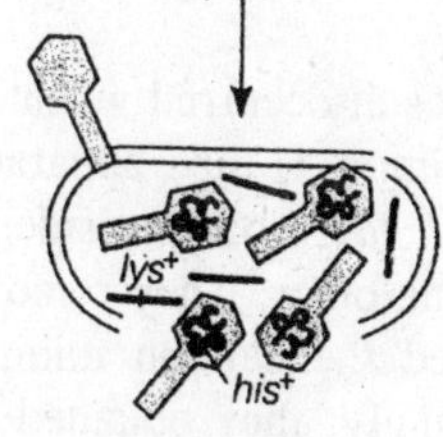

Occasionally, bacterial DNA fragments are packaged in a phage capsid.

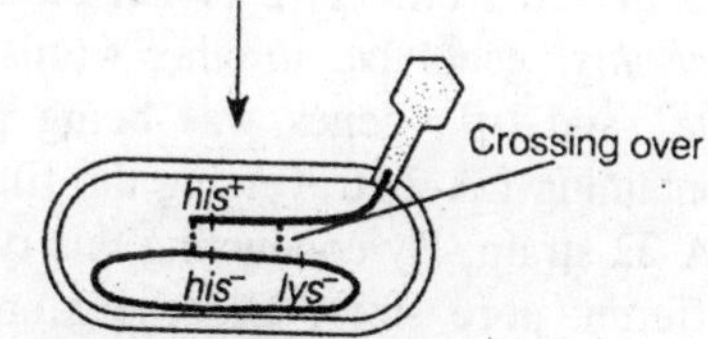

Transducing phages infect new host cells, where recombination due to crossing over can occur.

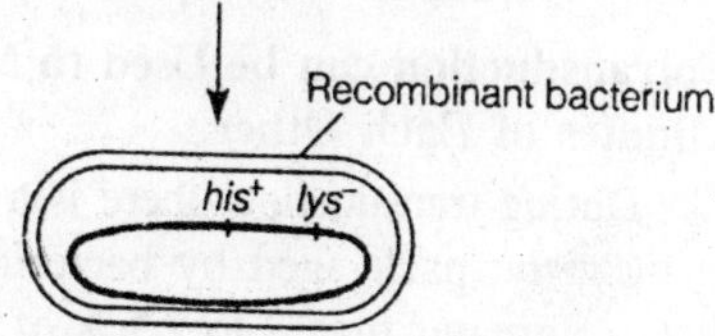

The recombinant bacterium has a genotype (his^+ lys^-) that is different from the recipient bacterial cell (his^- lys^-).

Fig. 9.5. Transduction in bacteria.

duction is called *generalized transduction*. Transduction was first discovered by Joshua Lederberg and Norton Zinder in 1952 while working at the University of Wisconsin in Madison. In an experimental strategy, they mixed together two strains of the bacterium *S. typhimurium*. One strain, designated LA-22, was *phe*$^-$, *trp*$^-$, *met*$^+$, and his$^+$ (unable to synthesize phenylalanine or tryptophan but able to synthesize methionine and histidine); the other strain, LA-2, was *phe*$^+$, *trp*$^+$, *met*$^-$, and *his*$^-$ (able to synthesize phenylalanine and tryptophan, but unable to synthesize methionine or histidine). When they placed this mixture of cells on plates with minimal growth media lacking these four amino acids, approximately one cell in 100,000 was ob served to grow. The genotype of the surviving bacterial cells must have been *phe*$^+$ *trp*$^+$ *met*$^+$ *his*$^+$. Therefore, Lederberg and Zinder concluded that genetic material ha been transferred between the two strains.

A novel result occurred when Lederberg and Zinder repeated this experiment using a U-tube apparatus. They placed the LA 22 strain (*phe*$^-$ *trp*$^-$ *met*$^+$ *his*$^+$) on one side of the filter and LA-2 (*phe*$^+$ *trp*$^+$ *met*$^-$ *his*$^-$) on the other. They removed samples from either side of the tube and plated the cell on minimal plates lacking the four amino acids. Surprisingly, they obtained colonies from the side of the tube that contained LA-22 but not from the side that contained LA-2. From these results, they concluded that some filterable agent was being transferred from LA-2 to LA-22 that converted LA-22 to *phe*$^+$ *trp*$^+$ *met*$^+$ *his*$^+$ genotype. In other words, some filterable agent carrying the *phe*$^+$ and *trp*$^+$ genes was being produced on the side of the tube containing LA-2, traversing the filter, and then being taken up by the LA-22 strain. By conducting this type of experiment using filters with different pore sizes, Lederberg and Zinder found that the filterable agent was slightly less than 0.1 μm in diameter, a size much smaller than a bacterium. They correctly concluded that the filterable agent in these experiments was a bacteriophage.

Cotransduction can be Used to Map Genes that are Within 2 Minutes of Each Other

During transduction, there is a maximum size of the DNA segment that can be pack aged by bacteriophages. P1 cannot package pieces that are greater than 2 to 2.5% of the entire *E. coli* chromosome, and P22 cannot package pieces that are greater than 1% of the length of the *S. typhimurium* chromosome. If two genes are close together along the chromosome, a bacteriophage may package a single piece of the

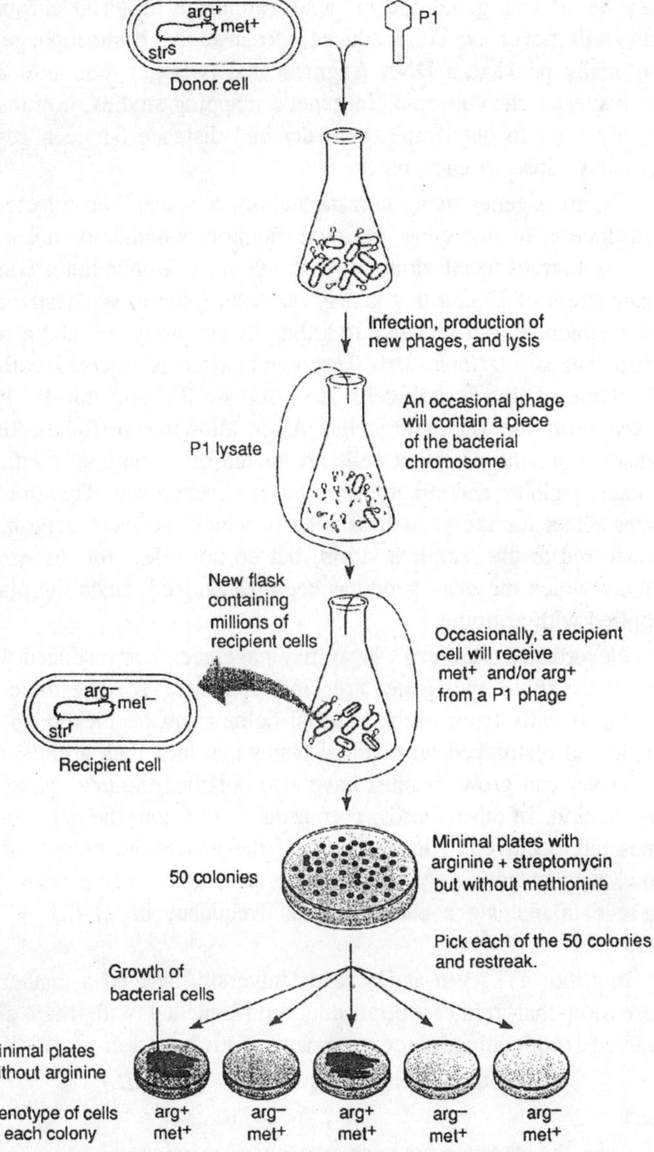

Fig. 9.6. The steps in a cotransduction experiment.

chromo some that carries both genes and transfer that piece to another bacterium. This phenomenon is called *cotransduction*. The likelihood that two genes will be cotransduced depends on how close together they lie. If two genes are far apart along the bacterial chromosome, they will never be cotransduced, because the bacteriophage cannot physically package a DNA fragment that is larger than 1 to 2.5% of the bacterial chromosome. In genetic mapping studies, cotransduction is only used to determine the order and distance between genes that lie fairly close to each other.

To map genes using cotransduction, a researcher selects for the transduction of one gene and then monitors whether or not a second gene is cotransduced along with it. As an example, let's consider a donor strain of *E. coli* that is arg^+ met^+ str^s (able to synthesize arginine and methionine, but sensitive to killing by streptomycin) and a recipient strain that is arg^- met^- str^r. The donor strain is infected with phage P1. Some of the *E. coli* cells are lysed by P1, and this P1 lysate is mixed with the recipient cells. After allowing sufficient time for transduction, the recipient cells are plated on a minimal medium that contains arginine and streptomycin but not methionine. Therefore, these plates select for the growth of cells in which the met^+ gene has been transferred to the recipient strain, but do not select for the growth of cells in which the arg^+ gene has been transferred, since the plates are supplied with arginine.

Nevertheless, the arg^+ gene may have been cotransduced with the met^+ gene if the two genes are close together. To determine this, a sample of cells from each bacterial colony can be picked up with a needle and restreaked on minimal plates that lack both amino acids. If the colony can grow, it must have also obtained the arg^+ gene during transduction. In other words, cotransduction of both the arg^+ and met^+ genes has occurred. Alternatively, if the restreaked colony does not grow, it must have only received the met^+ gene during transduction. These data indicate a cotransduction frequency of $21/(21 + 29) = 0.42$.

In 1966, T.T. Wu at Harvard University derived a mathematical expression that relates cotransduction frequency with map distance obtained from conjugation experiments. This equation is

$$\text{Cotransduction frequency} = (1 - d/L)^3$$

where

d = the distance between two genes in minutes

L = the size of chromosomal pieces (in minutes) that the phage carries during transduction.

(For P1 transduction, this size is approximately 2% of the bacterial chromosome, which equals 2 minutes.)

This equation assumes that the bacteriophage randomly packages pieces of the bacterial chromosome that are similar in size. Depending on the type of phage used in a transduction experiment, this assumption may not always be valid. Nevertheless, this equation has been fairly reliable in computing map distance for P1 transduction experiments in *E. coli*. We can use this equation to estimate the distance between the two genes:

$$0.42 = (1 - d/2)^3$$
$$(1 - d/2) = \sqrt[3]{0.42}$$
$$1 - d/2 = 0.75$$
$$d/2 = 0.25$$
$$d = 0.5 \text{ minutes}$$

This equation tells us that the distance between the met$^-$ and *arg*$^+$ genes is approximately 0.5 minutes.

Genetic mapping strategies in bacteria often involve data from both conjugation and transduction experiments. Conjugation is commonly used to determine the relative order and distance of genes, particularly those far apart along the chromosome. By comparison, transduction experiments can provide very accurate mapping data for genes that are fairly close together.

Bacteria can also Transfer Genetic Material by Transformation

A third natural mechanism for the transfer of genetic material from one bacterium to another is known as *transformation*. This process was first discovered by Frederick Griffith in 1928 while working with strains of *Streptococcus pneumoniae*. During bacterial transformation, a living bacterial cell will take up a fragment of DNA released from a dead bacterium. This DNA fragment may then recombine with the bacterial chromosome, producing a bacterium with genetic material that it has received from the dead bacterium.

Since the initial studies of Griffith, we have learned much about the events that occur in transformation. Only certain bacterial cells, known as *competent cells*, can be transformed by extracellular DNA. Temperature, ionic conditions, and nutrients in the growth media can greatly influence whether or not a bacterium will be competent to take up genetic material from its environment.

In recent years, geneticists have unraveled some of the steps that occur when competent bacterial cells are transformed by genetic material in their environment. First, a large fragment of genetic material binds to the surface of the bacterial cell. Before entering the cell, however, this large piece of chromosomal DNA must be cut into smaller fragments. This cutting is accomplished by a bacterial enzyme known as an *endonuclease*, which makes occasional random cuts in the long piece of chromosomal DNA. At this stage, the DNA fragments are composed of double-stranded DNA.

The next step is for the DNA fragment to begin its entry into the bacterial cytoplasm. For this to occur, the double-stranded DNA interacts with proteins in the bacterial membrane. In some bacterial species, one of the DNA strands is degraded and the other strand enters the bacterial cytoplasm. The single-stranded DNA then aligns itself with the homologous location on the bacterial chromosome. In the example, the foreign DNA carries a functional *lac*$^+$ gene. This strand of DNA aligns itself with a nonfunctional (mutant) *lac*$^-$ gene already present within the bacterial chromosome. The foreign DNA then recombines with one of the strands in the bacterial chromosome of the competent cell. In other words, the foreign DNA replaces one of the chromosomal strands of DNA, which is subsequently degraded. During recombination, alignment of the *lac*$^-$ and the *lac*$^+$ alleles results in a region of mismatch called a *heteroduplex*. However, the heteroduplex is only a temporary situation. DNA repair enzymes in the recipient

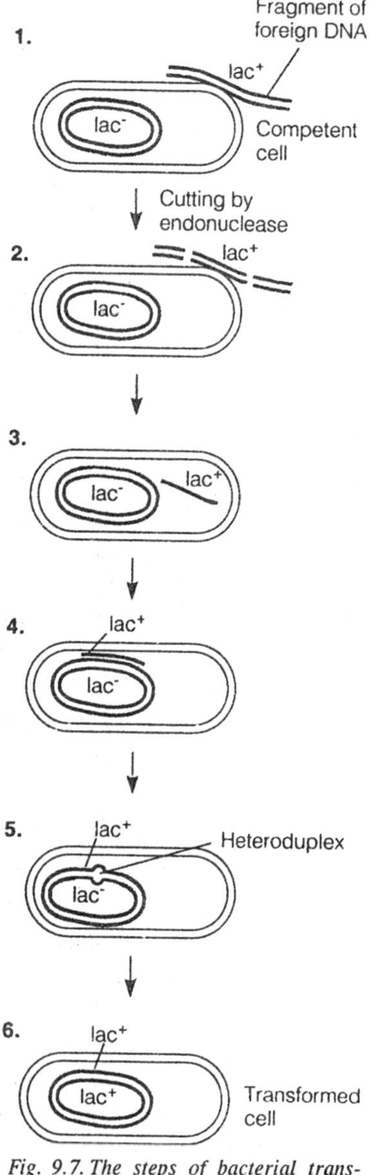

Fig. 9.7. The steps of bacterial transformation.

cell recognize the heteroduplex and repair it. In this case, the heteroduplex has been repaired by eliminating the mutation that caused the *lac*$^-$ phenotype, thereby creating a *lac*$^+$ gene. In this example, the recipient cell has been transformed from a *lac*$^-$ strain to a *lac*$^+$ strain.

Transformation has also been used to map many bacterial genes. Such gene mapping is conducted similarly to the cotransduction experiments described earlier. If two genes are close together, the cotransformation frequency is expected to be high, whereas genes that are far apart will have a cotransformation frequency that is very low or even zero. Like cotransduction, genetic mapping via transformation is only used to map genes that are relatively close together.

INTERAGENIC MAPPING IN BACTERIOPHAGES

Biologists do not consider viruses to be living, because they rely on a host cell for their existence and proliferation. Nevertheless, we can think of viruses as having traits, because they have unique biological structures and functions. Each type of virus has its own genetic material, which contains many viral genes. In this section, we will focus our attention on a bacteriophage called T4. Its genetic material contains several dozen different viral genes. These genes encode viral proteins that carry out a variety of functions. For example, some of the genes en code proteins needed for the synthesis of new viruses and the lysis of the host cell. Other genes encode the viral coat proteins that are found in the head, shaft, tail baseplate, and tail fibers. For example, five different proteins, designated by the numbers 34—38, assemble to form the tail fibers. The expression of T4 genes to make proteins 34—38 provides the bacteriophage with the trait of having tail fibers, enabling it to attach itself to the surface of a bacterium.

The study of viral genes has been instrumental in our basic understanding of how the genetic material works. During the early 1950s, Seymour Benzer at Purdue University embarked on a ten-year study that focused on the function of viral genes in the T4 bacteriophage. In this section, we will examine some of his pivotal results, which advanced our knowledge of gene function. We will also explore how he con ducted a detailed type of genetic mapping known as *intragenic* or *fine structure mapping*.

We have considered intergenic mapping earlier in this chapter. In that type of mapping, the goal is to determine the distance between two different genes. As shown here, determining the distance between genes *A* and *B* is an example of intergenic mapping. By comparison, intragenic mapping seeks to ascertain distances within the same gene.

For example, in a population, gene *C* may exist as two different mutant alleles. One allele may be due to a mutation near the beginning of the gene, the second to a mutation near the end. The goal of intragenic mapping is to determine the distance between the two mutations that occur in the same gene. In this section, we will explore the pioneering studies that showed the feasibility of intragenic mapping.

Lytic Bacteriophages Produce Viral Plaques; Mutations in Viral Genes can Alter Plaque Morphology

As they progress through the lytic cycle, bacteriophages ultimately produce new phages, which are released when the bacterial cell lyses. In the laboratory, researchers can visually observe the consequences of bacterial cell lysis in the following way. A sample of bacterial cells and lytic bacteriophages are mixed together. This mixture of cells and phages is then poured onto petriplates that contain nutrient agar for bacterial cell growth. Bacterial cells, which are not infected by a bacteriophage, will rapidly grow and divide to produce a "lawn" of bacteria. This lawn of bacteria is opaque (i.e., you cannot see through it to the underlying agar). In the experiment, seven bacteria cells have been infected by bacteriophages, and these infected cells are found at random locations in the lawn of uninfected bacteria. The infected cells will lyse and re lease newly made bacteriophages. These bacteriophages will then infect the nearby bacteria within the lawn. These cells will eventually lyse and also release newly made phages. Over time, these repeated cycles of infection and lysis will produce, around each site of an original phage infection, an observable clear area, or *plaque*, where the bacteria have been lysed.

A genetic analysis of any organism requires strains with allelic differences. Since bacteriophages are microscopic, it is rather difficult for geneticists to analyze mutations that affect phage morphology However, some mutations in the bacteriophage's genetic material can alter the ability of the phage to cause plaque formation. Therefore, we can view the morphology of plaques as a trait of the bacteriophage. Since plaques are visible with the naked eye, mutations affecting this trait lend themselves to a much easier genetic analysis. An example is a rapid-lysis mutant of bacteriophage T4, which tends to form unusually large plaques. These types of mutants were first identified by A.D. Hershey in 1946 while working at Cold Spring Harbor, New York. The plaques are large because the mutant phages lyse the bacterial cells more rapidly than do the wild-type phages. Rapid-lysis mutants form large, clearly defined plaques, as opposed to wild-type

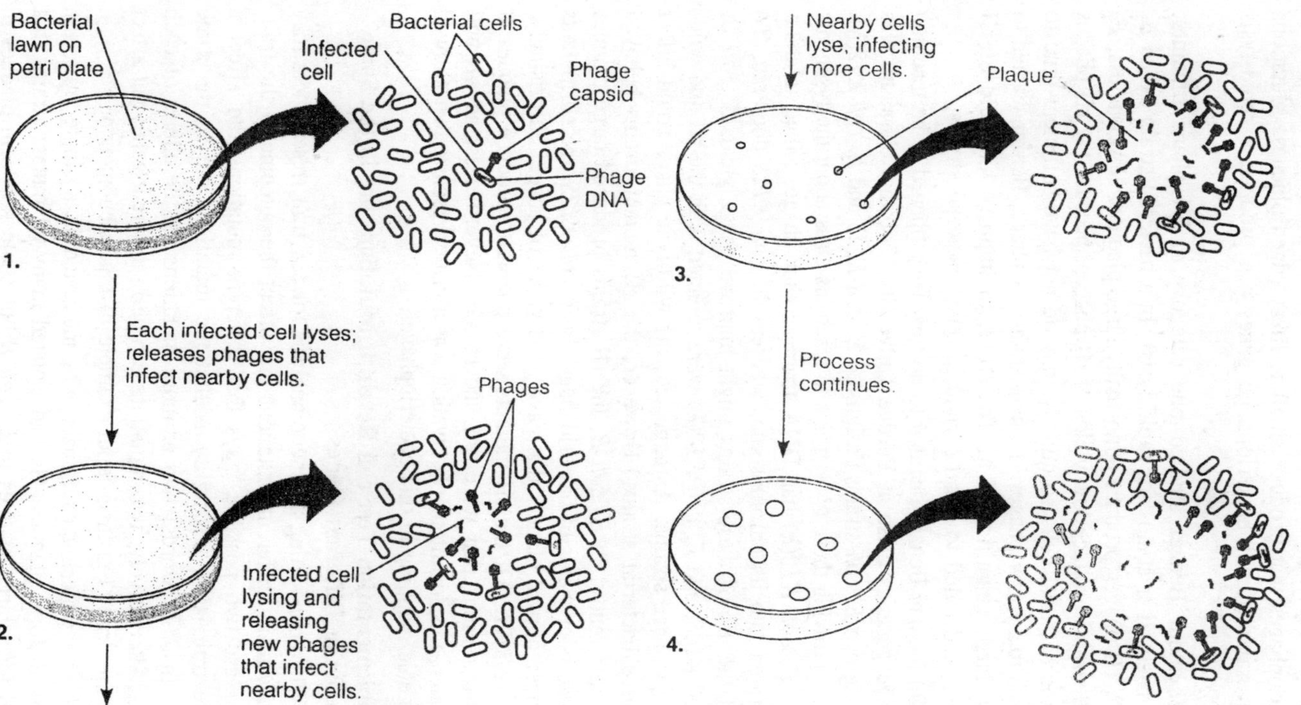

Fig. 9.8. The formation of phage plaque on lawn of bacteria in laboratory.

bacteriophages that produce smaller, fuzzy-edged plaques. Mutations in several different bacteriophage genes can produce a rapid-lysis phenotype.

Seymour Benzer studied one category of T4 phage mutants, designated rII (r stands for rapid lysis). In a bacterial strain called *E. coli B*, rII phages produce abnormally large plaques. Nevertheless, *E. coli B* strains produce low yields of rII phages, because the rII phages lyse the bacterial cells so quickly they do not have sufficient time to produce many new phages. To help study this phage, Benzer wanted to obtain large quantities of it. Therefore, to improve his yield of rII phage, he decided to test its yield in other bacterial strains.

On the day Benzer decided to do this, he happened to be teaching a phage genetics class at Purdue University. For that class, he was growing two *E. coli* strains designated *E. coli K12S* and *E. coli K12*(λ). He was growing these two strains to teach his class about the lysogenic cycle. *E. coli K12*(λ) has DNA from another phage, called lambda, integrated into its chromosome, whereas *E. coli K12S* does not. To see if the use of these strains might improve phage yield, *E. coli B*, *E. coli K12S*, and *E. coli K12*(λ) were infected with the rII and wild-type T4 phage strains. As expected, the wild-type phage could infect all three bacterial strains. However, the rII mutant strains behaved quite differently. In *E. coli B*, the rII strains produced large plaques that had poor yields of bacteriophage. In *E. coli K12S*, the rII mutants produced normal plaques that gave good yields of phage. Surprisingly, in *E. coli K12*(λ), the rII mutants were unable to produce plaques at all, for reasons that were not understood. Nevertheless, as we will see later, this fortuitous observation was a critical feature that allowed intragenic mapping in this bacteriophage.

Complementation Test can Reveal if Mutations are in the Same Gene or in Different Genes

When conducting a genetic analysis for any trait, researchers may identify many different mutations that affect the outcome of the trait. There are two possible ways that different mutations can affect a single trait. One possibility is that the mutations are in the same gene. In other words, two or more mutations can be alleles of each other. Alternatively, two mutations can be in different genes yet affect the same trait. Epistasis is an example of this phenomenon.

In his experiments Benzer was interested in a single trait, the ability to form plaques. He had isolated many rII mutant strains that could form large plaques in *E. coli B* but could not form plaques in

E. coli K12(λ). To determine the numbers of genes affecting plaque formation, he needed to know if all the rII mutations were in the same gene or if they involved mutations in different genes. To accomplish this, he conducted *complementation* experiments. In this type of approach, the goal is to determine if two different mutations (which affect the same trait) are in the same gene or in two different genes. The possible outcomes of complementation experiments involving mutations that affect plaque formation.

As shown here, distinct rII mutations in two different strains of T4 bacteriophage, designated strain 1 and 2, prevented plaque formation in *E. coli K12*(λ). To conduct this complementation experiment, bacterial cells were coinfected with the two different strains of phage. Two distinct outcomes are possible. If each rII mutation was in a different phage gene (e.g., gene *A* and gene *B*), a bacterial cell that is coinfected by both types of phages will have two mutant genes, but also two wild-type genes. If the mutant phage genes behave in a recessive fashion, the doubly infected cell will have a wild-type phenotype. In other words, coinfected cells will be lysed in the same manner as the wild-type strain. Therefore, this coinfection should be able to produce plaques in *E. coli K12*(λ). This is called complementation, be cause the defective genes in each rII strain are complemented by the corresponding wild-type genes. If, however, the two rII phage strains possess mutations in the same gene, they will not complement each other. For example, if both rII phages contain deleterious mutations in gene *A*, an *E. coli K12*(λ) cell that is coinfected by both phages will not be able to make plaques, because it cannot make a wild-type gene *A* product. This is called *non-complementation*.

By carefully considering the pattern of complementation and noncomplementation, Benzer found that the rII mutations occurred in two different genes, which were termed rII*A* and rII*B*. The identification of two distinct genes affecting plaque formation was a necessary step that preceded his intragenic mapping analysis, which will be described next. Benzer coined the term *cistron* to refer to the smallest generic unit that gives a negative complementation test. In other words, if two mutations occur within the same cistron, they cannot complement each other. Since these studies of the 1950s, it has become clear that a cistron is equivalent to a gene. In recent decades, the term gene has gained wide popularity while the term cistron is not commonly used. Nevertheless, it would be correct to refer to gene *A* as cistron *A* or gene *B* as cistron *B*.

Intragenic Maps were Constructed Using Data from a Recombinational Analysis of Mutants within the rII Region

The ability of a coinfection to produce many viral plaques is due to complementation. Non complementation occurs when two different strains have mutations in the same gene. However, at an extremely low rate, two non complementing strains of viruses can produce an occasional viral plaque if intragenic recombination has taken place. For example, coinfection experiment between two phage strains that both contain rII mutations in gene *A*. These mutations are located at different places within the same gene. Rarely, a crossover occurs in the very short region between each mutation. This produces a gene *A* with two mutations and also a wild-type gene *A*. Since this event has produced a wild-type gene *A*, the normal product of gene *A* will be produced and new phages can be made in *E. coli K12*(λ), resulting in the formation of viral plaques.

Even though intragenic recombination can take place, an experimental obstacle makes it difficult to measure. Since the distance between two mutations within the same gene is very short, the likelihood is extremely small that a crossover will occur in this region to produce recombinant chromosomes—perhaps less than one chance in 100,000. In conventional crosses involving eukaryotic organisms such as *Drosophila* or the pea plant, such a low rate of recombination is

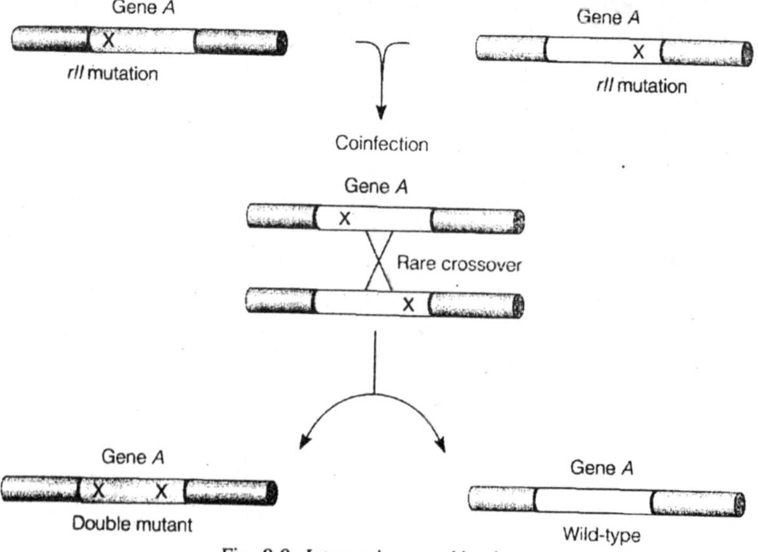

Fig. 9.9. Intragenic recombination.

very difficult to measure experimentally, since it would involve the analysis of hundreds of thousands or even mil lions of offspring. The accidental discovery that rII mutations behave differently in *E. coli B*, *E. coli K12S*, and *E. coli* K12(λ) provided an experimental system to detect recombinants that occur at a very low rate, even less than one in 1,000,000 times! In Benzer's own words, "I dropped everything else and embarked on this project."

The general strategy for intragenic mapping of rII phage mutations are shown. In steps 1-3, bacteriophages from two different non-complementing rII phage mutants (here, r103 and r104) were mixed together in equal amounts, and then infected into *E. coli B*. In this strain, the rII mutants could grow and propagate. When these two different mutants coinfected the same cell, intragenic recombination may occur, producing wild-type phages and double-mutant phages. However, these ultra genic recombinants were produced at a very low rate. Following coinfection and lysis of *E. coli B*, a new population of phages was isolated in step 4. This population was expected to mostly contain non recombinant phages. However, due to intragenic re combination, it would also contain a very low percentage of wild-type phages and doubly mutant phages.

To determine the relative amounts of parental and recombinant phages, Benzer took advantage of the observation that rII phages cannot grow in *E. coli* K12(λ). In step 5, he took his reisolated population of phages and used some of them to infect *E. coli B* and some to infect *E. coli* K12(λ). After plating in step 6, the *E. coli B* infection was used to determine the total number of phages, since rII mutants as well as wild-type phages can produce plaques in this strain. The overwhelming majority of these phages were expected to be non recombinant phages. The *E. coli* K12(λ) infection was used to determine the number of rare intragenic recombinants that produce wild-type phages.

The great advantage of this experimental system in detecting a low percentage of recombinants. In the laboratory, phage preparations containing several billion phages per milliliter are readily made. Among billions of phages, a low percentage (e.g., one in every 100,000) may be wild-type phages arising from intragenic recombination. The wild-type recombinants can produce plaques in *E. coli* K12(λ) whereas the rII mutant strains cannot. In other words, only the tiny fraction of wild-type recombinants would produce plaques in *E. coli* K12(λ). We can determine the frequency of recombinant phages by comparing the

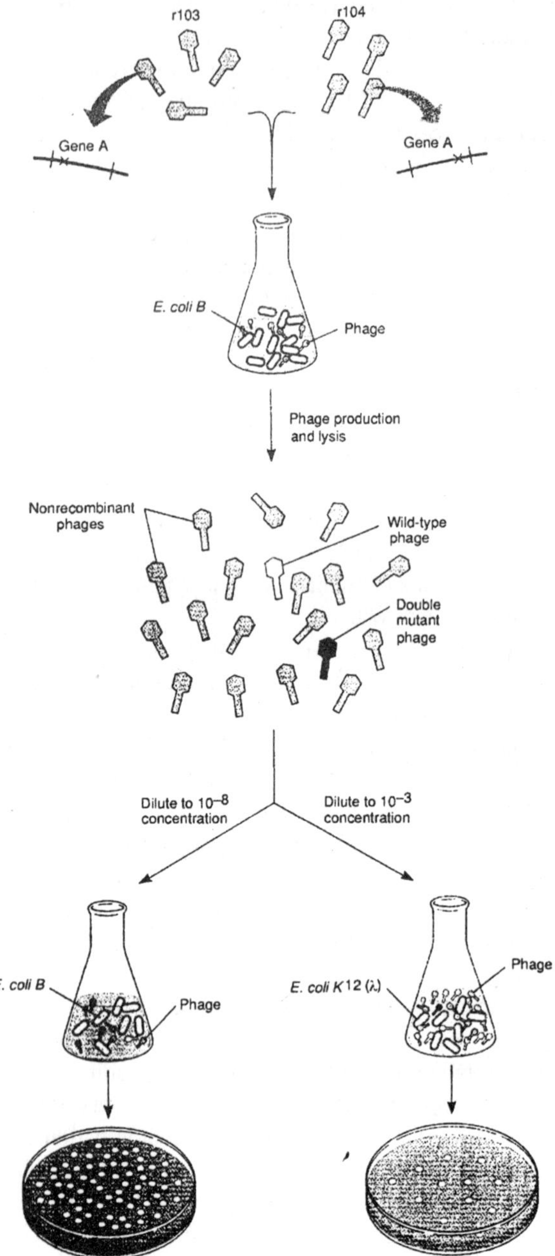

Fig. 9.10. Benzer's method of intragenic mapping in the rII region.

number of recombinant (wild-type) phages and the total number of phages. The total number of phages can be deduced from the number of plaques obtained from the infection of *E. coli B*. In this experiment, the phage preparation was diluted by 10^{-8} (1: 100,000,000), and 1 ml was used to infect *E. coli B*. Since this plate produced 66 plaques, the total number of phages in the original preparation was 66×10^8 6.6 $\times 10^9$ or 6.6 billion phages per milliliter. By comparison, the phage preparation used to infect *E. coli* K12(λ)) was only diluted by 10^{-3} (1 in 1000). This plate produced 11 plaques. Therefore, the number of wild-type phages was 11×10^3, which equals 11,000 wild-type phages per milliliter.

As we have already seen, genetic mapping distance is computed by dividing the number of recombinants by the total population (non recombinants and recombinants). In this experiment, intragenic recombination produces an equal amount of two types of recombinants: wild-type phages and doubly mutant phages. Only the wild-type phages are detected in the infection of *E. coli* K12(λ). Therefore, to obtain the total number of recombinants, the number of wild-type phages must be multiplied by two. With all this information, we can compute the frequency of recombinants using the experimental approach:

$$\text{Frequency of recombinants} = \frac{2\ (\text{Wild-type plaques obtained in } E.\ coli\ K12(\lambda)}{\text{Total number of plaques obtained in } E.\ coli\ B}$$

We can use this equation to calculate the frequency of recombinants obtained in the experiment:

$$\text{Frequency of recombinants} = \frac{2\,(11 \times 10^3)}{66 \times 10^9}$$

$$= 33 \times 10^{-6} = 0.0000033$$

Thus, there were approximately 3.3 recombinants per 1,000,000 phages.

The frequency of recombinants provides a measure of map distance. In eukaryotic mapping studies, we compute the map distance by multiplying the frequency of recombinants by 100 to give a value in map units (also known as centimorgans). Similarly, in these experiments, the frequency of recombinants can provide a measure of map distance along the bacteriophage chromosome. In this case, the map distance is between two mutations within the same gene. Like intergenic mapping, the frequency of intragenic recombinants is correlated with the distance between the two mutations; the farther apart they are, the higher the frequency of recombinants. If two mutations happen to be located at exactly the same site within a gene, they would not be able to produce any wild-type recombinants, and so the map distance would be zero. These are known as *homoallelic* mutations.

Deletion Mapping can be Used to Localize many rII Mutations to Specific Regions in the *rIIA* or *rIIB* Genes

Now that we have seen the general approach to intragenic mapping, let's consider a method to efficiently map hundreds of rII mutations within the two genes designated *rIIA* and *rIIB*. As you may have realized, the coinfection experiments are quite similar to Sturtevant's strategy of making dihybrid crosses to map genes along the *Drosophila* chromosome. Similarly, Benzer wanted to "cross" or coinfect different rII mutants in order to map the sites of the mutations within the *rIIA* and *rIIB* genes. During the course of his work, he obtained hundreds of different r mutant strains that he wanted to map. However, making all of the pairwise combinations would have been an overwhelming task. Instead, Benzer used an approach known as *deletion mapping* as a first step in localizing his rII mutations to a fairly short region within gene *A* or gene *B*.

This approach is easier to understand if we use an example. Let's suppose that the goal is to know the approximate location of an rII mutation, such as r103. To do so, *E. coli K12*(λ) would be coinfected with r103 and a deletion strain. Each deletion strain is a T4 bacteriophage that is missing a known segment of the *rIIA* and/or *rIIB* gene. If the deleted region includes the same region that contains the r103 mutation, it will be impossible for a coinfection to produce intragenic wild-type recombinants. However, if a deletion strain recombines with r103 to produce a wild-type phage, the deleted region did not contain the r103 mutation. In the example, the r103 strain produced wild-type recombinants when coinfected with deletion strains PB242, A105, and 638. However, coinfection of r103 with PT1, J3, 1241, and 1272 did not produce intragenic wild-type recombinants. Since coinfection with PB242 produced recombinants and PT1 did not, the r103 mutation must be located in the region that is missing in PT1 but not missing in PB242. This region is called A4 (A refers to the *rIIA* gene). In other words, the r103 mutation is located somewhere within the A4 region, but not in the other six regions (A1, A2, A3, A5, A6, and B).

First step in the deletion mapping strategy localized an rII mutation to one of seven regions; six of these were in *rIIA* and one was in *rIIB*. Other deletion strains were used to eventually localize each rII mutation to one of 47 short regions; 36 were in *rIIA*, 11 in *rIIB*. At this point, pairwise coinfections were made between mutant strains that had been localized to the same region by deletion mapping. For example, 24 mutations were deletion mapped to a region called A5d. Pairwise coinfection experiments were conducted among this group of 24 mutants to precisely map their locations relative to each other in the A5d region. Similarly, all of the mutants in each of the 46 other groups were mapped by pairwise coinfections. In this way, a fine structure map was constructed depicting the locations of hundreds of different rII mutations. As seen here, certain locations contained an abnormally high percentage of mutations compared with other sites. These were termed *hot spots* for mutation.

Intragenic Mapping Experiments Provided Insight into the Relationship between Traits and Molecular Genetics

Intragenic mapping studies were a pivotal achievement in our early understanding of gene structure. Since the time of Mendel, geneticists had considered a gene to be a unit of heredity that provided an organism with its inherited traits. In the early 1960s, however, the molecular nature of the gene was not understood. Since it was a unit of heredity, some scientists envisioned a gene as being a particle-like entity that could not be further subdivided into additional parts. However, intragenic mapping studies revealed, convincingly, that this is not the case. These studies showed that mutations can occur at many different sites within a single gene. Furthermore, intragenic crossing over can recombine these mutations, resulting in wild-type genes. Therefore, rather than being an indivisible particle, a gene must be composed of a large structure, which can be subdivided during crossing over.

Benzer's results were published in the late 1950s and early 1960s, around the same time that the structure of DNA was being elucidated by Watson and Crick. We now know that a gene is a segment of DNA that is composed of smaller building blocks called *nucleotides*. A typical gene is a linear sequence of several hundred to several thousand nucleotides. As the genetic map of indicates, mutations can occur at many sites along the linear structure of a gene; intragenic crossing over can recombine mutations that are located at different sites within the same gene.

There are three mechanisms for the transfer of genetic material from one bacterial cell to another. During *conjugation*, bacteria make direct physical con tact with each other. Donor cells can be either F^+ cells or Hfr cells. An F^+ cell contains a circular piece of genetic material, a *plasmid* called an *F* (fertility) *factor* that is transferred to the recipient (F^-) cell during mating. By comparison, an *Hfr* (for High frequency of recombination) bacterium transfers chromosomal DNA to the recipient cell. A second route of genetic transfer is *transduction*. In this case, a bacteriophage accidentally packages a portion of the bacterial chromosome, which is then transferred to another bacterium upon infection. Finally, a third mechanism of genetic transfer is *transformation*. For this to occur, a dead bacterial cell must release its genetic material into the environment. A living bacterial cell in a *competent* state subsequently imports the DNA, and then genetic recombination causes the imported DNA to replace segments of genetic material along the bacterial chromosome.

Bender constructed a *fine structure* genetic map of two bacteria phage genes, *rIIA* and *rIIB*. In the early 1960s, his fine structure map provided imp portent insights into the molecular nature of the gene. It revealed that a gene is not an indivisible particle. Rather, his results indicated that mutations can occur at many sites along the linear structure of a gene and that intragenic crossing over can recombine mutations that are located at different sites within the same gene. Research studies of genetic transfer in bacteria have provided a unique experimental strategy for mapping the linear order and relative locations of bacterial genes. Conjugation has been used to map the locations of many genes along the bacterial chromosome. In this approach, map distances are determined by the number of minutes it takes for a gene to enter a recipient cell during conjugation. In addition, cotransduction and cotransformation experiments have been commonly used to accurately map bacterial genes that are relatively close to each other on the chromosome.

As mentioned in the conceptual summary, intragenic mapping studies of T4 bacteriophages have provided great insight into the molecular nature of genes. A fine structure genetic map was constructed of two bacteriophage genes, *rIIA* and *rIIB*. This was accomplished using a coinfection strategy, in which the very low percentage of intragenic recombinants yielding wild-type phages could be identified by their unique ability to infect a strain of bacteria known as *E. coli* K12(λ). This approach illustrates the power of phage genetics compared with the analysis of off spring in eukaryotic species. It is technically easy to isolate huge numbers of phages. The selective inability of rII mutants to lyse *E. coli K12*(λ) allowed detection of the very few intragenic recombinants, which produced wild-type phages that could lyse *E. coli* K12(λ). In this way, the very short distance that occurs between mutations within a single gene could be determined.

10

Variation in Chromosome

The term *genetic variation* refers to genetic differences between members of the same species, or those between different species. Variation in specific gene is called *allelic variation*. Allelic differences are due to small changes (i.e., mutations) that occur within a particular gene. In this chapter, our emphasis will shift to larger types of genetic changes that affect the chromosomal composition of eukaryotic organisms. As we will see, these changes may affect the expression of many genes and lead to interesting changes in phenotypes.

In the first section of this chapter, we will examine how the structure of a eukaryotic chromosome can be modified, either by altering the total amount of the genetic material or by rearranging the order of genes along a chromosome. A substantial change in chromosome structure, possibly affecting more than a single gene, is referred to as a *chromosome mutation*. In most cases, a mutant chromo some can be detected microscopically; its structure will differ visually from a normal chromosome. In this chapter, we will examine how chromosome mutations occur, how they are transmitted from parent to offspring, and how they affect the phenotype of the individual who inherits them.

The rest of the chapter will be concerned with changes in the total number of chromosomes. A change in chromosome number is called a *genome mutation*. This type of mutation comprises two subtypes: changes in the number of sets of chromosomes, and changes in the numbers of individual chromosomes with in a set. Natural variation in the number of sets of chromosomes is relatively common among different species, particularly in the plant kingdom. Within the same species, changes in chromosome number within a set can also occur, but such alterations usually are detrimental. In this chapter, we will explore how variation in chromosome number occurs, and describe examples where it has significant phenotypic consequences.

Variation in Chromosome Structure

We will begin our discussion of chromosome variation by considering several ways in which the structures of eukaryotic chromosomes can be altered. The chromosomes found in the nuclei of eukaryotic cells are long, linear molecules that carry hundreds or even thousands of genes. In this section, we will examine how the composition of a chromosome can be changed. As you will see, segments of a chromosome can be lost, duplicated, or rearranged in a new way.

The study of chromosomal variation is important for several reasons. First, geneticists have discovered that variations in chromosome structure can have major effects on the phenotype of an organism. For example, we now know that several human genetic diseases are caused by changes in chromosome structure. In other cases, an individual possessing a chromosomal rearrangement may have a normal phenotype yet have a high probability of producing offspring with genetic abnormalities. Later in this section, we will examine irregularities in gamete formation that account for this phenomenon. Finally, changes in chromosome structure have been an important force in the evolution of new species. In this section, we will examine the cellular mechanisms that underlie changes in chromosome structure. We will explore unusual events during meiosis that affect how altered chromosomes are transmitted from parents to offspring. Also, we will consider many examples where chromosomal alterations affect an organism's phenotypic characteristics.

Natural Variation Exists in Chromosome Structure

Before we begin to discuss how chromosome structure can be altered, we need to have a reference point for a normal set of chromosomes. To determine what the normal chromosomes of a species look like, a *cytogeneticist* microscopically examines the chromosomes from several members of the species. Inmost cases, two phenotypically normal individuals of the same species will have the same number and types of chromosomes.

To determine the chromosomal composition of a species, the chromosomes in actively dividing cells are karyotyped. A *karyotype* is a micrograph in which all the chromosomes within a single cell have been arranged in a standard fashion. As seen here, humans contain 46 chromosomes (23 pairs), fruit flies have 8 chromosomes (4 pairs), and corn has 20 chromosomes (10 pairs). Except for the sex chromosomes, which differ between males and females, most members of the same species have very similar karyotypes. By comparison, distantly related species (e.g., humans versus fruit flies) have very different karyotypes. Nevertheless, a karyotype of 46 chromosomes is normal for humans, as is a karyotype of 8 chromosomes for fruit flies.

The chromosomes from any given species can vary considerably in size and shape. Cytogeneticists have various ways to classify and identify chromosomes. The three most commonly used features are size, location of the centromere, and banding patterns that are revealed when the chromosomes are treated with stains. By convention, the chromosomes are numbered according to their size, with the largest chromosomes having the smallest numbers. For example, human chromosomes 1, 2, and 3 are relatively large, whereas 21 and 22 are the smallest. An exception to the numbering system are the sex chromosomes, which are designated with letters (for humans, X and Y).

Another distinguishing feature of eukaryotic chromosomes is the location of the centromere. Chromosomes are classified as *metacentric*, *submetacentric*, *acrocentric*, and *telocentric*. Because the centromere is not exactly in the center of a chromosome, each chromosome has a long arm (designated with the letter *q*) and a short arm (designated with the letter *p*). In the case of telocentric chromosomes, the short arm may be almost nonexistent. When preparing a karyotype, the chromosomes are aligned with the short arms on top and the long arms on the bottom. Since different chromosomes often have similar sizes and centromeric locations (e.g., compare human chromosomes 8, 9, and 10), geneticists must use additional methods to accurately identify each type of chromosome. For detailed identification, chromosomes are treated with stains to produce characteristic banding patterns. A human karyotype in which the chromosomes have been treated with a chemical dye called *Giemsa stain*. In some chromosomal regions, the stain binds heavily and produces a dark band; in other regions, the stain hardly binds at all and produces a light band. As shown here, the alternating banding pattern, known as *G bands*, is a unique feature for each chromosome.

The banding pattern of eukaryotic chromosomes is useful in several ways. First, individual chromosomes can be distinguished from each other, even if they have similar sizes and centromeric locations. For example, compare the differences in banding patterns between human chromosomes 8 and 9. These differences permit us to distinguish these two chromosomes even though their sizes and centromeric locations are very similar. Banding patterns are also used to detect changes in chromosome structure. As discussed next, chromosomal re arrangements or changes iii the total amount of genetic material are more easily detected when viewing banded chromosomes. Also, chromosome banding may reveal evolutionary relationships among the chromosomes of closely related species.

Mutations can Alter Chromosome Structure

Now that we understand that normal chromosomes can come in a variety of shapes and sizes, we can consider how the structures of normal chromosomes can be modified. As mentioned earlier, a chromosome mutation is a substantial change in the structure of a chromosome. There are two primary ways that the structure of chromosomes can be altered. First, the total amount of genetic material within a single chromosome can be increased or decreased significantly. Second, the genetic material in one or more chromosomes may be rearranged without affecting the total amount of material. These alterations are categorized as deficiencies, duplications, inversions, and translocations.

Deficiencies and duplications are changes in the total amount of genetic material within a single chromosome. When a *deficiency* occurs, a segment of chromosomal material is missing. In other words, the affected chromosome is deficient in a significant amount of genetic material. Deficiencies are also referred to as *deletions*. In contrast, a *duplication* is the opposite situation—an amount of genetic material is repeated compared with the normal parent chromosome.

Inversions and translocations are chromosomal rearrangements. An *inversion* involves a change in the direction of the genetic material along a single chromosome. For example, a segment of one chromosome has been inverted, so that the order of four C-bands is opposite to that of the parent chromosomes. A *translocation* occurs when one segment of a chromosome breaks off and becomes attached to a different chromosome. When a single piece of chromosome is attached to another chromosome, this is called a *simple translocation*. In other cases, two different types of chromosomes can exchange pieces, thereby producing two abnormal chromosomes carrying translocations. This situation is referred to as a *reciprocal translocation*.

Loss of Genetic Material in a Deficiency Tends to be Detrimental to an Organism

A chromosomal deficiency occurs when a chromosome breaks in one or more places and a fragment of the chromosome is lost. A normal chromosome has broken into two separate pieces. The piece without the centromere will be lost and degraded, Therefore, this event produces a chromosome with a *terminal deficiency*. A chromosome has broken in two places to produce three chromosomal fragments. The central fragment has become lost (and degraded), and the two outer pieces have reattached to each other. This process has created a chromosome with an *interstitial deficiency*. Deficiencies can also be created when recombination takes place at incorrect locations between two homologous chromosomes. The products of this type of aberrant recombination event are one chromosome with a deficiency and another chromosome with a duplication.

The phenotypic consequences of a chromosomal deficiency depend on the size of the deletion and whether it includes genes (or portions of genes) vital to the development of the organism. When deletions have a phenotypic effect, they are usually detrimental. Larger deletions tend to be more harmful, because more genes are missing. Many examples are known in which deficiencies have significant phenotypic influences. In humans, for example, a genetic disease known as *cri-du-chat syndrome* involves a deficiency in a segment of the short arm of human chromosome 5. Individuals who carry a single copy of this abnormal chromosome (along with a normal chromosome 5) display an array of abnormalities including severe mental retardation, facial anomalies, and an unusual catlike cry (the meaning of the French name for the syndrome). Some other human genetic diseases, such as Angelman syndrome and Prader Willi syndrome are due to a deficiency in chromosome 15. Many types of chromosomal deletions have also been associated with human cancers.

Deficiencies can be Detected Using Cytological, Genetic, and Molecular Techniques

A variety of experimental techniques are used to detect a deletion within a chromosome. These include microscopic, genetic, and molecular methods. Microscopic techniques, which are relatively quick and easy, can detect chromosomal deficiencies large enough to be seen with a light microscope. Cri-du chat and Prader Willi syndromes are chromosomal deletions easily detectable via light microscopy. Fairly small deletions, which may involve only one or a few genes, are often difficult to detect with simple microscopy. However, more complicated microscopy techniques, such as in situ hybridization, have enhanced our ability to detect small deletions. When a mutation causes a phenotypic effect, genetic analysis can sometimes show that it is due to a deletion. Deletions in particular genes can be identified by their inability to revert back to the wild-type allele. In addition, deletions can sometimes be revealed by a phenomenon known as *pseudodominance*. This occurs when one copy of a gene has been deleted from a chromosome and the remaining copy of a recessive allele on the homologous chromosome is phenotypically expressed. Under these conditions, the individual is hemizygous for the recessive allele.

Duplications Tend to be Less Harmful than Deletions

Duplications result in extra genetic material. They are usually caused by abnormal events during recombination. Under normal circumstances, crossing over occurs at analogous sites between homologous chromosomes. On rare occasions, the crossover may occur at two different sites on the homologues. This results in one chromatid with an internal duplication and another chromatid with a deletion. The chromosome with the extra genetic material carries a *gene duplication*, because the number of copies of gene *C* has been increased from one to two. In most cases, gene duplications happen as rare, sporadic events during the evolution of species. Later in this section, we will consider how multiple copies of genes can evolve to produce a family of genes with specialized functions.

Like deletions, the phenotypic consequences of duplications tend to be correlated with size. Duplications are more likely to have phenotypic effects if they involve a large piece of the chromosome. In general, small duplications are less likely to have harmful effects than are deletions of comparable size. This observation suggests that having one copy of a gene is more harmful than having three copies. In humans, relatively few well-defined syndromes are known to be caused by small chromosomal duplications.

In 1936, Bridges Found that Gene Duplications Produced the Bar and Ultra-bar Eyes Phenotype in *Drosophila*

Early insight into the causes of gene duplications came from studies in *Drosophila* involving a trait that affects the number of facets in the eye. In 1914, Sabra Colby Tice of Columbia University found a fly that had a reduced number of facets. This trait was called bar eyes. A genetic analysis of the trait revealed that it is an X-linked trait that shows incomplete dominance. Females homozygous for the bar allele have a more severe phenotype than heterozygous females that have one bar allele and one wild-type allele.

In 1920, Charles Zeleny at the University of Illinois identified some rare mutants in a stock of flies that was originally homozygous for the *bar* allele. Some rare flies had eyes that were phenotypically normal (*bar revertants*), and other flies had eyes with even fewer facets than the *bar* homozygote. Zeleny called these flies *ultra-bar* (also known as *double-bar*). This trait also shows incomplete dominance, since a female fly that is homozygous for the *ultra-bar* allele has fewer facets than a heterozygous female fly carrying one *ultra-bar* allele and one normal allele.

Based on the results of genetic crosses, Alfred Sturtevant and Thomas Hunt Morgan of Columbia University initially suggested that the ultra-bar phenotype was due to a gene duplication in which two copies of the *bar* allele were on the same X-chromosome. Since it was (erroneously) thought that an ultra-bar female fly had two copies of the *bar* allele, yet displayed a more intense phenotype than a homozygous bar female that also had two copies of the *bar* allele, the term *position effect* was coined. This term refers to changes in phenotype that are caused by the positions of genes on a chromosome. In this case, it was suggested that having two *bar* alleles on the same chromosome produced a different phenotype compared with having two copies of the *bar* allele on separate X-chromosomes.

To gain further insight into the cause of the bar and ultra-bar phenotypes, Calvin Bridges at the California Institute of Technology investigated the bar/ultra-bar phenomenon at the cytological level. In cells of the *Drosophila* salivary gland, the chromosomes are easy to study under the microscope, because they replicate many times to form gigantic *polytene chromosomes*. The structure of polytene chromosomes will be described later in this chapter.

Because polytene chromosomes are so large, their banding pattern is very easy to see in great detail. It is thus possible to detect very small changes in chromosome structure. In the experiment described here, which was conducted in 1936, Bridges investigated changes in chromosome structure associated with the bar and ultra-bar phenotypes.

Hypothesis

The rare formation of the ultra-bar phenotype is due to a duplication of the bar allele. Information concerning the nature of the bar and ultra-bar phenotypes may be revealed by a cytological examination of polytene chromosomes.

Testing the hypothesis

Starting materials: A strain of flies homozygous for the bar allele and a homozygous normal strain.

1. Within the strain of homozygous bar-eyed flies, identify rare these that have normal eyes (bar revertants) or ultra-bar eyes.
2. Dissect the salivary glands from the larva of a normal strain, a homozygous bar strain, a bar-revertant strain, and an ultra-bar strain.
3. Prepare the salivary cells for the microscopic examination of the polytene chromosomes. It involves gently breaking open the cells, staining the chromosomes with dyes, and squashing the preparation on a microscope slide underneath a coverslip.
4. View the banding patterns of the polytene chromosomes under the microscope.

Interpreting the data

The cytological examination of region 16A provided direct insight into the nature of the bar and ultra-bar phenotypes. Bridges found that the bar phenotype itself is caused by a duplication of the genetic material in the 16A region of the chromo some. Furthermore, homozygous bar stocks can occasionally produce phenotypically normal flies (bar revertants) and ultra-bar flies by altering gene number. The polytene chromosomes of bar revertants showed that the 16A region had returned to the wild-type banding pattern. In other words, the duplicated region was re turned to a single copy. By comparison, the opposite situation occurred for the ultra-bar phenotype. In this case, an additional duplication occurred, so that there were three copies of the 16A region. As stated by Bridges, "The Bar-eye reduction [the number of facets] is thus seen to be interpretable as the effect of increasing the action of certain genes by doubling or triplicating their number."

The mechanism for the formation of the bar allele can be explained by unequal crossing over. The formation of *ultra-bar* and *bar-revertant* alleles can likewise be explained by unequal crossing over. As shown here, an unequal crossover between two X-chromosomes carrying the duplicated *bar* allele can result in one chromosome carrying one copy (*bar revertant*) and the other chromosome carrying three copies (*ultra-bar*):

The gene duplication and triplication seen with *bar* and *ultra-bar* alleles are also associated with position effects. A female that is homozygous for the *bar* allele has four copies of this region, and a female that is heterozygous for the *ultra-bar* allele (three copies) and the wild-type allele (one copy) also has four copies. However, a female that is heterozygous for the *ultra-bar* and normal alleles has fewer facets (45) than does a *bar* homozygote (70). This is a position effect—the positioning of three copies next to each other on an X-chromosome increases the severity of the defect. Position effects are caused by the influences of chromosome structure or genetic regulatory regions on the level of gene expression. In this case, each of the three genes in the *ultra-bar* allele is expressed at a higher level than it is when there are just one or two copies on the X-chromosome.

Duplications Provide Additional Material for Gene Evolution, Sometimes Leading to the Development of Gene Families

In contrast to the gene duplication that causes the bar phenotype in *Drosophila*, the majority of small chromosomal duplications have no phenotypic effect. Nevertheless, they are still very important, because they provide raw material for the addition of more genes into a species' chromosomes. Over the course of many generations, this can lead to the formation of a *gene family* consisting of two or more genes that are similar to each other. The members of a gene family are derived from the same ancestral gene. Over time, two copies of an ancestral gene can accumulate different mutations. Therefore, after many generations, the two genes will be similar but not identical. During evolution, this type of event can occur several times, creating a family of many similar genes.

When two or more genes are derived from a single ancestral gene, the genes are said to be *homologous*. Homologous genes make up a gene family. A well-studied example of a gene family illustrates the evolution of the globin gene family found in humans. The globin genes encode polypeptides that are subunits of proteins that function in oxygen binding. For example, hemoglobin is found in red blood cells; its function is to carry oxygen throughout the body. The globins gene family is composed of fourteen homologous genes that were originally derived from a single ancestral globin gene. According to an evolutionary analysis, the ancestral globin gene duplicated about 800 million years ago. Since that time, additional duplication events and chromosomal rearrangements have occurred to produce the current number of fourteen genes on three different human chromosomes.

Gene families have been important in the evolution of traits. Even though all of the globin polypeptides are subunits of proteins that play a role in oxygen binding, the accumulation of different mutations in the various family members has created globins that are more specialized in their function. For example, *myoglobin* is better at binding and storing oxygen, whereas the *hemoglobins* are better at binding and transporting oxygen via the red blood cells. Also, these different globin genes are ex pressed during different stages of human development. The ε- and ζ-globin genes are expressed very early in embryonic life, while the γ-globin gene exhibits its maximal expression during the second and third trimesters of gestation. Following birth, the γ-globin gene is turned off and the β-globin gene is turned on. These differences in the expression of the globin genes reflect the differences in the oxygen transport needs of humans during the embryonic, fetal, and postpartum stages of life.

Inversions Often Occur Without Phenotypic Consequences

We now turn our attention to changes in chromosome structure that involve a re arrangement in the genetic material. A chromosome with an inversion contains a segment that has been flipped to the opposite orientation. Geneticists classify inversions according to the location of the centromere. If the centromere lies within the inverted region of the chromosome, the inverted region is known as a *pericentric inversion*. Alternatively, if the centromere is found outside the inverted region, the inverted region is called a *paracentric inversion*.

When a chromosome contains an inversion, the total amount of genetic material remains the same as in a normal chromosome. For this reason, the great majority of inversions do not have any phenotypic consequences in the individuals who carry them. In rare cases, however, an inversion can alter the phenotype of an individual. Whether or not this occurs is related to the boundaries of the inverted segment. When an inversion occurs, the chromosome is broken in two places and the ends flip around to produce the inversion. If either breakpoint occurs within a vital gene, the function of the gene is expected to be disrupted, possibly producing a phenotypic effect. For ex ample, some people with *hemophilia* (type A) have inherited an X-linked inversion that has inactivated a gene for Factor VIII (a blood clotting protein). In other cases, an inversion (or translocation) may reposition a gene on a chromosome in a way that alters its normal level of expression.

Since inversions seem like an unusual genetic phenomenon, it is perhaps surprising that they are found in human populations in quite significant numbers. About 2% of the human population carry inversions that are detectable with a light microscope. In most cases, these individuals are phenotypically normal and live their lives without knowing they contain this abnormality. In a few cases, however, an individual with an inversion chromosome may produce (one or more) off spring with genetic abnormalities. This event may prompt a physician to request a microscopic examination of the individual's chromosomes. In this way, a phenotypically normal individual may discover that they have a chromosome with an in version. Next, we will examine why an individual carrying an inversion may produce offspring with phenotypic abnormalities.

Inversion Heterozygotes may Produce Abnormal Gametes Due to Crossing Over

An individual who carries one copy of a normal chromosome and one copy of an inverted chromosome is known as an *inversion heterozygote*. Such an individual, though possibly phenotypically normal, may have a high probability of producing abnormal gametes. The frequency of abnormal gametes depends on the size of the inverted segment. An inversion heterozygote with a fairly large inverted segment may produce a sizable number of abnormal gametes (perhaps 1/3 or even higher).

The underlying cause of abnormal gametes is crossing over within the inverted region. During meiosis I of gamete formation, pairs of homologous sister chromatids synapse with each other. For the normal chromosome and inversion chromosome to synapse properly, a loop, termed an *inversion loop*, must form to permit the homologous genes on both chromosomes to align next to each other despite the inverted sequence. If a crossover occurs within the inversion loop, highly abnormal chromosomes will be produced.

The consequences of this type of crossover depend on whether the inversion is pericentric or paracentric. This is a single crossover that involves only two of the four sister chromatids. Following the completion of mitosis, this single crossover yields two abnormal chromosomes. Both of these abnormal chromosomes have a segment that is deleted and a different segment that is duplicated. In this example, one of the abnormal chromosomes is missing genes *A*, *B*, and *C* and has extra copies of genes *H* and *I*. The other abnormal chromosome has the opposite situation; it is missing genes *H* and *I* and has an extra copy of genes *A*, *B*, and *C*. If these abnormal chromosomes are passed on to off spring, they may produce phenotypic abnormalities depending on the amount and nature of the duplicated/deleted genetic material.

The outcome of a crossover involving a paracentric inversion. A single crossover has occurred between two homologous sister chromatids; the other two sister chromatids have not participated in a crossover. This single crossover event produces a very strange outcome. One chromosome is produced that contains two centromeres. This is

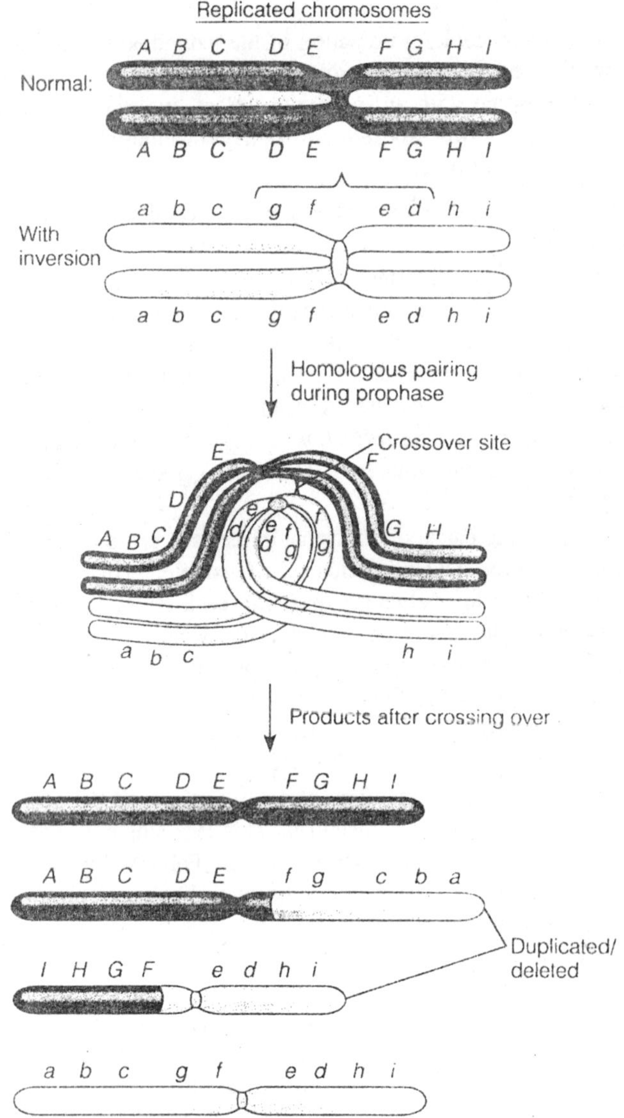

Fig. 10.1. Crossover within a pericentric inversion.

called a *dicentric chromosome*; the region of chromosome connecting the two centromeres is called a *dicentric bridge*. The crossover also produces a piece of chromosome without any centromere. This *acentric* (without a centromere) fragment will be lost and degraded in subsequent cell divisions. The dicentric chromosome is a temporary condition. When the two centromeres try to move toward opposite poles during anaphase, the dicentric bridge will be forced to break at some random location. Therefore, the net result of this crossover is to produce two normal chromosomes (namely, the ones that did not cross over) and two chromosomes that contain deletions. The chromosomes with deletions are the result of the snapping in two of the dicentric chromosome.

Translocations can be Balanced or Unbalanced; Unbalanced Translocations Usually have Detrimental Phenotypic Effects

Another type of chromosomal rearrangement is a translocation. As mentioned at the beginning of this section, reciprocal translocations involve an exchange of chromosomal fragments between two different chromosomes. A reciprocal translocation can be produced when two nonhomologous chromosomes cross over with each other. This type of rare aberrant event results in a rearrangement of the genetic material, though not a change in the total amount of genetic material. For this reason, a reciprocal translocation is also called a *balanced translocation*. Like inversions, balanced translocations are usually without any phenotypic consequences, because the individual has a normal amount of genetic material. In a few cases, balanced translocations can result in position effects in a fashion similar to inversions.

The inheritance of a simple translocation, in which one fragment of a chromosome is attached to another chromosome, can result in an unbalanced translocation. Unbalanced translocations are generally associated with phenotypic abnormalities or even lethality. An inherited human syndrome known as *familial Down syndrome* provides an example of this phenomenon. In this condition, a large segment of chromosome 21 is translocated to chromosome 14. In addition, this individual already has two normal copies of chromosome 21. This results in an imbalance in genetic material, since the individual has three copies of the genes that are found on a large segment of chromosome 21. As will be discussed later in this chapter, imbalances among many genes often lead to phenotypic anomalies. In familial Down syndrome, the person exhibits characteristics very similar to those of an individual with the more common form of Down syndrome, which is due to three entire copies of chromosome 21.

Individuals with Balanced Translocations may Produce Abnormal Gametes due to the Segregation of Chromosomes

Individuals who carry balanced translocations have a greater risk of producing gametes with unbalanced combinations of chromosomes.

Whether or not this occurs depends on the segregation pattern during meiosis I. In this example, the parent carries a balanced, reciprocal translocation and is likely to be phenotypically normal. During gamete formation, the homologous chromosomes attempt to synapse with each other. Because of the translocations, the pairing of homologous regions leads to the formation of an unusual structure that contains four pairs of sister chromatids, termed a *translocation cross*.

To understand the segregation of translocated chromosomes, pay close attention to the centromeres, which are numbered in the figure. During anaphase I of meiosis, each daughter cell will receive one of the two pairs of sister chromatids. For these translocated chromosomes, the expected segregation is due to the segregation of the centromeres; each daughter should receive a centromere located on chromosome 1 and a centromere located on chromosome 2. This can occur in two ways. One possibility is *alternate segregation*, this occurs when the chromosomes on opposite side of the translocation cross segregate into the same cell. One daughter cell receives two normal chromosomes, and the other cell gets two translocated chromosomes. Following meiosis II, four gametes are produced: two are normal and two have reciprocal (balanced) translocations.

Another possible segregation pattern is called *adjacent-1 segregation*. This occurs when adjacent chromosomes (one of each type of centromere) segregate into the same cell. When this occurs, each daughter cell receives one nor mal chromosome and one translocated chromosome. This produces four gametes, all of which are genetically unbalanced because part of one chromosome has been deleted and part of another has been duplicated. If the gametes produced from adjacent-I segregation unite with a normal gamete, the resulting zygote is expected to be abnormal genetically, and possibly phenotypically.

Alternate and adjacent-1 segregation are the likely outcomes when an individual carries a reciprocal translocation. Depending on the sizes of the translocated segments, both types may be equally likely to occur. In many cases, the gametes from adjacent-1 segregation cannot produce viable offspring, thereby lowering the fertility of the parent. On very rare occasions, *adjacent-2 segregation* can occur. In this case, the centromeres do not segregate as they should. One daughter cell has received both copies of the centromere on chromosome 1, the other both copies of the centromere on chromosome 2. This rare segregation pattern also yields four abnormal gametes that contain an unbalanced combination of chromosomes.

Variation in Chromosome Number

As we have seen in the preceding section, chromosome structure can be altered in a variety of ways. The total number of chromosomes, too, can vary. Eukaryotic species typically contain several chromosomes that are inherited as one or more sets. Variations in chromosome number can be categorized in two ways: variation in the number of sets of chromosomes, and variation in the number of particular chromosomes within a set.

Organisms that are *euploid* have a chromosome number that is an exact multiple of a chromosome set. In *Drosophila melanogaster*, a normal individual possesses eight chromosomes. The species is diploid, having two sets of four chromosomes each. We can also recognize that a normal fruit fly is euploid because eight chromosomes divided by four chromosomes per set equals two exact sets. On rare occasions, an abnormal fruit fly can be produced with twelve chromosomes, containing three sets of four chromosomes each. This alteration in euploidy produces a *triploid* fruit fly. Such a fly is also euploid, since it contains exactly three sets of chromosomes. Organisms with three

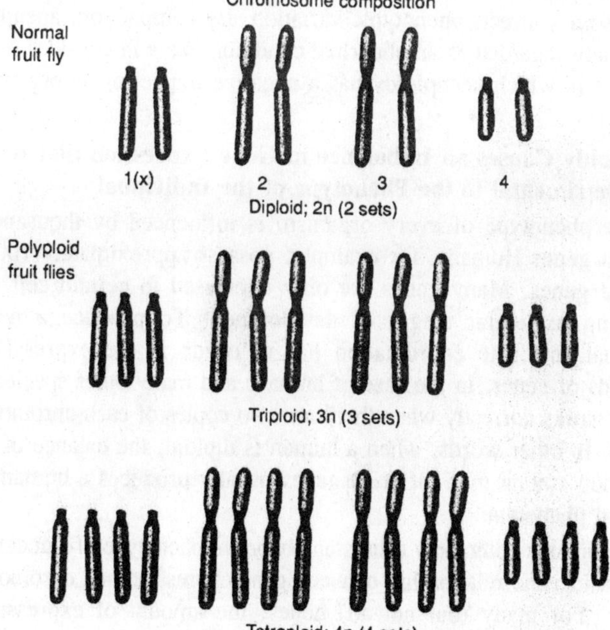

Fig. 10.2. types of variation in chromosome number.

or more sets of chromosomes are also called *polyploid*. Geneticists use the letter n to represent a set of chromosomes. A diploid organism is referred to as $2n$, a triploid organism $3n$, a *tetraploid* organism as $4n$, and so forth.

A second way in which chromosome number can vary is by *aneuploidy* (literally, not euploidy). This term refers to a variation that involves an alteration in the number of particular chromosomes, so that the total number of chromosomes it not an exact multiple of a set (not an exact multiple of n). For example, an abnormal fruit fly could contain nine chromosomes instead of eight because it had three copies of chromosome 2 instead of the normal two copies. Such a animal is said to have *trisomy*-2 or to be trisomic. Instead of being perfectly diploi (i.e., $2n$), a trisomic animal is $2n + 1$. By comparison, a fruit fly could be lacking copy of chromosome 1 and contain a total of seven chromosomes ($2n - 1$). The animal would have *monosomy-1*.

In this section, we will examine euploid and aneuploid variation in many eukaryotic species. We will learn that euploid variation among different species occurs occasionally in animals and quite frequently in plants. We will see how natural variation in the number of sets of chromosomes affects phenotypic variation. By comparison, aneuploidy is generally regardcd as an abnormal condition We will consider several examples in which aneuploidy has a negative impact of an organism's phenotype.

Aneuploidy Causes an Imbalance in Gene Expression that is often Detrimental to the Phenotype of the Individual

The phenotype of every organism is influenced by thousands of different genes Humans, for example, possess approximately 100,000 different genes. Many genes are only expressed in certain cell types or during particular stages of development To produce a normal individual, intricate coordination has to occur in the expression of thousands of genes. In the case of humans and many other species, the process works correctly when there are two copies of each chromosome per cell. In other words, when a human is diploid, the balance of gene expression among man different genes usually produces a human with a normal phenotype.

Aneuploidy commonly causes an abnormal phenotype. To understand why consider the relationship between gene expression and chromosome number. For many (but not all) genes, the amount of expression is correlated with the number of genes per cell. Compared with a diploid cell, if a gem is carried on a chromosome that is present in three copies instead of two, approximately 150% of the normal amount of gene product will be made. Alter natively, if only one copy of that gene is present due to a monosomy abnormality only 50% of the gene product will be made. Therefore, in trisomic and monosomic individuals, there is an imbalance in the level of gene expression between the majority of chromosomes found in pairs versus those that are not.

At first glance, the difference in gene expression between euploid and aneuploid individuals may not seem terribly drastic. Keep in mind, however, that a eukaryotic chromosome carries hundreds or even thousands of different genes. Therefore, when an organism is trisomic or monosomic, many gene products will occur in excessive or deficient amounts. This imbalance among many genes appears to underlie the abnormal phenotypic effects that aneuploidy frequently causes. In most cases, these effects are detrimental and produce an individual that is less likely to survive than a euploid individual.

The first person to recognize the harmful effects of aneuploidy was Albert Blakeslee at Cold Spring Harbor. In the 1920s, Blakeslee and his colleagues identified many examples of alterations in chromosome number in the Jimson weed (*Datura stramonium*). All 12 trisomies had capsules that were morphologically different from those of the normal diploid strain. These aneuploid plants also had many other morphologically distinguishable traits, including changes in leaf shape, size, and so forth. In many cases, the observed changes in chromosome number produced detrimental traits. For example, Blakeslee noted that the cocklebur plant (trisomy-6) is "weak and lopping with the leaves narrow and twisted."

Aneuploidy in Humans causes Abnormal Phenotypes

One important reason that geneticists are so interested in aneuploidy is its relationship to certain inherited disorders in humans. Even though most people are born with a normal number of chromosomes alterations in chromosome number occur fairly frequently during gamete formation. About 5-10% of all fertilized human eggs result in an embryo with an abnormality in chromosome number. In most cases, these abnormal embryos do not develop properly and result in a spontaneous abortion very early in pregnancy Approximately 50% of all spontaneous abortions are due to alterations in chromosome number.

In some cases, an abnormality in chromosome number produces an offspring that can survive. Several human disorders involve abnormalities in chromosome number. The most common are trisomies of chromosomes 21, 18, or 13, or abnormalities in the number of the sex chromosomes. Most of the known trisomies involve chromosomes that are relatively small (i.e., chromosomes 21, 18, and 13). Trisomies of the other human autosomes and monosomies of the autosomes usually produce a lethal phenotype that causes early spontaneous abortion.

Variation in the number of X-chromosomes, unlike the case for most other large chromosomes, is often nonlethal. The survival of trisomy-X individuals is explained by X-inactivation. In an individual with more than one X-chromosome, all additional X-chromosomes are converted to Barr bodies in the somatic cells of adult tissues. In an individual with trisomy-X, for example, out of the three X-chromosomes are converted to inactive Barr bodies. Unlike the autosomes, the normal level of expression for X-linked genes is from a single X-chromosome. In other words, the correct level of mammalian gene expression results from two copies of each autosomal gene and one copy of each X-linked gene. This explains how the expression of X-linked genes in males (XY) can be maintained at the same levels as in females (XX). It may also explain why monosomy-X and trisomy-X are not lethal conditions. The phenotypic effects involving sex chromosomal abnormalities may be due to the expression of X-linked genes prior to embryonic X-inactivation, or due to the imbalance in the expression of pseudoautosomal genes.

Some human abnormalities in chromosome number are influenced by the age of the parents. Older parents are more likely to produce children with abnormalities in chromosome number. For example, the incidence of Down syndrome rises with the age of the parents, particularly that of the mother. This syndrome was first described by the English physician John Langdon Down in 1866. The association between maternal age and Down syndrome was later discovered by L. S. Penrose in 1933, even before the chromosomal basis for the disorder was identified by the French scientist Jerome Lejeune in 1959. Down syndrome is most commonly caused by nondisjunction at meiosis I in the oocyte. The mechanism of nondisjunction will be described later in this chapter.

Different theories have been proposed to explain the relationship between maternal age and Down syndrome. One popular idea suggests that it may due to the age of the oocytes. Human primary oocytes are produced within the ovary of the female fetus prior to birth and are arrested at prophase I of meiosis I until the time of ovulation. Therefore, as a women ages, her primary oocytes have been in prophase I for a progressively longer period of time. This added length of time may contribute to an increased frequency of nondisjunction. About 5% of the time, Down syndrome is due to an extra paternal chromosome. Prenatal tests can deter mine if a fetus has Down syndrome or some other genetic abnormalities.

Table 10.1. Aneuploid conditions in humans

Condition	*Frequency*	*Syndrome*	*Characteristics*
Autosomal			
Trisomy-21	1/800	Down	Mental retardation, abnormal pattern of palm creases, slanted eycs, flattened face, short stature
Trisomy-18	1/6,000	Edward	Mental and physical retardation, facial abnormalities, extreme muscle tone
Trisomy-13	1/15,000	Patau	Mental and physical retardation, wide variety of defects in organs, large triangular nose
Sex chromosomal			
XXY	1/1,000 (males)	Klinefeltor	Sexual immaturity no sperm, breast swelling
XYY	1/1,000 (males)	Jacobs	Tall
XXX	1/1,500 (females)	Super female	Tall and thin, menstrual irregularity
X0	1/5,000	Turner	Short stature, webbed neck, (females) sexually undeveloped

Variations in Euploidy Occur Naturally in a few Animal Species

We now turn our attention to changes in the number of sets of chromosomes, referred to as variations in euploidy Most species of animals are diploid. In many cases, changes in euploidy are not well tolerated. For example, polyploidy in mammals is generally a lethal condition. In less complex vertebrates and invertebrates, however, a few examples of naturally occurring variations in euploidy occur. Male bees (drones) contain a single set of chromosomes; they are produced from unfertilized eggs. By comparison, female bees are diploid. Geneticists often refer to male bees as being "haploid," although in a strict genetic sense, the term haploid describes gametes that contain half the genetic material of the parent's somatic cells. An organism with a single set of chromosomes within its somatic cells is more accurately called *monoploid*.

A few examples of polyploid animals have been discovered. In some cases, animals that are morphologically very similar to each other can be found as a diploid species as well as a separate polyploid species. This situation occurs among certain amphibians and reptiles. As you can see, they look fairly similar to each other. Their differences in euploidy can only be revealed by an examination of the chromosome number in the somatic cells of the animals.

Variations in Euploidy can Occur in Certain Tissues within an Animal; Polytene Chromosomes are an Extreme example of Repeated Chromosome Doubling

Thus far, we have considered variations in chromosome number that occur at fertilization, so that all the somatic cells of an individual contain this variation. In many animals, certain tissues of the body will display normal variations in the number of sets of chromosomes. In particular, diploid animals sometimes produce tissues that are polyploid. The cells of the human liver, for example, can vary to a great degree in their ploidy. Liver cells can be triploid, tetraploid, and even octaploid ($8n$). This phenomenon is known as *endopolyploidy*. The biological significance of endopolyploidy is not completely understood. One possibility is that the increase in chromosome number in certain cells may enhance their ability to produce specific gene products that are needed in great abundance.

An unusual example of natural variation in the ploidy of somatic cells occurs in *Drosophila* and a few other insects. Within certain tissues, such as the salivary glands, the *chromosomes* undergo repeated rounds of chromosome replication without cellular division. For example, in the salivary gland cells of *Drosophila*, the pairs of chromosomes double approximately nine times ($2^9 = 512$). Repeated rounds of chromosomal replication produce a bundle of chromosomes that lie together in a parallel fashion. This bundle of many chromatids lying side-by-side is a polytene chromosome. They were first observed by E. G. Balbiani in 1881. In the early 1930s, Theophilus Painter and his colleagues at the University of Texas recognized that the size and morphology of polytene chromosomes provided geneticists with unique opportunities to study chromosome structure and gene organization.

Prior to the formation of polytene chromosomes, *Drosophila* cells contain eight chromosomes (two sets of four chromosomes each). In the salivary gland cells, the homologous chromosomes synapse with each other and replicate to form a polytene structure. During this process, the four types of chromosomes aggregate to form a single structure with several polytene arms. The central point where the chromosomes aggregate is known as the *chromocenter*. Each of the four types of chromosome are attached to the chromocenter near their centromeres. The X and Y and chromosome 4 are telocentric, and chromosomes 2 and 3 are metacentric. Therefore, chromosomes 2 and 3 have two arms that radiate from the chromocenter while the X and Y and chromosome 4 have a single arm projecting from the chromocenter.

Because of their considerable size, polytene chromosomes lend themselves to an easy microscopic examination. Ordinarily, we use light microscopy to visualize the highly condensed metaphase chromosomes seen during mitosis or meiosis. Since polytene chromosomes are so large, we can even see them during interphase, when normal chromosomes are not visible. In fact, a polytene chromosome during interphase is actually 100—200 times as large as the average metaphase chromosome. Polytene chromosomes exhibit a characteristic banding pattern. Each dark band is known as a *chromomere*. The structure of the genetic material within a dark band is more compact than in the interband region. More than 95% of the DNA is found within the chromomeres. The banding patterns of polytene chromosomes are much more detailed than those observed in metaphase chromosomes. Cytogeneticists have identified approximately 5000 bands along polytene chromosomes. At one time, each chromomere was thought to correspond to one gene. However, this idea was found to be incorrect. Polytene chromosomes have allowed geneticists to study the organization and functioning of interphase chromosomes in great detail. When a gene is deleted or duplicated in a mutation, researchers can map the change by observing abnormalities in the structure of polytene chromosomes. In addition, since polytene chromosomes can be observed during interphase, the expression of particular genes can be correlated with changes in the compaction of certain bands in the polytene chromosome.

Variations in Euploidy are Common in Plants; this Variation has allowed the Development of Many Agricultural Crops

We now turn our attention to the variations of euploidy that occur in plants. In contrast to animals, plants commonly exhibit polyploidy. Among ferns and flowering plants, about 30—35% of the species are polyploid. Polyploidy is also important in agriculture. Many of the fruits and grains we eat are produced from polyploid plants. For example, the species of wheat that we use to make bread, *Triticum aestivum*, is hexaploid (6*n*). In many instances, polyploid strains of plants display outstanding agricultural characteristics. They are often larger in size and more robust. These traits are clearly advantageous in the production of food. In addition, polyploids tend to exhibit a greater adaptability, which allows them to with stand harsher environmental conditions. Also, polyploid ornamental plants often produce larger flowers than their diploid counterparts.

Polyploids having an odd number of chromosome sets, such as triploids or pentaploids, are usually sterile. The sterility arises because they produce highly aneuploid gametes. To understand why aneuploidy occurs, consider what happens during anaphase Tin a triploid organism. Since there are three copies of each replicated chromosome, they cannot be divided equally between two daughter cells. For each type of chromosome, a daughter cell randomly gets one or two copies. For example, one daughter cell might receive one copy of chromosome 1, two copies of chromosome 2, two copies of chromosome 3, one copy of chromosome 4, and so forth. For a triploid species containing many different chromosomes in a set, it is very unlikely that any gamete will be euploid. If we assume that a daughter cell will receive either one copy or two copies of each kind of chromo some, the probability that a gamete will end up being perfectly haploid or diploid is $(1/2)^{N-1}$, where *N* is the number of chromosomes in a set. As an example, in a triploid species containing 20 chromosomes per set, the probability of producing a haploid or diploid gamete is 1 in 524,288. Thus, a gamete is almost certain to contain one copy of some chromosomes and two copies of the other chromosomes. This high probability of aneuploidy underlies the reason for triploid sterility.

Sterility can be an agriculturally useful trait, since it may result in a seedless fruit. For example, seedless watermelons and bananas are triploid varieties. The domestic banana, which is triploid, was originally derived from a normal diploid species and has been asexually propagated by humans via cuttings. The small black spots in the center of a domestic banana are degenerate seeds. In the case of flowers, the seedless phenotype can also be beneficial. Seed producers such as Burpee are developing triploid varieties of flowering plants. The triploid marigold is sterile and unable to set seed. According to Burpee, "they bloom and bloom, unweakened by seed bearing."

Natural and Experimental Ways to Produce Variations in Chromosome Number

As we have seen, variations in chromosome number are fairly widespread and usually have a significant impact on the phenotypes of plants and animals. For these reasons, researchers have wanted to understand the cellular mechanisms that cause variations in chromosome number. In some cases, a change in chromosome number is the result of nondisjunction. The term *nondisjunction* refers to the event in which the chromosomes do not separate properly during anaphase. As we will see, it maybe caused by an improper separation of homologous pairs in a tetrad, or a failure of the centromere to split during meiosis II or mitosis. *Meiotic nondisjunction* can produce gametes that have too many or too few chromosomes. If such a gamete fuses with a normal gamete during fertilization, the resulting individual will have an abnormal chromosomal composition in all of the cells of the organism. An abnormal nondisjunction event also may occur after fertilization in one of the somatic cells of the body. This second mechanism is known as *mitotic nondisjunction*. When this occurs during embryonic stages of development, it may lead to a patch of tissue in the organism that has an abnormal chromosomal composition.

Finally, a third common way in which the chromosome composition of an organism can vary is by *interspecies matings* to produce an alloploid organism. An *alloploid* organism contains sets of chromosomes from two (or more) different species. This term refers to the occurrence of chromosome sets (ploidy) from different (*allo-*) species.

In this section, we will examine these three mechanisms in greater detail. Also, in the past few decades, researchers have devised several methods to manipulate chromosome number in experimentally and agriculturally important species. As we will learn, the experimental manipulation of chromosome number has had an important impact on genetic research and agriculture.

Meiotic Nondisjunction can Produce Aneuploidy; Complete Nondisjunction can Produce Polyploidy

The phenomenon of meiotic nondisjunction was first described by Calvin Bridges, who compared inheritance patterns in *Drosophila* with the cytological presence of certain chromosomes. Nondisjunction event can occur during meiosis I or meiosis II. If it occurs during anaphase of meiosis I, an entire tetrad will migrate into one of the two daughter cells. All the gametes produced from this event will be abnormal. A second possibility is that nondisjunction can occur during anaphase of meiosis II. If this occurs, the net result will be two normal and two abnormal gametes. In this scenario, the individual produced from an abnormal gamete will be aneuploid (namely, either monosomic or trisomic for one chromosome). In rare cases, all the chromosomes can

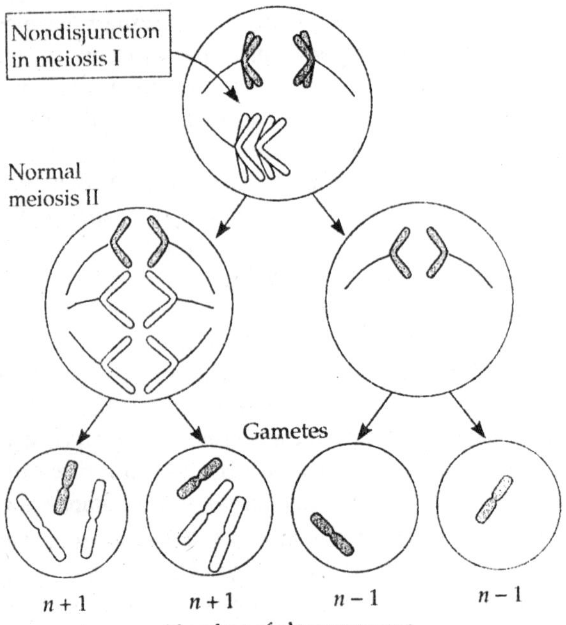

Fig. 10.3. Nondisjunction during meiosis I.

undergo nondisjunction and migrate to one of the daughter cells. The net result of *complete nondisjunction* is a diploid gamete and a gamete without chromosomes. While the gamete without chromosomes is nonviable, the diploid gamete might participate in fertilization with a normal haploid gamete to produce a triploid individual. Therefore, complete nondisjunction can produce individuals that are polyploid.

Mitotic Nondisjunction or Chromosome loss can Produce a Patch of Tissue with an Altered Chromosome Number

Abnormalities in chromosome number occasionally occur after fertilization takes place. In this case, the abnormal event happens during mitosis rather than meiosis. One possibility is that the sister chromatids could separate improperly, so that one daughter cell would have three copies of that chromosome while the other daughter cell would only have one. Alternatively, the sister chromatids could separate during anaphase of mitosis but one of the chromosomes could be improperly attached to the spindle, so that it would not migrate to a pole. If this happens, a chromosome will be degraded if it is left out side of the nucleus when the nuclear membrane re-forms. In this case, one of the daughter cells would have two copies of that chromosome,

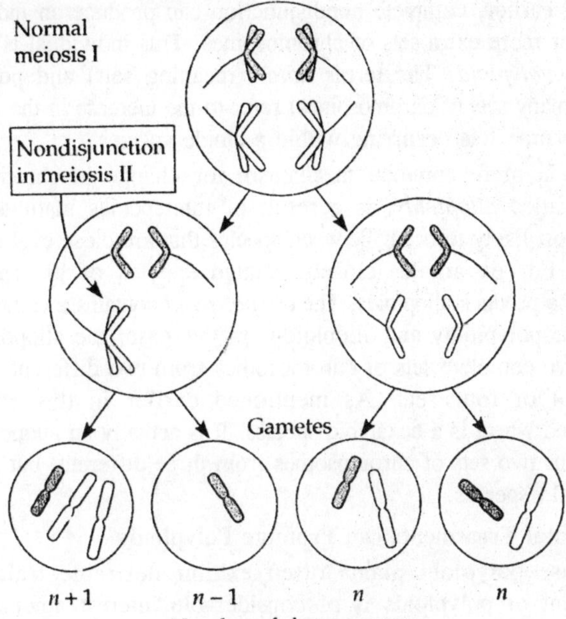

Fig. 10.4. Nondisjunction during meiosis II.

while the other would have only one. When genetic abnormalities occur after fertilization, part of the organism will contain cells that are genetically different from the rest of the organism. This condition is referred to as *mosaicism*. The size and location of the mosaic region will depend on the timing and location of the original abnormal event. If a genetic alteration happens very early in the embryonic development of an organism, the ab normal cell will be the precursor for a large section of the organism, In the most extreme case, an abnormality could take place at the first mitotic division. As an example, consider a fertilized *Drosophila* egg that is XX. One of the X-chromosomes may be lost during the first mitotic division, producing one daughter cell that is XO and one that is XX. XX flies develop into females XO flies develop into males. Therefore, in this example, one-half of the organization will become male and one-half will become female. This peculiar and rare individual is referred to as a *bilateral gynandromorph*.

Changes in Euploidy can Occur by Autopolyploidy, Alloploidy, and Allopolyploidy

Different mechanisms account for changes in the number of chromosome sets among natural populations of plants and animals. As mentioned earlier, complete nondisjunction can produce an individual with one or more extra sets of chromosomes. This individual is known as an *autopolyploid*. The terms *auto-* (meaning self) and polyploid (meaning many sets of chromosomes) refer to the increase in the number of chromosome sets occurring within a single species.

A much more common mechanism for change in chromosome number, called *alloploidy*, is a result of interspecies matings. This event is most likely to occur between species that are close evolutionary relatives. For ex ample, closely related species of grasses may interbreed to produce alloploids. The *allopolyploid* contains a combination of both autopolyploidy and alloploidy. In this case, the allopolyploid contains two complete sets of chromosomes from two different species for a total of four sets. As mentioned earlier in this chapter, domesticated wheat is a hexaploid species. It is actually an allopolyploid that contains two sets of chromosomes from three different, but closely related, wild species.

Experimental Treatments can Promote Polyploidy

Because polyploid plants often exhibit desirable traits, the development of polyploids is of considerable interest among plant breeders. Experimental studies on the ability of environmental agents to promote polyploidy began in the early 1900s. Since that time, various agents have been shown to promote nondisjunction and thereby lead to polyploidy. These include abrupt temperature changes during the initial stages of seedling growth, and the treatment of plants with chemical agents that interfere with the formation of the spindle apparatus.

The drug *colchicine* is commonly used to promote polyploidy. Once inside the cell, colchicine binds to tubulin (a protein found in the spindle apparatus) and thereby interferes with normal chromosome segregation during mitosis or meiosis. In 1937, Alfred Blakeslee and Amos Avery applied colchicine to plant tissue and, at high doses, were able to cause complete mitotic nondisjunction. This strategy can be used to produce new polyploid strains of plants. Colchicine can be applied to seeds, young embryos, or rapidly growing regions of a plant. This application may produce aneuploidy (usually an undesirable outcome), but it often produces polyploid cells, which may grow faster than the surrounding diploid tissue. If the parent plant is diploid, colchicine may cause complete mitotic disjunction, yielding tetraploid ($4n$) cells. As the tetraploid cells continue to divide, they generate a portion of the plant that is often morphologically distinguishable from the remainder. For example, a polyploid stem may have a larger diameter and produce larger leaves and flowers. Since individual plants can be propagated asexually from pieces of plant tissue (i.e., cuttings), the polyploid portion of the plant can be removed, treated with the proper growth hormones, and grown as a separate plant. Alternatively, the polyploid region of a plant may have flowers that produce polyploid seeds; a tetraploid flower will produce diploid pollen and eggs, which will combine to produce tetraploid offspring. In this way, the use of colchicine provides a straightforward method to produce autopolyploid strains of plants.

Alloploids are Often Sterile, but Allopolyploids are More Likely to be Fertile

Geneticists are interested in the production of alloploids and allopolyploids as ways to generate interspecies hybrids with desirable traits. For example, if one species of grass can withstand hot temperatures and a closely related species is adapted to survive through cold winters, a plant breeder may hope to produce an interspecies hybrid that combines both qualities (i.e., good growth in the heat and survival through the winter). Such an alloploid would be desirable in climates with both hot summers and cold winters.

An important determinant of success in producing an interspecies hybrid is the degree of similarity of the different species' chromosomes. In two very closely related species, the number of chromosomes might be identical or very similar. A karyotype of an interspecies hybrid between the roan antelope (*Hippotragus equinus*) and the sable antelope (*H. niger*) is presented. As seen here, these two closely related species have the same number of chromosomes. Moreover, the sizes and banding patterns of the chromosomes show that they correspond to one another. For example, chromosome 1 from both species is fairly large and has very similar banding patterns. This chromosome derived from both species likely carries many of the same genes. Analogous chromosomes from related species are called *homeologous* chromosomes (not to be confused with homologous).

The degree of similarity between the homeologous chromosomes also greatly influences whether an alloploid is fertile. This phenomenon was first recognized by the Russian cytogeneticist G. D. Karpechenko in 1928. He crossed a radish (*Rophanus*) and a cabbage (*Brassica*), both of which are diploid and contain 18 chromosomes. Each of these organisms produces haploid gametes containing 9 chromosomes each. Therefore, the alloploid produced from this interspecies mating contains 18 chromosomes. Since the radish and cabbage are not closely related, the nine *Raphanus* chromosomes are distinctly different from the nine Brassica chromosomes. During meiosis I, the radish and cabbage chromosomes cannot synapse with each other, resulting in a high degree of aneuploidy. Therefore, the radish/cabbage hybrid is sterile.

Karpechenko discovered a way to overcome the sterility of the radish/cabbage hybrid. The idea is to produce an allopolyploid (rather than an alloploid) with a diploid number of chromosomes from each of the two species. In the example here, a radish/cabbage allopolyploid would contain 36 chromosomes instead of 18. During metaphase I, the homologous chromosomes from each of the two species can synapse properly. When anaphase I occurs, the pairs of synapsed chromosomes can disjoin equally to produce gametes with 18 chromosomes each (a haploid set from the radish and a haploid set from the cabbage). These gametes with 18 chromosomes can combine with each other to produce an allopolyploid containing 36 chromosomes. In this way, the allopolyploid is a fertile organism. Unfortunately, it is not agriculturally useful, because its leaves are like the radish and its roots are like the cabbage!

Modern plant breeders employ several different strategies to produce allopolyploids. One is to start with two different tetraploid species. Since these make diploid gametes, the hybrid from this cross would contain a diploid set from each species. Alternatively, if an alloploid containing a monoploid set from each species already exists, a second approach is to create an allopolyploid by using agents such as colchicine.

Cell Fusion Techniques can be Used to Make Hybrid Plants

Thus far, we have discussed several mechanisms that produce variations in chromosome number. Some of these processes can occur naturally and have figured prominently in speciation and evolution. In addition, agricultural geneticists can administer treatments such as colchicine to promote nondisjunction and thereby obtain useful strains of organisms. More recently, researchers are devising cellular approaches to produce hybrids with altered chromosomal composition. As de scribed here, these cellular approaches have important applications in research and agriculture.

In the technique known as *cell fusion*, individual cells are mixed together and made to fuse. This method can be used in gene mapping. In agriculture, cell fusion can create new strains of plants. Cell fusion may allow the crossing of two plants that normally cannot interbreed. There are several reasons that interbreeding cannot occur. For example, one of the parents may be sterile. Also, two distantly related species may not be able to cross-pollinate. Similarly, within a single species there may exist" incompatibility alleles" that prevent certain strains from cross-pollinating or self-fertilizing. In many cases, cell fusion techniques have successfully circumvented such interbreeding problems.

The parent cells were derived from tall fescue grass (*Festuca arundinacea*) and Italian rye-grass (*Lolium multiflorum*). Prior to fusion, the plant cells from these two species were treated with agents that gently digest the cell wall without rupturing the plasma membrane. A plant cell without a cell wall is called a *protoplast*. The protoplasts are mixed together and treated with agents that promote fusion. Immediately after this takes place, a cell containing two separate nuclei is formed. This cell, known as a *heterokaryon*, will spontaneously go through a nuclear fusion process to create a *hybrid cell* with a single nucleus. After nuclear fusion, the hybrid cells can be grown on laboratory media and eventually regenerate an entire plant. The allopolyploid has phenotypic characteristics that are intermediate between tall fescue grass and Italian ryegrass. This type of approach is sometimes used by agricultural geneticists to produce intraspecies and interspecies hybrids.

Monoploids Produced in Agricultural and Genetic Research can be Used to Create Homozygous and Hybrid Strains

Plant breeders sometimes wish to have diploid strains of crop plants that are homozygous for all of their genes. One true-breeding strain can then be crossed to a different true-breeding strain to produce an F_1 hybrid that is heterozygous for many genes. Such hybrids are often more vigorous than the corresponding homozygous strains. This phenomenon, known as *hybrid vigor* or *heterosis*.

Seed companies often use this strategy to produce hybrid seed for many crops, such as corn and alfalfa. To achieve this goal, the companies must have homozygous parental strains that can be crossed to each other to produce the hybrid seed. One way to obtain these homozygous strains involves inbreeding over many generations. This may be accomplished after several rounds of self-fertilization. As you might imagine, this can be a rather time-consuming endeavor.

As an alternative, the production of monoploids can be used as part of an experimental strategy to develop homozygous diploid strains of plants. In 1966, Sipra Guha and Satish Maheswari at the University of Delhi produced monoploid plants directly from pollen (containing the haploid male gamete). Monoploids produced experimentally have been used to improve many agricultural crops such as wheat, rice, corn, barley, and potato. Experimental technique called *anther culture*, which can be used to produce a diploid strain homozygous for all of its genes. It involves alternation between monoploid and diploid generations. The parental plant is diploid but not homozygous for all of its genes. The anthers from this diploid plant are collected, and the haploid pollen grains within them are induced to begin development by a cold shock treatment. After several weeks, monoploid plantlets will emerge, and these can be grown on agar media in a laboratory. Eventually, the plantlets can be transferred to small pots. After the plantlets grow to a reasonable size, a section of the monoploid plantlet can be treated with colchicine to convert it to diploid tissue. A cutting from this diploid section can then be used to generate a separate plant. This diploid plant is expected to be homozygous for all of its genes, be cause it was produced by the chromosomal doubling of a monoploid strain.

In certain animal species, monoploids can be produced by experimental treatments that induce the eggs to begin development without fertilization by sperm. This process is known as *parthenogenesis*. In many cases, however, the haploid zygote will only develop for a short period of time before it dies. Nevertheless, a short phase of development can be useful to research scientists., the zebrafish (*Brachydanio rerio*), a common aquarium fish, has gained recent popularity among researchers interested in vertebrate development. The haploid egg can be induced to begin development by exposure to sperm rendered biologically in active by UV-irradiation.

We classify variations in chromosome structure as *deletions* (or *deficiencies*), *duplications*, *inversions*, and *translocations*. Deletions and duplications involve changes in the total amount of genetic material; inversions and translocations are genetic rearrangements. Deletions tend to be detrimental to the phenotype of the individual, although this depends on the size and location of the deletion. In some cases, a deletion heterozygote will exhibit *pseudodominance* of (normally recessive) genes located in the corresponding region of the non-deleted chromosome. In comparison, duplications tend to be less harmful. Gene duplications provide the raw material for the evolution of *gene families* in which a group of genes encode proteins that carry out similar yet specialized functions.

Inversions and translocations are chromosomal rearrangements; they often do not affect the phenotype of the individual who carries them.

Reciprocal translocations are sometimes called *balanced translocations*, because the individual has a normal amount of genetic material. In a few cases, inversions and translocations can affect phenotype because a breakpoint is within a vital gene or the rearrangement results in a *position effect* that alters gene expression or regulation. Inversions and translocations are often associated with fertility problems and a higher probability of producing abnormal offspring. Even though an individual carrying an inversion or balanced translocation may be phenotypically normal, crossing over and chromosomal segregation may lead to the production of gametes that do not have a balanced amount of genetic material. Such gametes are likely to produce phenotypic abnormality or even lethality.

Chromosome number is another critical factor in determining the phenotype of an organism. In the condition known as *aneuploidy*, an individual may have an extra chromosome (trisomy) or may be missing a chromosome (monosomy). This usually is detrimental to the phenotype. For example, various human genetic diseases, such as Down syndrome (trisomy-21), are due to irregularities in chromo sorre number. Likewise, in plants, aneuploidy also significantly affects the phenotype of an individual.

Variations in the number of sets of chromosomes are also common, particularly in the plant kingdom. This has dramatically influenced agriculture. Many of our modern crops are *polyploid* plants. These frequently exhibit characteristics superior to those of their diploid counterparts. Polyploids with an odd number of chromosome sets are usually sterile, and these are useful in producing seedless varieties of plants. In animals, some cells of the body may be *endopolyploid*–that is, they have more sets of chromosomes than other somatic cells. An extreme example are the *polytene chromosomes* found in *Drosophila*.

Changes in the chromosome number can arise via several different mechanisms. In natural populations, the most important of these are *nondisjunction* and *interspecies matings*. Nondisjunction produces gametes with alterations in chromosome number, which can lead to aneuploidy or even polyploidy. Also, nondisjunction or chromosome loss can occur in cells after fertilization to produce an individual that is a genetic *mosaic*. Another way to produce new combinations of chromosomes is by interspecies matings. These can produce *alloploids*, which have one set of chromosomes from each species, or *allopolyploids*, which have two or more sets from each species. Allopolyploids are more likely to be fertile when the chromosomes are found in homologous pairs.

The primary experimental strategy for studying variation in chromosome structure and number is the cytological examination of chromosomes. A karyotype is a photographic representation of the chromosomes from actively dividing eukaryotic cells. When preparing a karyotype, the chromosomes are usually stained with a dye such as Giemsa, which gives individual chromosomes their own characteristic banding pattern. By observing the banding patterns and number of chromosomes under a microscope, a cytogeneticist can determine if an individual carries a change in chromosome structure or number.

Experimental methods are also available to cause changes in chromosome number. For example, drugs such as colchicine can alter chromosome number by promoting nondisjunction. In addition, laboratory methods can produce hybrids by cell fusion techniques. This can be useful in making fertile interspecies hybrids. Also, monoploid plants and animals can be produced by the experimental activation of haploid gametes.

11

Physical Structure of Protein

Proteins are the nitrogen containing substances of immense importance (*proteos denotes of primary importance*) to the living beings. These are required by the living beings for the formation of *body tissues*, *enzymes*, *hormones*, *immunoglobulins* and other *intracellular* and *extracellular proteins*. Majority of the proteins are high molecular weight substances having very complex structures. On hydrolysis, proteins give *amino acids*, and some times certain non-protein residue(s) in addition to the amino acids. Usually twenty different amino acids are obtained at the most in the protein hydrolysates. Thus, amino acids are the 'building stones' of the protein molecules. Amino acids in the different protein molecules remain arranged in different but definite sequences which impart a specific type of property in these molecules.

Biological Functions of Proteins

Proteins play crucial roles in virtually all biological processes. The significance and remarkable scope of their functions are exemplified in:

Enzymatic Catalysis

Nearly all chemical reactions in biological systems are catalyzed by specific macromolecules called enzymes. Some of these reactions, such as the hydration of carbon dioxide, are quite simple. Others, such as the replication of an entire chromosome, are highly intricate. Nearly all enzymes exhibit enormous catalytic power. They usually enhance reaction rates by at least a millionfold. Indeed, chemical transformations rarely occur at perceptible rates in vivo in the absence of enzymes. Several thousand enzymes have been characterized, and many of them have been crystallized. The striking fact is that all known enzymes are proteins. Thus, proteins play the unique role of determining the pattern of chemical transformation in biological systems.

Transport and Storage

Many small molecules and ions are transported by specific proteins. For example, hemoglobin transports oxygen in erythrocytes, whereas myoglobin, a related protein, transports oxygen in muscle. Iron is carried in the plasma of blood by transferrin and is stored in the liver as a complex with ferritin, a different protein.

Coordination Motion

Proteins are the major component of muscle. Muscle contraction is accomplished by the sliding motion of two kinds of protein filaments. On the microscopic scale, such coordinated motions as the movement of chromosomes in mitosis and the propulsion of sperm by their flagella also are produced by contractile assemblies consisting of proteins.

Mechanical Support

The high tensile strength of skin and bone is due to the presence of collagen, a fibrous protein.

Immune Protection

Antibodies are highly specific proteins that recognize and combine with such foreign substances as viruses, bacteria, and cells from other organisms. Proteins thus play a vital role in distinguishing between self and nonself.

Generation and Transmission of Nerve Impulses

The response of nerve cells to specific stimuli is mediated by receptor proteins. For example, rhodopsin is the photoreceptor protein in retinal rod cells. Receptor molecules that can be triggered by specific small molecules, such as acetylcholine, are responsible for transmitting nerve impulses at synapses—that is, at junctions between nerve cells.

Control of Growth and Differentiation

Controlled sequential expression of genetic information is essential for the orderly growth and differentiation of cells. Only a small fraction of the genome of a cell is expressed at any one time. In bacteria, repressor proteins are important control elements that silence specific segments of the DNA of a cell. A quite different way in which proteins act in different entiation is exemplified by nerve growth factor, a protein complex that guides the formation of neural networks in higher organisms.

Classification of Proteins

A satisfactory classification of the proteins has not been possible till now as the chemical structure of most of the proteins is not known at present. The following classification is based merely upon solubilities and other physical properties of the proteins. On this basis, the proteins have been classifed in three groups, namely *simple proteins*, *conjugated proteins* and *derived proteins*.

According to Structure

Fibrous proteins

These proteins are associated with cellular elements and often serve the function of supporting specific structures of the cell. Examples are wool, silk fibroin, collagen (connective tissue), myosin (muscle), keratin (hair) and fibrin (blood clot). These proteins are largely insoluble in aqueous media and have high molecular weights that cannot be accurately estimated because of difficulties encountered in their purification. They appear as fibers made up of linear molecules that are arranged roughly parallel to the fiber axis. They are amorphous and some are capable of stretching and contracting. Human fibrin has the molecular dimensions of 38×700 Å.

Globular proteins

In contrast to fibrous proteins, the globular proteins are soluble in aqueous media and can be isolated in the crystalline state. Although not necessarily spherical, they are less asymmetric than fibrous proteins and consist of polypeptides (chains of amino acid residues) that are held together by cross-linked groups or in an aggregated state. Such aggregates are held together in a three-dimensional structure by relatively weak non-covalent bonds.

According to Solubility

Albumins

These proteins are *soluble* in water and dilute salt solutions, and can be coagulated on heating. These can be precipitated from their solutions upon *full saturation* with ammonium sulphate. Albumins thus salted-out may be purified by the process of dialysis. The coagulated albumins are insoluble in water, dilute acid, alkali and salt solutions.

Coagnlation starts above 75°C but this temperature differs for albumins obtained from different sources. The common examples of albumins are *ovalbumin*, *serum albumin*, *lactalbumin*, *myoalbumin*. The plant tissues have also been reported to contain albumins.

Globulins

These proteins are insoluble in water and soluble in dilute salt solutions, but can be coagulated on heating. These can be precipitated from aqueous solutions merely by fifty percent saturation with ammonium sulphate. These are found both in the animal and plant tissues. The examples of globulins are *ovoglobulin* (eggs), *lactoglobulin* (milk), *fibrinogen*, *alpha*, *beta* and *gamma globulins* (all in serum), *myosin* and *tropmyosin* (both in muscles), *edestin* (hempseed) and *excelsin* (Brazil nut).

Globulins may be precipitated merely by diluting globulin solutions since these are soluble in dilute salt solutions but insoluble in salt-free water or extremely dilute salt solutions. Globulins may also be precipitated merely by dialysis of the globulin solutions. Alubmins may be separated from globulins by using this technique.

Globins

These are neutral type of histones which cannot be precipated by adding ammonium hydroxide as histones can be precipitated. Such proteins can easily ombine with heme forming hemoglobin.

Glutelins

These are insoluble in neutral aqueous solutions but soluble in dilute acid or alkali. Examples are glutenin (wheat) and oryzenin (rice).

Prolamines

Prolamines are *water insoluble* but *soluble* in 70 percent ethanol. These proteins are also insoluble in absolute alcohol and other neutral solvents. Such proteins are mainly found in the cereals. The examples of such proteins are *gliadin* of the wheat protein, zein (*corn protein*) and *hordein* (*barely protein*). Gliadin is found to be poor in lysine content. *Zein* and *hordein* are poor in lysine, tryptophan and valine content. The amide nitrogen content of prolamines is found to be very high.

Histones

More basic than most proteins, the histones tend to form complexes with acidic compounds in the cell (nucleic acids). They are soluble in water and insoluble in dilute ammonia solution. Examples are thymus histone (also called nucleohistone because it is found combined with nucleic acids and scombrone (mackerel.).

Protamines

Compared with most proteins, these are relatively small molecules. The protamines are soluble in water and basic in character. They are found associated with nucleic acids in the sperm of fish and are often called nucleoprotamines. Examples are salmine (salmon), sturine (sturgeon), clupeine (herring), and cyprinine (carp).

Albuminoids

These are characterized by their *marked insolubility* in water and in all other neutural solvents. The *keratins*, *elastins*, *collagens* and *keratohyaline* are all the examples of albuminoids. *Keratins* are present in the hairs, nails, horns, hoofs and feathers. The outermost layer of skin is also formed by keratin. *Keratohyaline* is present in the layer of skin. Keratohyaline is later on converted into keratin. These proteins are rich in arginine, lysine and histidine content. These can be hydrolysed only by concentrated acids and alkalies. Although these cannot be usually digested in the human alimentary canal but some of the moths (*cloth moths*) and micro organisms can digest such proteins. *Collagen* is found to exist in the connective tissues and in the bones, and are insoluble in all the neutral solvents. *Elastins* are found to be present in the yellow elastic fibers of the connective tissues. The various ligaments are purely elastins. These can be digested by *pepsin* and *trypsin*. The insolubility of the keratins has been very useful because it prevents dissolutions of body in water, or dilute acids and alkalies.

Conjugated Proteins

These are also known as compound proteins. Conjugated proteins are those proteins which contain in their molecular structure, in addition to protein, some non-protein organic substance(s) called prosthetic group or a metal. These proteins have also been subclassified into the following groups.

Glycoproteins

Those proteins which contain carbohydrate in their molecular structure are included in this group. These include *mucopolysaccharides* and *mucoproteins*. The mucopolysaccharides contain predominantly carbohydrate and less protein, whereas the mucuproteins contain more protein and less carbohydrate. The *mucoproteins* include *ceruloplasmin* which is a blue copper containing protein, transferrin which is a iron transferring protein, *ossemucoprotein* of bones, tendomucoproteins which is a iron transferring protein, osseomucoprotein of bones, *tendomucoproteins* which are found to be present in the tendons, *chondromucoproteins* which are found to be present in the cartilage, and *mucin* which is found in the digestive tract.

Lipoproteins

These are those proteins which contain in their molecular structure, in addition to protein, a *lipid substance*. These are found to be soluble in the lipid-solvents. There exists a loose combination between protein and lipid. Such type of proteins occur mainly in the plasma, brain and eggs. In the plasma, these remain bound to mainly globulins. If such combinations contain α-globulin, these are known as the α-lipoproteins, and if β-globulins, then these are called β-lipoproteins.

Nucleoproteins

In addition to nucleohistones and nucleoprotamines, there is a third group of proteins capable of binding nucleic acids. These nucleoproteins are not basic and hold the nucleic acid by secondary valence bonds. They occur in microorganisms and are soluble in isotonic salt solution.

Chromoproteins

These proteins are pigmented owing to the prosthetic nonprotein group. They include hemoglobin (containing heme, an iron-protoporphyrin), ceruloplasmin (copper), hemocyanin (copper), ascorbic acid oxidase (copper) and ferritin (iron).

Dehydrogenases

These are conjugated protein enzymes that possess oxidizing activity because of the presence of prosthetic groups such as NAD^+ (nicotinamide adenine dinucleotide), $NADP^+$ (nincotinamide adenine dinucleotide phosphate), FMN (flavin mononucleotide), and FAD (flavin adenine dinucleotide).

Phosphoproteins

These proteins contain *phosphoric acid* in their molecular structure in addition to amino acids. Nucleoproteins and lipoproteins which do also contain phosphoric acid are not included in this group. The important examples of such proteins are *casein* and *vitellin*. Casein is found to be present in the milk, and vitellin is present in the egg-yolk.

Metalloproteins

Such proteins contain *metal(s)* alone which remains attached to the protein. The examples of such protein are *ferritin* (metal portion iron), and *carbonic anhydrase* (Zn).

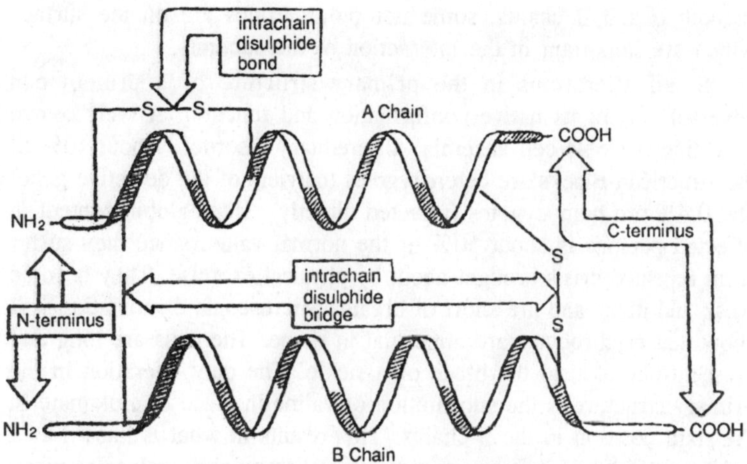

Fig. 11.1. Molecular structure of insulin.

Myoglobin and Hemoglobin

Kendrew in 1950 studied the native conformation of myoglobin, the first globular protein the native conformation of myoglobin, the first globular protein to be studied by the X-ray crystallographic technique. Myoglobin, a heme protein from muscle is similar to hemoglobin in structure and function. Perutz studied the three dimensional structure of hemoglobin. Myoglobin, a single polypeptide with 153 amino acid residues has overall dimensions of 45Å + 30Å + 30Å. About 78% of the structure is in α -helical form and there are no β-pleats. In the case of hemoglobin also more than 70% of the structure is α-helix. This is not however, a characteristic feature of all globular proteins. α-Chymotrypsin, a proteolytic enzyme has relatively high proportion of β-pleats (45%) and low amount of α-helix (14%). Lysozyme, another globular protein has 40% α-hlelix ad 12% β-pleats. Myoglobin has eight stretches of α-helix interspersed with non-ordered segments. The heme group is located in a crevice between two helices. The prosthetic group is on the surface facilitating oxygen binding. Most of the hydrophobic side chains are buried inside and the polar residues are on the surface. As indicated earlier, hemoglobin is made up of two α-chains and two β-chains. The overall conformations of myoglobin, α-and β-chains of hemoglobin are similar. It is probable these three polypeptides are derived from a single ancestral protein by gene mutation. Interaction between α-and β-chains of hemoglobin is very strong whereas, interaction between homologous chains is weak. Thus, the tetrameric protein can easily be dissociated to αβ dimers.

In both α and β chains, some non-polar groups are on the surface which are important in the interaction of the subunits.

Small alterations in the primary structure of a protein can adversely affect its native conformation and function. A well known condition is sickle cell anaemia, a hereditary disorder. About 10% of the American Blacks are heterozygotes (carriers of the defective gene) and 0.4% are homozygotes (affected directly). Hemoglobin content in affected persons is about 50% of the normal value, since they suffer from repeated crisis brought about by physical exercise. They become weak and dizzy and are short of breath. Microscopic examination will show that erythrocytes are abnormal in shape. The cells are long and crescent-like akin to the blade of a sickle. The only alteration in the primary structure is the substitution of valine in place of glutamate in the sixth position in the β-chains. This results in what is known as a 'sticky path' which causes aggregation of hemoglobin molecules when O_2 content is low.

Protein Denaturation

Since the conformation of a protein is solely dependent on week valence forces it can be disrupted by a variety of physical and chemical agents. The process is known as denaturation. The organized structure is lost and the protein assumes a highly disordered form. The protein will lose its biological activity. It becomes more susceptible to proteolytic attack. Many globular proteins are rendered less soluble on denaturation. An interesting instance of a protein losing its biological activity on denaturation is with reference to monellin, a protein 300 times sweeter than socrose. Monellin isolated from an African plant *Dioscorephyllum cumminsis* is made up of two polypeptide chains made up of 44 and 55 amino acid residues, non-covalently associated. On denaturation the protein loses its sweet taste. If the denaturation process is not very drastic the process becomes reversible, once the denaturing agent is removed. This phase is known as renaturation.

Moist heat is powerful denaturing agent. Hydrogen bonds are easily disrupted by heat. Extremes of acidity and alkalinity at moderate temperature, disrupt electrostatic interactions and cause conformational changes. Heavy metal ions like Hg^{++} and Pb^{++} can complex with negative charges or sulphydryl groups. The basis of administering egg white immediately to counteract lead poisoning is based on the complexation of egg proteins with the toxic metal ion. Polar organic solvents like ethanol also can cause denaturation, if temperature is not controlled. Trichloroacetic acid and perchloric acid are two common laboratory reagents used for denaturation and precipitation of proteins. Sodium dodecyl sulphate (SDS, $CH_3 (CH_2)_{10} CH_2 - OSO_3^- Na^+$) another reagent used in protein analysis is also a powerful denaturing agent . It can dissociate subunits by disrupting non-polar interactions. Urea ($H_2N - CO - NH_2$) and guanidine hydrochloride [$H_2N - C (NH_2) = N^+ H_2Cl^-$] at high concentrations (6.0 - 8.0 M and 2.0 - 3.0 M respectively) act as denaturing agents. Unlike commonly believed, urea does not act by disrupting hydrogen bonding. It acts by interfering with non-polar interactions.

Plasma Proteins

Hemoglobin the major protein in blood (12-15 g/100 ml) is confined to the red cells. Plasma, the cell-free fraction is also rich in proteins (6.3-7.5 g/100 ml). A large array of structurally and functionally different proteins is present in plasma. There are carrier proteins like albumin, transferrin and apolipoproteins. Quantitatively the second important group of proteins after albumin are the immunoglobulins, which are defence proteins. Another group of proteins known as protein inhibitors accounts for 10% of total plasma proteins. A variety of clotting factors which are mostly precursors for proteolytic enzymes involved in blood coagulation are present in relatively low concentrations in plasma. There are circulating protein hormones like insulin and thyroid stimulating hormone in very minute amounts. Enzymes which are mostly nonfunctional in plasma, are also present in traces.

Several techniques are employed for the qualitative and quantitative separation of plasma proteins. A common technique used in clinical laboratories for the separation of serum (rather than plasma to eliminate fibrinogen) is zone electrophoresis on paper, agar gel or cellulose acetate strips at pH 8.6. Five fractions in the order of increasing mobility towards anode namely albumin, α-1, α-2, β and -γ globulins are usually obtained by this technique. Each globulin fraction is comprised of more than one protein which can further be separated by sophisticated techniques.

(i) After the electrophoretic run the protein bands are stained to visualize the proteins with suitable dyes. Proteins bind tightly to colored dyes through electrostatic and hydrophobic interactions.

(ii) Semiquantitation of the protein bands by scanning in a densitometer.

Albumin the major plasma protein, accounts for about 55-60% of the total proteins. It is synthesized exclusively in liver and a healthy liver can synthesize 10-15 g of albumin per day. The life span of an albumin molecule is about 20-25 days. Nearly 40% of plasma calcium

Table 11.1. Plasma proteins

Proteins	*Concentration G/100 ml*	*Mr kDa*	*Function*
Prealbumin	0.03	61	Transport of thyroxine
Albumin	3.2 - 4.2	68	Diverse functions
α_1-Acid glycoprotein	0.10	44	Acute phase protein
α_1-Proteinase inhibitor	0.25	54	Elastase inhibitor
α_2-Macroglobulin	0.20	720	Nonspecific proteinase inhibitor
Haptoglobin	0.10	85	Binds hemoglobin
Ceruloplasmin	0.02	150	Copper transport
Prothrombin	0.02	63	Blood clotting
Transferrin	0.30	85	Transport of iron
Plasminogen	0.05	140	Retraction of fibrin clot
Fibrinogen	0.30	340	Precursor of fibrin clot
γ-Globulins	0.8-1.7	-	Immune reaction

is bound to albumin. Albumin is involved in the transport of free fatty acids from adipocyte to liver. Bilirubin, steroid hormones and many water insoluble drugs are also bound and transported by albumin. Along with other plasma proteins albumin acts as a buffer. Albumin has a major role in osmotic regulation and fluid distribution. It accounts for about 80% of the total colloidal osmotic pressure (25 mm Hg) in blood plasma. One g of albumin can hold 18.0 ml of water. Decreases in albumin level will cause fluid accumulation in the interstitial space and soft tissues resulting in edema. Prolonged malnutrition, kidney diseases associated with protein loss in urine, liver cirrhosis and extravagation as in burns will cause this condition. However, in analbuminemia a rare genetic disorder, persons do not develop edema and are apparently healthy. In this condition globumin level increases and arterial blood pressure is lowered to compensate for the absence of albumin.

The predominant component of α_1-globulin (0.3-0.5 g/100 ml) is a glycoprotein known as α_1-proteinase inhibitor which is a powerful inhibitor of neutrophil elastase. Elastase when not regulated can cause tissue breakdown and loss of elasticity in the lung. Two variants of this protein (S and Z) which are far less effective against elastase are known mainly in the Scandinavian countries. Persons with these modified α_1-proteinase inhibitors develop emphysema. α_1-Acid glycoprotein is so called because of its low isoelectric point. The concentration of this protein is significantly increased in plasma in inflammation and other acute disease conditions. Nearly 30% of the α_2-fractions and 40% of β-fraction are accounted for by apolipoproteins, which are described later. The functions of transferrin and haptoglobin which belong to the β and α_2-globulin fractions are also detailed later. Ceruloplasmin a copper containing protein belongs to α_2-globulin fraction. A major protein of this fraction is α_2-macroglobulin which has the capacity to trap and remove from circulation a large number of proteinases and can hence play a regulatory role.

γ-Globulins

This group of proteins which are unique to vertebrates are also called immunoglobulins. Unlike most other plasma proteins which are synthesized in liver, immunoglobulins are made in β-lymphocytes and plasma cells of lymph nodes, bone marrow and spleen. They bind specifically to antigenic sites on other molecules. The antigens, which provide the binding sites, can be proteins, pollysaccharides, nucleic acids or even relatively low molecular weight compounds, which are of foreign origin to the body. Thus, bacterial and viral components can act as antigens and trigger antigen-antibody reactions.

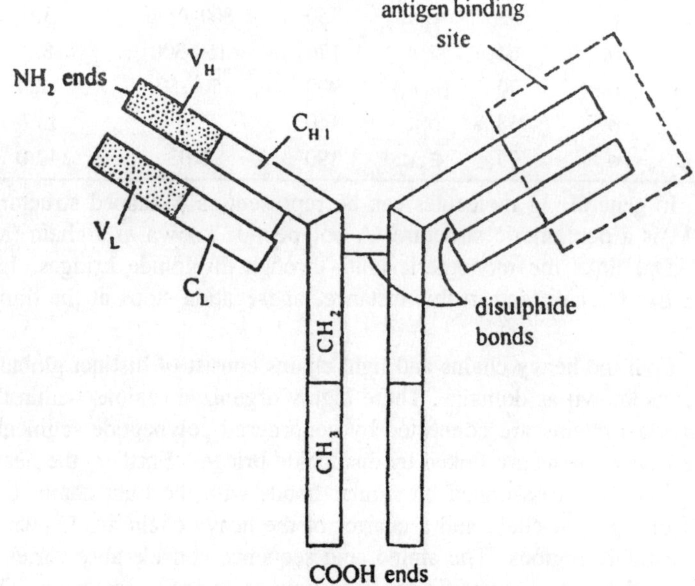

Fig. 11.2. Molecular structure of an immunoglobulin molecule.

Knowledge of immunoglobulins came from the studies on protein in plasma and urine in patients suffering from myelomatosis (immunocytoma tumors). In this condition, γ-globulin level is increased in serum. Characteristic proteins known as Bence-Jones proteins are excreted in large amounts in urine. These proteins precipitate on heating urine samples to 45-50°C but redissolve at higher temperatures. They were identified as low molecular weight proteins (light chains) which are constituent units of immunoglobulins. Two types of light chains known as κ and λ chains are present in immunoglobulins and in humans the former predominates. Each immunoglobulin molecule is a heterotetramer made up of two light chains and two heavy chains. Light chains are simple proteins whereas, the heavy chains are glycoproteins. The light and heavy chains are synthesized as separate molecules and are assesmbled to functional immunoglobulins in the cells of their origin. The immunoglobulins are classified into five groups based on the type of heavy chain.

Table 11.2. Classification of immunoglobulins (Ig)

Group	*Heavy Chain*	*Mr kDa*	*Native form*	*Total Mr, kDa*	*Plasma concentration mg/100 ml*	*Percent carbohydrate*
Ig G	γ	53	$\gamma_2 \kappa_2$	150	800-1200	3.0
Ig A	α	64	$\alpha_2 \kappa_2$	170	150-300	8.0
Ig M	μ	70	$(\mu_2 \kappa_2)$	900	50-150	12.0
Ig D	δ	58	$\delta_2 \kappa_2$	160	4	13.0
Ig E	∈	75	$\in_2 \kappa_2$	190	0.03	12.0

In general, Ig molecules can be represent as Y-shaped structure. Ig M is a pentameric structure. A polypeptide known as J-chain (Mr 15 kDa) links the monomeric units through disulphide bridges. IgA also has J- chain and in this instance, aggregation stops at the dimer stage.

Both the heavy chains and light chains consist of distinct globular regions known as domains. These highly organized regions within the individual chains are connected by nonordered polypeptide segments. The heavy chains are linked by disulphide bridges. Further, the heavy chain is also cross-linked by similar bonds with the light chain. One half of the light chain and a quarter of the heavy chain are known as the variable regions. The amino acid sequence considerably varies in this region and are specific for each type of antibody molecule. This is known as the idiotypic variation. The rest of the molecule is known as the constant region in which the amino acid sequences are almost identical in each class of immunoglobulin. The antigden binding site is known as Fab site consisting of light chains and the N-terminal half of the heavy chain. The remaining part of immunoglobulin known as Fc also has important biological functions. For example, the Fc region of immunoglobulin G is responsible for triggering pathways of the immune response that leads to the lysis of unwanted organisms. An example is the complement system that is activated which consists of a series of proteinases.

IgG is mainly responsible for humoral immunity. It is the only immunoglobulin that can cross through the placenta. IgA which is present in some secretions is thought to provide surface immunity. Ig A secretion is facilitated by its specific binding to a protein known as secretory component. IgM is the receptor in the B-lymphocytes and helps in established humoral immunity. IgD is also found at the surface of B-lymphocytes but its function is not known. IgE is found in mast cells and basophils. The concentration of IgE increases in response to allergic reactions.

Disorders of immunoglobins are numerous. Agammaglobulinemia is a rare X-chromosome associated genetic disease affecting only the males. In this condition, there is virtual absence of immunoglobulins in blood plasma. The affected persons are highly susceptible to bacterial infection but react almost normally to viral infections. Hypogammaglobulinemia may be restricted to a single class of immunoglobulins or may involve under-production of all the five types. In myelomas, increased production of a restricted class of immunoglobulins or of a single specific immunoglobulin is seen. Immunoglobulin level in blood is increased generallly in infections. Sometimes the body rejects its own proteins which become antigenic. This results in the autoimmune disorders. Systemic lupus erythomatosis and some types of rheumatoid arthritis are examples. It is probable, buried antigenic sites (epitopes) in endogenous proteins get exposed or the 'self' proteins bind with exogenous triggers and become antigenic in these conditions.

Primary Structure

One of the great achievements of modern chemistry has been the development of techniques for determining the precise sequence of amino acids in a protein. The first protein to have its sequence of amino acids determined was the hormone insulin. Its molecular formula is $C_{254}H_{377}N_{65}O_{75}S_6$. This is small as proteins go. Even so, it took Dr.

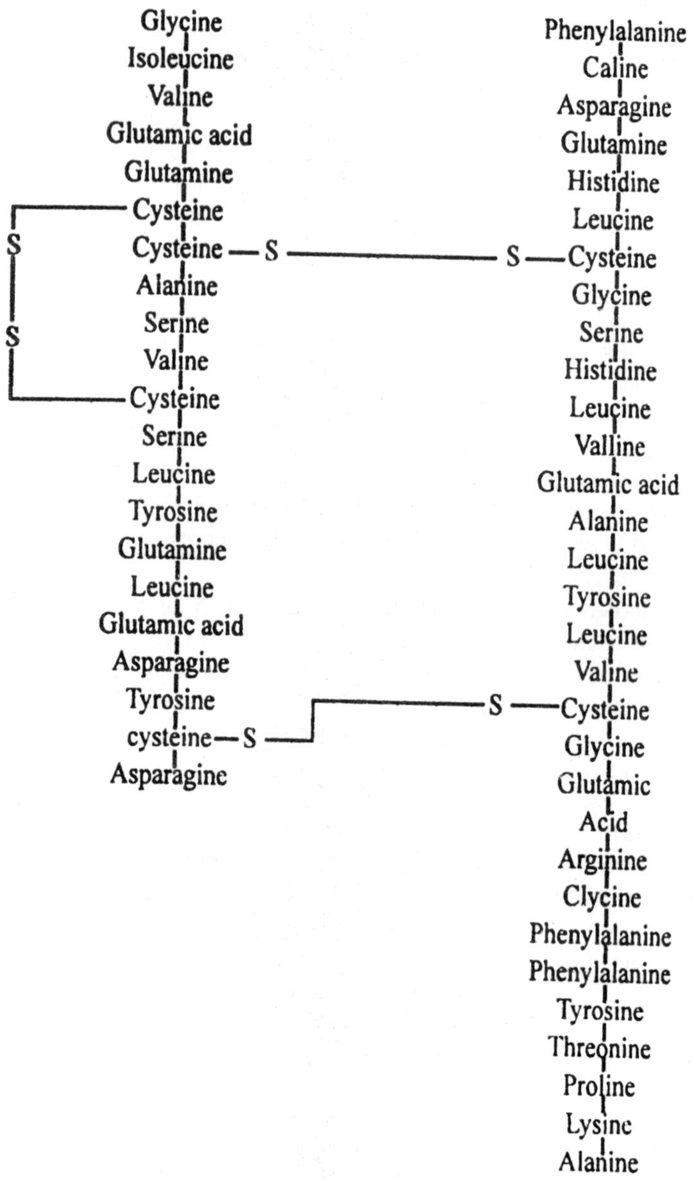

Fig. 11.3. Sequence of amino acids in the human insulin molecule, the molecule consists of two polypeptide chains held together by two disulfide bridges.

Frederick Sanger and his colleagues at the University of Cambridge in England 10 years (1944-1954) to work out the exact sequence of amino acids in the protein. Insulin consists of two polypeptide chains containing a total of 51 amino acid residues.

The amino acid cysteine occurs at six positions in the insulin molecules. Wherever two cysteines are close to each other, they can be oxidized (each losing a hydrogen atom). As a result a covalent bond forms between their respective sulfur atoms forming a *disulfide bridge*. In this way two different polypeptides can be drawn into a loop. Sanger found one *intra* chain and two *inter*chain disulfide bridges in the insulin molecule.

Since the days of Sanger's pioneering work, the techniques of protein sequencing have developed rapidly. It is now possible to have much of the job done automatically by machines. The sequence of amino acids is now known for hundreds of different proteins. The sequence of amino acids in a protein, together with the location of any disulfide bridges, is called the *primary structure* of the protein.

Let us now examine the primary structure of *lysozyme*. Lysozyme is an enzyme found in an egg white, tears, and other secretions. It is responsible for breaking down the polysaccharide walls of many kinds of bacteria, and thus it provides a measure of protection against infection.

The lysozyme in egg white is a simple polypeptide containing 129 amino acid residues. There are four pairs of cysteines, establishing disulfide (S-S) bridges between positions 6 and 127, 30 and 115, 64 and 80, and 76 and 94. The presence of these covalent linkages tells us immediately that we cannot represent the polypeptide as a straight, rigid chain. The chain must fold on itself to allow the pairs of cysteines to be close to each other.

Secondary Structure

To discover the actual configuration of a protein molecules in three-dimensional space, we must turn to another analytical technique, that of x-ray crystallography. A crystal consists of an orderly, stacked arrow of ions or molecules. If a beam of x-rays is passed through a crystal, some of the x-rays will be reflected by atoms in the crystal. Because of the orderly arrangement of the atoms, the reflections will also be orderly. A simple analogy would be the orderly pattern produced by a street light at night when viewed through the grid of a window screen. By examining the pattern of reflections produced as the beam is directed at the crystal from a variety of different angles, it is possible (espically with the help of a computer) to determine the arrangement of atoms in that crystal.

The first proteins to be analyzed by x-ray crystallography were certain structural proteins like the alpha-keratins of wool and fibroin, the protein secreted by the silkworm. These proteins were good choices for study because of their regular, self-repeating structures.

X-ray analysis of alpha-keratins revealed several interesting facts. The peptide linkage itself turned out to be very rigid, with all its atoms lying in a plane. The only opportunities for flexibility in a polypeptide occur at the bonds to the alpha carbon—that is, the carbon that carries the R group. In the alpha-keratins this flexibility is exploited by the formation of a helical twist to the polypeptide chain. Several features of this helix should be noted. (1) The R groups of the amino acid residues all extend to the outsides. (2) The helix makes a complete turn every 3.6 residues. (3) The helix is right-handed; as it recedes, it twists in a clockwise direction. (4) The –C=O (carbonyl) group of each peptide bond extends parallel to the axis of the helix and points directly at the –NH group of the peptide bond four amino acids below it in the helix. A hydrogen bond forms between these groups: –C=O . . . H–N–. This precise three-dimensional arrangements of amino acids is called the *alpha helix*. It is one of the most common examples of *secondary structure* in a protein.

What makes the alpha helix possible is the large number of hydrogen bonds. The strength of a single hydrogen bond is only about 5% of that of a covalent bond. But the presence of a hydrogen bond between each amino acid in the chain, and the one that is four amino acids away, provides sufficient total bond strength to make the alpha helix a very stable structure. However, it should be possible by breaking these intrachain hydrogen bonds to pull the helix out in much the same way that a spring can be extended. And, in fact, wool fibers can be stretched to about twice their normal length thanks to the molecular properties of the alpha helix.

Fibroin is the protein that silkworms use to spin the threads of their cocoon. It, too, has been subjected to x-ray analysis. In fibroin the polypeptide chains are extended. A number of chains lie parallel to each other, held together by the hydrogen bonds that form between the – C = O and –N–H groups of one chain with the –N–H and – C = O groups of the adjacent chain. In silk it would be better to describe the chains as being antiparallel because adjacent chains run in opposite directions—that is, from N-terminal to C-terminal and vice versa. A series of antiparallel stands lying side by side make up a beta-pleated sheet. It is another important and commonly found example of secondary structure. Because the chains are fully extended, we would not expect to be able to stretch them without breaking covalent bonds. It is for this reason that silk is not extensible. However, the layers of beta-pleated sheet in silk fibers make them very supple.

The alpha helix and the beta-pleated sheet are two of the most common examples of secondary structure, but other orderly arrangements of amino acid residues also occur in polypeptides. All examples of secondary structure are a direct reflection of the particular amino acids and their order that are used in the synthesis of the polypeptide. The chains of fibroin, for example, consist mainly of alternating glycine (hydrophobic) residues. This arrangement enables the chains to rest closes together in the beta-pleated sheet configuration. On the other hand, a chain containing a series of alanine residues will spontaneously fold into an alpha helix with the CH_3 groups of the alanines projecting to the exterior of the helix. Stages, as with cellulose. The fact that the protein is extremely resistant to stretching is an essential part of its functioning. For example in tendons, bone, skin, teeth, and connective tissue. Proteins which entirely in the form of helical coils, such as keratin and collagen, are exceptional.

Tertiary Structure

Usually the polypeptide chain bends and folds extensively, forming a precise, compact 'globular' shape. This is the protein's tertiary structure and it is maintained by the interaction of the four types of bond already discussed, namely ionic, hydrogen and disulphide bonds as well as hydrophobic interactions. The latter are quantitatively the most important and occur when the protein folds so as to shield hydrophobic side groups from the aqueous surroundings, at the same time exposing hydrophilic side chains, as described above.

The tertiary structure of a protein can be determined by X-ray crystallography. By early 1959, and after many year's work, John kendrew and Max Perutz had built the first atomic model of myoglobin showing secondary and tertiary structures using this technique. They received the Nobel Prize for their work in 1962:

Primary structure — single polypeptide chain of 153 amino acids, the sequence was elucidated in the early 1960s;

Secondary structure — about 75% of the chain is α-helical (8 helical sections);

Tertiary structure — non-uniform folding of the α -helical chain into a compact shape;

Prosthetic group — haem group (contains iron).

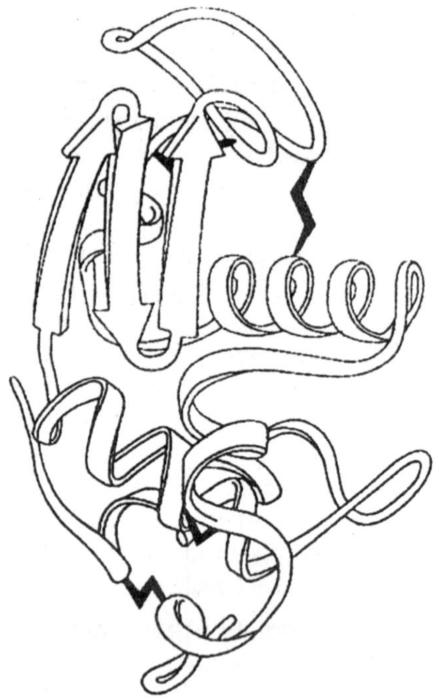

Fig. 11.4. Tertiary structure of lysosome.

Myoglobin is formed in muscle where its function is to store oxygen. Oxygen combines with the haem group as in haemoglobin. The haem group gives muscle its red appearance. The elucidation of tertiary structure is still very time-consuming. Use of computers and other techniques to predict tertiary structure, based on knowledge of primary and secondary structures, is a fast-growing area of molecular biology. From this follows the possibility of designing proteins with particular shapes for particular functions, with important applications in industry and medicine.

Quaternary Structure

Many highly complex proteins consist of more than one polypeptide chain. The separate chains are held together by hydrophobic interactions and hydrogen and ionic bonds. Their precise arrangement is known as the *quaternary structure*. Haemoglobin shows such a structure. It is the red oxygen-carrying pigment found in the red blood cells of vertebrates. It consists of four separate polypeptide chains of two types, namely two α chains and two β chains. These resemble myoglobin in structure. The two α-chains each contain 141 amino acids, while the two β chains each contain 146 amino acids. The complete structure of haemoglobin was worked out by Kendrew and Perutz.

As is typical of globular proteins, its hydrophobic side chains point inwards to the centre of the molecule, and its hydrophilic side chains face outwards, making it soluble in water. A mutation which causes one of the hydrophilic amino acids to be replaced by a hydrophobic amino acid, thereby reducing its solubility, is responsible for the disease sickle cell anaemia. The protein coats of some viruses, such as the tobacco mosaic virus, are composed of many polypeptide chains arranged in a highly ordered fashion.

Denaturation and Renaturation of Proteins

Denaturation is the loss of the specific three-dimensional shape of a protein molecule. The change may be temporary or permanent, but the amino acid sequence of the protein remains unaffected. If denaturation occurs, the molecule unfolds and can no longer perform its normal biological function. A number of agents may cause denaturation as follows.

Heat or radiation. eg infra-red or ultra-violet light. Kinetic energy is supplied to the protein causing its atoms to vibrate violently, so disrupting the weak hydrogen and ionic bonds. Coagulation of the protein then occurs.

Strong acids and alkalis and high concentrations of salts. Ionic bonds are disrupted and the protein is coagulated. Breakage of peptide bonds may occur if the protein is allowed to remain mixed with the reagent for a long period of time.

Heavy metals. The positively charged ions of heavy metals (cations) form strong bonds with the negatively charged carboxyl groups on the R groups of proteins and often disrupt ionic bonds. They also reduce the protein's electrical polarity (its overall charge) and thus increase its insolubility. This causes the protein to precipitate out of solution.

Organic solvents and detergents. These reagents disrupt hydrophobic interactions and form bonds with hydrophobic (non-polar) groups. This in turn causes the disruption of hydrogen bonding. When alcohol is used as a disinfectant it functions to denature the protein of any bacteria present.

Renaturation

Sometimes a protein will spontaneously refold into its original structure after denaturation, providing conditions are suitable. This is called renaturation, and is good evidence that tertiary structure can be determined purely by primary structure and that biological structures can spontaneously assemble according to a few general principles.

12

Physical Arrangement of Genes

Genes are virtually never found in the form of a free double helix of DNA. Instead, they are packaged. Packaging can involve special associations of different regions of nucleic acid, superhelical twisting, and association with particular RNAs and proteins. This packaging fulfills a number of functions. For one thing, it enables the genetic instructions to be stored in a small place. Both the folding of the nucleic acid and the strong negative charges on the phosphate groups are factors in this condensation of genetic material.

Double-stranded DNA is not actually rigid, but it has definite constraints on its flexibility. Each nucleotide subunit has its own negatively charged phosphate, and, since like charges repel one another, the close packing of these groups requires a number of positive charges to be bound by ionic bonds to the nucleic acid in order to neutralize the charge repulsion. Polyamines and or special, highly basic proteins fulfill this function in most cases.

Another function of packaging is to insure the protective inertness of the genes themselves, which is in marked contrast to the lack of protection of the mRNA during translation. A third function of the packaging is to facilitate proper distribution of the genes to the daughter cells at cell division. A fourth function is to promote synapsis when it is appropriate (that is, usually during meiotic prophase). Fifth, it is quite possible, though not proven to date, that packaging facilitates the regulation of eukaryotic DNAs. On the other hand, the mere attachment of positively charged proteins or polyamines to the phosphate groups might present some geometrical problems in the approach of DNA polymerase for replication, correction endonucleases for repair, or RNA polymerase for transcription. The packaging is managed so as to avoid conflict with these basic life functions.

VIRUSES

Viral genetic material, whether DNA or RNA, exists in two distinct states, which differ greatly in their packaging: the inert *virion* and the active *vegetative state*. The virion is essentially crystalline, having no metabolic activities. Viruses are usually classified taxonomically based on the properties of their virions.

The nucleic acid of viruses interacts with itself in different ways, depending on the virus. Among the RNA viruses, there are three basic structures of the virion nucleic acid: (1) double-stranded RNA, which is divided into 10 different separate (not attached together) segments (for example, mammalian reovirus), (2) single-stranded RNA in a covalently closed circle (for example, in mouse endomyocarditis or EMC virus), or (3) single-stranded RNA in linear form. The single-stranded, linear RNA may be wound smoothly into a helix as in tobacco mosaic virus (TMV) or may assume a complex, flowerlike structure by forming base-paired *hairpin loops*, like f2, Qβ, or R17 bacteriophages. The RNA of the virion, in any case, is complexed with capsomeric proteins, the components of its protein coat. The coat or capsid may be helical or polygonal in design. Many RNA viruses are also *enveloped*; that is, the host cell membrane, modified by the virus, becomes wrapped around the core of the virion to form the complete virion particle.

Among the DNA viruses, there are four basic structures of the virion nucleic acid: (1) linear and single-stranded, as in ϕM13, (2) circular and single-stranded, as in ϕX174, (3) double-stranded and circular, being twisted into a *supercoil*, like polyoma tumor virus or (4) double-stranded and linear, like Herpes virus. The double-stranded, linear DNA viruses can have different kinds of arrangements of the genetic sequences. Herpes viruses have one copy of each genetic region and are double-stranded throughout. Other DNA viruses, for example T7 phage, have *terminal redundancy*. The sequence at one end is an exact copy of the sequence at the other end. In English, a terminally redundant sentence might read, "I did my experiment I did." In T7, all the phage particles contain DNA with the same terminal redundancy. Other phages, for example T2, T4, and T6 (the T-even phages) are *circularly permuted* as well as terminally redundant. In terms of the same sentence given above, T-even phage would have some genomes reading as previously and others reading "Did my experiment I did my," others reading "My experiment I did my experiment," and others reading "Experiment I did my experiment I." If you analyze the four variants given, you can see that the italic portions contain the same four words. If the four italic words in each of these four different sentences were cut off and the two ends were attached together into a circle, the four circles of words would be the same. For this reason, the genomes are called circularly permuted. Terminal redundancy, as before, refers to the fact that the two ends contain the same sequence.

Another structure characteristic of some double-stranded DNA viruses, for example, lambda (λ) phage, is called *sticky ends*. These are complementary regions of single-stranded DNA at the two ends of the linear, double-stranded DNA sequence. If these two single-stranded regions were to form base pairs with each other, as they do in the vegetative state, the whole genome would be a circle with only one nick or break along each of its two strands. In the virion state, evidently this type of circle does not occur.

In DNA viruses, the charge on the DNA can be neutralized by polyamines or specific internal proteins, or both (for example, in T phages). The protein capsid of the virion may be helical, polygonal, or complex (as in the T phages with complex head and tail structures). Again, as in RNA viruses, some of these viruses can be enveloped in host cell membrane fragments.

Both RNA and DNA viruses have an active state, the vegetative state. During this time, no complete virions are present in the infected cell, since the nucleic acid is separated from its capsid during the earliest stages of the infection. The parasitic nature of viruses is evident during the vegetative stage, since the nucleic acid of the virus takes over all or part of the transcriptional and translational apparatus of the host cell, pirating energy to perform its replication. Many viruses do not change in nucleic acid structure when they infect a cell but merely dissociate their nucleic acid from the capsid package. Other viruses do reorganize their nucleic acid structure after infection. Immediately after infection, lambda joins its sticky ends and ligase forms a covalent bond between them, producing a covalently closed circle of double DNA.

Another example is found in bacteriophage Qβ whose single-stranded RNA [called (+) by convention] serves as a template for formation of a complementary (–) RNA strand. The double helical RNA product is called the *replicative form* (RF) of Qβ. It is never

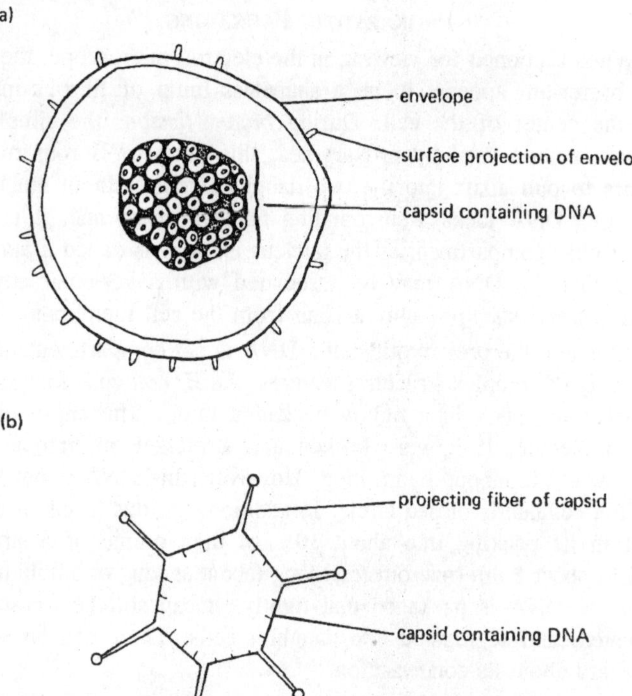

Fig. 12.1. Shapes of virions of some DNA viruses: (a) virion of varicella—Herpes zoster; (b) virion of adenovirus type 5.

found in virions but only in the vegetative state. When the RNA-dependent RNA polymerase (replicase) catalyzes more RNA syntheses from the RF as template, the product includes mostly (+) strands. The single-stranded RNA viruses of the leukovirus group have only the (+) strand in the virions, and after infection, (-) DNA complementary to their genome is synthesized under catalysis by reverse transcriptase. The (-) DNA is then replicated to form a double helix of DNA having both (+) and (-) strands. Then, the RNA polymerase transcribes this double helix, using the (-) strand as a template, to produce single-stranded (+)-strand RNAs for new virions. Many other virions change their organization in the vegetative state; these examples will give a feeling for the range of possibilities.

In all cases, the viral nucleic acid is packaged differently for inertness than for replication and expression. The degree of differences between the two varies from virus to virus.

PROKARYOTIC PACKAGING

When sectioned for viewing in the electron microscope, the DNA of a bacterium appears to be a shapeless lump of fibrous material near the center of the cell. During *binary fission*, the simple cell division method used by prokaryotes, this lump of fibrous material appears to pull apart into the two daughter cells without much ado. Since this DNA lacks a surrounding nuclear membrane, it is not a true cellular compartment as the nucleus is, so it is called a *nucleoid*. Notice that the DNA may be associated with a vesicular structure called a *mesosome*, probably arising from the cell membrane.

Although the prokaryotic cell's DNA is not compartmentalized, it has plenty of complex structural features. An *E. coli* cell, for example, maintains its DNA in a tightly packaged lump. The entire circular DNA molecule, if it were broken and stretched out into a linear form, would be about 1 mm long. However, this DNA is not linear; it is in a covalently closed circle. In addition, various levels of coiling result in its packing into about 10% of the volume of a structure which is about 2 μm (micrometers) long (about as long as a millimeter!). When the DNA is packaged that tightly, it can still be transcribed, replicated, and segregated into daughter cells. There can be nothing haphazard about its condensation.

An early study by Vogel showed that mutagenesis tended to affect certain regions, which were widely separated on the genetic map, simultaneously. The suggestion he made was that the nucleoid was folded in such a way that these regions are in close proximity to one another in three-dimensional space, although they were widely separated when the circle is completely unfolded. Subsequently, many investigators attempted unsuccessfully to isolate a structured nucleoid from *E. coli*.

In 1972, Stonington and Pettijohn succeeded in preparing *E. coli* nucleoids, in their tightly coiled form. Analysis of these structures showed that the DNA was double helical and supercoiled, and that RNA was required to stabilize the supercoiling. Notice that RNase releases loops but DNase releases the supercoiling. Although relatively few supercoiled loops (held together by RNA linkers) are shown in the model, many loops probably exist. An electron micrograph taken by Worcel and Burgi in 1973 shows the loosened structure of an isolated nucleoid associated with a scrap of the bacterial membrane. This membrane may be derived from the mesosome. Pettijohn and his collaborators have shown that the nucleoid structure does not interfere with the access of RNA polymerase to the DNA for purposes of

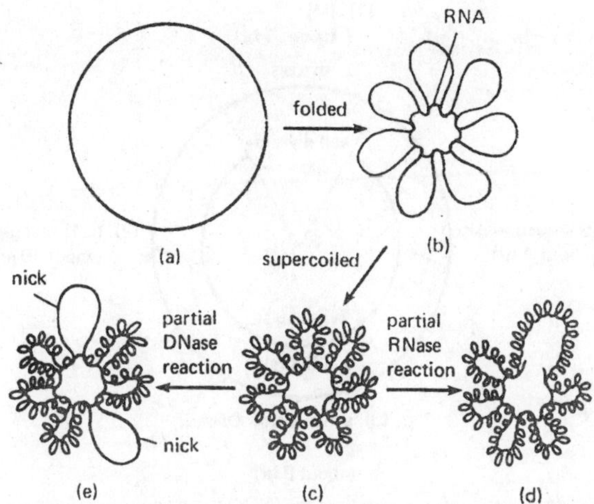

Fig. 12.2. Model for the arrangement of the DNA and RNA portions of the E. coli nucleoid, in its condensed state. (a) circular, unfolded chromosome; (b) folded chromosome; (c) folded and supercoiled chromosome; (d) RNase; (e) effects of attacking structure with RNase.

transcription as the nucleoid is isolated. It may be that a tighter state, presently uncharacterized, exists *in vivo*.

A number of investigators have examined the proteins of the membrane scrap that is tightly bound to the nucleoid. These proteins are a subgroup of those in the whole *E. coli* membrane, and it may be that they are important in initiating DNA replication.

Bacteria do not contain the special basic nuclear proteins (*histones*) that eukaryotic cells have. They have substantial quantities of polyamines, however. These very likely neutralize the charge on the DNA phosphates, and, with particular proteins that have been recently discovered, thereby function in much the same manner as histones do. Although the bacteria lack histones, Griffith has been able to show that the bacterial DNA has a beaded appearance (with 100 Å beads) like that we will be describing for eukaryotic DNA. In prokaryotes, the DNA must be able to assume this structure without the influence of histones. The bacterial basic proteins may play a role similar to histones of eukaryotes in this packaging.

Eukaryotic Chromosomes During Interphase

Cell Cycle

As mentioned previously, in contrast to prokaryotes, eukaryotes have a membrane surrounding their DNA. In fact, it is only during interphase that this membrane is present. It is convenient to divide

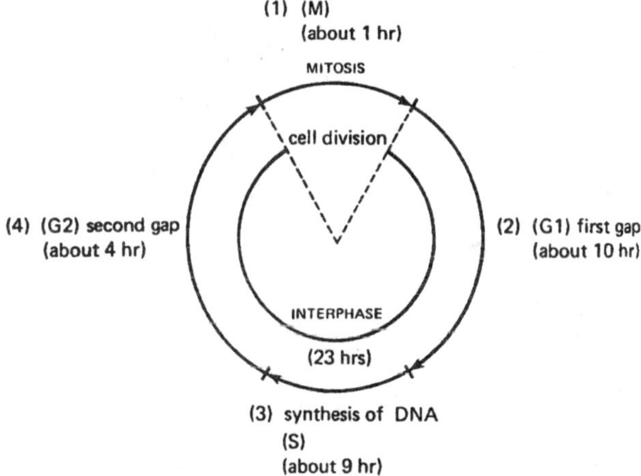

Fig. 12.3. The cell cycle of a mammalian cell dividing once each 24 hours.

the cell division cycle into four phases. Mitosis (M phase), the actual division, is the shortest. Each daughter cell then enters the gap 1 (G_1) period of interphase. Latei in interphase, the DNA is replicated during the synthesis (S) phase. The cell does not divide immediately after its DNA is replicated; instead, it enter a second gap (G_2) period of inter phase at the end of G_2 mitosis (M) occurs again. You should not consider the gap to be resting phases, for the cellular life (transcription, translation, interaction with the environment) take place during the G_1 and G_2 phases the packing the DNA during all three phases of interphase has profound implication from gene expression and its regulation.

Unineme Chromosomes

The *chromatin* (DNA plus associated proteins and RNAs) during interphase is often described as extended. In eukaryotic cells the chromatin is divided into chromosomes, and during the M phase, each of these chromosomes is very tightly coiled up so that the chromosomes are shortened. When G_1 occurs the coils are relaxed, and each chromosome is hundreds of times longer than during M. Nevertheless, during interphase, there is still a coiled substructure in chromatin. This coiled substructure consists of two levels of coiling: double strands of DNA, and nucleosomes. The first level of coiling is the double helix itself. Let us consider the arrangement of the DNA double helix before discussing nucleosomes.

The DNA from a particular chromosome could be in a number of separate linear or circular pieces (*multineme*) or could be in only a single piece, running from end to end of the chromosome (*unineme*).

One of the experiments demonstrating most clearly that chromosomes are unineme is that of Kavenoff and coworkers in 1973. Long DNAs takes longer than short DNAs to relax after an environmental stress. Kavenoff used this difference in relaxation time to measure the longest DNA molecules in a preparation of DNA. DNA was prepared from a number of different genetic strains of *Drosophila*, each differing in the length of the longest of the four chromosomes. These strains included different species in the genus *Drosophila* as well as strains that probably arose from the macro-lesion type of mutations. The *Drosophila* strains that Kavenoff compared differed in the amount of DNA in their longest chromosome. This was demonstrated by means of staining the DNA and using a very tiny spectrophotometer beam, aimed through a

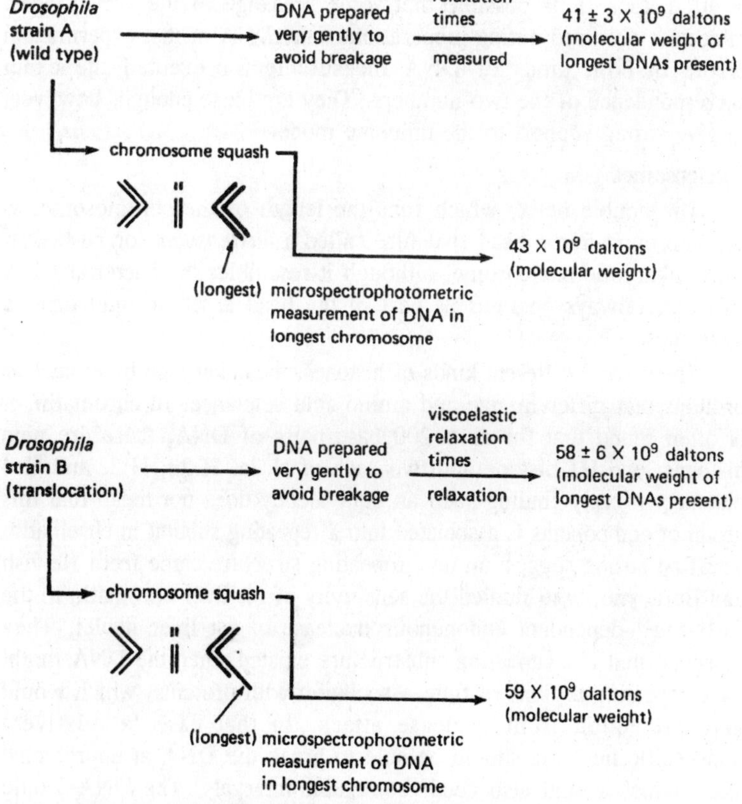

Fig. 12.4. Portion of an experiment supporting the unineme model of chromosome structure, as performed by Kavenoff and colleagues.

microscope at the longest chromosome. It was possible to show that the longest chromosome in strain A had 41 $\times$ 10^9 daltons molecular weight of DNA in it, whereas the longest chromosome in strain B had 59 $\times$ 10^9 daltons molecular weight of DNA. The lengths were proportional: strain A's longest chromosome was longer than strain B's longest chromosome. Notice that Kavenoffs choice of the longest chromosome to study was very clever: if the relaxation times showed that the longest DNAs found were as large as the amount of DNA in the longest chromosome, the longest chromosome must have been unineme, since a DNA as large as that could not reasonably be part of one of the other, substantially shorter, chromosomes of the cell. In fact, the longest DNA in preparations from strain A had 41 $\times$ 10^9 daltons molecular weight, whereas the longest from strain B had 58 $\times$ 10^9 daltons. It is possible that some breakage of the very longest molecules occurred during preparation of the DNA or that experimental errors in both kinds of DNA measurement prevented the exact correspondence of the two numbers. They are close enough, however, to give strong support to the unineme model.

Nucleosomes

The double helix, which runs the length of the chromosome, is coiled around into a bead structure called a *nucleosome* (or nu-body). This eukaryotic nucleosome, although it resembles the bacterial DNA structure, always contains as part of the bead a set of eight histone molecules.

There are 5 different kinds of histones, the eukaryotic basic nuclear proteins that differ in size and amino acid sequence. In chromatin, it is often found that for each 200 base pairs of DNA, there are nine histones; one H1 histone and two each of H 2a, H 2b, H 3, and H 4 histones. Merely finding such an equivalency does not mean that this group of components is associated into a repeating subunit in chromatin. The first strong suggestion of a repeating structure came from Hewish and Burgoyne, who studied the sensitivity of rat liver chromatin to the Ca^{2+}-Mg^{2+}-dependent endogenous nuclease of rat liver nuclei. They reasoned that if a repeating substructure existed, then the DNA might have repeating regions of tight association with proteins, which would give protection from nuclease attack. In that case, a relatively nonspecific nuclease should be able to break the DNA at unprotected sites, which would also occur at regular intervals. The DNA would be broken into a family of lengths, which would be multiples of the length of the protected region of DNA within a repeating unit.

The experiments of Hewish and Burgoyne involved exactly that design. After nuclease attack, the DNA was purified free of the histones and other proteins and the different lengths of DNA were separated via electrophoresis. The DNAs in the gel after electrophoresis were located by staining with the fluorescent dye, ethidium bromide. The DNAs present were 200 base pairs long, 400 base pairs, 600 base pairs, and higher multiples of 200 base pairs long. Hewish and Burgoyne concluded that a regular repeating unit of chromatin organization might occur, in which an unprotected, nuclease-sensitive site was found every 200 base pairs. The nuclease would not break the DNA at every possible sensitive site, so different lengths would be produced. However, each length would be a multiple of 200 base pairs.

Once Hewish and Burgoyne had made this observation, others quickly developed the field. An elegant study correlating the electron microscopic appearance with the biochemical properties of nucleosomes was done with an animal virus, SV40. This DNA virus is double-stranded and circular, with a supercoil twist. It is replicated in the nucleus of the infected cell during its vegetative phase. The circles are associated with host cell histones to form nucleosomes. The length of the DNA circle of the virus can be measured extremely accurately in the absence of the histones and in their presence. The circles are 4 as long with histones, thus the DNA must be coiled. In addition, the 100 Å beads, looking like nucleosomes, can be seen. The number of beads per circle is always equal to the number of 200 base-pair lengths of DNA in the viral genome. DNase breaks apart the short bridges between the beads, giving lengths of DNA that are multiples of 200 base pairs. RNase has no effect on the structure, and the histones are present in the same proportions as in regular eukaryotic DNAs.

Location and State of Histones and Nonhistone Proteins

The structure of a single nucleosome has been established by means of extensive studies of histone- histone associations and by particle scattering techniques applied to the location of the DNA. Also, comparisons have been made between nucleosomal structures of different organisms and between differentiation states (for example, embryos and adults or different adult tissues) of a single organism.

Model of a *core* unit, consisting of two each of the histones H 2a, H 2b, H3 and H4, around which is wrapped a 140-base-pair length of DNA. The H1 histone's position is uncertain, but it probably interacts with two adjacent beads, clamping them together. There are various lengths of DNA between the beads. In mature rat liver, there are 60

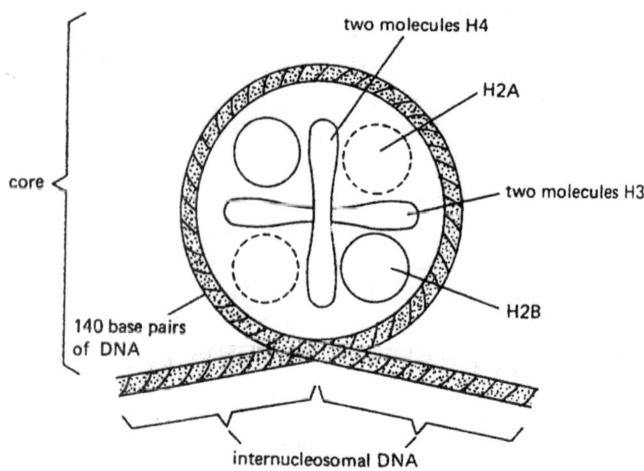

Fig. 12.5. Substructure of nucleosomal particle, showing that two each of four different histones interact with 140 base pairs of DNA in the core.

base pairs between core units. Of these 60 base pairs of this *internucleosomal DNA*, 30 base pairs may be considered to belong to each of the cores.

As far as we can tell at present the most variable feature of this structure is the length of the internucleosomal DNA. In fungi, only core lengths are found (the whole repeating unit is 140 base pairs long), whereas in most other organisms the internucleosomal DNA is 20 to 60 base pairs long. Internucleosomal DNA lengths evidently change during the early development of sea urchins. Another correlation with differentiation is that this internucleosomal length varies among different regions of mature rat brain. Notice that the histone/DNA ratio as well as the internucleosomal DNA length can vary.

We now come to questions of structure and function interaction. You might suppose that it would be useful to package DNA in units of function, that is, genes. A nucleosomal unit is not big enough to contain a gene. Since an average gene is around 1000 base pairs long, it should be packaged into five nucleosomes. Furthermore, the nucleosome structure is changed but not disrupted during transcription of genes, as shown by experiments on transcription of hemoglobin genes. These active genes, just like the generalized chromatin, are converted to *n*(200) base pair lengths by nucleases, (like micrococcal or endogenous nuclease); therefore, actively expressing genes are still packaged with histones. However, there must be a more open, less protected structure of genes that are being transcribed, since DNase-1 can selectively chop up such genes. The histones may, infact, have less charge-neutralization capacity in transcribing areas, due to modification (acetylation, for example) of some of the positively charged amino acids in the histones. This control mechanism could open the chromatin structure for transcription via repulsion by phosphate negative charges on DNA.

Another mechanism that might open the DNA-histone structure is for one or both of these components (DNA and histone) to interact with some specific non histone nuclear proteins. The non-histone proteins would then be a group of specific on-control proteins for transcription of particular genes. Several consequences can be inferred from this hypothesis. First, each differentiated tissue should have a distinct group of non-histone proteins, that this prediction is fulfilled—each tissue or organism contains a unique set of these nonhistone nuclear proteins.

Second, any regulatory non-histone proteins (NHPs) should be found in association with active chromatin but not with quiescent chromatin. One experiment by Comings and colleagues that support this notion was an analysis of non-coding, highly repetitive DNA—a portion of the DNA that is never transcribed—which showed that this DNA lacked nonhistone proteins. Another experiment supporting this model of regulatory function for nonhistone proteins was performed by Elgin and Silver. This experiment is rather complex, but it involves a number of techniques often used in molecular biology research today, so it is worth describing.

The chromosomes studied were a special type of interphase chromosomes found in salivary glands, intestinal cells, and a few other cells of Dipteran insects. The chromosomes are extended and not condensed, but they are *polytene*—they contain about $2^{10} = 1024$ strands of DNA that are virtually identical. The strands are all lined up parallel to one another in each chromosome. Places along the length of the chromosome where genes are located contain more DNA and are called bands; places between genes, called *interbands*, contain less DNA. The chromosomes can be viewed by staining or can be dried for electron microscopy. The general appearance of such polytene chromosomes and the results of Silver and Elgin's experiment, to be described in the following paragraph. If the NHPs bind specifically to active chromatin, we would expect them to be concentrated in certain bands that are puffed out because of transcription

The design of Silver and Elgin's experiment. First, NHPs were prepared from the *Drosophila* and purified so that they were free of

DNA and histones. Then the NHPs were injected into rabbits. The rabbits made antibodies to the NHPs, which appeared to the rabbits to be foreign invaders. Elgin and Silver collected these antibodies to NHPs from the blood serum of the rabbits. We will call these antibodies "rabbit anti-NHPs." These rabbit anti-NHPs can specifically recognize and bind tightly to the *Drosophila* NHPs. But neither the NHPs nor the rabbit anti-NHPs can be recognized under the microscope, so the location of the NHPs could not yet be pinpointed. Next, Elgin and Silver used a fluorescent marker, which could be seen under the microscope. The fluorescent dye was covalently linked to a type of antibody prepared by injecting rabbit antibodies into goats and then collecting the goat serum, which recognizes and binds specifically to rabbit antibodies. This structure is called fluorescent goat-antirabbit antibody. The location of NHPs could now be recognized by means of this fluorescence, since the NHPs bind the rabbit anti-NHP and they, in turn, bind the fluorescent goat-antirabbit-antibody.

The actual experiment, then, involved preparation of a nicely spread-out display of polytene *Drosophila* salivary gland chromosomes. These chromosomes contained NHPs, concentrated at whatever sites they usually occupy. Then, the chromosomes were treated with rabbit anti-NHPs, which were bound at the NHPs sites. The excess rabbit anti-NHPs were washed out. The fluorescent goat antirabbit antibodies were added next. These bound to the rabbit anti-NHPs. Now, the areas near the NHPs were fluorescent when viewed under the microscope. The photograph in the result—the NHPs evidently are concentrated in the areas of actively transcribing genes, since certain puffed bands are highly fluorescent. In addition, an area known to contain nongenetic (unexpressed) DNA has no detectable NHP (fluorescence).

Some of the NHP of the nucleus may well be in association with newly transcribed hnRNA. Histones and nonhistone proteins may also play a role in replication of eukaryotic DNA. The Okazaki fragments in eukaryotes may have an assembly state that is approximately nucleosome sized, but others are both smaller and larger. The newly replicated DNA is associated with a slightly looser nucleosome structure than the other DNA. Another interesting aspect of replication is that not all eukaryotic DNA replicates at the same time, and the nongenetic or highly inactivated (*heterochromatic*) DNA is replicated later in S phase than the normal (*euchromatic*) DNA. Even euchromatin is replicated in a definite order. The order has only been established so far in a few cells, such as cells that are becoming polytene, but it

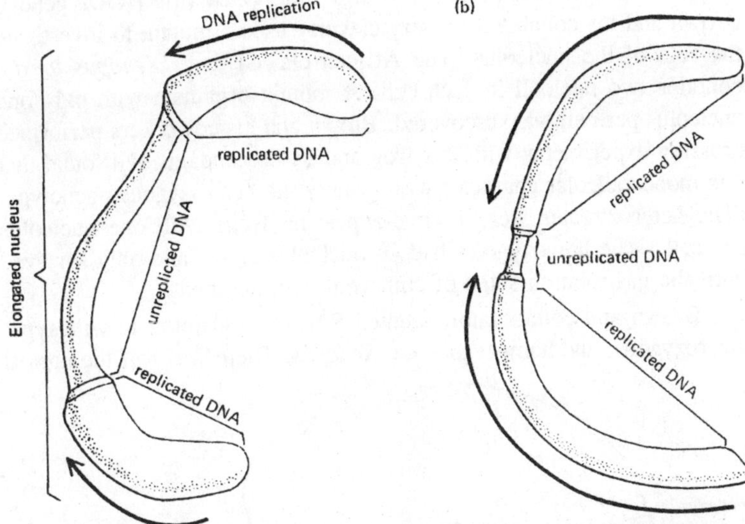

Fig. 12.6. Replication of DNA in the protozoan Euplotes passes through the nucleus in a wave: (a) mid-replication, with S phase 60 per cent complete; (b) late replication—S phase 90 per cent complete.

may well be generally true. At different times during early development of insect cells, the replication of DNA was studied. The different bands replicate in a definite order, but the order does not follow the order of the genes on the chromosome. Replication is ordered in a somewhat different way in the nucleus of *Euplotes*, where it moves in a wave from one end of the nucleus to the other. The studies of synchronized yeast cells by Halvorson have led to his suggestion that yeast genes are replicated in the same order in each division cycle. Yeasts are unusual among eukaryotes in having a large number of very short chromosomes.

In summary, it seems that whole cell regulation rather than intra-chromosomal organization may control the order of replication of individual genes. The manner in which the replicated DNA is separated into two chromatids within a chromosome is not known. An interesting study by Langan and collaborators suggests that H1 (the histone that is not intrinsic to the nucleosome bead) is phosophorylated just before cell division.

Nucleoli

When cells are stained for nucleic acids during interphase the nucleolus can be seen as a very darkly staining area within the nucleus. The components of nucleoli are dispersed during mitosis. The nucleolus consists of RNA and proteins, with a little DNA (the rRNA genes). Brown and his collaborators very cleverly used a mutant to investigate the role of the nucleolus. The African clawed frog, *Xenopus laevis*, contains two nucleoli in each cell. A mutant organism with only one nucleolus per cell was discovered. Brown and his coworkers performed crossing experiments with this frog and its descendants and found that this mononucleolar character was actually the heterozygous phenotype. (The heterozygotes were normal-appearing frogs with one nucleolus per cell.) The homozygotes had no nucleolus at all, and only survived until the gastrulation stage of embryonic development.

Brown and collaborators studied RNA transcription in wild type, heterozygous, and homozygous nu^- *Xenopus*. There was half the normal

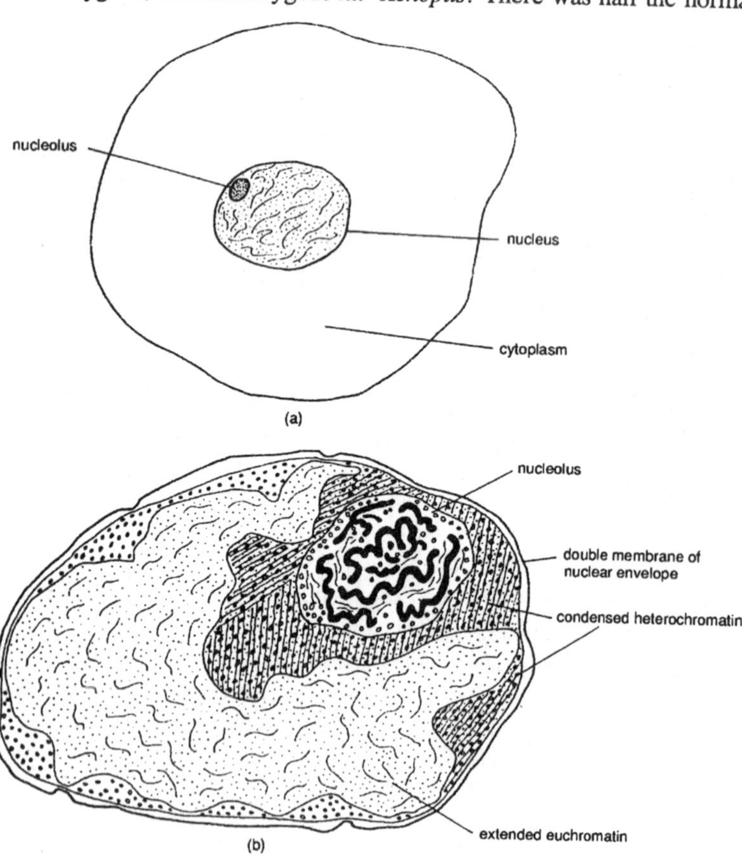

Fig. 12.7. Appearance of nucleoli via light and electron microscopy. (a) Light microscopic view. (b) Electron microscopic view.

rRNA transcription in heterozygotes and no rRNA transcription in *nu⁻* homozygotes. There was also less rRNA in the *nu⁻* strain. The nucleolus thus seemed to be the site of rRNA transcription, that is, the rDNA or RNA genes. The *nu⁻* strain had a homozygous deletion (macrolesion mutation) at these genes. Another way to describe nu- strain is that the *nucleolus organizer region* (NOR) has been deleted. Since the ribosomal subunits are at least partially assembled from rRNAs and ribosomal proteins at the nucleolus, there is an aggregate of ribonucleoprotein there. Before the role of the nucleolus was clear, cytologists referred to the process as *organizing* the nucleolar material, rather than coding for the rRNA, and this terminology is still widely used. In some oocytes, many extra copies of rDNA are *amplified* from the nucleolar organizer.

In another study demonstrating a correlation between rRNA coding capacity and the nucleolus, Ritossa and Spiegelman used the technique of RNA-DNA hybridization. This technique is based on the ability of RNA to form base pairs with one of the DNA strands of the gene

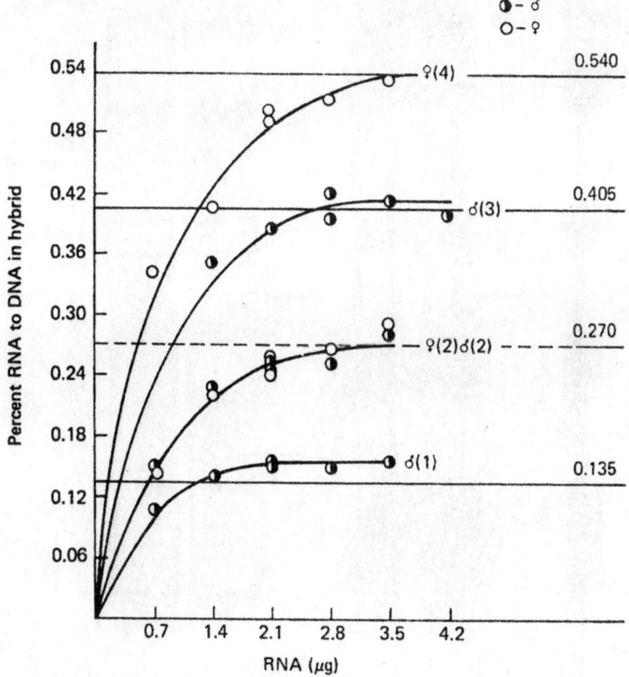

Fig. 12.8. The number of nucleolar organizing regions in different Drosophila strains is proportional to the amount of rDNA in the strains.

from which it is transcribed. Ritossa and Spiegelman studied a group of *Drosophila* strains that differed in the number of nucleolar organizers they contained. They showed that the amount of DNA that could base pair with rRNA was proportional to the number of NORs the fly strain had.

The nucleolus is the site not only of rRNA transcription but also of its processing and of the interaction of ribosomal proteins with it. The ribosomal proteins are coded for by their own genes, which produce mRNAs that are translated in the cytoplasm. There the nascent ribosomal proteins enter the nucleus and go to the nucleolus for processing. How this locational specificity is achieved is presently a mystery.

Special Chromosomes and Special Chromatin States in Interphase

The most widely studied special chromosomes of interphase are probably the polytene chromosomes. As mentioned earlier these polytene chromosomes are extended but are composed of multiple parallel DNA

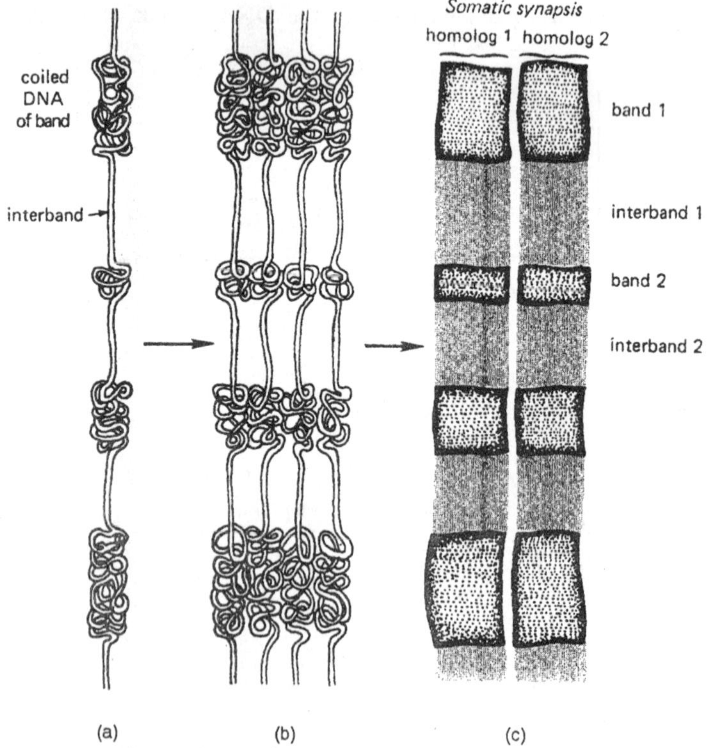

Fig. 12.9. Drawing of bands and interbands of a polytene chromosome.

strands, having essentially the same genetic material in the same order. Most of the DNA in these chromosomes has been replicated ten times in the absence of normal mitosis, so 1024 strands of DNA exist in each of the chromosomes (first one strand, which replicates to give two, each of which replicates to give four, and so on). The control system allowing S phase to occur repeatedly without M is not understood at present.

One of the unexpected features of polytene chromosomes is that the homologs are synapsed. Recall that *synapsis* is a feature of meiotic prophase, a type of nuclear division usually leading to production of gametes. These polytene chromosomes are not condensed but extended; these cells will not even undergo mitosis, nor have they any relation at all to germ cell production. Analysis of the common features of these cells' chromatin and that of meiotic cells might well lead to interesting conclusions about the mechanisms of synapsis.

Another interesting feature of the polytene chromosomes is that their DNA is not all replicated to the same degree. The DNA that is under-replicated is of at least two types: the centromeric DNA, which contains no genes, and the rDNA at the nucleolus organizer regions. These regions tend to be replicated late in each round, and it is possible that they fall further and further behind at each round of replication, finally failing to be replicated at all in some rounds.The lack of actual cell division in these cells means that the replicated DNA s need never be separated from each other, so differences in the degree of replication need not create special problems.

A special kind of highly condensed interphase chromatin is present in all chromosomes. It is called *heterochromatin* in contrast to the extended euchromatin. The heterochromatin may be *constitutive*

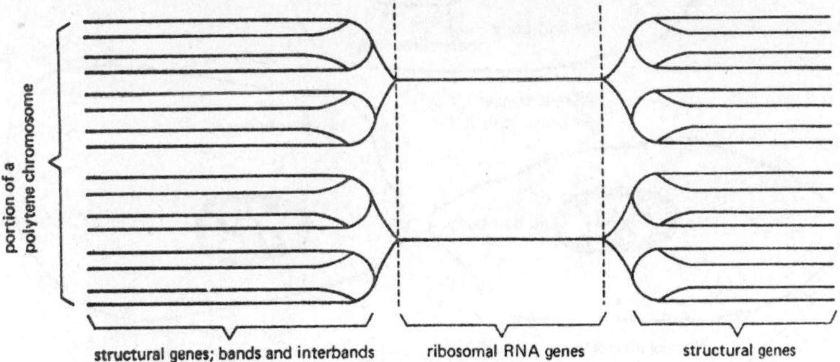

Fig. 12.10. Under-replication of rDNA during polytenization results in a lesser representation of this region in polytene chromosomes.

heterochromatin—always condensed in every interphase cell, for example, the centromeric DNA. Or, it may be *facultative heterochromatin*—meaning that this particular DNA is extended (euchromatic) in some cells and condensed (heterochromatic) in others. The constitutive heterochromatin in *Drosophila* salivary gland cells aggregates together so that all the four pairs of chromosomes are stuck together by a clump of heterochromatin called the *chromocenter*. The reason for this heterochromatin stickiness is not known.

An example of facultative heterochromatin is provided by *X-chromosome inactivation*. Mary Lyon first proposed that a dark-staining clump of heterochromatin called the *Barr body*, which occurs in the nucleus of most females was an inactivated, heterochromatic X chromosome. She suggested that the pair of Xs in a female contributes more copies of these genes than are needed after early development is complete. Some time during late development, then, one X in each cell is condensed into a Barr body. According to the *Lyon hypothesis*, the choice of which X is made heterochromatic is random. However, it has been shown to be random in some cases and nonrandom in other cases (for example, in embryonic membranes). Females are thus *mosaic* in terms of gene action. Some cells have the maternal group of X-linked genes turned on, whereas other cells have the paternal group of X-linked genes turned on. Strenuous attempts to reverse X inactivation in tissue culture have failed. The process of heterochromatin formation may thus be irreversible or nearly irreversible.

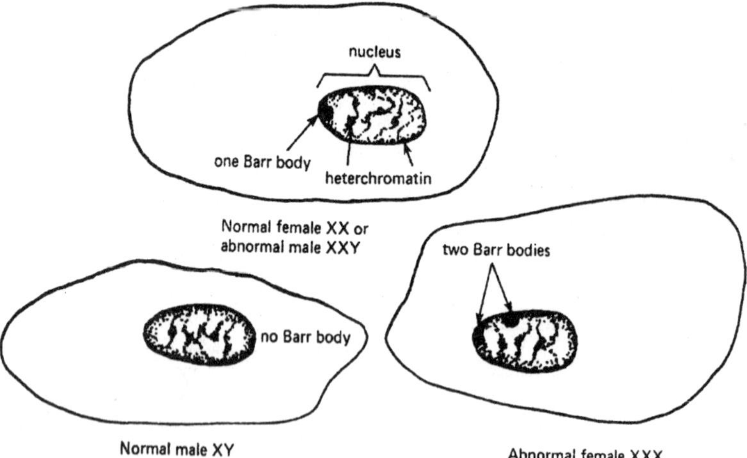

Fig. 12.11. Barr bodies are produced from all the X chromosomes except one, which remains active.

Experiments by Gurdon, involving transplantation of mature nuclei (probably containing facultative heterochromatin) into enucleated eggs, show that some of such nuclei can (in frogs at least) support development of complete, normal adults. A particularly interesting aspect of Gurdon's experiments suggests that reversal of heterochromatization is a slow process. He found that a mature nucleus only rarely succeeded in dividing fast enough to keep pace with the rapid cleavage divisions early in development. This observation may be related to heterochromatinization since heterochromatin usually replicates last in the S phase. If Gurdon took a nucleus from one of the embryos whose development stopped because of slow nuclear division and transplanted that nucleus into an enucleated egg, the success in cleavage was much greater than before. A possible explanation is that the heterochromatin condensation had already been partly reversed, so that the nucleus was more nearly in the euchromatic state of a normal embryonic nucleus.

Eukaryotic Chromosomes During Cell Division

Coiling, Chromomeres, and Banding

During mitosis or meiosis, the prophase is the stage during which the chromosomes become shorter and thicker. It has long been proposed, by DuPraw and others, that this process is one of multiple coiling. The hypothesis of a solenoidal structure, with coils of coils, had a renaissance since nucleosomal substructure has been discovered. Recall that nucleosomes already have two layers of coiling: (1) the double helix and (2) the helical wrapping of the double helix around the histone bead. A string of nucleosomes, with each internucleosomal DNA bridge interacting maximally with its neighbouring histones, is thought to form a 100 Å *unit fiber*. This fiber may then be coiled, and that coil maybe coiled again. Coiling proceeds for approximately seven levels, resulting in about a 500-fold shortening. The nucleosome remains the basis of all this structure; it is not disrupted or distorted.

During the process of prophase coiling, the chromatin attains a beaded appearance on a much larger scale than nucleosomes—a scale that is visible through a light microscope, whereas nucleosomes require an electron microscope. Because these beads stain very darkly, they were named *chromomeres*. The chromomeres may be equivalent to the bands of polytene chromosomes. As coiling proceeds, the chromomeres coalesce into fewer and fewer darkly staining regions.

Even where the chromosomes are maximally condensed at the end of prophase (that is, at metaphase), a banding pattern characteristic of each individual chromo some can be seen after staining with special techniques. The acetic acid-saline Giemsa staining technique, which shows *G banding*, has been the basis of an international system of human chromosome classification. Roughly the same regions are stained by quinacrine mustard, producing fluorescent *Q bands*. Q banding is especially strong in heterochromatic regions; the Y chromosome, which is almost all heterochromatin, is very bright in this procedure. A modification of the Giemsa procedure stains the portions that remain unstained in G or Q banding. This technique is called reverse banding or *R banding*. All of these techniques have proved very useful in mapping genes via parasexual techniques.

Centromeres and Kinetochores

In condensed chromosomes, each can be seen to have a very narrow region where the spindle fibers will attach. This region is the

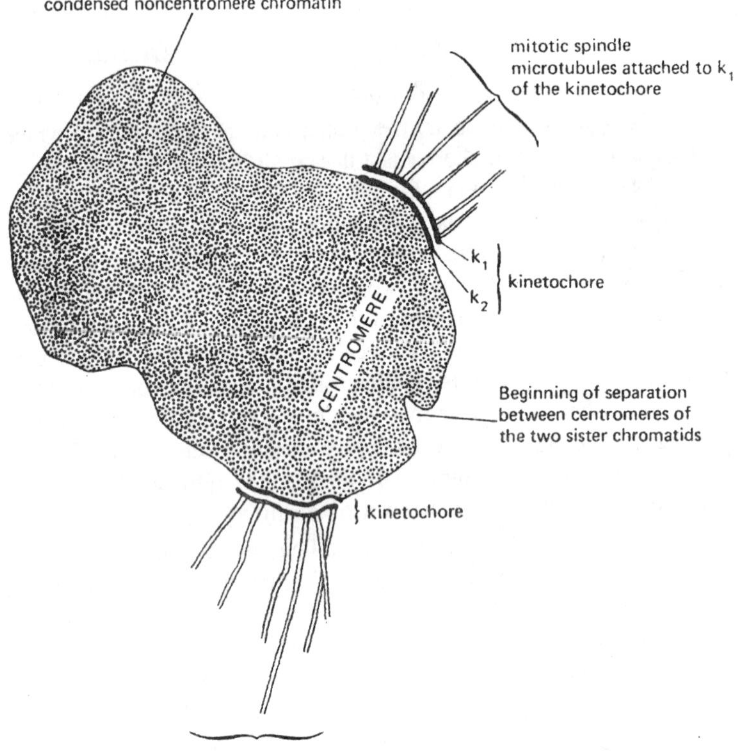

Fig. 12.12. The appearance of the centromere and the associated kinetochores during mitotic metaphase.

primary constriction or *centromere*. The DNA of this region contains no genes and is heterochromatic in interphase. The nucleosomes at the centromere evidently lack non-histone proteins (NHPs). An interesting speculation is that the corn abnormal 10 chromosome, causes a depletion of NHPs at various sites along the chromosome. These sites become fake centromeres.

The centromere need not be at the center of the chromosome. In fact, chromosomes can be classified by their centromere placement. Terminal placement of the centromere is called *telocentric*, central placement of the centromere is called *metacentric*, and placement very close to the terminus is called *acrocentric*. Each category can also be further subdivided. The shorter arm of an acrocentric chromosome is called *p* and the longer arm is called *q*.

The function of the centromere is evidently to allow organization of a kinetochore. The kinetochore is a complex structure, evidently largely of protein, in the form of a plaque on the surface of the chromosome where spindle fibers can attach.

Synapsis

Recognition of homologous pieces of DNA occurs readily in viruses and prokaryotes, so evidently it does not require a complex structure. The mechanism by which two completely base-paired, identical double helices of DNA might recognize each other probably involves partial base pair separation under the influence of special proteins. The gene product of the *E. coli rec* A gene, for example, allows interhelix base pairs to form in this prokaryote. In eukaryotes, homologous DNAs are sequestered or packaged with proteins into separate chromosomes. It may be that one or more proteins of the eukaryotic chromosome actually serve to inhibit synapsis, the sticking together of homologous chromosomes in perfect register. In any case it is rare, but not completely unknown, for synapsis to occur at times outside of meiotic prophase I.

In eukaryotes, synapsis is the major DNA-DNA recognition process. The structure of synapsed chromosomes is complex. The *synaptinemal complex* (SC) contains RNA, protein, and presumably DNA. It has been proposed that DNA strands or loops of chromatin extend through the SC into the chromatin of the homologous chromosome. A type of lump visible in the electron microscope and called a *recombination nodule* appears to be equivalent to a chiasma as seen in the light microscope. Still, the only solid evidence that the homologous DNAs come into contact with each other is genetic: recombination between linked genes evidently occurs while the chromosomes are synapsed. Suggestive evidence comes also from cytogenetics: chiasmata appear to be derived from breakage and reunion of synapsed homologous chromosomes. A promising approach to the study of this process is genetic: mutants affecting meiosis have been selected, particularly in fungi, *Drosophila*, and nematodes, and are now under extensive study. The chromatin components that are important for synapsis may be pinpointed by looking for the differences between such mutants and wild type. Another promising approach is genetic in a larger sense. The structure of the SC is being compared in many different species, and the common factors are likely to be those that were genetically conserved in evolution because they are crucial for meiotic success.

One caveat is that evidently DNA sequence homology need not be extensive to result in synapsis, since X and Y chromosomes, with only a little homology, synapse (albeit end-to-end) at meiosis.

Special Chromosomes and Chromatin Regions in Cell Division

The study of comparative genetics and cytogenetics has often contributed heavily to the understanding of major genetic processes. In cell division, the most unusual chromosome structures have provided invaluable information about chromosomes in general. Recall, for example, that the interphase chromatin oddity, the polytene chromosome, was important to our understanding in the same way. In addition the lampbrush chromosomes formed during meiotic prophase in amphibian oocytes (egg-cell precursor cells) have been very fruitful study objects for geneticists. These chromosomes are condensing, but they are fluffy with side loops.

Early in the study of lampbrush chromosomes, it was proposed that the loops each contained one or more genes whereas the chromatin at the axis of the chromosome was spacer DNA. This proposal was supported by the observation that the loops were all being transcribed into RNA. Later results showed that genes were also located in the axis portion of lampbrush chromosomes. Presently, it is thought that the genes whose products are needed in early development are transcribed during meiotic prophase and the mRNA is stored in the egg. Genes whose expression is needed later in development are not being transcribed at this stage.

Other special structures that occur later in meiotic prophase I in amphibian oocytes are multiple nucleoli. These nucleoli are very numerous and are scattered around the periphery of the nucleus in the area near the nuclear membrane. Miller showed that these nucleoli were not attached to the NOR (nucleolus organizer region) but each contained a separate circle of rDNA that was being actively transcribed to form rRNA. As usual, rRNA processing and ribosome assembly was occurring at the transcription sites, so nucleoli (ribonucleoprotein aggregates) could be seen cytologically. A part of Miller's experiment. Isolated nucleoli were disrupted with detergents to form "bracelets." The ring portion of the bracelet disappeared when DNase was added; the beads of ribonucleoprotein were diminished in size by RNase or pronase.

Even in more typical or average cells, the fate of nucleoli during cell division is interesting. During prophase, the nucleoli persist (which is how the NORs are discerned, since one chromosome cannot be distinguished from another during interphase). After prophase, when the nuclear membrane is beginning to disappear, the nucleolar material disperses. It is not clear whether all ribosomes are completed before dispersal or not. Neither is it clear whether the NOR starts from scratch to form a nucleolus after telophase or whether some of the previous nucleolar components return for further processing after cell division is complete.

INDEX

S

T